I0823250

BENEATH THE WAGE

ALSO IN THE *NEAR FUTURES* SERIES

Portfolio Society: On the Capitalist Mode of Prediction
IVAN ASCHER

Undoing the Demos: Neoliberalism's Stealth Revolution
WENDY BROWN

Markets in the Making:
Rethinking Competition, Goods, and Innovation
MICHEL CALLON

Counterrevolution:
Extravagance and Austerity in Public Finance
MELINDA COOPER

Family Values:
Between Neoliberalism and the New Social Conservatism
MELINDA COOPER

Discounting the Future:
The Ascendancy of a Political Technology
LILIANA DOGANOVA

Rated Agency: Investee Politics in a Speculative Age
MICHEL FEHER

Hayek's Bastards:
Race, Gold, IQ, and the Capitalism of the Far Right
QUINN SLOBODIAN

Market Civilizations: Neoliberals East and South
QUINN SLOBODIAN & DIETER PLEHWE

Beneath the Wage: Tips, Tasks, and Gigs in the Age of Service Work

Annie McClanahan

ZONE BOOKS
633 Vanderbilt Street, Brooklyn, New York 11218

Distributed by Princeton University Press,
Princeton, New Jersey, and Woodstock, United Kingdom

Library of Congress Control Number 2025038063

To Margaret *for understanding*

To Lulu *for joy*

To Mom *for everything*

Everyday life as the terrain of ever-changing alienations also holds the key to their dismantling.

—KRISTIN ROSS, *The Commune Form*

CONTENTS

Introduction

We live in an age of service work. According to the Bureau of Labor Statistics (BLS), only 20 percent of the US population performs "goods-producing" labor (manufacturing, extraction, and agriculture), while the other 80 percent do "services-providing" labor, from truck driving to financial management, teaching to janitorial work. What, if anything, do those jobs have in common? After all, the BLS's "services-providing supersector" includes jobs with the highest salaries, as well as those with the lowest wages; it contains enduringly professionalized occupations (lawyers, doctors), but also historically precarious jobs (home health-care workers, hotel cleaners). Nonetheless, a glance at the twenty most common jobs in the United States—all but one of them in the services-providing sector—does let us begin to generalize about service work. The list includes retail sales workers, fast-food employees, cashiers, cooks, clerks, and restaurant servers, as well as registered nurses, health aides, and elementary school teachers. Most of these jobs involve in-person work that cannot yet be automated. Nor can most of these jobs be outsourced, though they are disproportionately likely to be performed by immigrant, nonwhite, and female-identified workers. They are highly likely to involve some degree of "temporal instability": constantly changing shifts and schedules, unpredictable working hours, and involuntary part-time work. And they are mostly low-waged jobs: 75 percent of those earning the minimum wage or less are in the service sector, and workers in nonprofessionalized service-sector occupations are more likely to live below the official poverty line than any group other than farmworkers.

This book offers a new history and theory of contemporary service work. Today's service workers regularly toil for nonhourly methods of wage payment. They are subject to indirect yet insidious forms of domination, from the "self-management" of performance-based wages to the impersonal surveillance of platforms and apps. They are more likely to work in temporary jobs or as gigworkers. Their work is less likely to be protected by maximum-hour and minimum-wage laws. And they are a test case for the ways that even jobs resistant to full automation can still be transformed by technologies of speedup and intensification. In all these ways, service work requires us to rethink our basic understanding of wages, management, labor-saving technology, and regulation. This book does just that, focusing less on service work's "affective" or "performative" dimensions and more on how it is paid, how it is controlled, and how it is mechanized. I do so by identifying what I contend are three paradigmatic types of contemporary service labor: superexploited tipwork, deskilled clerical microwork, and informalized gigwork.

While theories of service work have tended to neglect its labor process, histories of labor have tended to ignore service work entirely. This book argues that service work is not a footnote in the story of modern capitalism, but an indispensable shadow history of labor exploitation. Long considered an anomaly or anachronism and understood less as a class formation than as a feeling, low-waged service work is in fact key to understanding the nature of work and life under capitalism. Instead of treating low-wage service work as marginal or exceptional, *Beneath the Wage* argues that service work is an enduring and structuring form in the history of wage labor. It maintains that service work is best understood as a gendered and racialized method of labor exploitation. It suggests that service work's long-standing exclusion from regulation requires us to imagine different strategies for political mobilization. And it contends that representations of service work—from pop culture to radical labor imaginaries—help reveal the connections between everyday life and the broader social relations that produce our shared subsistence.

Each chapter of *Beneath the Wage* analyzes the history, culture, and politics of one of these exemplary forms of contemporary service work. Chapter 1, on tipwork, studies the history of tipping since the eighteenth century, looks at the rise of TV shows about low-waged tipwork (from reality TV to the episodic narratives of absurdist comedy), and recounts the use of mutual aid among tipworkers to produce an abolitionist vision of solidarity. Chapter 2, on microwork, excavates the history of piece-rate wages, explores conceptual poetry produced by workers on platforms such as Amazon Mechanical Turk, and describes how subcontracted, outsourced microworkers, while denied the centralized "shop floor" of factory labor, use "work-to-rule" sabotage against the employers who exploit them. In Chapter 3, on gigwork, I reconstruct the contradictory fantasies and anxieties around freedom and control that have long been associated with the spatial mobility of "circulation gigwork," examine how those fantasies and anxieties have shaped contemporary novels written about and by gigworkers, and offer an account of how and why service-worker unions are dispensing with the productivist language of "fair wages" and beginning to center so-called noneconomic demands concerning housing, policing, borders, and the climate crisis. In the book's conclusion, I subject my own kind of service work—university teaching—to scrutiny, exploring the sharp turn toward online higher education in the wake of the COVID-19 pandemic, and I imagine the kinds of political mobilization that might combat deskilling and automation in the portion of the service sector I know best.

My title, *Beneath the Wage*, evokes the contradictions that attend service work as waged labor. Michael Denning has influentially argued that the "fetishism of the wage" also depends on the production and normalization of "wageless life."[1] *Beneath the Wage* expands this claim to understand service work as a form of waged life that is nonetheless denied the minimal protections and legitimation extended to waged industrial work. Service work is an activity, not a product: its "output" can be alienated neither from the body of the service worker herself nor from the body of the person she serves. Like goods-producing manufacturing labor, however, service work has been commodified, socialized, and subjected to the impersonal domination of the wage. But unlike manufacturing work, it has also been largely excluded from the paradigm of "free labor." Service workers, I suggest, are thus "beneath" the wage in the sense that like other wage workers, they are compelled to earn a living, but they are also "beneath" the wage in the sense that they are excluded from wage labor's promises of freedom, autonomy, and equality.[2]

Service work's seemingly anomalous or anachronistic status has also been used to exclude it from labor standards, reforms, and regulation. In the period of rapid industrial growth and innovation that began in the early twentieth century, US law and regulation provided most manufacturing workers with minimum hourly wages, maximum working time regulations, collective bargaining agreements, and a range of protections attached to the new category "employee." At the same time, however, the United States was *also* innovating a service sector defined by precarious tip wages, long working days governed by task efficiency, and the uncertainty attached to the equally new category "independent contractor." This book thus focuses primarily on the US context because it is here that we can see most clearly how and why service work, specifically in its status as labor that does not involve "the production of goods for commerce," was excluded from regulations designed for a period of rapid industrial growth.[3] Put otherwise, I want to offer a counterhistory of wage labor in what Giovanni Arrighi famously termed the "long twentieth-century" of US industrial hegemony: instead of focusing on the manufacturing workers whose labor was highly rationalized, mechanized, and regulated, I attend to the role of newspaper boys whose precarious working conditions gave rise to the legal concept of the "independent contractor"; to Black "domestics" washing windows as day laborers; to piece-rate female "outworkers" stuffing envelopes in their own homes.

But I am also interested in what happened *after* that period of industrial growth, as the service sector was increasingly compelled to power capital accumulation on its own in the wake of deindustrialization. A low-productivity service sector cannot produce adequate economic growth under capitalism, which is why we are now many decades in to a "long downturn," or accumulation crisis.[4] *Beneath the Wage* is about what work looks and feels like in the present age of productivity stagnation. It contends that slowing productivity growth manifests in the worker's labor process as a nearly unbearable temporal speedup, that technological stagnation is lived as intensified domination, and that an inertial economy is experienced as wages so low that the worker's everyday existence becomes perilous. In this context, the idea of being "beneath the wage" suggests not just that service work is typically lower waged, less secure, and more subordinated than many other types of work, but also that attention to service work reveals the domination, precarity, and exhaustion concealed beneath *all* waged work under capital.

Beneath the Wage also explores how low-waged service work has occasioned vital and distinctive strategies for political solidarity beyond either legislative reform or traditional "fair wage" demands. Service work yokes our everyday lives to the broader communal relations that ensure our common survival. This is truer today than ever before. Precisely insofar as service work has been increasingly socialized under capitalism, and precisely inasmuch as the service sector has been forced to expand as a result of deindustrialization, contemporary service work structures forms of collective survival and subsistence across and within the proletarian class as a whole, creating new forms of nonbiological connection between households and the larger social order, between intimates and strangers, between the act of providing service work and the fact of depending on the service work of others.

Bringing together the historical, cultural, and political dimensions of service work, *Beneath the Wage* is inspired by the method of Marx's chapter "The Working Day" from *Capital, Volume One*. There, Marx attempted to capture "the voice of the worker, which had previously been stifled in the sound and fury of the production process."[5] To do that, he listened for the "voices"—real and imagined—of workers, capitalists, and even machines in a variety of sources: in the "Blue Books" produced by the English and Scottish factory regulators; in the margins of public health documents and news reports; in the defensive statements of factory owners themselves; and in the works of William Shakespeare, Charles Dickens, and Charlotte and Emily Brontë.[6] From this array of texts, Marx fashioned a robust theory of life both in and beyond the factory, explaining how everything from the invention of shift systems to the price and quality of bread was connected in a world organized around the industrial wage.

Beneath the Wage strives to create an analogous portrait of our world of service work by drawing on a similarly diverse range of sources. I tell the story of how contemporary service work has been structurally and phenomenologically transformed by methods of wage payment and measures of output, by the pressure of technological speedup and surveillance, and by the insecurity of schedules and contracts and compensation. I do so by way of an archive that is at once fictional and documentary, historical and technical, theoretical and political. I look at how politicians described the problem of regulating restaurant work in the early twentieth century and how contemporary gigworkers have responded to legislation around their "independent contractor" status. I read economists and scientific managers talking about efficiency and incentives and subcontracted workers describing what it's like to work under the lash of piece-rate wages. I attend to traditional "aesthetic" forms (prestige television dramas, conceptual poetry, literary autofiction), to "pop" forms such as reality TV, comedy, and advertisements, and to workers' writing about their own labor.

Part of what I hope to get by treating such a wide variety of texts is a fuller understanding of how service work operates at the level of both individuals and systems—and, further, of the ways that service work uniquely mediates between these two levels. Recognizing the link between individual particularity and classed generality—between the concrete and the abstract, experience and totality, theory from above and praxis from below—is, this book argues, vital both to comprehending service work and to organizing around it. I've sought to assemble an unruly set of sources that can help us do that. Describing service work from a variety of perspectives, these sources create a bridge between everyday life and the social totality.

Most Marxist theories of aesthetics have tended to focus on our need for "cognitive maps" capable of illuminating the "hidden abode of production" and of rendering the vast scales of globalized commodity production. But coming to grips with our age of service work requires us to register intimacy and totality at once. How do we map the forms of capitalist exploitation that happen when we are handed a bag of groceries or a cup of coffee, when we have our blood pressure taken or our homework graded, when we ask for our office trashcan to be removed or our data set to be coded? What does it mean that many service workers also pay others to serve them, as when the bartender takes an Uber home from work or the Uber driver stops off for a drink? To understand these relations, we need texts capable of describing not only awesome distances, but also temporary solidarities; not only the vast scales of the centralized factory, but also the minor knowledges of how things move hand to hand; not only the veiled secret of the "hidden abode," but the ever-present fact of the everyday forms of labor that are directly before us.

EXISTING THEORIES OF SERVICE WORK

No book has more influenced our contemporary understanding of service work than Arlie Hochschild's 1983 *The Managed Heart: On the Commercialization of Human Feeling*. Hochschild's study of female Delta flight attendants identifies a new form of in-person service she terms "emotional labor." *The Managed Heart* opens with a passage from Marx's *Capital* on child labor in a nineteenth-century wallpaper factory. Marx, Hochschild writes, was concerned not just with what the factory worker was paid and how many hours he had to work, but also with "the human cost of becoming an 'instrument of labor.'" Both the factory worker who produces tangible goods and the service worker whose product is a "state of mind," she argues, are alienated from some fundamental aspect of the self: the factory worker from his own body, the emotional laborer from her very "soul." Although she starts out by emphasizing this continuity in the alienation of labor, however, Hochschild is ultimately more interested in the *differences* between manufacturing labor and service work. For the flight attendant, she argues in a key paragraph, "*the emotional style of offering the service is part of the service itself,* in a way that loving or hating the wallpaper is not a part of producing [it]. Seeming to 'love the job' becomes part of the job; and actually trying to love it, and to enjoy the customers, helps the worker in this effort." Whereas the wallpaper manufacturer was not required to like his job—was not, indeed, required to have or express any particular feelings at all—the service worker must not just "*seem* to 'love the job'" but "actually try to love it." Flight attendants must "develop feelings for the parts [they] play" and "participate in the illusion" to be believable. For Hochschild, service workers thus engage in a kind of "double pretending" through which they come to experience the "state of mind" they perform and produce as if it is their own, real emotion. This "social engineering," she contends, requires a mutually reinforcing circuit between the authentic private self and the performed or "engineered" public self. Focused on the "timeless" question of "what an emotion is and how we can manage it," *The Managed Heart* is not a theory of labor exploitation, but rather an account of "the costs and benefits of managing emotion."[7]

Despite Hochschild's surprisingly minimal engagement with questions of labor process and class in *The Managed Heart,* a generation of sociologists has used the book to describe service work as labor that conscripts "the spirit and the soul of the worker."[8] With the "transition from an industrial to a service economy," one theorist notes, the "subjectivity of the worker becomes central to the production process"; interactive service work, another contends, is less about the body than it is about workers' "looks, words, feelings, thoughts, attitudes, and demeanor."[9] For these scholars, as for Hochschild, control over the "hearts and spirits" of workers requires service employers to gain the "consent" of workers and to ensure they "internalize" the discipline of service work.[10] Because service workers' performed feelings often become "real feelings" when ritually repeated, it is claimed, service workers lose their "authenticity and singularity," as their "sense of self" becomes entangled in the success of their employer.[11] Often, as in Hochschild's account, arguments about the entangled self are used to distinguish the clear-eyed production worker from the more self-deluded service worker. Whereas "the assembly line worker could openly hate his job," the service worker's forced performances produce feelings of "inauthenticity" and "estrangement" to the point where workers may no longer be able to "distinguish their 'real' selves from their 'on-stage' selves."[12]

Although Hochschild was focused more on estrangement than exploitation, her ideas about the false consciousness and affective confusion of service workers also show up in autonomist and post-Marxist theories of contemporary service work.[13] In his book *Dead Man Working*, for example, Carl Cederstrom cites Hochschild to argue that "the injunction to be authentic" means service workers "can no longer draw the line between what is fake and genuine." Mark Fisher similarly claims that under the regime of service work, "it is no longer possible to just turn up at work and be miserable" and that service workers must instead perform "a happy smile [and] ritualized submission."[14] Maurizio Lazzarato contends that the requirement to perform affect "also directly acts on the subjectivity of employees," who come to believe "the promises made to them."[15] Contemporary service work, argues Frédéric Lordon, demands that emotions be not just "outwardly enacted, but 'authentically' felt" and thus defines a "post-Fordist regime" in which work is governed by "new affective sensibilities."[16]

As Lordon's reference to a "post-Fordist regime" implies, many of these post-Marxist critics also argue that the "affective" qualities of service work make it an entirely new form of accumulation via affective exploitation—a new "postmodern social factory" in which feelings themselves become "a source of value," in Cederstrom's language. Eva Illouz similarly identifies service work as a new phase of "emotional capitalism."[17] For Lazzarato, the rise of "immaterial labor" whose "raw material . . . is subjectivity" renders prior Marxist theories of value and exploitation obsolete. Michael Hardt, likewise, argues that "affective labor" is now "the highest value-producing form of labor," and Antonio Negri describes "an economy of desire" in which "affective flows" become "productive nexuses."[18] In their immensely influential coauthored book, *Empire,* Hardt and Negri together contend that work involving "the creation and manipulation of affect," as well as other forms of care, communication, and creativity, are "driv[ing] the postmodernization of the global economy."[19]

These accounts of the postindustrial service economy as an entirely new form of value accumulation draw on a longer Marxist-feminist tradition committed to rethinking the division between value-productive and reproductive labor. The first wave of influential Marxist-feminist accounts of reproductive labor focused primarily on unwaged housework (although, as I will discuss in the next section, Black Marxist-feminists such as Angela Davis were at the same moment producing vital theories of waged domestic work). Housework, Silvia Federici's 1974 manifesto *Wages Against Housework* fiercely contends, is the site of "the most subtle and mystified violence that capitalism has ever perpetrated." Like Hochschild's *The Managed Heart, Wages Against Housework* attends to the "affective" dimension of domestic care work, but in a more explicitly political key, arguing that housework is made to *appear* as a "labor of love" so that women can be denied a legitimating wage.[20] Leopoldina Fortunati's *The Arcane of Reproduction,* published in Italian in 1981 and translated into English in 1995, offers a more structural account of unwaged housework, arguing that the female labor market of housework and sex work is posited as "non-value," but is actually necessary to the production of surplus value because it produces the use value of labor power itself.[21] Fortunati refutes political or normative distinctions between productive labor and reproductive labor and illuminates the role of gender in constituting and naturalizing those distinctions. Yet while Fortunati treats reproductive labor as a vital *part* of the productive process, she does not suggest that it is *independently* productive.[22] The male worker's body is the "dead labor" the housewife manufactures in the "arcane of reproduction," making her the concealed source of some of the value he in turn produces in the "abode of production."[23] Noting the zero-sum contribution of reproductive labor to production, then, we can distinguish between Fortunati's account and the claims of thinkers such as Lazzarato, Illouz, and Hardt and Negri, who argue that affective work has become "self-valorizing," capable of producing an entirely new kind of capitalist value outside the sphere of productive labor.

This distinction between productive and reproductive labor might seem somewhat scholastic, were it not for its connection to the question of value production in a period of deindustrialization. Put simply, what happens when almost everyone is working in the arcane of reproduction, but almost no one is laboring in the abode of production? Important recent books by Nancy Fraser, Jason Smith, and Gabriel Winant have noted that far from catalyzing a new era of dynamic and self-sustaining affective value production, the rise of service work suggests an ever-intensifying crisis in capital accumulation. For Fraser, that crisis is a "crisis of care": the simultaneous decline of the Fordist "family wage" and decimation of governmental social welfare provisioning in the 1970s required formerly unwaged "housewives" to enter waged work (often low-waged service work) and thus also to rely on the even lower-waged (and often racialized and feminized) care work of others, producing an intractable contradiction between capitalism's reliance on reproductive labor and its increasing inability to support or sustain it.[24] For Smith and Winant, in turn, the rising service sector is at once cause and effect of a global "long downturn"—the stagnation not only of technological innovation (productivity gains), but also of accumulation as such (rates of growth). When manufacturing employment started its precipitous decline beginning the early 1970s, they note, the service sector initially absorbed a lot of that cast-off labor. Yet because in-person service work "require[s] an intuitive, embodied, and socially mediated form of knowledge or skill," Smith argues in *Smart Machines and Service Work: Automation in an Age of Stagnation*, there are "technological, moral, and even legal limits" to its mechanization and automation. As more and more labor is allocated to this relatively low-waged, low-productivity sector, he contends, economic growth has slowed or even completely stalled out.[25] Winant's *The Next Shift: The Fall of Industry and the Rise of Health Care in Rust Belt America* similarly connects the rise of care work to the collapse of industrial manufacturing. In a deindustrialized economy, Winant argues, "high-employment, low-profit industries—such as health care, education, and social services—experience . . . limited opportunities for productivity gains, a problem inherent to the provision of human services."[26] Relatedly, Maya Gonzalez and Jeanne Neton's influential 2013 essay "The Logic of Gender" connects the Marxist-feminist tradition to more recent scholarship on service work by clarifying the relationship between the unwaged "housewife" of the past and the low-waged child-care provider of the present.[27] Contemporary service work's low wages, Gonzalez and Neton argue, can be explained not only by its economically and technologically "unproductive" nature, but also by its historic devaluing, a history intimately connected to its naturalization as "women's work."[28]

Attending to histories of industrialization and deindustrialization, to contemporary crises of productivity and profitability, and to how service work came to be devalued and dominated, this body of scholarship is vitally important to *Beneath the Wage*. Only by theorizing contemporary service work *as* labor—and in the context of or by comparison with other kinds of labor—can we understand its low and precarious wages, its feminization and racialization, its exclusion from contracts and regulation, and the ways service workers themselves have been forced to labor perpetually harder, faster, and longer.

THE PREHISTORY OF SERVICE WORK

As I have already suggested, service work is not a footnote in the story of modern capitalism, but an indispensable shadow history of labor exploitation. Today's service work has roots in the history of domestic servitude: the maids, nannies, and household servants who were (and are) controlled through direct domination, yet also exploited through wages and labor markets.[29] As Evelyn Nakano-Glenn argues in her influential essay "From Servitude to Service Work," the history of how and under what conditions "racial-ethnic women were employed as servants to perform reproductive labor in white households" bears intimately on a contemporary era in which "racial-ethnic women are disproportionately employed as service workers," performing labor-intensive, low-wage work while being subjected to a repertoire of racialized and gendered techniques for exploitation.[30] This section briefly sketches the history of domestic servitude in order to show how contemporary service work continues to be shaped by the methods of wage payment, discipline, management, and regulation that were first innovated for preindustrial domestic servitude in Britain and enduringly racialized in the United States.

Centuries before theories of contemporary service work as "immaterial labor," classical political economists such as Adam Smith were already writing about domestic servitude as work that "does not fix or realize itself in any permanent subject; or vendible commodity" and instead "perish[es] in the very instance of [its] performance," without "leav[ing] any trace or value behind."[31] Classical political economy's substantialist theory of value—the idea that value inheres in the physical object as the crystallization of embodied labor—inevitably resulted in normative distinctions between goods-producing work and the more ephemeral output of domestic servitude. [32] As Carolyn Steedman argues, because servants "did not 'really' work or make . . . *vendible objects,*" classical political economists such as Smith and John Locke could not conceptualize them as working class.[33] Far less beholden to a substantialist definition of productivity than his predecessors, Marx argued to the contrary that those whose work is "consumed as services and not in products separable from the worker" could also be "directly exploited in a capitalist manner." Yet despite acknowledging that as of the time of *Capital*'s writing, the "servant class" was larger than the number of workers employed in textile factories, mines, and the metal industries *combined*, Marx nonetheless tended to treat domestic servants as a feudal holdover largely irrelevant to a theory of the capitalist mode of production. Servants were part of a "transitional stage," he argued, and were "of microscopic significance when compared with the mass of capitalist production."[34]

Domestic servitude also seemed at odds with capitalist work discipline, management, compensation, and productivity, concepts that were defined almost exclusively in relation to industrial manufacturing. As the historian E. P. Thompson famously argues, eighteenth-century industrialization transformed time itself by requiring working days of a fixed length and the rationalized regularity of "clock time."[35] While Thompson focuses on the standardization of labor time, Eric Hobsbawm's classic essay "Custom, Wages, and Workload in Nineteenth Century Industry" describes the standardization of wages measured by time.[36] Both Hobsbawm and Thompson yoke the temporal discipline of rationalized, mechanized industrial labor to the increased use of formal wage contracts. Yet neither time wages nor this kind of rationalized, predictable time discipline apply to domestic service. As historian Leonard Schwarz suggests, in the eighteenth and nineteenth centuries, the time-based wage was gendered, age specific, and "did not apply to those who lived in their employers' houses: farm servants, apprentices, domestic servants. The latter received board wages" and "had no legal time of their own."[37] Guides to servants' behavior from this period generally say nothing about hours of work, since domestic servants were paid by the year and had no legal control over their hours or their pace of work.[38] To the extent that time functioned as a mode of labor discipline for domestic servants, it did not enforce what Thompson calls "bourgeois exactitude," but instead made working time infinitely elastic.[39] Because the servant is hired "without any particular time limited" for their labor, the eighteenth-century jurist William Blackstone argues, they "shall serve... as well when there is work to be done as when there is not."[40] Those considered "menial servants"—from the Latin *intra moenia*, or "within the walls" of the household—did not experience Thompson's "distinction between their employer's time and their 'own' time."[41]

Blackstone's writings on the rights and responsibilities of domestic servants and their masters would soon become the basis for new laws and regulations governing manufacturing labor. Yet domestic servants also quickly became one of modern labor law's most vexing problems.[42] Eighteenth-century British common law had given masters an immense amount of control over their servants, and industrial-era employment law translated that "open-ended duty of obedience" into the employer's right to control all aspects of the employee's labor process, whether directly or via managers and overseers. At the same time, actual domestic servants were excluded from the very laws and regulations originally modeled on their working conditions. For instance, the 1875 Employers and Workman Act—a reform that enabled the modern trade-union movement in Britain—borrowed heavily from the 1867 Master-Servant Act, yet the 1875 law explicitly excluded domestic servants from its scope. By the end of the nineteenth century, domestic servants were largely omitted from legal categories such as "laborer," "apprentice," and "workman." As those formerly distinct types of laborers were drawn together into a single term—"employee"—and codified as a legally protected group in the twentieth century, domestic servants would be set ever further apart, providing the constitutive outside to the protected legal categories that enabled the rise of industrial wage labor in Britain.[43]

The history of domestic servitude and labor law is strikingly similar in the US context. Much as British jurists had struggled over how or whether to define domestic servants as workers, the issue of how and whether to regulate domestic servitude so beleaguered America's late nineteenth-century middle class that it was termed "the Great American question."[44] The answer to that question would be the same in the United States as in Britain. Much as the "ephemeral" nature of domestic servitude had excluded it from the British tradition of classical political economy, twentieth-century domestic servitude in the United States was excluded from regulation because it did not produce a material commodity alienable from its maker. A 1930 New York State court opinion ruling against a domestic servant seeking recognition as an employee, for instance, held that "there is no tangible, commercial product of domestic service, it ministers only to the necessity, comfort, and convenience of the employer."[45] Also as in Britain, waged domestic servitude in the early twentieth-century United States could not be understood as labor because neither its time discipline nor its compensation had been rationalized in the ways goods-producing labor had. A 1917 Bureau of Labor Statistics report notes that because the domestic worker's "whole time... belongs to her employer," her labor could not be regulated in the manner of work done in "the factory, the store, and the office."[46] Nonwhite domestic servants in the United States were particularly vulnerable to the intensity and insecurity endemic to work that was not legally or politically recognized *as* work. They typically received part or even all of their compensation as "in-kind" payments, rather than standardized cash wages, and they experienced what historian Cecelia Rio describes as a life of "around-the-clock duty" characterized not by rationalized time, but by diffuse and unpredictable obligation.[47]

As this last detail suggests, the US context had its own specificity, too. Servitude was a particularly vexing problem in the United States because it suggested the nation hadn't actually broken from European "feudal" relations. Most importantly, the fear (or fantasy) of domestic servitude's anachronism was profoundly racialized in the

United States. The association of "menial" domestic labor with chattel slavery had outlasted slavery's formal abolition. After emancipation, waged domestic work was still predominantly performed by Black and other nonwhite women in the North as well as the South. Domestic servitude, Jacqueline Jones argues, "recapitulated the mistress-slave relationship in the midst of industrializing America. As paid labor became increasingly associated with the time-oriented production of goods, the black nurse, maid, and cook remained something of a labor-force anachronism."[48] Sarah Haley powerfully describes the link between domestic service and "carceral servitude" in this period. "The 'proprietorial notions of the self' grounding white liberal notions of freedom"—notions that emerged in no small part from the fetishistic affirmation of work that produced tangible commodities—ensured that "caprice governed the economic decisions of white domestic managers," she writes.[49] In her history of postbellum Black women's labor, Tera Hunter similarly contends that "white Southerners had a stake in the persistence of individualized, manual, low-wage household labor."[50] Angela Davis, in her powerful critique of the *Wages for Housework* manifesto cited in the previous section, notes that "in the United States, women of color—and especially Black women—have been receiving wages for housework for untold decades." Black women, Davis contends, "have had to do their own housekeeping and other women's home chores as well.... As paid housekeepers, they have been called upon to be surrogate wives and mothers in millions of white homes."[51]

Domestic service was thus excluded from the emerging contractual understanding of free labor in the postbellum United States because it was naturalized as labor "innate" to women of color, because it was subject to intimate, "individualized" domination instead of impersonal modern management, and because it was unprotected by either tradition or law.[52] Similar reasoning was used to exploit migrant women. Beginning in the mid-nineteenth century, Grace Chang notes in *Disposable Domestics*, migrant women were essentially "imported into the

United States from the Third World" to labor as domestic servants. Migrant women were perceived to be "naturally" suited both to the hard work of care, cleaning, and cooking and to the unrecognized status of that work. Programs such as the "Americanization" schemes of 1910s and 1920s, which conscripted Mexican immigrant women into domestic work in the US Southwest, were grounded in the fiction that the work of migrant domestics was not actually work at all, but rather "training" or "rehabilitation," and that domestic servants' white bosses were not employers subject to labor regulations, but rather "hosts" or even "friends."[53]

This brief history of domestic servitude shows us how certain kinds of work are made to seem less like work. Despite the realities of domination and precarity, domestic servitude in the United States and Britain was centrally understood, in Steedman's words, as "an emotional and affective relationship rather than a class relationship."[54] This early substitution of affect for class offers a surprising point of origin for the claims of contemporary theorists that "emotional laborers" willingly "internalize" the affects they are compelled to perform. Well before the rise of capitalism, the servant's relationship to the master already functioned as a ready metaphor for voluntary submission to the natural and divine authority of the father, the king, and God. Servants weren't just called upon to obey, but rather to "internalize obedience and be faithful in their hearts," as Sarah Maza explains in her history of domestic service in the seventeenth century.[55] Sometimes, this kind of willing submission could appear as a virtue (as in descriptions of service to Christ). Just as often, this sort of "voluntary servitude"—the degrading quality of consenting to your own domination—is what has made servants appear to be the abject other of the capitalist wage laborer: content in their submissiveness, complicit in their unfreedom, stubbornly premodern.

Of course, one does not need to look hard to find ample evidence that domestic servants were neither complicit in their exploitation nor content with it. It is a grievous error to think that political consciousness and therefore political organizing are possible only in the context of the formal wage contract. Although often denied legal protection, formal regulation, political representation, and collective bargaining rights, domestic servants have frequently been a radical faction in labor movements and beyond. In her book *Between Women: Domestics and their Employers,* the feminist sociologist Judith Rollins argues that the domestic servants who have long been depicted as subordinate, invisible "non-persons" are actually anything but. Over years of conversations with nonwhite domestic servants, Rollins found a high level of class consciousness and a canny "awareness of the Other" that she compares to Frantz Fanon's account of the colonized subject who is fully prepared to fight for his own liberation.[56] Historian Ashley D. Farmer likewise describes a revolutionary vanguard of "militant Negro domestics" who forged a vital network of radical Third-Worldist solidarity. In in the 1940s and 1950s—a period in which 80 percent of Black women were employed as domestic workers—Black feminist Marxists such as Louise Thompson Patterson, Claudia Jones, and Alice Childress organized through the Communist Party, the Southern Negro Youth Congress, the National Negro Labor Council, and the independent Domestic Workers Union (DWU). These women were theorists as well as organizers, developing their own conceptual paradigms to describe the exploitation specific to nonwhite, female domestic servants. Such paradigms included the concepts of "triple exploitation" (Patterson's term, which would become the basis for later influential theories of "intersectional" oppression) and "super-exploitation" (Jones's term, which as others have done, I hope to build on throughout this book).[57] Although domestic servants were frequently sidelined by the mainstream labor movement (a 1970 AFL-CIO report claimed it was "impossible" for the organization to include domestic workers, who "have several different employers in the course of a week"), they continued to organize both within and beyond traditional unions.[58] As Magally Miranda has argued, domestic workers are today showing all workers what it looks like to build collectivity outside the standard context of the shared workplace or the union shop and across the dividing lines of regulated, unregulated, waged, and unwaged labor.[59]

This is a book about service work in the twenty-first century: the work of restaurant servers and baristas, outsourced clerical workers and app-bound gigworkers. This kind of work may seem far afield from the work that's been done by domestic servants for centuries. But if we want to understand why service work is often treated as if it's not work at all, why this kind of low-wage work is gendered and racialized in specific ways, why service workers are often seen as submissive, instead of as exploited, and why theories of service work focus on service workers' feelings instead of on their formation as a class, the answers to these questions lie in the longer history of domestic servitude. Likewise, if we want to understand the working conditions of contemporary service work—its vulnerability to domination and subordination, its low and uncertain wages, its marginalization in law and politics—we must see that these conditions, too, originated in the working lives of domestic servants. Finally and perhaps most importantly, if we want to understand how jobs that have been constitutively excluded from political and legal protections might nevertheless foster their own forms of radical consciousness, political organizing, and communal solidarity, we would do well to pay attention to the collectivist practices of the servant workers who once occupied that same precarious, informally waged, and legally unrecognized position.

SERVICE WORK AND LABOR PROCESS THEORY

If we focus too much on what service workers do (smile, create, care, emote), we risk overlooking the conditions in which they do it. This book is an attempt to understand those conditions. It is interested in how service workers are paid (wages), how their work is controlled (management), and how that work is mediated by technology (mechanization). I borrow these three concepts—wages, management, and mechanization—from the tradition of labor process theory. Most famously developed by Harry Braverman in his monumental book *Labor and Monopoly Capital: The Degradation of Work in the Twentieth Century*, "labor process" describes the way workers themselves experience waged work and especially how they are stripped of skill, pride, and control over their own labor.[60] I have found labor process theory an invaluable resource for understanding the general tendency of work under capitalism to be devalued and degraded.[61] Yet much as theories of service work have rarely focused on its labor process, theories of labor process have rarely focused on service work.[62] *Beneath the Wage* hopes to change that. Doing so, I'll argue, doesn't just afford us new insights into the functioning of the service sector. It also helpfully decenters manufacturing labor from our understanding of capitalist wage labor as such, revealing important connections between low-wage service work and other types of labor that are not goods-producing. Like farmwork, service work often uses nonhourly methods of wage payment that fail to provide a stable or even adequate living for workers. Like truck drivers and other goods-circulating workers, service workers tend not to be surveilled by a stopwatch-holding scientific manager, but instead are forced to work harder and faster via decentralized, indirect management. And although service work remains less mechanized than manufacturing labor, technology is today being used to degrade and outsource not only low-waged service work but also professionalized care work such as teaching and health care.

Service work is also distinct from goods-producing labor insofar as it has been excluded from labor movements and labor reforms. To understand this aspect of service work's history, I add a fourth concept to the list above: regulation. Because regulatory reforms such as the 1937 Fair Labor Standards Act (FLSA) were made possible by changes in the management and technology of industrial manufacturing, laws dealing with minimum wages and maximum hours are often simply treated as a given in labor process theory. Service work, by contrast, has typically been excluded from such regulation. Service work's constitutively unregulated status is, I'll argue, the last defining aspect of its labor process.

The three chapters of this book shed light on these structuring conditions of service work. Chapter 1 focuses on wages and management (the history of superexploitative tip wages and their relationship to direct domination in service work). Chapter 2 considers wages and machinery (piece-rate wages and the deskilling and outsourcing of clerical task work). Chapter 3 takes up management and machinery ("independent" gigwork's reliance on the time-disciplining technology of algorithms and apps). In all three chapters, I emphasize how exploitation and domination have been intensified by service work's exclusion from labor regulation. Out of these close studies of service work's labor process, I ultimately aim to develop a broader theory of the dominant tendencies of capitalism in the twenty-first century. In service work's irregular wages, we see a widening trend toward *superexploitation*. In its methods of indirect management, we see the unmistakable process of *intensification*. In its complex relation to machine-driven automation, we see a pronounced shift toward *deskilling*. And in its eluding of regulation, we see the triumph of *informalization*. These conceptual pairings—and their role in illuminating the past and present of low-waged service work—are worth explaining in a bit more detail.

SUPEREXPLOITATION (WAGES)

It is essential to understand not just *how much* service workers are paid, but also simply *how*. This attention to the method of wage payment is among this book's most important contributions to labor history and theories of the labor process. Whereas most scholarship on wages focuses simply on the amount of the wage, theories and histories of the method of wage payment look at whether wages are regulated or formalized, how frequently wages are paid and in what form (monetary or nonmonetary), and in what way the amount is calculated (by time, output, performance, or something else). The method of wage payment is often particular to a given historical epoch and is determined by social, political, and cultural forces—including, I argue, racialization and feminization—as well as by the level of technological development in the economy or sector.

We tend to associate industrialization with formal contracts and standardized wages, but in fact even late nineteenth-century labor arrangements tended to rely as much on unwritten, casual agreements as on formal contracts.[63] Wage agreements, in particular, were variable and disparate. Prior to generalized industrialization, manufacturing wages were often paid "in kind" (in food, beer, or lodging). In the extractive economy, payment in coal, by-products, and credit remained common well after the rise of the factory system.[64] Even when wages were paid in cash, the quantity due could be measured in a range of ways. By the early nineteenth century, wages were most often measured either by time (hourly, daily, or weekly wages) or by individual output (task-based or piece-rate wages). Yet other ways of calculating compensation persisted until the early twentieth century, including premium-bonus systems, task-bonus systems, weighing and measuring, profit sharing, payment by earnings, and sliding scales.[65] It wasn't until assembly-line technology allowed workers' output to be totally determined by machine speed that the specific type of hourly wage Melinda Cooper aptly describes as the "Fordist family wage" could be codified in the United States by the FLSA and become the dominant method of measuring wages in the manufacturing sector.[66]

Despite this complex history, contemporary political economists, cultural critics, and even historians have tended to treat the regulated, cash-based, hourly wage as a conceptual, political, and historical norm.[67] *Beneath the Wage* argues to the contrary that "wage" does not name a singular coherent category, but something multiple, variegated, and historically specific. Even after the passage of the FLSA, nonwhite female domestic servants were paid neither by the hour nor by the task, but instead in an unpredictable mix of irregular cash wages and in-kind payment (room and board, leftovers, and hand-me-downs). Likewise, manufacturing work performed by "low-productivity" workers with disabilities, work where workers are spread out across large spaces (as in farmwork), and work where workers are "self-managed" (as in goods-circulating work such as like truck driving) all continue to be paid via piece rates. Piece-rate and task-rate wages are particularly important to new forms of platform-based digital "microwork," so named for the amount of the wage as well as the size of the tasks. And for in-person service workers from railway porters to waitresses, the precapitalist practice of giving small gratuities to household staff persisted long after the rise of advanced industrialization. Legally codified at mid-century as a legitimate form of wage payment, tips paid directly by the customer remain a crucial aspect of the in-person service sector.

Following the work of Marxist development economists, I use the term "superexploitation" to characterize service work's unique methods of wage payment. Superexploitation involves two distinct but often overlapping processes.[68] First, superexploitation happens when workers' compensation does not cover their cost of living: when, in Marx's terms, wages do not fully or predictably provide the "means of subsistence...sufficient to maintain [the worker] in [their] normal state as a working individual."[69] Second, superexploitation happens when workers are simply compelled to work harder during a shift, producing what Marx describes as an increase in the "tension" or "density" of working time, or what development economists describe (in language we might query) as the "greater exploitation of the worker's physical strength."[70]

There are myriad debates over the specific terms used to describe these methods of surplus value extraction and over what a term such as "superexploitation" can tell us about waged industrial work. I am less interested in these conceptual nuances and more curious about what the idea of superexploitation allows us to see about the relation between wages, work intensity, and the entanglement of race, gender, and class. Superexploitation bears down with special force on workers who are not paid a guaranteed hourly wage and whose wages are not legally regulated. It is further enabled by the racialization and feminization of labor, which likewise become justifications for a hierarchy of wage forms.

My use of the term draws particularly on the radical analytical and political insights of Claudia Jones. Born in Trinidad and Tobago, Jones migrated to the United States as a child and in 1945 became the first Black woman to become a member of the Communist Party of the USA.[71] As both a labor organizer and a journalist, Jones explored "the militancy of the Negro woman" in light of the Black Belt Thesis, which held that formerly enslaved Black workers in the South were an internal colony. Jones emphasized the interlocking systems of capitalism, chattel slavery, and patriarchy most vividly represented by the Black female domestic servant. As she puts it in her 1949 essay "An End to the Neglect of the Problems of the Negro Woman!" the "super-exploitation of the Negro woman worker is revealed not only in that she receives, as a woman, less than equal pay for equal work with men, but also in that the majority of Negro women get less than half the pay of white women." Black women had been pushed out of industrial manufacturing work after the end of World War II, she notes, and were most likely to be "hit hardest" by increased cost of living, leading to their "exclusion from virtually all fields of work except the most menial and underpaid."[72]

Beneath the Wage uses the concept of superexploitation to describe the specificity of the wage relation in the service sector: a sector where workers are compelled to work for less than they can subsist on and where nonstandard methods of wage payment enable racialized and feminized forms of exploitation. As a way of naming variations within the wage form, superexploitation draws our attention to the violence and precarity that are a part of every wage relation, even when those features are concealed beneath the regularity of hourly wages and the "fairness" underlying wage regulation.

INTENSIFICATION (MANAGEMENT)

Histories of the wage in manufacturing labor typically connect its particular forms of "work discipline" to the standardization of time (working days with a fixed length and measured by clocks), to the modernization of wage agreements ("a fair day's work for a fair day's pay"), and to the rationalization of management.[73] Taylorist scientific management, Braverman argues, required "the gathering together of the workers in a workshop and the dictation of the length of the working day; the supervision of workers to ensure diligent, intense, or uninterrupted application," and "the setting of production minimums." Only after work had been centralized, standardized, and rationalized could stopwatch-holding managers dictate "the precise manner in which work is to be performed."[74]

The time discipline and scientific management famously described by Braverman, Thompson, and Hobsbawm is not easily applied to service work, which often involves unpredictable work hours and irregular efficiency, more "self-management," and a less rationalizable—even immeasurable—"output."[75] Yet it would be a mistake to think that labor discipline doesn't matter in the service sector. Indeed, labor discipline is if anything more important in service work than in goods-producing work. Whereas manufacturing achieves productivity gains by replacing humans with machines, the service sector must "coerce more labor out of a given hour by means of refinements in supervision, oversight, and workplace discipline," Jason Smith notes.[76] *Beneath the Wage* explores how this coercion works: how, in an attempt to eke out more productivity, nontechnological techniques of labor *intensification* are used to make service workers' days longer and their pace of work faster. Tips ensure that in-person service workers are highly attuned to the temporal demands of those they serve; indeed, one suggested origin for the word "tip" is that it was an acronym for "to insure promptitude."[77] Task wages, likewise, are used to control subcontracted or outsourced workers who labor in their own homes, far from the view of managers or supervisors. Modern platform gigwork, in turn, has innovated a postindustrial time discipline often described as the "obligation to be available," ensuring that workers remain subordinated to a working day whose only limit is the limit of the human body.[78] Across all kinds of service work, moreover, we find heavy use of part-time work and other "just-in-time labor" arrangements that, Joel Suarez explains, allow employers to "suppress labor costs in service industries where productivity largely came through more employment rather than [technological] investment."[79]

My description of these techniques as "intensification" is intended to evoke a form of labor control that combines the direct domination with which service work is often associated and the more indirect, "scientific" forms of managerial and technological control typically associated with manufacturing labor. By arguing that service work synthesizes "preindustrial" forms of coercion and more "modern" methods of machine-mediated scientific management, I am also intervening in an ongoing critical debate about the so-called "neofeudal" qualities of twenty-first-century service work and gigwork. In a widely discussed 2020 essay, Jodi Dean uses the term "neofeudalism" to describe a present mode of accumulation characterized by "non-capitalist dimensions of production—expropriation, domination, and force." One of the central features of the contemporary economy, she suggests, is the economic dominance of a "vast sector of servants."[80] Dean thus describes the service economy by analogy to what she describes as preindustrial and ostensibly noncapitalist domestic servitude. As my own emphasis on the history of domestic servitude suggests, there is much in this analogy that is useful and indeed vital. Yet Dean offers no historical account of the relationship between preindustrial domestic service and contemporary service work. As a result, she implies a *return* to an older form of exploitation, rather than a *continuity*. This risks treating service work as an exceptional, anachronistic, or "non-capitalist" type of labor. In fact, as I've tried to show, it is a significant and persistent part of the history of capitalism. What I describe throughout this book as a long "age of service work" is an attempt to center this historical continuity as well as the coconstitution of manufacturing labor and service work, which exert pressure on one another not simply as "uneven" forms—one declaring itself "modern," one seemingly anachronistic but also in combination. That continuity and coconstitution are particularly present when we consider strategies of intensification, which have often originated in the service sector *before* passing into the sphere of manufacturing. The forms of control and rationalization used to manage service workers today are neither residual and "pre-capitalist" nor evidence of a return to a "feudal" mode of accumulation. Instead, they are evidence of capitalism's defining and continuous need to ensure that work rarely slows and never stops.

DESKILLING (TECHNOLOGY)

"Automation" is the word on everyone's lips. Yet it is a truism that automation doesn't really work in the service sector. The idea that service work is technologically stagnant (meaning it is immune to the kind of technological advancements that might eventually allow a task to be fully automated) has been central to many recent theories of the sector. Aaron Benanav describes service work as impervious "to the incremental process innovations that generate rapid rates of productivity growth," while Astra Taylor claims that service-sector technology is little more than "fauxtomation."[81] Many of these accounts have drawn on mid-century macroeconomist William Baumol's theory of "cost disease" to describe the problem of increasing productivity through technology in the service sector. In a famous 1967 essay, Baumol argues that manufacturing is "technologically progressive": technological innovations and economies of scale from the assembly line to new computing technology allow "output per man hour" to increase both consistently and rapidly in the goods-producing sector. The service sector, by contrast, is composed mostly of "nonprogressive" activities, "which by their very nature, permit only sporadic increases in productivity." Because it is difficult, if not impossible, to increase service work's output significantly, the service sector tends to lag behind "productivity in the remainder of the economy."[82]

Baumol's work was prescient. While service-sector productivity increased during the mid-century industrial boom because of new communications and information technology, in the 1970s it fell even more precipitously than manufacturing productivity did, and it essentially never rebounded. Service work's "technologically stagnant" character is partly due to the specific tasks it involves. As Baumol notes, for instance, one can neither speed up nor scale up jobs such as teaching or orchestra conducting, because the resulting decline in the quality of the product "would be viewed with concern by critics and audience alike."[83] More often, it is simply not technologically possible to supplement or replace human service workers with machines. Although we have been imagining robot maids since at least *The Jetsons*, engineers have yet to develop robots capable of doing many of the basic tasks commonly performed by domestic servants (or by mothers). As of this writing, no one has yet been able to make a machine that can competently sort and fold a basket of laundry. (Tesla did announce in January 2024 that it had finally created a robot capable of folding a shirt, but it turned out that the robot was remotely controlled by a human operator, making it more akin to Taylor's "fauxtomation" than to a new Fordist assembly line.)

It is generally true that you can't automate a lot of service work. But that does not mean there is no link between service work and labor-saving technologies. On the contrary, there's a crucial connection between them. I argue that this connection is best captured by the concept of *deskilling*. Deskilling refers to the process whereby a job is broken up into smaller parts or otherwise simplified so that it can either be performed by less-skilled (or just lower-waged) workers or be fully automated. Deskilling reduces workers' autonomy and control over their own labor, allowing managers and indeed machines themselves to determine not just *what* is done but also *how*.

It is important to begin any discussion of deskilling by noting that it is not a quality of the worker or even of the work itself: a job can be "deskilled" and yet continue to require an immense amount of skill to perform. Rather, deskilling is a process that affects a type of worker or even an entire profession over time. To give the example I explore in this book's Coda, the deskilling of university teaching labor might begin when a teacher has to replace a skill she already has (teaching in the classroom) with a new skill (recording online lectures); teaching *as a whole* is then "deskilled" when her employer decides she can be replaced with her own recorded online lectures plus an underpaid student "learning assistant." Similarly, because the digital microwork described in Chapter 2 tends to be performed by people living outside the Anglosphere, it requires workers to have English-language skills that are far beyond the foreign-language knowledge of most US professionals. Yet this work has been "deskilled" in the sense that it has been broken up into the smallest possible units so that a single project can be spread out across hundreds or even thousands of workers, each doing as little as a single keystroke. Deskilling is also important to the labor process of platform gigwork, where managerial labor and control over workers is now handled by the platform itself. Whereas taxi drivers or truckers once relied on their own experience and "road knowledge," today, apps tell them what to do, where to go, and how to get there while also monitoring their speed, location, and efficiency.[84]

Moreover, while service work has not historically been the site of major technological innovations—and while technology is unlikely to ever have the kind of immediate, exponential impact on service-work productivity that technologies such as the assembly line had on manufacturing—recent developments in data processing and machine learning are nonetheless transforming labor in many parts of the sector. The GPS capabilities of circulation gigwork platforms, for instance, have resolved long-standing problems in logistics by ensuring that tens of thousands of delivery workers are taking the fastest routes to multiple destinations and thus guaranteeing maximum spatial and temporal efficiency. The deskilling of clerical work that happens on microwork platforms simply wasn't possible prior to innovations in computing and communications technology. Nor was the asynchronous online college lecture possible prior to widespread high-speed internet and high-quality cameras becoming standard features of personal computers.

The digital deskilling of service work is a good example of what Benanav terms "labor-substituting" technologies in contrast to the "labor-replacing" technologies of full automation.[85] Yet I would also argue that contemporary service work indicates that the distinction between these two ways of describing the technological mediation of labor may not be as stable as we think. After all, reducing the number of workers required to complete a given task *is* "labor-replacing," even if some human workers are still required. Work that has been persistently and significantly deskilled can be more easily automated, especially if what Baumol identified as the "quality" limit has been overcome. For instance, once an employer has decided that instead of paying one professional translator to translate a document, they will instead hire dozens of deskilled "microworkers" to translate a single sentence of the text each—because the cheaper cost is worth the decreased quality—then it becomes easier for that same employer to decide to use AI to do the same job, even if the AI makes more mistakes. Drawing on the idea of what some economists are now calling "so-so automation"—technologies that generate only small productivity improvements, replace jobs that were already low waged, and contribute very little to overall economic growth—*Beneath the Wage* argues that that labor-replacing automation, technological stagnation, and a low-growth economy are bound together in the contemporary service sector by the ubiquitous process of deskilling.

INFORMALIZATION (REGULATION)

As I have already suggested, service and retail workers as a whole were initially exempted from federal regulations surrounding working hours and wages because they did not make "vendible goods." Even when the FLSA and other New Deal reforms were expanded in the mid-1960s, large portions of the service work economy, especially jobs such as domestic service and home health care, were exempted from reform.[86] Hourly wages were a good fit for work with standardized time discipline and output. But work that lacked that standardization because of its nonphysical products, unpredictable hours, and reliance on self-management—in other words, service work—could seemingly not be included under these new regulations. Likewise, the distinction between "employees" and "independent contractors" was based on the difference between goods-producing manufacturing workers—centralized in one space and controlled by scientific managers—and goods-circulating service workers, whose work was ostensibly more independent and autonomous and who were thus excluded from the legal rights granted to formally waged workers.[87]

This book theorizes service work's constitutive exclusion from state regulation as *informalization*. Informalization is a process whereby a kind of work is explicitly excluded from laws, regulations, and contractual guarantees. Visible across the long history of service jobs, informalization describes the legal and political status of a wide range of workers: early twentieth-century domestic workers paid in hand-me-downs, tipworkers vulnerable to time theft, subcontracted clerical outworkers and digital microworkers performing unregulated work in their own homes, twenty-first-century "independent contractors" spending unpaid hours on gigwork platforms just waiting for work.

Perhaps the most important thing that the concept of informalization helps us grasp is how the absence of legal regulation in service work has kept the sector tethered to the racialized, gendered, xenophobic, and ableist logics that served to differentiate it from industrial labor in the first place. Informalization secures the idea of service work as exceptional, whether in the sense that it is mostly performed by women and nonwhite workers or in the sense that it is premodern, somehow outside of or improper to the sphere of capitalism itself. Service work has never been understood as free labor; instead, like unwaged reproductive work, it has been perceived as the natural domain of women and nonwhite subjects whose "substandard" productivity or skill did not make them fit for "real" work. These were some of the reasons that service work was exempted from contracts and labor laws; then, in a perverse cycle, the absence of contracts and labor laws became yet another sign of service work's exceptionalist or anachronism. This is the cycle of informalization: the way regulation shapes service work simply by way of its absence.

POLITICS AND THE CULTURE OF SERVICE WORK

The forms of superexploitation, intensification, and deskilling specific to low-waged service work are, I have suggested, intimately tied to its regulatory informalization. Yet I am aware that my focus on regulation risks valorizing legal reforms such as the FLSA, treating them as a simple solution to exploitation, and not as part of the larger *system* of exploitation. A similar ambivalence haunts Marx's account of the Factory Acts in his "Working Day" chapter. On one hand, he sees this regulation as a victory for the English working class—a "modest Magna Carta... which at last makes clear 'when the time which the worker sells is ended, and when his own begins.'" On the other hand, he is clear that maximum-hours reforms only prove that the state operates in the service of capital: the regulatory state may "curb capital's drive towards a limitless draining away of labour-power by forcibly limiting the working day," but it is still ultimately an institution "ruled by capitalist and landlord."[88] In fact, he suggests, regulations are how the state transcends intracapitalist conflict between individual firms in order ensure the stability of the mode of accumulation as a whole.

I stake out a similar position. There is no question that service work's informalization makes it uniquely vulnerable to superexploitation. But this is not cause to celebrate regulation as the solution to the problem of service work's precarity, domination, or low wages. If, as I suggested above, the particular forms of regulation forged in an age of US-led industrial hegemony were specific both to the labor process of goods-producing work and to the political possibilities available in an age of productivity growth, service work must innovate its own demands, as well as its own organizing forms. Indeed, one aim of this book is to show how the history of informalized, superexploited service work requires us to update the long-standing assumption that the hourly wage-earning, goods-producing worker is the embodiment of the working class as such. Such metonymy has long justified the subordination of other political interests and desires—from racial equality and gender emancipation to anticolonial and anti-imperialist movements—to the struggles of formally waged male manufacturing workers, and it has privileged the shop floor as the place where class struggle happens and indeed where class itself is made. *Beneath the Wage* is an attempt to reject the emphasis on one particular kind of wage—and one particular kind of worker—in our understanding of class struggle. The world of waged work is more various than we have acknowledged. So, too, is resistance to the wage.

To this end, *Beneath the Wage* pays particular attention to the distinct organizing strategies, tactics, and demands being forged by contemporary service workers. These present-day struggles are themselves informed and illuminated by the longer histories of domestic-worker and service-worker organizing. Feminist labor historian Dorothy Cobble has noted that long before the rise of what we now call "gigwork," waitresses' unions eschewed traditional worksite-specific organizing in favor of what she terms "occupational unionism," which demanded workers' broad right to autonomy over their labor process and the need for livelihood security outside single-employer contracts.[89] Contemporary service-worker activism, I suggest, is similarly pushing the boundaries of industrial unionism. Workers whose exploitation depends on "independent contractor" classification have organized not just as members of a trade or industry, but around this shared legal status, from delivery gigworker organizations such as Los Deliveristas Unidos to cleaning-worker groups such as Liberty Cleaners. Tipworker groups such as One Fair Wage, discussed in Chapter 1, are likewise organizing and creating solidarity networks around shared vulnerability to a specific wage form, connecting baristas and bartenders to nail salon workers and parking lot attendants. Organizations such as the Tech Workers

Coalition, meanwhile, are going beyond even "wall-to-wall" union organizing by mobilizing not only professionalized and salaried tech workers, but also informalized, outsourced microworkers paid by the piece.

There is also a long tradition of service workers organizing collectively beyond and outside of traditionally "economic" workplace demands. The mid-century Domestic Workers Union (DWU) described above, for instance, was international, intersectional, and radically multi-issue. DWU member Claudia Jones's famous essay on superexploitation describes not only the case of Dora Jones, who was kept as a domestic worker in conditions indistinguishable from chattel slavery, but also the case of Rose Lee Ingram, a Black sharecropper given a life sentence for defending herself against lynching. Similarly, as I discuss at the end of Chapter 3, radical rank-and-file service workers are today making demands not just for higher wages or better working conditions, but also for the rights of workers with disabilities, for the rights of queer and trans workers to gender-affirming health care, for police abolition, immigration reform, ecological justice, and divestment from the military-industrial complex.[90] Cobble describes these kinds of organizing as "relational unionism," a movement committed to the belief that "the reproduction of people and the planet are as important as making things and dominating nature through tools and technology." This book's Coda explores new opportunities for relational unionism in my own sector, higher education, arguing that we should focus our resistance to labor-saving technology not just on our own working conditions as teachers, but also on students' right to a high-quality education.

For a long time, service workers have been innovators of community building, collective survival, and mutual aid. Because the DWU was organizing informalized domestic workers hired to do day labor all over the city, it combatted the decentralized and ever-changing nature of these workers' employment by drawing on urban institutions such as social clubs and hiring halls and by building on traditions in Black folk culture. In this way, they forged what historian Dayo Gore describes as "strategies of survival and communities of support" outside formal union structures. We find similar strategies in the world of service work today, especially among the most marginalized workers. In Chapter 1, I describe the sex workers and club dancers organized via autonomous groups such as Soldiers of Pole and the Haymarket Pole Collective, whose practices build on the DWU's tactics for communal survival. Like the DWU, contemporary service-worker organizations aren't just mobilizing toward collective bargaining; they're also working within communities, focusing their efforts on the most vulnerable members and fighting for decriminalization and prison abolition. Sex workers are taking care of each other through networks of mutual aid such as the Sex Workers Outreach Project (SWOP), sharing resources from cash money to clothing and from rental assistance to bags of groceries, Narcan, and meals.

Contemporary service-worker organizing has powerful historical roots, but it also emerges out of some distinctively contemporary conditions. These include the combination of declining productivity and stagnant growth on the one hand, and skyrocketing subsistence and reproduction costs on the other. To understand these conditions, I have found it helpful to borrow the idea of "metabolic rift" developed in Marxist ecological thought. Metabolic rift theory describes how capitalism exhausts the two resources it needs most—nature and workers—by disrupting natural and social cycles of self-subsistence and social renewal. Separated from nature, workers can neither sustain themselves nor prevent the destruction of the natural world from which their sustenance once came. In parallel, service workers today experience what we might term a "reproductive rift": domestic workers are unable to afford housing; child-care workers are unable to afford child care; delivery gigworkers are unable to afford groceries. Thinking of these situations as instances of reproductive rift help us understand why organized service workers are not merely emphasizing their right to a "fair share" of their own productive output, but instead demanding wages adequate to rising subsistence costs.

The political strategies of contemporary service workers are one of this book's primary subjects. Another of its main subjects is how the political situation of service work has been taken up in art and culture. Many Marxist scholars continue to draw on Theodor Adorno's famous account of aesthetic autonomy—what Nicholas Brown glosses in a Kantian vein as art's fundamental purposeless and hence resistance to commodification.[91] This book is after something different, more akin to what poet and activist Mark Nowak describes as "social poetics": texts in which workers themselves document and critique their own working conditions and that often "coalesce around the formation of new relationships, new empathies, new narrators, new cultures, and new organizational formations."[92] *Beneath the Wage* pays careful, interpretive attention not just to the kinds of texts literary and cultural critics typically take seriously and read closely—novels and poems and prestige TV—but to a larger archive as well, one that includes the various ways that service workers have described their work in historically situated and vividly documentary detail. These texts also engage and dramatize service work's longer histories. They do so by appropriating past aesthetic forms, such as the picaresque and the georgic; by illuminating historically enduring features of service work, especially those persistently yoked to race and gender; and by recasting modes of working-class knowledge production such as the workers' inquiry—often perceived as a genre of industrial labor—for a new world of low-waged service work. Each chapter in this book thus attends to the history of the various genres and traditions through which workers themselves have described their work, and it is interested in how those traditions are recast and remediated in the context of contemporary labor. Contrary to the Hochschildian image of service workers as "participating in the illusion" of their own performances, contemporary cultural representations of service work register a notably clear-eyed understanding of service work—its low wages and its precarity, its forms of domination and intensification, its technologies of deskilling and subordination. These texts limn the contours of new forms of sociality, forms that are both antagonistic and immanent to the superexploitative conditions in which they have been produced and thus distinct from the aspirations once generated by the "free" laborer of industrial capitalism. Careful attention to this archive reveals the threads that bind the iron laws of capital to workers' own daily experience, which today takes place less often on the shop floor and more often before a sink of dirty dishes.

What this book calls "the age of service work" is not just a new way to describe the recent present. Nor is it yet another name for the postindustrial era that began in the 1960s when services-providing labor expanded while goods-producing labor contracted, ushering in a "long downturn" of falling profits. Instead, this phrase is a prompt to rethink the whole history of capitalism's wage through the paradigm of low-waged service work. Once we realize that service work is neither exceptional nor anachronistic, we will begin to grasp that its defining features (superexploitation, intensification, deskilling, informalization) are not residual processes or temporary exceptions, but the abiding and enduring tendencies of wage labor under capital.

CHAPTER ONE

Tipwork and TV

What are we watching when we watch reality TV? Despite the genre's oft-deplored frivolity, we're often watching other people do their jobs. Alongside romance and real estate, work has been an immensely popular subject for reality shows, including workplace-competition shows, small-business-advice shows, workplace dramas, and dangerous-jobs voyeurism. Beginning in the twenty-teens, however, a new kind of work started to show up on reality TV: service work. *Vanderpump Rules* (about the staff of SUR restaurant in Los Angeles); *Après Ski* and *Timber Creek Lodge* (about the staff of high-end ski lodges); *Below Deck, Below Deck Mediterranean,* and *Below Deck Sailing Yacht* (about the "yachties" who work and live on chartered superyachts) all document the lives and labor of leisure and hospitality workers. On these shows, we see workers trying to fulfill the needs, desires, and whims of wealthy customers and clients by doing jobs ranging from bartending and gourmet food preparation to working as deckhands or lodgehands. We see them prepare elaborate meals, plan theme parties, serve cocktails and coffee, set up picnics on the beach and excursions to the slopes. They also do a lot of chatty conversing, undertake some strategic flirting, and pretend to care about the customers' birthdays and anniversaries.

But something else interesting happens on most of these shows: the formal presentation and distribution of a tip. Although wages or salaries are rarely mentioned on the other workplace reality shows described above, they are central to in-person-service reality TV. On *Below Deck,*

Figure 1.1. Distributing the group tip on *Below Deck*.

as the guests depart, the staff receive handshakes and hugs and claim that the guests were great pals and will be missed. Then the guest who arranged and paid for the trip presents the captain or manager with a fat envelope stuffed with cash, a group tip for the staff. Later, at the "tip meeting," the captain reviews their individual and group performance and—while they wait with bated breath—tells the staff the amount of the collective tip (see fig. 1.1). As the captain doles the bills out, the yachties respond with either relief or disappointment about the amount.

By ending the storyline of each "charter" with this crucial moment of wage payment, *Below Deck* makes explicit that all the work done on the ship, from flirting to washing dishes, is just a means to a monetary end. The staff, it becomes obvious, have a knowing and entirely material relationship to the emotional performances required of them by their customers. Moreover, because the amount of the tip is uncertain, its payment feels neither like a preordained moment of narrative closure nor like the obligatory restoration of ethical equilibrium. Instead, by registering the payment of the tip as a moment of suspense, *Below Deck* draws our attention to the precarious experience of working for an unguaranteed and unpredictable wage.

As the recent popularity of these shows suggests, tipwork is on the rise. Employment in the full-service restaurant industry has grown almost four times faster than overall private-sector employment in the last three decades, and the restaurant and food service industry is the nation's second-largest private sector employer. Today more than one in ten US workers (around 16 million total) are employed in the leisure and hospitality sector, and in 2023, more than 6 million restaurant and hospitality workers in the US relied on tips.[1] Tip wages are also crucial to the gigwork sector: Amazon Flex, Caviar, Instacart, and DoorDash all use a "tip credit" structure, counting tips toward guaranteed compensation. As of 2024, more than 7 million Americans were working a tip-dependent platform-based gig job. Around 10 percent of the US workforce thus currently relies on tips for a significant portion of their income, while nearly half have worked for tips at some point in their lifetime.[2]

Yet when we talk about service work, we rarely talk about wages, and when we talk about wages, we rarely talk about tips. We have had still fewer opportunities to talk about solidarity and organizing among tipworkers themselves, since in-person service work has historically been marginalized within the traditional labor movement. An exception to that marginalization is the activist and advocacy organization One Fair Wage (OFW). Founded in 2013, OFW is an offshoot of the Restaurant Opportunities Center (ROC), a group created in 2001 by labor lawyer Saru Jayaraman after 9/11 brought New York City's service industry to a temporary standstill.[3] In addition to supporting leisure and hospitality unions such as UNITE-HERE and working with fast-food and other nonunionized service workers for an increase in the federal minimum wage, OFW has been particularly committed to advocacy and activism around the problem of tip wages. As OFW puts it in their mission statement,

> The service sector is one of the largest and fastest-growing sectors of the United States economy, but also the lowest paying. The restaurant

> industry includes 7 of the 10 lowest-paying jobs in the country. In fact, people who work in the industry are twice as likely to need food stamps as the rest of the US workforce, and three times as likely to live in poverty.... [The] federal minimum wage for tipped workers today [is] $2.13 an hour... [T]hese workers include not only restaurant servers, bussers, hosts, bartenders, but also workers in nail salons, hair salons, car washes, airports, and parking lots. And now app-based companies like InstaCart, DoorDash, Uber, and Lyft are also pushing for subminimum wages for their employees, arguing that their customer tips should count toward their workers' payments.[4]

As OFW notes, tip wages are more likely to leave workers in poverty. Yet OFW's mission is to organize not just around the *amount* of wages service workers receive, but also the *type* of wage they are paid. As this chapter will explain, service work's low wages are intimately connected to the common use of tips as a method of wage payment. Since the turn of the twentieth century, tip wages have been kept artificially low both by regulatory exclusion and by concerted lobbying efforts on the part of the leisure and hospitality industries.[5] Moreover, much as receiving tips draws together everyone from head steward to deckhand on *Below Deck*, tipwork is common to a wide range of subsectors and job categories.[6] For OFW, shared dependence on tip wages defines and indeed constitutes a class, one that includes not only restaurant workers, but also salon workers, parking attendants, and the ever-growing numbers of gigworkers.[7]

This chapter uncovers a historical and cultural archive wherein tipwork is framed as a specific type of service work, one that demands new ways of thinking about wages. Tipwork, I contend, is an unacknowledged and underexplored part of the history of wages, of the contemporary cultural imaginary around labor, and of service workers' own political formations. I argue that contemporary tip wages must be understood in the context of longer histories of waged domestic servitude. I begin with the parallel histories of tipping and of the regulated hourly wage, arguing that the creation of the hourly wage as a political norm depended on distinctions between those who earned time-based wages and those who were paid in tips. Histories of the Fair Labor Standards Act (FLSA) rarely focus on the exclusion of service workers. Nor do they attend to enduringly racialized and feminized legal distinctions between tips and more formalized, contractually guaranteed, and federally regulated methods of wage payment. Yet tipworkers—from immigrant hotel housekeepers to Black Pullman porters and "redcaps"—were central to debates over labor reform in the early twentieth century, even as they were also excluded from the regulations that emerged out of those debates.

The second part of the story I tell about tips concerns pop culture: the way we think and talk about work and the way a crucial pop-cultural medium—television—registers transformed understandings of work in a period when more and more people are working for insecure, informal tip wages. I suggest that TV representations of work life have long contributed to cultural beliefs about the meaning of work and wages, especially the belief that work is (at best) about vocation, upward mobility, and meaning, or (at least) about a repetitive tedium that provides certainty, freedom, and security via a guaranteed wage. What I term "tipwork TV," by contrast, turns away from narratives of professional development and vocational stability and instead formalizes the episodic, fragmented, and profoundly insecure experience of working for tips.

Tipwork TV also rejects the idea that in-person service workers are subject to particularly demeaning forms of false consciousness—what Arlie Hochschild has influentially described as the "double pretending" whereby service workers come to *believe* the emotions they are required to perform.[8] The third section of this chapter explores the history of the claim that service work is particularly alienating or degrading, tracking the metaphor of the submissive service worker from sixteenth-century political philosophy to twenty-first-century critical theory. I then turn to the political imaginaries and political praxis of contemporary tipworkers, who contest service work's feminized "servility" and point us to the limits of traditional demands for "fair wages" in the service sector more broadly.

TIPS, TIME DISCIPLINE, AND THE REGULATION OF THE HOURLY WAGE

Historians of capitalism such as E. P. Thompson and Eric Hobsbawm influentially argue that implementing capitalist labor discipline also required standardizing time. Yet because they focus primarily on manufacturing—where standardized work time and time-based wages are common—these histories can't tell us much about either the wages or the disciplining of service workers. Service work's output is often unquantifiable or immaterial, and its working time cannot be measured or rationalized in the same way manufacturing working time can.[9] To understand the history of time, work discipline, and wages as they have shaped in-person service work, we must look not to the history of manufacturing work, but rather to the history of domestic servitude.

Servants and other domestic workers do not "experience a distinction between their employer's time and their 'own' time," as Thompson describes industrial temporality.[10] Instead, the disciplining of service labor depends precisely on the absence of any such distinction: work discipline for eighteenth-century and nineteenth-century domestic servants was not shaped by "bourgeois exactitude," but by the master's ability to make work time limitless and endless.[11] Servants were also not compensated by time. Indeed, because more British workers labored as domestic servants than in manufacturing during most of the "industrial" nineteenth century, time-based wages were limited to "certain people, usually fit adult men, at a particular period of their lives," historian Leonard Schwarz explains. Farmhands, apprentices, domestic servants, and others were far more likely to receive "in-kind" wages—from lodging to leftovers—and "had no legal time of their own."[12]

In the United States, the tradition of in-kind payment for domestic work persisted into the early twentieth century and was racialized as well as gendered.[13] As Jacqueline Jones argues in her powerful history of Black women's domestic labor in the postbellum South, in-kind wages were used to justify the exclusion of Black female domestic workers from the protections of wage regulation. Because they weren't involved in "the time-oriented production of goods," she notes, Black women in domestic service were typically paid irregularly and often received payment in the form of a room to sleep in, hand-me-down clothes, and leftover food.[14] The "Black Codes"—which continued to govern the conduct of "free" Black workers even after formal emancipation—held that "no written contract shall be required when the servant voluntarily receives no remuneration except for food and clothing."[15] Historian Cecelia Rio notes that Black domestic servants thus experienced neither a legal nor a practical difference between work time and leisure time. "Legally required to be on call twenty-four hours a day, seven days a week," they were subordinated to what a Black female domestic worker described in 1912 as "a treadmill life."[16]

In-kind payment was seen as a solution to the unquantifiability of domestic workers' work time and to the immeasurability of their output. But as in-person service shifted from private to public spaces, in-kind wages for service workers were soon replaced with another unpredictable method of wage payment: tipping. Most historians believe the modern practice of tipping was established in Britain during the early eighteenth century to supplement in-kind wages for household servants who also had to serve visiting guests. Overnight and weekend guests in private houses would make small cash payments, called "vails," to the domestic staff of the house to ensure that the servants would be as attuned to the temporary guests as to their permanent masters. Later in the eighteenth century, the rise of coffeehouses and restaurants meant that services once performed exclusively in private homes were increasingly conducted in public, and the practice of tipping not only survived but indeed enabled this historical transition. There are many competing accounts of the origins of the word "tip," but among the most common is that the word was first used in a Fleet Street coffeehouse frequented by Samuel Johnson, which had a bowl on the table with the words "To Ensure Promptitude" (TIP) inscribed on it.[17] Although this origin story is likely apocryphal, it does suggest that tip wages helped consolidate a method of discipline in service work. Service work requires attention to time, but its temporality is subjective and variable, hence the qualitative "promptitude," instead of the more quantitative "pace": what one customer appreciates as salutary efficiency another might find annoyingly overattentive; one customer might gobble a meal in a few minutes, while another might linger for an hour.

The portion of the population employed in domestic service had sharply declined by the end of the nineteenth century, but the number of commercial eating and drinking establishments, hotels, and trains increased dramatically. Household servants had been controlled by constant surveillance, an intimate form of work discipline augmented by the in-kind and "board" wages that made servants fully dependent on their masters. But the waitresses, coat check girls, railway porters, and shoeshine boys of the new service economy did not have one ever-present master; instead, they served a constant churn of temporary customers. As the twentieth century dawned, not only did more people work for tips than ever before, but more working-class and middle-class consumers found themselves in tipping situations.[18]

Almost as soon as tipping became standard public practice, however, it was subject to condemnation. Even paying a tip could be "degrading" to the customer, while receiving them was even worse. Cultural historian Kerry Seagrave quotes a 1905 criticism of tipping that insists, "Mark the servility of the girl's [waitress] attitude and her meek and lowly 'Yes Sirs' and 'No sirs!'... She makes him her superior by kow-towing to him and accepting a tip.... Tips and servility go together."[19] The tipworker's willingness to render herself "meek and lowly" seemed to remove her from the modern, "rational" discipline of the clock, the wage, and the contract, making her seem more like a serf or a chattel slave than like a "free laborer." As the Orientalist term "kow-tow" suggests, fears about tipping also reflected anxieties about the increased employment of Chinese, Japanese, and Filipino immigrants in service-sector jobs ranging from domestic servants to railway porters. Tipping was also commonly derided as a form of "baksheesh," yoking it not just to the fear of Asianized or Arabacized submissiveness, but also to ethnicized civic corruption.[20]

Although tipping was much more common in the United States than elsewhere, early twentieth-century reformers also saw tipping as particularly un-American because it encouraged antidemocratic social and class distinctions that were supposed to have been left behind in Europe. A 1938 opinion essay by Alvin Harlow titled "Our Daily Bribe" thus argues that tipping "doesn't belong in a democracy" and is "a product of lands where for centuries there has been a servile class." Harlow is particularly appalled at the idea that tipping itself had become democratized, such that even "low-income folk" were doing it: "clerks and salesgirls eating twenty-cent lunches at a soda fountain [are] tipping the soda jerker five or ten cents."[21]

Of course, Harlow's description of the United States as a place without a "servile class" ignores the history of American chattel slavery, a history materially as well as discursively linked to the racialization of tipping. By the early twentieth century, a significant portion of tip-earning workers were Black, and most nonagricultural Black workers were performing service work of one kind or another.[22] William Scott's 1916 *The Itching Palm: A Study of the Habit of Tipping in America*, for instance, expresses discomfort with the idea that Black workers had been emancipated from chattel slavery only to become "slaves" of a different kind: "The Negro was servile by law and inheritance," Scott propounds, whereas "the modern tip-taker voluntarily assumes, in a republic where he is actually and theoretically equal to all other citizens, a servile attitude for a fee."[23] Writing twenty years later, Harlow concurs: "One hundred years and more ago," he writes, "there was practically no tipping of white persons in the United States.... We had no 'servants' then: the waiter and the hostler and the coachman regarded themselves as…free citizens whose means of livelihood were as honorable as anyone else's."[24] For Scott and Harlow, then, not only is tipworking associated with Blackness and with unfree labor, the (Black) tipworker's "servility" seems to threaten the precarious status of "free labor" as such.

Anxiety about tipwork, race, and free wage labor was likely also linked to a concomitant debate about a specific group of "modern tip-takers," namely, the Pullman train porters. The Pullman Company was the largest single employer of Black men in the United States between 1900 and 1920, and the company's preference for Black workers was itself a legacy of chattel slavery. In 1915, Pullman general manager L. S. Hungerford explained that "these old southern coloured men," being mostly former "house servants," were "adapted to waiting on the passengers, give them better attention and [have] a better manner."[25] The Pullman Company was also the most outspoken defender of tip wages in early-twentieth-century policy and reform debates. In 1915, the Federal Commission on Industrial Relations held hearings to investigate whether "the standard salary of the [Pullman] porters…is such that the porters are obliged to secure tips from the public in order to live."[26] The president of Pullman, Abraham Lincoln's son Robert Todd Lincoln, acknowledged that "'this arrangement of tips is not a nice one at all." But, he went on to say, tipping "is an old custom…and one to which the colored race is accustomed…and the public seems to be fond of it."[27] Because service work was seen as a holdover from the informal dependencies of domestic service and chattel slavery, the "old custom" of tip wages was likewise enduringly racialized.

The fear that tips would foster "servility" was feminized as well as racialized. As the male-dominated manufacturing sector expanded rapidly, in-person service work—especially the kinds of low-waged jobs most often paid in tips—was increasingly coded as "women's work." Anti-tipping legislation tended to be framed not as labor reform, but rather as a way to protect female workers from sexual impropriety, in part because tipwork was intimately associated with sex work. Labor historian Dorothy Cobble quotes a Progressive Era reformer critical of the "relation of subservience and patronage" between tip-earning waitresses and their male customers. Those who relied on tips, a union organizer predicted, would become "servile, slavish, mealy-mouthed and beggarly, and succumb to 'the easier way' of loose morals."[28] Waitressing was often judged an "improper trade" for women because tips were paid directly by the customer in cash: this made food-service labor seem more intimate than other kinds of work and tip wages more sexually exploitative than their hourly equivalent. Sociologist Frances Donovan's 1920 ethnographic study *The Women Who Wait*, for example, argues that because the waitress is unable to fulfill her true desire for marriage and domesticity, she settles instead for a life of "unclean jokes" and "semi-prostitution."[29]

Tipwork was thus represented as a premodern method of wage payment that needed to be modernized and reformed to befit an industrial democracy liberated from the legacies of both European feudalism and American chattel slavery. Yet as New Deal reforms and regulations took effect in the late 1930s, those regulations would say and do essentially nothing about tipwork: far from fading into obscurity, this "old custom"—associated with both servility and moral corruption—would instead become even *more* common. Applied to manufacturing labor, maximum-working-hours and minimum-wage laws aimed at nothing less than "extend[ing] the frontiers of social progress," as President Franklin Delano Roosevelt put it in a 1937 speech.[30] By contrast, in-person service work continued to be represented as a preindustrial holdover untouched by and unavailable to progressive modernization. Whereas manufacturing labor could be modernized *through* regulation, in-person service work's anachronism was an alibi for *not* regulating it.[31]

To understand how and why service work could be excluded from New Deal regulation, it's useful first to consider labor reform prior to the Fair Labor Standards Act (FLSA). The earliest attempts to regulate labor at the federal level, in the late nineteenth and early twentieth centuries, had focused particularly on female workers and on reproduction, instead of production. The case for wage regulations in the United States in this period centered on a moral and often patriotic demand that citizen-workers should be able to reproduce themselves both individually and as a population.[32] Focusing on health and moral virtue, reformers concentrated their efforts on outlawing child labor and on the regulation of women's wages as a way to prevent "social evils" ranging from the "spread of infections" to the "sapping and decay of patriotism."[33] In 1908, the Supreme Court affirmed the right of states to regulate women's working hours, asserting that the collective interest in the health of future generations justified interfering with women's freedom of contract and the right to free enterprise. In the 1910s and early 1920s, many states passed their own minimum-wage laws for women across occupations, from service workers in laundries, hotels, and restaurants to female workers in the garment industry and manufacturing.

However, the more conservative courts of the next few decades would view the regulation of labor less favorably, striking down prohibitions of child labor as well as state-level minimum-wage rules for women workers. Even organized labor groups, especially in the skilled trades, were suspicious of any federal infringement on collective bargaining rights, in part because male labor organizers had come to perceive regulation as feminizing.[34] It would take the devastating effects of the Great Depression, including fears about the emasculating effects of male unemployment, to persuade politicians and labor organizations alike of that the benefits of regulation outweighed the perceived costs.[35] Beginning in the early 1930s, Roosevelt began talking about the risk of falling wage rates, and in 1935, his administration passed the National Labor Relations Act (NLRA), which guaranteed private-sector workers the right to organize unions, engage in collective bargaining, and strike.

To ensure the support of Southern legislators, however, the NLRA ultimately included two key occupational exclusions: "The term 'employee'... shall not include any individual employed as an agricultural laborer, or in the domestic service of any family or person in his home."[36] These occupational exclusions were clear proxies for race: the vast majority of Southern farmworkers were Black, and 80 percent of domestic servants were Black women.[37] Although most historians have focused on the exclusion of Black farmworkers, the NLRA was also a crushing defeat for Black and other nonwhite domestic workers. Historian Peggie Smith quotes a domestic worker's letter to Roosevelt expressing her disappointment: "When you mention a code for Domestics, they arrogantly tell you it will and can never be done. I wonder why it is that the same God made us made the rest of mankind and yet when it comes to hours and wages there is such a difference."[38]

Despite the exclusions built into the NLRA, however, it did pave the way for larger labor reform: following its passage, the Supreme Court finally reversed course on federal wage regulation in 1937, in the case *Parrish v. West Coast Hotel.* Although arguably crucial to New Deal labor regulation, *Parrish* is rarely discussed in histories of labor reform—perhaps because it reveals a path *not* traveled. Elsie Parrish was a chambermaid in a Washington hotel being paid less than the state-mandated women's minimum wage of $14.50 for a forty-eight-hour week. When Parrish sought redress under Washington's minimum-wage protections, the hotel argued that the state's wage regulations were an unconstitutional violation of its due-process rights. The court ultimately ruled in favor of Parrish, holding that the regulation of labor contracts did not violate the due-process clause and that the government could indeed regulate labor federally as part of its mandate to serve the public good.[39] Within weeks of the Parrish decision, Congress began to debate the bill that would come to be called the Fair Labor Standards Act (FLSA).

Roosevelt's initial message to Congress called for a bill protecting agricultural as well as industrial workers, but the bill as ultimately written would, like the NLRA, exclude agricultural workers almost entirely. The implicit reason for this exclusion was the desire of Southern legislators to preserve the Jim Crow economic system. But the explicit argument against regulating farm work—not just in the South, but in Northern and Western states, too—was that wage-and-hour regulations were suited only to manufacturing labor. Lobbyists and legislators alike argued that because farm work is seasonal and needs to be "flexible" with respect to labor demand and hours of operation, it could not be subject to the "rigid rules laid down" for "big city factories."[40] Chapter 2 will return to the link between agricultural labor and service work. For now, I simply want to draw attention to the claim that because agriculture is not rationalized and time disciplined, policies written to regulate manufacturing labor could not be applied to it. This language would soon show up in debates about regulation of service workers as well.

The FLSA didn't include the NLRA's language about domestic workers because it included an even more consequential carve-out: not just in-home domestic servants, but the entire service sector, was excluded from the FLSA, including retail workers and those who performed in-person service in public establishments. This exclusion was necessary because the FLSA did not ground its claim to constitutionality on the precedent set by *Parrish*, whose defense of the state's authority to regulate the terms of labor contracts was relatively broad, but instead on a case decided two weeks after *Parrish*, *NLRB v. Jones and Laughlin Steel Corporation*, which concerned the rights of steel workers to unionize under the NLRA.[41] Unlike *Parrish*, *Jones and Laughlin* is famous as a cornerstone of New Deal regulation. *Parrish* had addressed the broader question of the public interest in regulating labor (covered under the states' police powers) and argued that freedom of contract had no constitutional basis. *Jones and Laughlin* did neither. Instead, it used the far narrower Commerce Clause—which gives Congress the authority to "regulate commerce . . . among the several states"—to justify the constitutionality of federal wage-and-hours regulation. But because the Commerce Clause gave Congress authority to legislate *only* in matters pertaining to interstate transport, the FLSA could apply only to labor directly involved in interstate "commerce." And much as eighteenth-century contract law had few protections for those who didn't make "vendible goods," the FLSA defined "commerce" solely as "the production of [physical] goods."[42] The FLSA thus did nothing to regulate employment in the service sector, including the low-waged jobs typically held by women: laundry service, hairdressing, retail, domestic service, or hotel and restaurant work.[43] Although the Elsie Parrish case had arguably provided a key legal precedent, the FLSA completely failed to provide federal wage or hour regulations for workers like Parrish. At the very moment that the tendential domination of the large factory system over more casual arrangements was allowing mostly male and mostly white manufacturing workers to demand fair wages, nonwhite and predominantly female service workers were still receiving their wages in tips and hand-me-downs.

The exclusion of service workers rarely occupies much space in accounts of the 1938 FLSA. Nor did it occupy much space in the congressional debates about the act: in records of these debates, service workers appear almost exclusively in the negative, as the chair of the House Labor Committee, Mary Norton, is repeatedly called upon to remind her colleagues that retail and service employers are not regulated by the act and thus not worth discussing.[44] Indeed, the entire framework of average hourly wages central to the FLSA was borrowed from the world of manufacturing. As we will see in Chapter 2 discussion of piece-rate wages, the hourly wage was not yet a universal norm in manufacturing in 1937. Nonetheless, the "regulatory hour" provided the FLSA with what historian Richard Epstein describes as a "stable and homogenous measure" especially well suited to manufacturing labor.[45] Once written into regulation, hourly wages became more common in practice, as well, at least in industrial workplaces where straightforward "clock in/clock out" labor processes and standardized time shifts were the norm. Technological developments such as the Fordist assembly line, as well as Taylorist management practices, further helped manufacturers standardize workers' output and thus their wages.[46] But service work had a less measurable output, was less standardized by technologies such as the assembly line, and was less likely to rely on the temporalities of work discipline that helped rationalize the clock-punching labor of manufacturing.[47] Service work required a working day that was not divided by the hour, both to preserve maximum flexibility for the employer and to ensure the maximum duration of the service worker's working time.[48] None of that flexibility and variability seemed suited to the "fair wages" language of the FLSA.

Post–New Deal debates about the regulation of service work thus focused not just on who had a right to minimum wages and what that minimum should be, but also on the method of wage payment itself: What *did* wages measure in the service sector, and what form should they take? It is at this point that we see the debate about tips return again. Yet because tips had by this point become common custom, the question was no longer whether they were a legitimate type of wage but instead how to count them as wages. The 1933 National Recovery Act (NRA), Roosevelt's first attempt to establish minimum wages, had held that lower wages could be paid to service workers because their tips would make up the difference. The NRA was declared unconstitutional in 1935 and was essentially replaced by the 1937 FLSA, which said nothing about how tips ought to be counted, because it simply excluded most service work. But the FLSA *did* cover at least one type of employees paid in tips: the railway and ship baggage handlers known as "redcaps."

The redcaps, who were predominantly Black, were initially not classified as employees at all but rather as "privileged trespassers," allowed to hire themselves out for whatever tips they could earn. In early 1938, however, the redcaps were recognized as employees by the Interstate Commerce Commission. Because of the specific legal status of railway and transportation workers under the FLSA, the redcaps were also covered by the act's hours-and-wages regulations in a way few other service workers were. Almost immediately after the passage of the FLSA, the railroad and shipping companies began threatening the redcaps with dismissal if they wouldn't sign forms stating that they earned their full federally mandated minimum wage in customer tips.[49] In response, the redcaps organized into the International Brotherhood of Redcaps (IBOR) and began sending telegrams to Roosevelt telling him of the unlawful dismissals and insisting that their tips should not be counted as wages.[50] In 1941, the issue went to the Supreme Court in *Williams v. Jacksonville Terminal Co.* and *Pickett v. Union Terminal Co.*[51] As a 1941 report notes, "the Court found no clear-cut objective [in the FLSA] on the question of tips: tips were neither specifically included in nor specifically excluded from wages."[52] In a five-to-three decision, the court determined that tips could be counted toward federally regulated guaranteed wages. The court also noted, however, that such a ruling followed the letter of the FLSA but might not serve workers' "social welfare" as intended by the act. Immediately following the 1941 decision, many reformers thus called on state and federal legislatures to amend the FLSA so that the tips of covered employees could not be counted toward the minimum wages due to them. Writing in favor of these reforms, Mary Anderson, director of the US Women's Bureau, argued that "if we are to have legal minimum wages, [the employer] must have total legal responsibility for paying them.... It is he alone who can be prosecuted if the law is not complied with."[53] In the main, however, these demands would go unheeded, not least because of the lobbying power of the travel and hospitality industries.

The status of tipped employees would not become the site of federal reform again until 1966, when large-scale amendments to the FLSA drew many service workers under wages-and-hours regulations. Departing from the narrow constitutional interpretation of the 1938 FLSA, the 1966 amendments formalized a more expansive dimension of "commerce" and narrowed or repealed exemptions for employees of hotels, restaurants, laundries, and food service, increasing the number of workers included under the act by around 30 percent.[54] The debates on these inclusions were fierce. As they had argued with respect to domestic servants decades earlier, legislators claimed it was impossible to include the restaurant and hotel industries in regulations designed for industrial workers. Once again, the debate centered on questions of time discipline and the method of wage payment. As Representative Edward Gurney put it, restaurant workers' "work hours are different and ... there are a great many fringe benefits in connection with their work."[55] Another discussion concerned whether restaurant workers should be paid for time spent "unproductively" in cleaning, washing their hands, or waiting for customers to finish their meal. The amendment ultimately excluded restaurant workers from overtime regulation because, as Representative Roman Pucinski put it, "it is difficult to control the eating habits of patrons."[56]

But the main issue in 1966 was the same as it had been during the 1940s-era redcap debate: were tips to be considered part of wages, or were they simply an additional gratuity? Representative Pucinski yoked the seemingly self-evident feminization of this labor to the technical problem of how to compensate it: "We recognize one thing. Certainly, a girl earns tips. But a line must be drawn at some point as to where the tips are actual earnings and where they are gratuities for extra-good service."[57] On the one hand, as Representative John Dent noted, "the responsibility for paying the employees always belongs to the employer" and not to the customer; on the other hand, in the words of the Representative John Kluczynski, "the employer and the employee are partners in the earning of tips."[58]

The proposed solution was a "tip-credit wage" that would allow employers to count tips as a "credit" toward a percentage of the federally guaranteed minimum wage.[59] While specific language about tips as wages was new to the 1966 FLSA, the tip-credit wage fell under a larger category that had existed since the original 1938 legislation: the "subminimum wage." During the debate over the FLSA, Southern Democrats had proposed an explicitly racialized wage differential for "substandard" Black workers. This was ultimately rejected, but the FLSA did allow some workers to be paid a "subminimum" wage based on their ostensibly lower "productivity": learners, apprentices, and those "whose earning capacity is impaired by age or physical or mental deficiency or injury" could be paid a fraction of the prevailing federal minimum wage. Reformers and scholars have noted that for workers with disabilities, the subminimum-wage provision—which still exists today for workers with disabilities, for incarcerated workers, for students, and for those who perform piece-rate industrial "homework"—functioned to "perpetuate the labor practices of the Industrial Revolution that the FLSA was intended to upend," including the use of piece-rate wages and production targets, which guarantee that "workers either exhaust themselves with the effort of meeting them or fail to make as much income as they needed."[60] (I will return to this problem in Chapter 2's history of piece-rate wages.)

As if attempting to determine precisely how much overwork and underpayment was acceptable for in-person service workers, the congressional debate around the tip-credit wage featured a fierce battle over what percentage of the minimum wage could be covered by tips. Arguing that employers ought to be allowed to count tips toward the *entire* minimum wage (essentially giving them access to free labor), Representative Charles Goodell argued that "tips in this country are greater than you think. Tipped employees are already the aristocrats of the hotel and restaurant industries."[61] Here, Goodell cunningly reverses the representation of tip earners as "servile" or "slavish," presenting tipworkers as so privileged that they require no federal protection. Goodell's regressive amendment ultimately failed, but as the bill made its way toward resolution, the percentage of the guaranteed wage that could be covered by tips steadily nudged upward from the originally proposed 35 percent. Echoing the debates of the 1930s, the National Restaurant Association (NRA) claimed that the negative impact of the bill would be mostly felt in the South and proposed a 50 percent credit.[62] The NRA was by then becoming an extraordinarily powerful lobby, and they ultimately prevailed: in 1966, the tip-credit wage was set at half of the prevailing federal minimum wage, so long as employers could prove the difference was made up by customer tips averaged out across the employee's working hours.

In 1996, under further pressure from the NRA, President Bill Clinton's Small Business Job Protection Act would change the tip-credit wage again. No longer would the "subminimum wage" for tipworkers be indexed to 50 percent of the federal minimum wage; it would instead be set at a permanent $2.13/hour, which was half of the federal minimum wage as of 1991. In his objection to this part of the legislation, Senator Edward Kennedy wondered why the restaurant industry—with its profits—should be allowed this special treatment.[63] It's not difficult to answer Kennedy's rhetorical query. Lobbying contributions by the NRA had increased 250 percent between 1987 and 1996, making it one of the most powerful industry lobbies in the nation.[64] In 1996, the NRA was headed by Herman Cain, former CEO of Godfather's Pizza and future presidential candidate. During the debate about the changes to the FLSA, Representative Jon Christensen read the entirety of a statement by Cain in opposition to any increase in the subminimum wage. Cain claimed that an increase would make it harder "to hire people who lack basic work skills"—the same argument that had been made in support of racialized and gendered wage differentials in the 1930s.[65] The debate among legislators over whether tipworkers should be paid a standard minimum wage focused yet again on questions of time discipline, such as whether waiters should be paid for time spent doing tasks such as folding napkins or prepping their workstations.

Because the 1996 law set the subminimum wage at a fixed $2.13/hour, the federal tip-credit wage is today only 29 percent of the federal minimum wage (fig. 1.2). Even as prices rise or the federal minimum wage is raised, employers of tip earners have their low labor cost locked in, while tipworkers themselves are increasingly likely to fall into poverty.[66] Only seven states require that tipworkers be paid the standard state minimum wage; twenty-six have established their own subminimum wage, but most set it at $5.00/hour or less. Poverty rates for tipped workers are more than twice as high as poverty rates for nontipped workers, and the median wage for tipworkers (including tips) is $15.81, as compared with $24.95 for workers overall.[67] More than one in ten

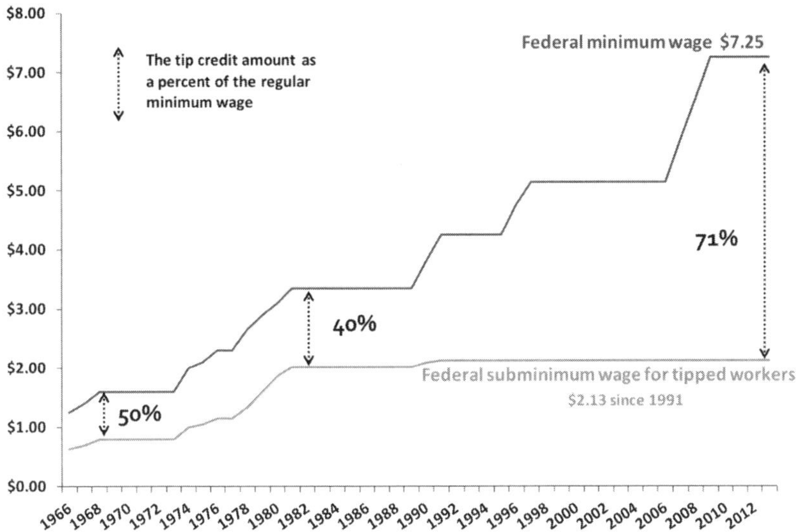

Figure 1.2. Federal minimum wage and subminimum wage for tipped workers (1966–2013). [Source: Sylvia A. Allegretto, "Waiting for Change: Is It Time to Increase the $2.13 Subminimum Wage?" IRLE Working Paper No. 155-13 (2018), https://irle.berkeley.edu/publications/working-papers/waiting-for-change-is-it-time-to-increase-the-2-13-subminimum-wage.]

tipworkers report earning less than the federal minimum wage, even including tips: the requirement to "top-up" employees' wages to the federal minimum is notoriously hard to enforce, making tipped workers uniquely vulnerable to wage theft.[68] In states that pay the subminimum wage, 25 percent of tipped restaurant workers of color live in poverty.

Much as the Pullman Company made customers themselves responsible for ensuring workers' living wages, the subminimum tip wage has been a massive labor-cost subsidy for the restaurant and hospitality sector. Shifting a larger portion of workers' incomes to tips saves employers from having to pay a fair wage and the state from having to guarantee one. Tips also reduce the cost of managing and monitoring service workers: if your income depends on providing fast, attentive, careful service, you will probably "oversee" yourself quite effectively, a process Jasper Bernes evocatively terms "self-harrying."[69] Tip wages are also a crucial method of time discipline. Restaurants might be open from morning until late at night, but they do most of their business in a three-hour window around dinner, and tip wages ensure that workers must be present for all those hours without being paid. Tip wages create "flexibility" in an industry in which the labor process is organized as a series of asynchronous tasks. Restaurants can also cut workers at a moment's notice, allowing management to be reactive to the wage cost relative to the day's likely profits while leaving workers in a state of total precarity.

The subsidy provided to the hospitality and restaurant sector via the subminimum wage thus arguably contributed to the transformation of the US economy from a manufacturing to a service economy and aided the growth of the restaurant industry as a major portion of US employment (fig. 1.3). The number of people working in food services has doubled since the early 1990s. Today one in nine workers is employed in the "Leisure and Hospitality" sector and the combination of retail, leisure, hospitality, and "personal" service makes up around a quarter of all employment.

The subminimum-wage/tip-credit structure has also shaped contemporary app-mediated gigwork. Chapter 3 of this book explores in more detail the technology, management, and regulation specific to platform-based circulation gigwork, but for the purposes of this chapter—and following the lead of the One Fair Wage campaign's statement quoted above—I here include platform gigwork under the broader category of tipwork. Most apps—including Uber, Lyft, TaskRabbit, GrubHub, Instacart, Caviar, and Postmates—offer customers a "suggested tip amount" of 15 to 20 percent, and tips are a significant portion of gigworkers' income. Gigwork also replicates many of the key features of tipwork: no paid leave, insurance, retirement benefits, or overtime protections; unpredictable scheduling; and a disproportionate use of part-time status.[70] Like in-person service workers, gigworkers forced to hustle for tips don't need much management to work hard and

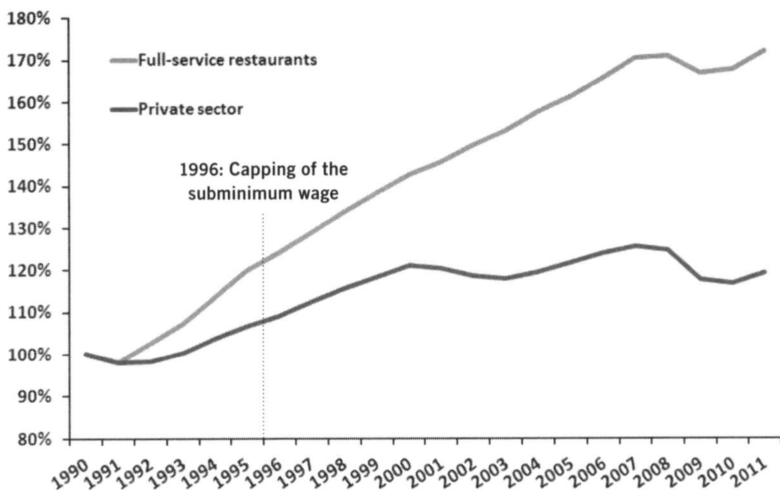

Figure 1.3. Employment growth in the private sector and full-service restaurant industry before and after the capping of the subminimum wage (1990–2012). [Source: Sylvia A. Allegretto, "Waiting for Change: Is It Time to Increase the $2.13 Subminimum Wage?" IRLE Working Paper No. 155-13 (2018), https://irle.berkeley.edu /publications/working-papers/waiting-for-change-is-it-time-to-increase-the-2-13 -subminimum-wage. Edited to add marker for 1996 capping of subminimum wage.]

fast, because they won't get paid otherwise. Gigworkers' reliance on tips makes life in the gig economy not only desperate, but dangerous, because the employment model's "flexibility" incentivizes potentially fatal levels of bodily risk.[71] In 2018, for instance, Caviar deliverer Pablo Avendano was killed while biking on a rainy night after receiving a message from the service encouraging couriers to come out despite the bad weather by promising high tips.[72] In gigwork, then, tip wages are not a holdover from preindustrial or "neofeudal" labor. They are instead a form of capitalist rationalization and time discipline in a sector where labor costs would otherwise be quite high relative to profits.

As I described above, after the passage of the FLSA, ship and railroad companies tried to force redcap porters to sign agreements claiming they were independent contractors working for tips instead of employees working for wages. The contemporary gigwork sector has done almost the exact same thing to protect itself from any federal regulation. Companies such as GrubHub, Postmates, Uber, Lyft, TaskRabbit, DoorDash, Instacart, and Amazon Flex have all taken advantage of the independent contractor model to adopt their own version of a subminimum wage. Amazon Flex, Caviar, Instacart, and DoorDash use a "tip-credit" structure whereby tips are discounted from the worker's guaranteed compensation. With DoorDash, the guaranteed per delivery rate includes tips: the more the worker earns in tips, the less the company has to pay. Amazon Flex—a third-party delivery program—claims to guarantee drivers a relatively high minimum wage, but in fact, the company counts tips toward that payment even as it conceals the actual payment structure so that workers can't tell what portion of their wage is coming directly from tips.[73] Instacart, for example, has sometimes used a pay structure that reduces the "wage" paid to the shopper to less than a dollar an hour when the customer tip is high.

Tipwork is also no less racialized and feminized today than it was in the early twentieth century. In the mid-2010s, female-identified workers made up more than 70 percent of all tipped workers and 66 percent of tipped restaurant workers, but they made fifty cents per hour less than workers who identified as male in equivalent positions. Female workers in states that use the tip-credit subminimum wage experience significantly higher rates of sexual harassment, and the restaurant industry generates more sexual harassment claims than any other US employer. As one server put it in a legal report about the problem of sexual abuse for tipworkers, "There is a lot of sexual harassment [but] you just kind of brush it off. . . . I just want my tip, I don't want anything to mess up my tip."[74] Black tipped workers consistently earn less than their white counterparts: during the COVID-19 pandemic, Black service workers reported a more significant decrease in their tips than did white service workers, and they experienced far more hostility when they attempted to enforce public health protocols.[75] Migrant laborers, likewise, are vulnerable to time theft and wage theft by platform gigwork companies that use the absence of regulation in tip-based gigwork both to recruit and to superexploit workers without work permits. Niels van Doorn and Darsana Vijay, among others, argue that gigwork platforms have integrated migrants into low-wage labor markets via tipwork's principles of "efficiency, self-dependency, and flexibility."[76]

Just as "in-kind" payment, including "wages" that took the form of leftovers and hand-me-downs, was once used to justify the exclusion of Black female domestic workers from the protections of wage regulation, today, discourse about the wages of tipworkers often features the racialized and feminized language of "gratitude" as an alternative compensation for work that can't be recognized *as* work. In the summer of 2020, Instacart workers took to social media to complain about the fact that tips—which many customers were using to compensate "essential workers" for taking a health risk—were being subtracted from their guaranteed wages. In response, Instacart put together a website "honoring the essential stories" of fifty gigworkers for the platform, almost all of them women and nonwhite men, and celebrated users of the platform who had "shown gratitude" to their shoppers by giving them hand-made blankets, cards, and homemade pie (fig. 1.4).[77]

Instacart borrowed from a strategy used a few years earlier by hotel-chain giant Marriott, who partnered with former California First Lady Maria Shriver (founder of the nonprofit A Woman's Nation) to create The Envelope Please program. Noting that the mostly female, immigrant and/or non-white room-cleaners rely on tips, and often live in poverty, the noprofit created cards for hotel rooms that encouraged hotel guests to "express their gratitude by leaving tips and notes of thanks for hotel room attendants in designated envelopes provided in their rooms."[78] Drawing on the tradition of treating tips as a "gratuity" fundamentally different from wages—even as they used tips *toward* wages—and yoking service-work with racialized and gendered forms of direct subjugation, these "person-to-person" initiatives shifted responsibility from the company to the customer in a manner that mirrored the strategy of the Pullman company a century earlier.

Figure 1.4. "Beyond the Cart" campaign from Instacart (2021).

In his influential essay on wages and industry, Hobsbawm describes the idea of a "fair day's wage for a fair day's work" as a "rule of the game" that both workers and employers came to learn at the beginning of the twentieth century and that was codified in labor regulations such as the FLSA.[79] In industrialized manufacturing, workers could indeed "lear[n] to regard labor as a commodity," because both their labor and the commodities they produced could easily be perceived as the concrete embodiment of their work—an "output" separable and alienable from the bodies of workers and customers. Employers, for their part, could "lear[n] the value of intensive rather than extensive labor utilization," because they could increase productivity ("usually a synonym for output per man-hour") via Fordist assembly lines and Taylorized management.[80] Yet none of these conditions apply to service or retail workers. Even after industrialization, in-person service workers still labored in a relatively low-technology sector where labor costs were relatively high, where work processes were less easily rationalized or deskilled, and where racialized and gendered wage differentials had created the conditions for legal and political exclusion and informalization. We thus ought to modify Hobsbawm's phrase by noting that the "rule" of regulated, hourly wages has actually been limited to *one* kind of "game": industrialized manufacturing labor in the fully developed world. Moreover, the codification of a "rule" for that kind of labor was made possible precisely because waged manufacturing work could be contrasted to *other* kinds of labor that were largely excluded from regulation, formalization, and labor organization.

The economic, political, and legal frameworks that justified those exclusions were themselves the product of what labor historian Phyllis Palmer terms "a contest over cultural meanings." The cultural meaning of service work, I have argued, shows up in a tradition of political economy that excludes service work because the output is not a "vendible commodity," in a tradition of common law that treats hired servants as appendages of their masters, in efforts to use occupational exclusions around service work as a proxy for racial exclusions, and in the longstanding representation of feminized service work as sex work.[81] But if wages today are increasingly likely to fall outside Hobsbawm's political "rules," we are clearly playing a new game. Since the early 1990s, nearly half of job growth has been in low-paid service work, which means more and more people work for very uncertain wages.[82] Compared with hourly workers, tipworkers are disproportionately less likely to be unionized, more often work in competition with one another or alone, and are more likely to be managed either by an app or by the customers who pay their wages. Tipworkers have none of the protections of the contract and few of the protections of federal regulation. They are subject to wage and time theft and are unlikely to have health insurance, paid leave, overtime protections, wage regulation, health and safety protections, or stable schedules. They work under a distinct form of time discipline that requires a high level of self-managed speedup and that subjects them to the variable and subjective temporal perceptions of customers. The consequences of this new kind of "game," the next section will argue, show up not only in contemporary policy and politics, but also in pop culture: in the various ways we think and talk about work, even when we're not working.

SERVICE WORK ON TV

Tipwork increasingly appears not just on reality TV, but on scripted series, too, where it shapes both the content and the form of genres from the prestige drama to the absurdist comedy. Since the 1970s, I will argue, representations of work life on television have typically given narrative arc to Hobsbawm's "rules," framing work as the development of skills recognizable by and in the market, as something to take pride and even pleasure in, as a source of social and individual meaning, or as a formal arrangement that rewards effort with security. TV shows about work have thus traditionally linked character directly to occupation: what you do is who you are.[83] What I term "tipwork TV," by contrast, formalizes the new "game" of informalized wages where one has not a single occupation or boss or task, but many. If, as critic Madeline Lane-McKinley puts it, "what we watch [on TV] reflects back to us the social totality of work," then tipwork TV provides a particularly canny and compelling register of what work is like now.[84]

The "First Golden Age of Television" in the 1950s and 1960s was dominated by variety shows and domestic sitcoms, and "workplace TV" didn't come into its own until the 1970s. Workplace TV was thus concomitant with the rise of the service sector itself. We might posit, indeed, that workplace TV came into its own *because* of the shift to service work: the kind of manufacturing labor covered by federal wage regulations (the kind that plays by the "rules of the game" evoked above) has almost always seemed too tedious for television. "No one would watch a show called *Keypunch* [or] *Assembly Line*," Ella Taylor argues, because such jobs are "devoid of the dramatic charges of incident and interaction that enliven narrative."[85] Manufacturing work is hard to narrate for precisely the same reasons it is easy to regulate: it is repetitive, predictable, highly rationalized, and takes place under the same conditions every day. Service work, by contrast, is hard to regulate for the same reasons it is replete with narrative incident: it is arrhythmic, unpredictable, and highly variable.[86]

Of course, the category of "service work" itself is also quite variable, including both higher-waged (mostly salaried) professional jobs such as performing surgery and lower-waged (often tipped) jobs such as waiting tables. Initially, both high-waged and low-waged service work showed up primarily on sitcoms. Workplace comedies from the 1970s blended the familiar domestic storylines of the 1960s with new workplace content via the genre of the "work-family series." Series such as *The Mary Tyler Moore Show, The Bob Newhart Show, M*A*S*H*, and *WKRP in Cincinnati* featured workplaces that included both professionalized service workers (surgeons, psychologists, producers) and more deskilled, lower-waged service workers (clerks, retail workers, receptionists). These shows also, Taylor argues, represented the workplace as a domestic "utopia" defined by "close emotional ties between coworkers."[87] Even the most explicitly "working-class" sitcoms of the 1970s (shows such as *Laverne and Shirley* and *All in the Family*), Lane-McKinley notes, "blend[ed] the workplace with the household, constructing a romantic vision of work life."[88]

As workplace TV came into its own in the 1980s and 1990s, however, representations of low-waged service work and representations of professionalized service work were increasingly split into two distinct genres. Salaried, white-collar labor appeared mostly on dramas. As Michael Tueth observes, the workplace dramas of the 1980s focused on white-collar professionals: "psychologists, physicians, educators, politicians, designers, lawyers, journalists."[89] Michael Szalay similarly argues that the prime-time TV of the 1980s and 1990s was dominated by workplace dramas such as *Hill Street Blues, ER, LA Law,* and *The West Wing* that focused on "high-minded professionals" deeply committed not only to their jobs, but also to each other.[90] These series—precursors to what would soon be called "quality" TV—attached the genre prestige of the drama to the occupational prestige of professional work. Some, especially those focused on the work of public-service professionals (doctors, district attorneys, detectives) were episodic "procedurals." But many more were serial, featuring plots that carried over week after week. These serial workplace dramas featured characters who developed, Michael Newman suggests, from "innocence to experience," a narrative arc "based on a more novelistic progression of events over a long direction, with episodes like chapters in an ongoing saga rather than self-contained stories."[91] The workplace drama thus captured the work lives of professionals and managers whose work was historically less vulnerable to mechanization and rationalization and who were much more likely to be paid a salary, instead of an hourly wage.[92]

Middle-class salaried service work, by contrast, still tended to appear on sitcoms (*Coach, Head of the Class, 9 to 5, Murphy Brown,* and *Night Court*), while some of the most important and popular sitcoms of this period, *Cheers, Alice, Newhart,* and *Taxi,* were specifically about lower-waged in-person-service workplaces. Notably, however, on these series, service work tended to be depicted either as entrepreneurial (being a server who also owns the business, like Sam on *Cheers* and Bob and Mary in *Newhart*) or as a vocation (like Alex on *Taxi*). Like the "work-family" series of the 1970s, the service-work sitcoms of the 1980s suggested that the service workplace was a surrogate family—one that included bosses and customers as well as coworkers (fig. 1.5).[93]

The service-work-family trope also shows up in a less obvious archive of "working-class" shows from this period, namely, the startling number of domestic-service sitcoms from the 1980s and early 1990s: *Benson, Dudley, I Married Dora, The Nanny, Mr. Belvedere, Charles in Charge, Who's the Boss?, Diff'rent Strokes, Frasier, Gimme a Break, Silver Spoons, Murphy Brown,* and *Fresh Prince of Bel-Air.* None of these series are likely to appear on lists of "working-class sitcoms," but they all feature in-home domestic workers as primary characters or even protagonists. That they have largely been excluded from the category "working-class sitcom" is arguably symptomatic of our collective inability to see domestic service as working-class labor, an inability that I have already suggested was likewise central to service-work's exclusion from regulation and reform. There were of course far fewer *actual* domestic servants in the 1980s and 1990s than there had been a few decades earlier.

Figure 1.5. The entrepreneurial service family on *Cheers*.

But it would be wrong to assume that the popularity of the domestic-servant sitcom in this period did not reflect economic changes. Rather, these narratives were an anxious response to the entrance of white, middle-class women into waged work in the postindustrial 1970s, which in turn required more households than ever before to rely on *out-of-home* service workers (mostly nonwhite women) to do tasks from child care to cooking.[94] On series such as *Dudley* and *I Married Dora*, L. S. Kim argues, the figure of the racialized domestic is used to uphold traditional ideals of "work, the home, the family, patriarchy, middle-classness, and whiteness," as if creating a bulwark against the reality of rapid change.[95] On *Charles in Charge*, *Mr. Belvedere*, *Who's the Boss*, and *Murphy Brown*, by contrast, the real-world feminization of both waged and unwaged care work is displaced onto the fantasy of white men hired to perform child care (fig. 1.6).

On series in which the domestic servant or care-work provider marries into the family they serve (*I Married Dora*, *The Nanny*, *Charles in*

Figure 1.6. Male waged domestic work on *Charles in Charge.*

Charge, Who's the Boss, Frasier, and *Silver Spoons*), domestic servants are quite literally integrated into the family. The fiction that waged domestic employees are members of the family had recently been evoked to explain the unregulated status of in-home service work. As Senator Peter Dominick put it in when the regulation of domestic labor was being reconsidered: "What do we do about the cleaning lady that comes in? She enjoys herself. She gets together with the family and has a coke or a glass of milk."[96] Although the 1974 expansion of the FLSA included more domestic workers than ever before, it specifically excluded babysitters, "companionship service," and all employees who lived in the home of their employers—in other words, virtually all the domestic servants who would show up on sitcoms a decade later.[97]

The domestic-service comedies named above are thus the least recognized examples of the "working-class sitcom" in the 1980s and

1990s. The *most* recognized working-class sitcom of that period, of course, is *Roseanne*. *Roseanne* is rarely discussed as a specifically "service-work" comedy, but Roseanne's transition from factory worker in the first season to bartender and fast-food server in the second and third seasons arguably allegorizes the shift in US employment from manufacturing work to low-waged service that had begun in the mid-1970s and was well underway by the late 1980s when the show premiered. Yet by the show's fourth season, neither Roseanne nor Dan were waged ("working-class") employees at all. In season four, they co-owned a family business (a bike shop). In season five, they were each owner-managers of a sole-proprietor enterprise: a diner and a house-flipping business. By the end of 1997's final season, Roseanne had become a creative professional writing autofiction. Roseanne's series-arc transformation thus also mirrors the fantasy work necessary to *disavow* the consequences of the aforementioned shift from manufacturing to service: the show turns service work from a working-class job into an entrepreneurial investment and then into creative vocation (fig. 1.7).[98]

In any case, *Roseanne*'s conclusion presaged a broader turn in TV at the turn of the millennium. In 2005, Tueth mused that perhaps the TV workday was over because "it [was] time to play."[99] By the early 2000s, working-class comedies such as *Roseanne* and *Married with Children* were again ceding ground to sitcoms such as *Friends*, *Will & Grace*, and *Sex and the City* that focused on professional or creative work.[100]

Tueth's optimistic speculation—not to mention the shows he describes—feels symptomatic of the financial bubble years of the late 1990s and early 2000s, but that bubble would eventually pop. Thereafter, people not only worked more than ever, they worked for lower wages and more and more often for tips. Since the millennium, the fastest-growing sector of the economy has been low-waged service jobs, and most of the new jobs created in the decade or so after the 2007–2009 financial crisis were "alternative employment," aka gigwork. Beginning in the 2010s, then, we find more and more TV characters

Figure 1.7. From manufacturing to service on *Roseanne*.

working low-waged service work or performing gigwork. *American Vandal, Atlanta, The Bear, BoJack Horseman, Broad City, Crashing, Easy, Girls, The Good Place, High Maintenance, Insecure, It's Always Sunny in Philadelphia, Master of None, Party Down, Silicon Valley, Sex Lives of College Girls, Succession, Unbreakable Kimmy Schmidt, Togetherness, Two Broke Girls, Search Party,* and *White Lotus* have all featured characters earning tips by driving for Uber, serving drinks, working for TaskRabbit or Instacart, making espressos, delivering consumer goods, and waiting tables.

Virtually all these series depart from the rosy picture of the "workplace family" and entrepreneurial opportunity common to service-workplace series from the 1970s to 1990s, offering instead a clear-eyed representation of service work as precarious and highly exploited.[101] We find this clarity even on shows that are not explicitly *about* service work, but that are nonetheless committed to acknowledging its background presence in the lives of the rich, such as the hit HBO dramas *Succession* and *White Lotus.*

Succession's camera often lingers on the work being done behind the scenes—caterers folding napkins, cooks chopping vegetables, bussers carrying stacks of dishes (fig. 1.8). *Succession* refuses the "upstairs/downstairs" structure of a show such as the PBS drama *Downton Abbey,* which also is about a wealthy family headed by a strong patriarch pondering the legacy of the family brand and teetering on the cusp of historical irrelevance: on *Succession,* servers are rarely given speaking lines, let alone plotlines. By not giving narrative space to both server and served, *Succession* insists instead that a fundamental inequality structures both the material economy of its world and the narrative economy of its plot.[102] *Succession*'s silent background service workers thus recall the representation of servants in the nineteenth-century novel, whose status as minor characters sets into relief the "rich" characterization of their masters.[103] As in the nineteenth-century domestic novels described by Alex Woloch, on *Succession,* "the servant vanishes into the duty he or she performs."[104]

Figure 1.8. Service in the background on *Succession.*

Whereas *Succession* attends to the silent physical work performed in the background, *White Lotus*'s first season focuses on the emotional labor required of those who serve the vacationing rich. (The second season largely drops these kinds of characters and replaces them with a plot centered on two female sex workers, a choice that we will have cause to return to later in this chapter.) Yet on *White Lotus* as on *Succession,* the serving class is important mostly insofar as they reflect the venality or desires of the served.[105] In this way, *White Lotus* suggests a Hochschildian understanding of emotional labor that requires affective performances so sincere even the performer can no longer distinguish between her own feelings and those of her customers. Belinda, the massage therapist on *White Lotus,* cannot be granted real emotional complexity on a show that *also* wants to grant real emotional complexity to Tanya, the wealthy white woman Belinda must contort herself to please. Tanya can be given depth and arc: at the end of season 1, after giving Belinda a large cash tip, she leaves the island and goes on to new narrative plotlines (including on the next season of the show). Belinda, by contrast, ends the season just as she began, waving and welcoming new guests in an endless loop, recall-

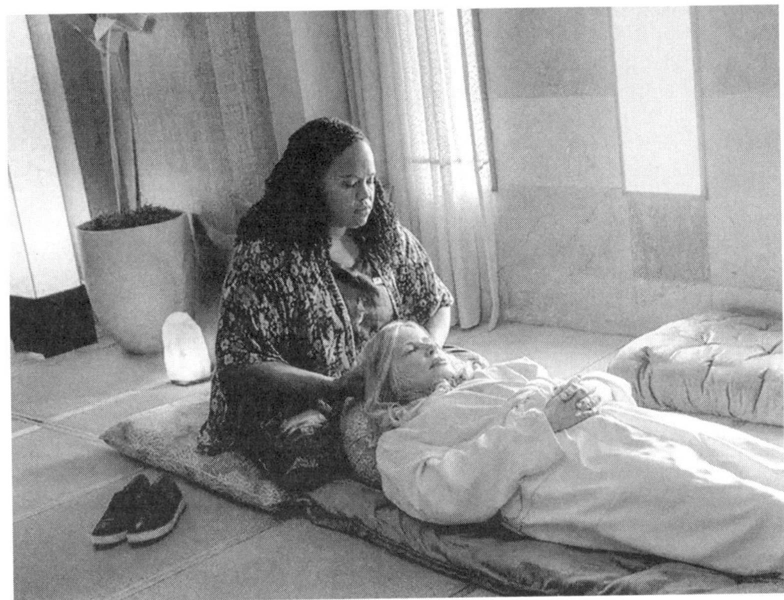

Figure 1.9. Static service workers on *White Lotus*.

ing my earlier reference to the Black domestic worker's self-described "treadmill life" (fig. 1.9).

Prestige series such as *White Lotus* and *Succession* clearly reject both the sentimental ideology of "one of the family" narratives and the false equality of the "upstairs/downstairs" character economy, features common to previous in-person service shows from *Charles in Charge* to *Downton Abbey*. Yet as a result, *Succession* and *White Lotus* cannot help but suggest that while the rich have marital problems and family dramas and existential crises, low-waged service workers have only their low-waged service work. We find a different effort to grapple with the tradition of service-work TV and the "workplace family" on *The Bear*, whose first two seasons dramatize the labors of Carmy Berzatto, an award-winning high-end chef, to turn his family's beloved sandwich counter into a high-end restaurant. Like Sam on *Cheers*, Newhart on

Newhart, and Roseanne on season five of *Roseanne*, Carmy isn't just the chef, but also the owner—indeed, the series is at least as much about the risky venture of investing in a restaurant as it is about the experience of working in one. Like those earlier shows, Carmy's is also very much a family business (both literally and metaphorically). Unlike on *Cheers*, however, the connection between work and family on *The Bear* is not the site of comfort, but the source as well as the symptom of trauma. Perhaps the series' most famous episode, "Fishes," involves a vivid flashback of Carmy's mother cooking while getting increasingly drunk and emotionally erratic. Punctuated by a persistently ringing kitchen timer, the episode connects this family incident to the ruthless time discipline involved in kitchen work, which is also depicted throughout the series with repeated images of clocks, buzzers, and a sign that reads, menacingly, "Every Second Counts."

Yet *The Bear* also suggests that Carmy's trauma might be *healed* via a blend of (work) family and self-managed entrepreneurship. To do so, it substitutes the "upstairs/downstairs" plot with what we might term, using restaurant lingo for distinguishing kitchen staff from waitstaff, a "front-of-the-house/back-of-the-house" plot. Most of the show's narrative energy is on the back-of-the-house workers—the chefs, sauciers, and pastry chefs whose relationship to their work recalls Szalay's description of the professional work on 1980s and 1990s "prestige TV": "high-minded professionals working earnestly on behalf of the public interest rather than profits." The front-of-the-house workers—that is, the tipworkers, those least likely to have either the entrepreneurial or the vocational commitments of Carmy and his co-owners—are as backgrounded and as silent on *The Bear* as they are on *Succession* (fig. 1.10).

The exception to this minor characterization of front-of-the-house service workers is a plotline involving Richie, Carmy's feckless cousin, who learns to practice and apply the workplace principle of "service" to his own personal growth: "I just like being able to serve other people now. You know? I think that's why restaurants and hospitals use the same word: 'hospitality.'" Ultimately, the very phrase that previously

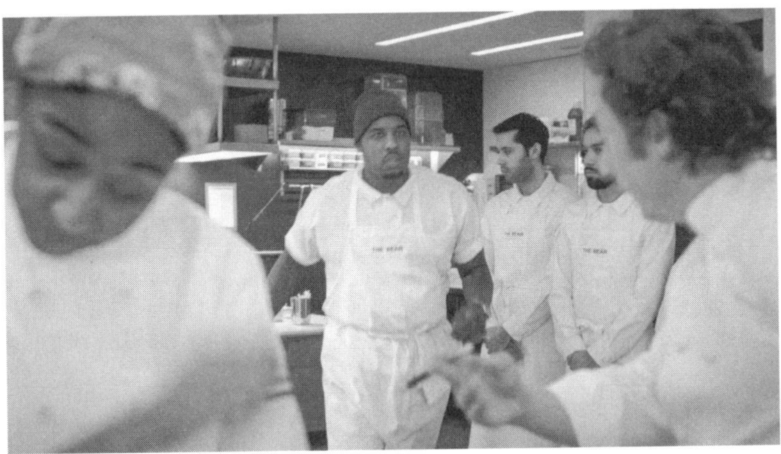

Figure 1.10. Silent servers in the background on *The Bear.*

connoted restaurant work's punishing time discipline—"Every Second Counts"—is repurposed to mean finding personal meaning via customer service.

For TV that more directly responds to the experiences of tipworkers, then, we may have to turn away from prestige dramas about customers and owners and bosses and look instead to the tipwork comedy: *Unbreakable Kimmy Schmidt, Insecure, High Maintenance, Easy, American Vandal, Atlanta, Silicon Valley, Party Down, The Sex Lives of College Girls, Crashing, Master of None,* and *Broad City.* Tip-waged gigwork appears so explicitly in these contemporary sitcoms that the real-life apps themselves are named: Uber and TaskRabbit on *Unbreakable Kimmy Schmidt,* Lyft on *Insecure,* Postmates on *American Vandal* (fig. 1.11). Often, those who work in tipwork are shown using the services of other tipworkers, as when "The Guy"—the weed deliverer on *High Maintenance*—orders takeout food or goes to a bar.

The precarity implied by tip wages often shows up explicitly, too. The first episode of *Party Down,* for instance, ends as *Below Deck* does, with the distribution of a group tip, but because their boss has

Figure 1.11. Gigwork brands on *Silicon Valley.*

encouraged them to "bet on themselves" by using a tip jar instead of accepting a predetermined 20 percent of the final bill, each member of the catering staff is given a measly fourteen dollars at the end of a long night (fig. 1.12). At the end of an early episode of *The Sex Lives of College Girls*, in turn, Kimberly—whose financial aid package requires her to work at an on-campus café—ends up as a plus-one at a fancy party where her fellow café workers are moonlighting as cater waiters. After Kimberly helps them earn better tips by announcing to the other guests that the waiters are all students on financial aid, they offer her a cut. They also welcome her into the service working class by reminding her not to tip the coat-check guy in language that evokes the history of domestic servitude: "The help don't tip the help!"

Tipwork TV comedies enframe ideological fantasies, too, of course. Sometimes, TV representations of tipwork perpetuate the myth that it is a salutary "flexible" alternative to formal employment, one that enables workers to pursue other vocational trajectories. "Kimmy Goes to College" in season 3 of *Kimmy Schmidt*, for instance, includes some clearly satirical details about gigwork—in a montage sequence of odd

Figure 1.12. Distributing the group tip on *Party Down*.

jobs, we see Kimmy blow up a large inflated rat of the kind unions often use for picket line actions, implying that she's temping as a picket-line walker—but by the end of the episode, Kimmy's peripatetic wage hunting has gotten her a full scholarship to Columbia. Elsewhere, precariously waged service work is just another gig to make ends meet before you make it big in the culture industry. Thus, we find Pete, the would-be comic on *Crashing*, working as a street barker for a comedy bar and compensated based on how many customers he brings in; Ern, the aspiring music producer of *Atlanta*, working a commission-dependent sales job; and Odinaka, a character who appears in an episode of season 2 of *Easy*, driving for Uber while performing stand-up.

But even when these series treat tipwork and gigwork optimistically, the abiding feeling of exhausting overwork often disrupts the fantasy. Although the Odinaka episode on *Easy* is playfully titled "Side Hustle," it turns out that the aspiring comedian has two tipwork jobs in addition to his vocational aspirations: he works days as a Chicago tour guide and nights driving for Uber ("It doesn't pay *much*, but..." he trails off vaguely). Since far more of the episode is dedicated to his work in these two jobs than to his stand-up, it becomes unclear which is the temporary "side hustle" and which is his permanent—or permanently contingent—form of employment.

Tipwork TV also foregrounds the bodily risks involved in "flexible" tipwork. On season 2 of *High Maintenance*, for instance, "The Guy" has his bike stolen and must rely on a friend who also works as an Uber driver to ferry him around (for a cut of the tips, of course). When The Guy is badly injured on the job, we discover that he has health insurance only because his ex-wife agreed to keep him on her plan. The rise of tipwork and gigwork is thus often explicitly yoked to rising costs of reproduction: Issa, protagonist of the aptly-titled *Insecure*, drives for Lyft in the evenings after her full-time non-profit job so she can save up enough for a security deposit on an apartment.[106]

These comedies clearly depart from the professional emphasis of the 1970s through the 1990s salaried workplace drama. Like post-2000 prestige TV, they were written in a period of postindustrial financial and labor crisis. But they do not feature prestige TV's residual nostalgia for Fordism or the "family wage," largely because they do not feature baby-boomer patriarchs such as Tony Soprano, who can remember, and thus mourn the loss of, better days for white, male, waged workers in the United States.[107] They are instead the genre correlative of the "recession millennial," a generation that recognizes such promises as bankrupt. Compared with previous generations, millennials are poorer, more indebted, less likely to own a home, more likely to live with their parents, less likely to have full-time work, less likely to have a job for which a college degree is required and, above all, far more likely to work in low-paid service work or gigwork. For these workers laboring outside even the minimal protections of the minimum wage, there are no binding forms of social or contractual obligation on offer. This means that we never see a boss and almost never see a manager on tipwork TV; it also means there are far fewer conventional family relationships on these shows than there are on work-family series or domestic workplace dramas. On tipwork TV, family ties are likely to look as they do on *High Maintenance*: being so broke you have to ask your ex-wife to keep you on her insurance.

Tipwork TV comedies reject the formal conventions of the workplace drama, with its narrative of development and possibility, and that narrative's flip side, the "purgatorial" feeling of regression and nostalgia Szalay discerns in *The Sopranos*. Instead, they embrace the sitcom's interest in the absurd, the embodied, and the surreal, as well as comedy's ability to register confusion, uncertainty, and the contrary emotional states that arise when one must pretend to feel one thing while actually feeling another (thus clarifying, contra Hochschild, that service workers do *not* actually confuse the performance of feeling with sincere emotions).[108] Indeed, as Carolyn Steedman argues, the structure of service-work humor has long relied on these contrary tendencies—on the fantasy of relation or connection versus the fact of withdrawal and indifference: "The servant joke in general... is based on a deep conviction and wish that they are watching you; but it turns out to be the case that you are watching them, but perhaps not carefully enough to learn the lesson [they] teach, which is that they're not really very interested in you; not interested in making a story out of nothing."[109] On *Succession* and *White Lotus*, the servant is a minor background figure, "vanish[ing] into the duty he or she performs" and there only to provide a silent relief against which the rich protagonists' venality or inner emptiness can be illuminated. But on tipwork comedies from *Below Deck* to *Insecure*, the customer is the uninteresting, minor character: comic solely insofar as they mistakenly imagine themself as central to the narrative, the customer vanishes as soon as they pay a tip (or don't).[110]

Tipwork TV comedies also refuse to "make stories"—or at least to make a certain kind of narrative coherence—out of tipwork's chaotic precarity. In this way, tipwork TV departs from some of the formal conventions of the traditional situation comedy because it is precisely the stable "situation" that has been left behind in contemporary tipwork TV. The diner waitress had coworkers; the Postmates deliverer does not. The taxi driver had a dispatch center; the Uber driver has an iPhone. Under these conditions, it is scarcely surprising to find few representations of familial relationships between managers and tipworkers on tipwork TV: tipworkers' *actual* families, after all, are significantly more likely to rely on public benefits than are the families of their bosses. Whereas the sitcom's ability to disrupt and then restabilize working conditions by the end of each episode suggested a faith in contractual stability, the characters of tipwork TV are far more insecure. And whereas the sitcom has often tended to imagine a work life made livable and meaningful through what Lane-McKinley describes as "pranks, inside jokes, and other forms of casual everyday humor" and to reimagine the workplace as the site of either romance or familial intimacy, tipwork TV offers a far less cozy account of working conditions, a far more attenuated faith in upward mobility, and a far less comfortable sense of employment's stability.[111]

Tipwork TV's disorderly, episodic, paratactic narratives and its protean, resilient characters thus suggest a form at once new and old, one I term the "tipwork picaresque." Traditionally, the picaresque is an episodic narrative of only partially connected events depicting the adventures of a hero (or antihero) forced to endure an intolerably chaotic and unpredictable world.[112] The picaro, Matthew Garret contends, is "jostled by experience: pushed around, battered, abused, carried from one adventure (one scene of abjection, however it might strain toward laughter), to another."[113] The picaro's protean errancy is largely due to the kind of labor he performs, namely, temporary service. Pierre Vilar thus attaches the rise of the genre to "the inflation of the nonproductive tertiary sector" in the sixteenth century.[114] In the classic picaresque from that period *Lazarillo de Tormes*, Lazarillo describes himself as the "servant of many masters."[115] The picaro's relationship with those "many masters" requires him to "assum[e] whatever appearance the world forces on him," Stephen Miller argues. Like the domestic servant, the picaro must be constantly available to the master and must be whatever the master wants him to be. The master, in turn, is responsible for the servant's welfare. Yet in most picaresques, either the master or the picaro ends up deviating from this informal arrangement, such that the picaro is often paid too little to live on or not paid at all. The picaresque thus yokes poverty not to labor exploitation, but rather to subsistence and indeed to hunger. In this way, Peter Linebaugh suggests, it is a fundamentally "proletarian" genre—not a narrative about work and its meaning, but a narrative about what it means to have to work to survive.[116]

Like the classic picaro, moving from master to master and forced to rely on his wits, informalized service workers are vulnerable both to harassment by customers and to wage and time theft by bosses. And like the classic picaresque—whose characters were often not only servants, but also sex workers and thieves—the contemporary tipwork picaresque captures this insecurity by analogizing *informalized* service work to *criminalized* service work.[117] In *Easy*'s "Side Hustle" episode, the story of tipworker Odinaka runs in parallel to the story of Sally, a sex worker. The episode sets up a series of explicit parallels between her work and his, including a crosscut between Odinaka scooping up the cash tips from his tourist-bus gig and Sally putting an envelope with the cash she's paid by a client on top of her refrigerator (fig. 1.13). In a season 2 episode of *High Maintenance*, likewise, a customer aptly named "Johnny" taunts and threatens The Guy by asking, "You want me to leave the money on the counter like you're a hooker?": because The Guy is working as a weed deliverer (which was at the time still illegal in New York City), like a sex worker, he has little recourse against customers who refuse to pay (fig. 1.14). Attuned to the basic measures of proletarian survival under conditions where wages are uncertain, the tipwork picaresque thus captures the lived precarity of being excluded from the political, legal, economic, and cultural forms that have often defined "working class." (I return to the comparison of tipwork to sex work in the next section.)

The tipwork picaresque is thus keyed to represent subjects whose working lives are defined by temporary and uncertain working conditions, characters whose stories are not so easily wrestled into the arcs

Figure 1.13. Cash tips on *Easy*.

of development and education that structure conventional narratives of professional achievement. It formalizes this insecurity by playing with the picaresque's capacity for narrative fragmentation. The "New York, I Love You" episode of Netflix's *Master of None* offers a particularly compelling example of this formalization. Generally, *Master of None* is a somewhat conventional bildungsroman, but season 2's "New York,

Figure 1.14. Cash tips on *High Maintenance.*

I Love You" episode departs from the show's predominant plotlines and from its protagonist, Dev. The episode begins with Dev and his friends discussing a movie they want to see, but quickly moves away from them and instead follows different characters who shift abruptly from the scene's background into its foreground: Eddie, a doorman; Maya, a bodega cashier; and Samuel, a taxi driver. The arc of the episode follows a kind of associative logic that reflects both the endless and atemporal time discipline of tipwork and the radical uncertainty that defines jobs structured by repeated encounters with temporary bosses: Dev passes Eddie on the street, we leave Eddie behind when he walks past Maya's bodega, and Maya is second in line for Samuel's cab. In a powerful sequence about the relationship of these minor characters to the economy of the city—and to the economy of plot—a resident of the building where Eddie works shouts at him, "You have one job to do. One!" to which Eddie replies, "Actually sir, I have many different

Figure 1.15. A jack of all trades on *Master of None*.

jobs for many different people" (fig. 1.15). Although he is denied developed protagonicity, Eddie is thus the real "jack of all trades" evoked by the series' title. As the seventeenth-century Spanish picaresque *The Rogue* described its own nonprotagonist, Eddie "is all the World: know him alone / And then yee know a Multitude in One." For the picaro, nothing is more constant than inconstancy.[118]

What affective comportment is required to survive this wild inconstancy? Tipwork TV is comic, to be sure, but, again like the classic picaresque, this is not the happy stasis of the comedic fool. Subject to constant change—indeed, existential peril—the picaro must instead embody the detached endurance of tragicomedy.[119] In *Our Aesthetic Categories*, Sianne Ngai argues that service work is most effectively represented by characters such as Jim Carrey in *The Cable Guy*: a "zany" figure whose wild energy registers service work's blending of work and play and whose bodily contortions reflect the demand that service workers be constantly "flexible."[120] We certainly see this type of zaniness in tipwork TV, especially on shows such as *Broad City* and *Kimmy Schmidt*. Yet the contemporary tipwork picaresque also captures a more muted way of being in the world, that is the pragmatic disconnection necessary to endure tipwork when one has no fantasy of escaping from it.[121] An affable but flat affect likewise permeates the tipwork picaresque's pragmatically passive nonprotagonists. In *High Maintenance,* for instance, The Guy is the center, but never the agent, of an essentially plotless narrative. Even his namelessness indicates a refusal of conventional developmental characterization: he is both Everyman and, as Miller describes the classic *picaro,* "every man he has to be," defined purely in anonymous nonrelation to those he serves ("I'm gonna call The Guy").

Moreover, The Guy's affective mood features none of the zany's coked-up stimulation, but instead the more passive stoner stoicism of a world without upward mobility. In an episode from the first season titled "Trixie," for instance, we meet a young couple who work in restaurants, but supplement their low wages by renting out a space in their tiny apartment on Airbnb. Exemplary "recession millennials," they become gigwork hoteliers and thus sacrifice sanity for a modicum of security: "We were gonna be adults this year, live by ourselves, and I don't know how else we're gonna pay the rent unless we do this." Stressed out, they call The Guy to deliver some weed and invite him to sit in their cramped loft and smoke with them while they all talk about their jobs. "I'm never doing another service job again. *Ever,*" The Guy says emphatically, only to correct himself in stoner trail-off, "Well I mean I guess this is a service job, but. . . ."[122] The Guy's disconnected geniality is nothing like Ngai's excessive zaniness, perhaps because like many service workers, he is a service worker who often serves other service workers. His stoner "chill" thus registers as a gesture of solidarity toward his tipworking customers, who need no tip-soliciting performance.[123] The Guy's affect doesn't suggest an indistinction between work and play, but rather a blurring of the character positions of server and served.[124]

As we discover later in the same episode, it also suggests the passive pragmatism necessary to endure the fragmented experience of precarious labor under "many masters." The unnamed female customer

Figure 1.16. Serving service workers on *High Maintenance*.

of The Guy tells a story about a particularly bad night waiting tables: "I'm bored, I'm alone, so I'm trying to engage them. . . . I bring them their enchiladas and they eat and then leave with their whopping 8 percent tip. Then they leave, and I'm sittin' there, just, like, reading my Jane Austen novel, and then ten minutes later she comes *back* in. . . ." (fig. 1.16). The story ends with the customer making a crude sexual gesture at her while slamming the door. Here, we see the kind of emotional distance necessary to endure a certain kind of tipwork, a distance that has less to do with an incessant flow of activity and more to do with prolonged experiences of boredom and routine punctuated by unpredictably hostile encounters. To survive this kind of time discipline, the series suggests, it is necessary to separate oneself from the experience entirely. Offered in a tone of emotional distance and without either punchline climax or narrative closure, the unnamed server's story recalls the "perpetual authority" the household master had over the servant's time, as well as the asynchrony and irregularity of shift time that makes restaurant work seem unregulatable.

Shows such as *High Maintenance, Crashing,* and *Easy* are structured around relationships that are briefly intimate but lack lasting consequence, an inconsequentiality redoubled by the ephemerality of the episodes themselves, which introduce us to characters we will never meet again in a seemingly random way. Such encounters are definitive of the tipwork picaresque, in which brute necessity—the story of survival, of being thrown from master to master—becomes the contingency of social encounters. These social relations are also not so different from the kind an Uber driver might experience a dozen times in a single night. On the one hand, she will be rated via intimate and subjective measures like "Entertaining" or "Good Conversation" or "Cool Music." On the other hand, the system for "matching" her with her riders is all about the pure algorithmic contingency of geographic proximity (fig. 1.17). The tipwork picaresque thus formalizes the "independence" of tip-earning gigworkers enshrined in labor law. As Chapter 3 will explain in much more detail, contemporary labor law distinguishes between actual employees and mere gigworkers by saying that the latter are independent, inessential to the company's main business, and only temporarily necessary to its operation.[125] In this legal framing, we see all the features of the social worlds represented on tipwork TV: contingent, incidental, impermanent.

The wage implied a relatively clear and stable social relation—and thus also made clear the antagonism—between bosses and employees. Such stability and clarity are not always available to tipworkers and gigworkers, as when the bartender calls an Uber to get to work or the Postmates deliverer stops for a drink on her way home. Yet this confusion also opens up new forms of political belonging at the points of consumption and circulation, including forms of solidarity that might violate the laws of private property that likewise undergird the wage contract. "New York, I Love You" thus ends with a modest, but remarkably

Figure 1.17. Temp work and temp characters on *Insecure*.

powerful image of marketplace mutual aid, via thef, among the marginally employed. One of Samuel's friends, who works at a fast-food restaurant, opens the restaurant after hours and steals food for Samuel and a group of randomly met acquaintances. In the closed restaurant on a darkened street, the service workers drink and dance on the tables.

"Obsession with hunger, obsession with feasting—these are the twin poles of the *picaro's* dreams," Vilar contends.[126] Feast and famine, theft and gift, are likewise the overlapping logics of service work sociality in "New York, I Love You." We find a similar image of service workers oscillating between precarious survival and bacchanalian surfeit on an episode from season 4 of *Broad City* punningly titled "Just the Tips." The episode centers on protagonist Ilana's new waitressing job, where she has learned to succeed not by being "servile," but by sadistically abusing her customers and thus forcing them to want her approval. In the episode, "the tip" describes not just Ilana's wages, but also her French-tipped fingernails, which she uses to spear cheese cubes and snort coke. Later in the episode, "the tip" also refers to the tip of her friend Jaime's penis, which he is considering circumcising. "Just the Tips" thus exaggerates and wildly literalizes the connection between tipwork and affective or bodily intimacy. *Broad City*'s body humor recalls the genre Rebecca Wanzo influentially terms the "precarious-girl comedy," in which characters' "constant association with that which is considered gross (like dirt, vomit, and feces) is habitually a sign of... emotional and economic insecurity."[127] This episode similarly uses comedic abjection to think about the relationship between service work and the body of the service worker, but with less self-abasing pathos and more utopian pleasure, drawing yet again on the picaresque's commitment to carnivalesque disorder and reversals of fortune—to feasts, as well as famines. Ilana piles her tip cash on her bed and rolls around naked on it; at the end the episode, she also goes on a tipping spree of her own, flirtatiously stuffing the cash she's been given in tips into the back pockets and shirt collars of the male caterers and bartenders at a party (fig. 1.18). Here, the connection between service work and the erotic body becomes a way to celebrate the horizontal intimacy of tip wages, which promiscuously flow from one tipworker to another in a kind of carnivalesque mutual aid.

To the extent that low-waged work shows up on TV, I have suggested, it shows up mostly as service work: the variability, intimacy, and uncertainty of service work have made it hard to regulate, but easy to narrate. The service workplace TV of the 1970s to the 1990s reckoned with the challenge of understanding service work *as* work by suggesting that the service workplace wasn't *really* a workplace, but instead a haven in a heartless world—a place where "everybody knows your name" and where, from bosses to customers to tipworkers themselves, "our troubles are all the same." As low-waged service work came to occupy a greater share of the occupational field in the first decades of the twenty-first century, however, service workers themselves began to show up in new ways on TV. On dramas, in-person service work is represented as its own kind of "hidden abode." On series such as *Succession* and *White*

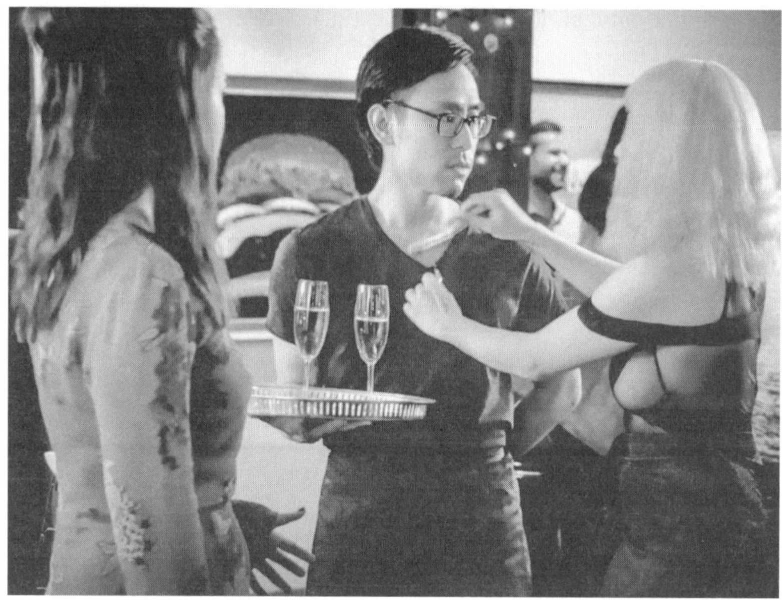

Figure 1.18. Using tips to tip the waiter on *Broad City*.

Lotus, in-person service workers make both life and narrative possible for the owners and bosses, the customers and clients, who perform the job of being primary characters. On tipwork comedies, by contrast, the picaresque's preference for the episodic over the continuous, for dispersal over development, and for fleeting spatial encounter over extended temporal association is used to formalize the experiences of a service-working class likewise defined by precarity—defined, that is, not by subjection to the formalized wage, but rather by exclusion from it.

SEX WORK, "ESSENTIAL WORK," AND THE FEMINIZATION OF SERVICE

On tipwork TV, the vulnerability associated with in-person service is turned into comedy. Comedic images of bodily abjection—the unnamed restaurant server in *High Maintenance* laughing ruefully about a customer's juvenile sexual gesture and Ilana comparing her cash tips to her French-tipped fingernails—are used both to evoke and to resist abiding anxieties about intimate, feminized service work. Those anxieties, as we saw in the first section of this chapter, are neither new to contemporary service work nor specific to tipwork TV; rather, they have long been associated with the difficulty of detaching the products of service work from the body or the "self" of the service worker. Because in-person service work does not produce "vendible commodities," it appears not just unrationalizable and unregulatable, but even premodern or nonmodern. As a result, in-person service work cannot be recognized as "free labor," and service workers themselves appear uniquely dominated, unfree, and even abject.

In the final section of this chapter, I draw on feminist theorist Heather Berg's critique of "sex-work exceptionalism"—the idea that sex work is a uniquely degrading form of work—to identify a similar kind of "service-work exceptionalism."[128] Like sex-work exceptionalism, service-work exceptionalism confuses the exclusion of service workers from law, political economy, and traditional political organizations with the idea that service work is thus more degrading than other forms of wage labor. Service-work exceptionalism and sex-work exceptionalism are not just analogous, but also bound together: service-work exceptionalism depends on the association of service work *with* sex work. In-person service work and sex work both involve labor whose "product" is connected to the body or being of the worker, both incorporate direct and seemingly intimate forms of domination, and both depend on informal cash wages. In the remainder of this chapter, I want to explore the discursive and material history of service-work exceptionalism and to think about the different ways that service workers (including sex workers) have reckoned with its consequences.

Earlier in this chapter, I cited sociologist Frances Donovan's 1920 study of waitresses, with its claim that the rise of tipping presaged a "social breakdown" that would inevitably draw certain classes of workers into immorality or vulgarity as a means of survival. We find similar anxieties about feminized service work in critics writing about service work a full century later. Describing the imperative that workers "suffer with a smile," for instance, Marxist cultural critic Mark Fisher draws on a sex-work metaphor to explore the forms of exploitation specific to postindustrial service work. "To understand work now," he writes, "consider the pornographic practice of bukkake. Here, men ejaculate in women's faces, and the women are required to act as if they enjoy it, to lasciviously lick the semen from their lips as if it is the most delicious honey.... The humiliation is not adequate unless they are *seen* to be performing an enjoyment they don't actually feel."[129] Carl Cederström and Peter Fleming similarly narrate the thoughts of an imagined service worker who, when his work demands performances of "authenticity," thinks of the sex workers he saw "in a documentary" who "seemed somehow resigned to lending their bodies to some unrefined truck driver who'd come in for a quick fuck."[130] Frédéric Lordon's *Willing Slaves of Capital* likewise uses the sex worker / service worker comparison to think about contemporary work more broadly: "Neoliberal capital is the world of the girlfriend experience," he contends, referring to the particular sex-work arrangement in which the sex worker performs a more "personal," comprehensive form of erotic and romantic attention.[131] In *Sugar Daddy Capitalism*, Fleming claims to discern a whole new epoch of accumulation defined by the "personalization of labor": the "all too human power relationships" whereby "the boss no longer demands just your objective time," but "also wants your arse." Through an extended allegory that seems to exceed his own rhetorical control, Fleming argues that neoliberal freedom may look like "two people meeting to make a 'deal,'" but in fact, it's nothing more than "a dimly lit hotel room" inside of which "awaits an overweight man in a bathrobe" who is "willing to help you get that lucky break... for a price."[132] Again and again, labor that is feminized, that is disconnected from standard forms of time discipline, and that involves direct forms of control or subordination tends to produce misogynist and homophobic social panic.[133]

Feminist theories of service work as affective labor do not feature the scandalized—but also implicitly titillated—descriptions of service work as sex work that we find in writers such as Fleming and Lordon. But service-work exceptionalism—the idea that service work makes one uniquely vulnerable to violations of autonomy and authenticity—does show up there in ways I think are worth querying. As I discussed in the Introduction, the most influential theorist of affective work is sociologist Arlie Hochschild, whose book *The Managed Heart* uses flight attendants to understand work where the product is not a tangible good, but "a state of mind." Emotional labor, she suggests, requires workers to experience their "engineered" feelings as real. They must "develop feelings for the parts [they] play" and "participate in the illusion" to be believable. This is why Hochschild compares performances of emotional labor by in-person service workers to method acting. Like the method actor, who must persuade herself before she can persuade her audience, the flight attendant must perform a kind of "double pretending."[134]

Perceived not as simply *pretending* to "'love the job,'" but as *"actually trying to love it,"* service workers cannot help but seem like deeply mystified subjects of false consciousness—more fundamentally unfree than workers who do not have to invest their deepest "self" in their labor. As a result, the service worker becomes an exemplary case for a broader question about what Hochschild calls "social engineering," but we might also simply term "ideology": why do subjects consent to their own domination?

The association of service work with this kind of "voluntary servitude" is an old one. As I suggested in the Introduction, servitude has long functioned as a ready metaphor for willing submission to divine and natural authority because servants seemed freely to give their masters control over their feelings, desires, and performances of self. Sixteenth-century political philosopher Étienne de La Boétie's famous *The Politics of Obedience: The Discourse of Voluntary Servitude*, for instance, explains why some subjects "willingly" submit to political tyranny whereas others resist by comparing the former to "cowardly and submissive" servants and the latter to independent goods producers. "The tiller of the soil and the artisan discharge their obligation when they do what they are told to do," he argues, whereas those who "serve the tyrant," must "not only obey orders; they must anticipate his wishes; to satisfy him they must foresee his desires; they must... accept his pleasure as their own, neglecting their preferences for his, distorting their character and corrupting their nature."[135] We can immediately see in these lines one origin for Hochschild's claim about service workers' self-mystified "double pretending." Indeed, Lordon's *Willing Slaves of Capital* draws directly on La Boétie's account to explore the "passionate servitude" of contemporary service work, a "new 'voluntary servitude'" wherein "the productive performance is primarily a 'human' performance, affective and behavioural" and "the enslaved consent" to their own exploitation.[136]

In-person service workers, especially those who earn tips, have thus been made to appear as wage labor's *other*—as dangerously servile and unfree. But they have also, and often at the same time, been used to *typify* how wage labor alienates workers from their own bodies and desires. Even in the late nineteenth and early twentieth centuries, discourse against tipping didn't *just* express anxiety about "menial" service work. It also registered fears about what it meant to depend on wages at all. As historians Daniel Rodgers and Lawrence Glickman have demonstrated, nineteenth-century American workers were still profoundly ambivalent about what it meant to work for wages.[137] They saw wage labor as dangerous and demeaning, a departure from the American ideals of autonomy and independence emblematized by the independent craftsman or producer. An 1877 labor reformer quoted in Glickman's history of living-wage discourse, for instance, claims that wages "make the employer a despot and the employee a slave, a system that... enfeebles the mind, corrupts the morals, and propagates misery, vice, and crime."[138] From the mid nineteenth century until the passage of the New Deal, formal, contractual wages were thus described in the exact same terms that would later be used to describe tips: as "wage slavery" (a racialized language of servility used to connect wage work to demeaning dependency) or as "prostitution" (a feminized language of threatened masculinity used to identify wage labor with abjection and subjugation).[139] Anxieties about waged work in general were thus displaced onto anxieties about tip wages in particular in order that formal, regulated wages might seem acceptable to white, male, skilled industrial workers dreaming of becoming bosses themselves someday.

So how have service workers themselves reckoned with this discourse and these anxieties? How, more specifically, have service workers been able to describe and indeed resist the forms of informalization, domination, and precarity specific to tipwork without at the same time succumbing to a service-work exceptionalism that might make them appear uniquely abject, uniquely degraded, uniquely powerless? Here, I want to explore two very different approaches to this problem by looking to the labor organizing practices and discourses of service workers and sex workers themselves.

Let me begin where this chapter began, with the labor group One Fair Wage (OFW). As part of its campaign against subminimum tip wages during the COVID pandemic, OFW created an emblematic character: "Elena the Essential Worker." Pictured in classic Rosie the Riveter pose, fist cocked, Elena doesn't wear Rosie's factory-worker-blue jumpsuit but is dressed instead in restaurant whites and a cook's apron (fig. 1.19).

Unlike the Rosie of the iconic image, Elena is Black, and as her "bio" tells us, "Elena was born thirty years ago and immigrated to the United States with her family as a young girl. She is a single working mom with two young children who are her world. She believes fiercely in creating worker power at the grassroots level and fighting for a better tomorrow for her children and all those experience poverty, dangerous working conditions, and subminimum wages."[140]

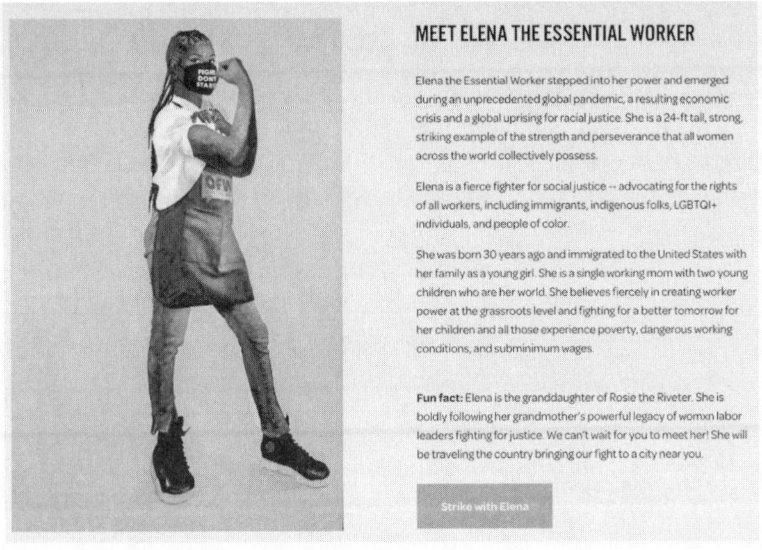

Figure 1.19. One Fair Wage's Elena the Essential Worker campaign.

Drawing a connection between Elena's maternal role and her political agency, the OFW campaign recalls older sentimental narratives about women's labor and their reproductive citizenship. Like images of industrial workingwomen in the late nineteenth century, Elena figures a refusal to treat white, male manufacturing workers as the quintessential wage laborers.[141] Yet the image does so by associating pandemic-era female service workers not with the histories of domestic servitude or service work, but instead with the history of industrial labor. The campaign's remediating evocation of Rosie the Riveter is particularly complicated in this context. The image of Elena visually evokes the iconic Westinghouse Electric image created as part of the War Manpower Commission's propaganda efforts by designer J. Howard Miller in 1942 (fig. 1.20).

Elena's biography concludes with the "fun fact" that "Elena is the granddaughter of Rosie the Riveter. She is boldly following her

Figure 1.20. The Westinghouse Electric Rosie the Riveter created by J. Howard Miller for the War Manpower Commission, 1942.

grandmother's powerful legacy of womxn labor leaders fighting for justice."[142] OFW was not alone in using Rosie as a symbol for "essential workers." Beginning in spring 2020, as COVID lockdowns began, the Westinghouse Rosie—now wearing a mask as well as a bandana—came to symbolize the courage of the nurses, teachers, and care workers who continued to work during the pandemic (fig. 1.21).

The link created here between pandemic-era "essential work" and the original World War II campaign was more than just handy iconicity or historical coincidence: like the image of Rosie, the term "essential work" *also* originated with the War Manpower Commission. During World War II, as during the pandemic, this classification was mostly a form of labor discipline.[143] Workers whose labor was classified as essential to the war effort were not permitted to change jobs.[144] During the COVID pandemic, the "essential worker" classification likewise conscripted workers, many of them service workers, into working in

Figure 1.21. Various pandemic Rosies.

dangerous conditions. Most of the jobs classified as "essential" in 2020 were low waged, without paid leave, and held by workers of color. While some businesses offered workers temporary "hero pay," classification as "essential" almost never led to an increase in compensation. The category's meaning—essential to what or whom?—was intentionally vague: while canneries or meat-packing plants are arguably essential to social provisioning, it's somewhat harder to understand why restaurants are.[145] Classification as "essential," and the sentimental representation of essential workers as "heroes," was thus mostly a way to avoid regulatory oversight, to subject low-wage workers of color to extremely hazardous working conditions, and to discipline a labor force that otherwise might have had unprecedented political leverage.

So why did OFW and many other worker organizations embrace the term "essential work"—the same term that some companies themselves were using to prevent workers from organizing or from receiving a living wage? I want to suggest that OFW and the other campaigns using Rosie as a visual touchstone were trying to reject the social imaginary that would distinguish between labor of goods production and the labor of service provision—the very social imaginary that led to the exclusion of service workers such as Elsie Parrish from labor regulation in the first place. In an essay about the history of the FLSA's exclusions, Palmer notes that agricultural workers eventually "reconceptualized their work as 'industrial'" to push back against a legal and political discourse that had framed their labor as too preindustrial to be recognized by modern labor law. We find a similar strategy in OFW's use of Elena the Essential Worker. Aligning Elena with the industrious nationalism of Rosie the Riveter, the OFW campaign explicitly situates the feminized service worker in a genealogy of productive, industrial, working-class labor. Service workers are *not* different from industrial workers, the image implies; rather, they share the same lineage and history.

In so doing, OFW attempts to radicalize the feminization of service work by disavowing service-work exceptionalism. By making tip wages central to its campaign, it resignifies service work, offering a critique that focuses not on affective and emotional submission, but instead on the political economy of the method of wage payment itself. Indeed, OFW suggests that one might imagine organizing workers not around shops or trades or crafts or even sectors, but rather around shared exploitation under a specific wage form. Tips, they note, are a method of superexploitation not just for restaurant workers and gigworkers but also for "workers in nail salons, hair salons, car washes, airports, and parking lots," as well as "workers with disabilities, incarcerated workers, and youth workers."

A different scene of labor militancy, however, might allow us to ask what is *lost* when tipwork is framed in relation to apparently virtuous, productive industrial labor and thus protected from the analogy to ostensibly demeaning, unproductive affective or embodied work. In its list of tip-earning occupations, OFW does not mention sex work. But some of the most dynamic organizing among contemporary service workers today is being done by sex workers, porn workers, and club dancers, many of whom rely on tips or other forms of direct payment. As Berg writes in *Porn Work: Sex, Labor, and Late Capitalism*, "a burgeoning movement in sex-work activism and scholarship frames work itself as the problem with sex work and uses sex work as a lens through which to critique the conditions of work under capitalism."[146] Juno Mac and Molly Smith likewise describe how "the bravery and resilience of sex workers... played a part in many [historic] liberation struggles," from the feminist movement and queer rights to socialist and worker organizing, and note that "the [contemporary] sex worker movement... buzzes with energetic grassroots organizing."[147]

Much of this recent organizing has, like OFW's organizing of service workers, centered on demands for legal recognition under labor law and on the need for wage protections for tipworkers in particular. The club dancers organizing through the workers organization Soldiers of the Pole, for instance, describe having to pay club fees and to give around 30 percent of their tips back to the club. The Soldiers of

Pole strikers chanted, "If you don't stop stealing tips / we're not gonna show our tits!" Here, then, we are reminded that sex work is not a metaphor for tipwork, but rather simply an instance of it.[148] Soldiers of the Pole emerged in the wake of the *Dynamex Operations West, Inc. v. Superior Court* decision, a unanimous ruling of the California Supreme Court that made it harder for California employers to exploit the "independent contractor" classification. Yet even after *Dynamex*, club owners could still take advantage of the flexibility of informalized tips and put new rules in place that made dancers' working conditions *worse* than they had been before *Dynamex*. Dancers were forced to report earning a minimum set by the club or be fired, and clubs began adding more required "tip-outs" to replace the old "house fees" model and taking an even larger share of tips, which they then used to meet the required minimum wage.

The clubs' response to *Dynamex* also ought to sound familiar. Recall, for instance, the redcaps who, *because* they were included under the FLSA, were forced to sign agreements claiming they were independent contractors and were required to count tips toward their hourly minimum wage. This history also reminds us that it is not enough to include more workers into existing classifications for "employee" when so much of the legal regulation that ostensibly regulates and protects employees is withheld from service workers, especially those who work for tips.

Similar issues attend unionization. For instance, in 2022, dancers at a Los Angeles club called Star Garden became the first formally unionized erotic dancers in the United States by affiliating with the Actors Equity Association. This was a major victory for many workers in the industry. Yet sex worker organizations created by and for nonwhite performers, such as the Haymarket Pole Collective, argue that different, more horizontal and relational forms of organizing are required to support trans, Black, and immigrant dancers who may lack the kinds of paperwork (work permits, licenses, updated birth certificates) required by traditional collective bargaining agreements as well as by the formalized "employee" model.[149] Sex workers groups such as the Sex Workers Outreach Project (SWOP) have likewise formed radical solidarity not just around unionization or wages, but in the tradition of mutual aid, which extends and radicalizes the intimacy and horizontality that tipping exploits.

In his work on the relationship between race, class, and gender, Chris Chen notes that "The workers' movement—with its valorisation of wage-labour, work, and the worker as the subject of history—failed to grasp that wage-labour is not the only form of exploitation." Chen goes on to argue that racial and gender disparities have often been "reproduced as an inherent category of capitalism... *not primarily through the wage but through its absence*."[150] Despite significant differences in both their tactics and their aims, service-worker groups from OFW to SWOP are expanding this claim, understanding the wage to name not a singular coherent category, but rather something multiple and variegated. These differences *among* types of wages have also been shaped by the valorization of "productive" labor Chen describes, allowing tip wages and other insecure methods of wage payment to be excluded not only from the productivism that has long underwritten labor reform and regulation, but also from the history of the labor movement and from modern theories of work and exploitation. To be "waged," contemporary service workers insist, may still mean being exploited by wage relations that are unregulated, uncontracted, unguaranteed; internally differentiated by informalization and superexploitation; and the product of historical and enduring processes of racialization and feminization. Understanding the exploitation of service work thus requires attention not simply to *what* workers are paid, but also to *how*.

CHAPTER TWO

Microwork and Piece-Rate Poetry

In 2008, digital media artist Aaron Koblin got the attention of the tech sector by selling ten thousand sheep—or, more precisely, ten thousand drawings of sheep. For *Sheep Market,* his MFA project in UCLA's Media Arts program, Koblin hired roughly ten thousand people to each draw a sheep, paying them two cents per drawing. Koblin displayed the ten thousand drawings in various formats—as a group, on a gallery wall; individually, on a "conveyor belt" display—and sold prints of twenty-sheep blocks. His artist's statement makes some glancing references to Marxist theories of alienation, but the piece soon got noticed by Jeff Barr, vice-president and "chief evangelist" for Amazon Web Services.[1] Barr would frame *Sheep Market* in practical terms: "What a cool example of collaborative art!" Barr enthused, "Think of this as an example of how to quickly, easily, and inexpensively get 10,000 people to do something for you. Today it is sheep, but it could just as easily be choices of color combinations for car interiors, [or] evaluation of some logos for your business."[2] Koblin himself would go on to become a tech entrepreneur, cofounding a virtual-reality company, leading Google's Data Arts team, and being named one of the "100 Most Creative People in Business." By the time he described *Sheep Market* in a 2011 TED talk titled "Visualizing Ourselves with Crowd-Sourced Data," the references to Marx would be gone, and the emphasis would be on "the humanity of the creative process."[3]

So how *did* Koblin hire ten thousand people "quickly, easily, and inexpensively"? This seemingly impossible project—finding, hiring, and paying ten thousand artists!—was possible because Koblin used the then-brand-new digital platform Amazon Mechanical Turk (AMT), an online service that allows corporations, research teams, and individuals to hire so-called "microworkers" to perform deskilled digital clerical work.[4] Microwork was fairly new in 2008 when Koblin created *Sheep Market*, but today, at least 20 million workers around the globe regularly engage in some form of microwork. There are many microwork platforms—Appen, Clickworker, Survey Junkie, Hive, Scale, Lionbridge, and others[5]—but AMT, launched in 2005, was the first and remains the largest. As Jeff Bezos explains, "Normally, a human makes a request to a computer, and the computer does the computation of the task. But artificial artificial intelligences like Mechanical Turk invert all that."[6] AMT allows employers to break up larger projects into tiny, deskilled tasks using algorithmically managed work flows. The "requester" posts each task and its rate of compensation to the AMT platform. Microworkers (typically called Turkers) browse the listed tasks and chose which ones to perform. Although they are termed "human intelligence tasks" (HITs), most of the tasks on AMT are repetitive and tedious: sorting merchandise into categories based on color or style; transcribing voice recordings; matching websites to search terms; categorizing images, testing CAPTCHAs. AMT and other microwork platforms thus allow clerical service work to be done by workers in their own homes and using their own computers and internet connections. And AMT isn't just a model for subcontracting clerical work; it's also a way to outsource it. Microworkers are increasingly concentrated in the Global South, and their wages are shockingly low: a Pew Study estimates the global average hourly wage of microworkers is $1.25 an hour.[7]

Microworkers aren't actually *paid* by the hour, however: as Koblin's two-cents-per-sheep project reminds us, they are paid by the task. AMT may have invented microwork, but it didn't invent task-rate wages. More commonly called piece-rate wages, this method of wage payment considerably predates the hourly wage. A piece-rate wage is defined by the International Labor Organization (ILO) as any wage "paid by the unit performed (e.g., the number of tee shirts or bricks produced) instead of being paid on the basis of time spent on the job."[8] Piece rates are most common outside the developed world, especially in regions that skipped the phase of high industrialization and moved directly from agriculture to service work, such that the regulated hourly wage common in manufacturing never became the norm.[9] But piece-rate and task-rate payments are also on the rise in the developed world. According to one study, the proportion of jobs that use performance-based pay in the United States rose by 50 percent in the last decades of the twentieth century.[10] The kind of "circulation" gigwork Chapter 3 will describe, for example, typically relies on a mix of task-rate and tip wages, where the platform pays workers a per-mile and/or per-delivery "base rate" that is then supplemented with consumer tips. Much as scientific managers in the early twentieth century constantly adjusted piece-rate wages up and down to encourage higher rates of productivity, contemporary circulation gigwork companies use wage algorithms to tune their per-delivery task-rate wages to the subtle rhythms of labor supply and consumer demand.

The first section of this chapter explores the history of piece-rate and task-rate wages. As I suggested already in Chapter 1's history of tipwork, the regulated hourly wage is neither a conceptual nor a historical norm, but rather a wage form specific to mechanized, standardized, centralized, skilled manufacturing labor. Outside of manufacturing, from farm work to service work, performance-based wages such as tips and task-rate wages are remarkably common. Like tips, task-rate wages are a way to compensate workers not on the basis of time worked, but instead on output produced. Like tips, task-rate wages enable the intensification of labor: they compel workers to work faster, harder, and longer. Like tips, task-rate wages have been racialized and gendered, perceived as a method of wage payment especially well suited to immigrant workers, nonwhite workers, workers with disabilities, and women. And like tips, the exceptional status of task-rate wages has been codified into law. The history of task-rate wages thus reveals unexpected connections between the service work of waiting tables and the service work of data entry. Both are low waged; both are shaped by a history of informalization, feminization, and racialization; and both are subject to nonhourly methods of wage payment.

Yet task-rate wages also reveal important differences between in-person service work and deskilled clerical service work. In-person service work such as the tipwork described in the previous chapter is difficult or even impossible to rationalize, mechanize, outsource, or automate. Clerical service work, by contrast, has become steadily more rationalized and mechanized over the last century; in the last few decades, it has also been increasingly outsourced and even automated. Task-rate wages, I will argue, have enabled these changes because they allow employers to combine *techniques* of intensification with *technologies* of mechanization and automation. Whereas Chapter 1 situated contemporary tip wages in longer histories of domestic servitude, this chapter situates the task-rate wages paid to clerical microworkers in a more unexpected historical context: farm work. As Chapter 1 mentioned briefly, both farm work and service work were often excluded from labor reforms and regulation because their fundamentally "nonindustrial" labor processes were perceived as unregulatable. Yet unlike in-person service work, farm work was also in the process of becoming more like industrial work, increasingly and steadily rationalized and mechanized. Piece-rate wages, I suggest, were vital to this transition. Piece-rate wages allowed agricultural employers to combine brutal "preindustrial" methods of superexploitation (forcing workers to labor harder, longer, and more intensely) with new forms of scientific management and new technologies of mechanization and deskilling. Piece-rate wages also enabled and were enabled by the superexploitation of temporary migrant farmworkers through schemes such as the Bracero Program. Ultimately, I will contend, the use of piece-rate wages also led to greater levels of automation in the agricultural sector.

We can map a surprisingly similar history onto clerical service work. Like farm work, clerical service work once seemed immune to mechanization or significant increases in productivity. But by attending to the history of task-rate wages in clerical work—from the female clerical workers whose electric typewriters counted each tap of the carriage return key, to the "homeworkers" paid for each envelope they addressed, to today's outsourced microworkers paid a fraction of a penny for each click of a mouse—we can understand how technology allowed deskilled clerical service work to be rationalized, outsourced, and even automated.

As Koblin's piece also reminds us, it isn't just corporations who are hiring task-rate microworkers via AMT, it's also artists. As one critic wryly observes, "the history of people using AMT to make art is almost as old as the platform."[11] Among visual artists, xtine burroughs is among the most well known and prolific of the AMT users, producing works such as the video project *Mechanical Games*, the conceptual work *Meditations on Digital Labor*, the book/installation project *A Penny for Your Thoughts*, and the sound project *Endless Om*. Video artist James Coupe created *Video Art General Intellect Query III*, which not only used AMT, but was also the first piece of new-media art sold on Amazon Art Market. Other visual art examples include Andy Baoi's *The Faces of Mechanical Turk*, Clement Valla's *Seed Drawings*, Tara Kelton's *Autoportrait*, and Yuri Pattison's *Outsourced Views*. Works of AMT poetry have been published in the influential anthology *Against Expression*, edited by Craig Dworkin and Kenneth Goldsmith, and also include Markus Strohmaier's "In the daily life of a Mechanical Turk" and Suzi Grossman's "Scary Cat." Although never mentioned in Mark McGurl's *Everything and Less: The Novel in the Age of Amazon*, these projects are arguably the true art of "the age of Amazon."[12]

In part two of this chapter, I discuss two of these AMT art projects: Fred Benenson's "translation" piece *Emoji Dick* and Nick Thurston's conceptual poetry collection *Of the Subcontract*. These projects are typically understood in the context of conceptual art's long-standing fascination with work and commodification. They also exemplify a more recent neoconceptual interest in "cut-and-paste" art, outsourcing, and automation. Reading not just for concept, but also for genre, voice, and the poetics of social action, however, I want to situate the individual poems that make up these projects in a longer genealogy of proletarian poetry. These poems, I argue, illuminate the managerial and infrastructural conditions underwriting the microwork system (from algorithms to English-language hegemony), animating the relationship between the everyday, immediate experience of labor paid by the task and the technologies that make that form of labor exploitation possible.

The third section of this chapter uses the histories of both clerical microwork and task-rate wages to think through the broader problem of automation in the service sector. Recent influential accounts of service work by political economists Aaron Benanav and Jason Smith rightly note that service work has historically been immune to automation: defined by unpredictable and nonmechanizable activities, the service sector has been unable to make the large leaps in productivity that have cyclically transformed manufacturing.[13] But the history of deskilled clerical service work reveals something more complicated. Drawing on the affordances of the task-rate wage, microwork combines older techniques of sweating and informalization with the newer technological affordances of digital service labor. In the third part of this chapter, I use AMT microwork as a case study for testing Benanav and Smith's firm dichotomies between labor replacing and labor saving, between technological efficiency and managerial domination, between innovation and stagnation. I argue that although AMT still depends heavily on task-rate superexploitation and outsourcing, its "artificial artificial intelligence" has also aided the development of labor-replacing innovations in AI. In this way, microwork exposes the material links between the creation of new labor-substituting technology and the deskilling and mechanization of knowledge work across the globe. Because AI is automating what were already low-waged and low-productivity jobs, however, it is not creating significant economic growth or producing new kinds of jobs to compensate for the jobs it replaces. As a result, I suggest, microworkers are increasingly turning to various techniques of sabotage and machine breaking to register their resistance to being automated out of work.

TECHNOLOGY, TECHNIQUE, AND THE HISTORY OF TASK-RATE WAGES

Time-based wages promise workers consistent compensation regardless of productivity, performance, success, or demand. For this reason, at least two centuries of orthodox economists and capitalist employers have expressed their preference for performance-based wages, a broad category that includes tips, commission-based wages, and piece-rate or task-rate wages.[14] Like tips, piece-rate wages rely on a nontemporal form of labor discipline, allowing compensation to be indexed directly to performance. Because piece-rate workers are paid on the basis of individual output, piece-rate wages are a form of intensification: as Marx notes, "the quality and the intensity of [piece-rate] work [is] controlled by the very form of the wage."[15]

Marx also suggests that piece-rate wages are particularly useful when the work has been *partially*, but not *fully*, industrialized. The piece-rate worker must "strain his labour power as intensely as possible," which in turn "enables the capitalist to raise the normal degree of intensity of labor" by lengthening the working day.[16] For this reason, piece-rate wages are often associated with the kind of "absolute" surplus value characteristic of semi-industrialized labor processes. Marx's contemporary, the Ricardian political economist John Ramsay McCulloch, argues in a similar vein that task-rate wages allow employers to adjust wages based on what each individual worker "deserves" to be paid, a mapping of compensation onto output especially useful for production processes where mechanization is incomplete.[17] Piece-rate wages were also seen as ideologically as well as practically useful in inculcating capitalist labor discipline among workers new to industrial labor. The historical school of German economics, which produced the first systematic theory of wage forms, viewed piece work as "one of the most important processes in the course of the nineteenth-century emergence of capitalism." Early twentieth-century German economists Gustav Schmoller and Werner Sombart both argue that time-based wages are "irrational" because they guarantee compensation regardless of output. Piece-rate wages, they suggest, inspire the workforce with a capitalist spirit by assigning a specific and quantifiable benefit to diligent work.[18]

In the early industrial period described by Marx, piece-rate wages often coexisted with time-based wages, even within the same production process, as a way of separating low-skill manual work from higher-skill mechanized labor. In his history of the London clothing trades, James Schmiechen explains that preindustrial textile labor was divided between the "honorable 'flints,'" who did skilled work for hourly or daily wages in the master's shop, and the "dishonorable 'dungs,'" who performed unskilled labor for piece-rate wages.[19] This distinction between skilled workers (paid by time) and unskilled laborers (paid by the piece) persisted even as the textile sector industrialized. Under the "sweating," or "putting-out," system, textile producers hired subcontractors who would in turn pay female workers (and children) to perform deskilled piecework. A single garment might be cut and assembled by skilled, male machine tenders and then finished by women doing deskilled hand sewing in tenement sweatshops. The mechanized parts of the labor process often favored hourly or daily wages because workers were centralized and supervised and the machines themselves could guarantee a steady, standardized output. Sweatshops, by contrast, employed largely unsupervised workers whose output varied depending on individual skill, effort, and time spent working.[20] Peter Linebaugh describes the piece-rate wages paid to sweated workers as part of a larger "revolution in the labor process" necessary to the refinement of a system of industrial management.[21]

The labor process of these piece-rate outworkers was far less mechanized than to the work of the machine tenders, but piece-rate wages were not simply a holdover of preindustrial labor processes. Indeed, as I have already suggested, piece-rate wages are most effective when there has already been some industrial rationalization and deskilling. Unlike the less alienated and more holistic relationship between effort and output characteristic of preindustrial labor (what E. P. Thompson terms "task orientation"), industrial piece-rate wages require employers to put a specific value on relatively small differences in individual output.[22] Workers' output must be consistent enough that a boss can compare the output of different workers or between one day and the next. The work must also have been deskilled enough that effort (or even simply physical strength) is more determinative of output than is skill or experience. Likewise, piece-rate wages are best suited for labor processes so standardized that the *quantity* of the output is more variable than the *quality*. Otherwise, the benefits that come from increasing the quantity will be counteracted by the nearly-inevitable decline in quality that comes when you incentivize speed.[23]

The most influential theorist of and advocate for piece-rate wages was the father of modern "scientific" management, Fredrick Winslow Taylor. For Taylor, piece rates are not a substitute for modern management; rather, they are a highly effective *form* of management, especially where the labor process is largely rationalized but still in the process of being mechanized. If used alongside time-and-motion studies and a scientific theory of behavioral motives and economic compensation, Taylor argues, piece-rate wages can coordinate the financial incentives of workers and bosses. A "uniform standard rate of pay by the day," Taylor says, creates a "common tendency to 'take it easy,'" whereas a piece rate "not only pulls the man up from the top but pushes him equally hard on the bottom."[24] When wages are guaranteed regardless of output, Taylor's contemporary C. Bertrand Thompson notes, workers are ensured a "fair day's pay," but the employer is guaranteed nothing. The boss, Thompson notes, doesn't want "the mere command of the workman's *time* but a measurable *product*." With piece rates, then, "the employer pays for what he gets and the employee is paid for what he does. Both sides are satisfied and the production increases."[25] Edward Lazear, founder of the field of personnel economics, agrees: scientific incentive schemes "motivate those who want to work at high levels of effort as well as those who choose to work at lower levels of effort."[26]

Like tips, piece-rate wages were also the basis for racialized, gendered, and abilized wage differentials. As the distinction between the "flints" and the "dungs" evoked above suggests, piece rates have always been seen as particularly advantageous when a firm wants to hire unskilled workers, but doesn't want to expend the time and money to train them.[27] Because piece rates "placed on the worker the full burden of any inefficiency," David Montgomery writes, they were thought to be "especially effective in inducing high output" among immigrant workers and other new entrants to the labor market, especially women.[28] Female factory workers in the late nineteenth century were more than three times more likely to be paid by the piece, compared with male workers.[29] By the early twentieth century, piece-rate wages were common in industries such as meat packing, cigar making, and canning, all of which took advantage of an abundant pool of cheap immigrant labor.[30]

Within a few decades, however, technologies such as the assembly line led to an almost fully machine-paced labor process in manufacturing. As a result, piece-rate wages were steadily replaced by regulated hourly wages in that sector. Whereas piece-rate wages had enabled employers to hire workers at a range of skill levels and provided no incentive to train them, mechanization required a more coordinated and synchronized productivity among workers. The technology of integrated-line production depended on a steady, standard effort from each worker. Because these new machines were expensive to operate, employers preferred having a small number highly skilled workers, instead of many deskilled workers, to ensure the line didn't idle during bottlenecks.[31] Standardized production technologies ensured productive equality among workers and guaranteed output, regardless of workers' individual speed. As a result of these technologies, labor regulations such as the Fair Labor Standards Act (FLSA) could easily apply the "regulatory hour" as the basis for a "stable and homogenous measure" of productivity among skilled manufacturing workers.[32] Thus, while the 1938 text of the FLSA made no reference to piece-rate work, a 1944 Supreme Court ruling in *United States v. Rosenwasser* (a textile manufacturing business) held that there was "no real basis for excluding piece-rate [manufacturing] workers from the benefits" of the FLSA. It further noted that piece-rate wages had been relatively common at the time of the FLSA's passage and that "Congress necessarily had to create practical and simple measuring rods" so that piece-rate wages could be "translated... by computation to an hourly basis."[33]

As we have already seen, however, the FLSA of the 1930s to the 1960s excluded more workers than it included. Piece-rate wages, already intimately yoked to race, citizenship, and gender, helped facilitate some of those exclusions. Workers with disabilities, for instance, were not—and indeed are *still not*—covered by the requirement that piece-rate wages be "translated" into their hourly equivalent. New Deal–era Labor Secretary Frances Perkins demanded a "subminimum wage" for these "substandard workers" by using on the same productivist logic that had allowed her administration to defend a narrowly literal definition of "commerce" as the production of physical goods. The 1938 FLSA allowed "sheltered workshops" (employers that hire only workers with disabilities) to base their wage rates on the productivity of each individual worker using a piece-rate scheme. Later amendments to the FLSA would make the wage rates of workers with disabilities *worse*, not better, and even today, hundreds of thousands of workers for sheltered workshops such as Goodwill earn piece-rate wages far below the federal minimum wage.[34]

Piece-rate wages thus are most effective when labor has already been deskilled and can be performed by the cheapest workers available, whether they are immigrants, women, or others deemed "substandard." Piece-rate wages allow capitalists to profit from labor sweating and intensification, forms of superexploitation that operate in coordination with the kind of legal exclusions described above. Yet piece-rate wages are not an *alternative* to mechanization and automation, but rather a feature of labor processes that are *in the process* of transitioning from being very labor intensive to being more fully mechanized. We can understand these exclusions best by looking to the history of piece-rate wages in agriculture.

In Chapter 1, I discussed the way productivist ideologies justified the exclusion of tips from New Deal wage regulation. A very similar rhetoric defined the use of piece-rate wages in agriculture. During the New Deal era, Black employment in the South was still disproportionately concentrated in domestic service and agriculture: in the former, as we have seen, workers were often paid in leftovers and hand-me-downs; in the latter, practices such as sharecropping, debt peonage, and crop theft ensured that Black farmers labored under conditions little better than the chattel slavery from which they had been formally emancipated.[35] Attempting to write racial wage differentials into the law, Southern legislators sought to associate Black agricultural labor with the same "substandard" productivity that they were simultaneously ascribing to workers with disabilities. They also claimed that agricultural work—again like domestic service—was constitutively preindustrial and thus ill suited to wages-and-hours rules.[36] As one senator put it, "agricultural labor was not subject to the usual evils of sweatshop conditions of long hours indoors at low wages."[37] Ivan McDaniel, a lobbyist for the agricultural producers, argued during congressional debates over the FLSA that "the mechanized theories of industry do not fit in in agriculture, the rigidity of operations does not fit."[38] Much as service work had been excluded from the FLSA because it didn't produce "tangible goods," agricultural work was excluded because it didn't conform to the kinds of time discipline and rationalization common to modern manufacturing. As we saw in the previous chapter, legislators and lobbyists argued that restaurant workers couldn't have their hours regulated because "it is difficult to control the eating habits of patrons." A very similar claim was made about the fundamentally "natural" and nonrationalizable labor time of agricultural work: "The cow," one senator averred, "cannot be regulated by any law you set down here. She gives down her milk at 6 in the morning."[39] Having already insisted that the working hours of domestic workers had to accommodate the variability of demands on their time, lobbyists and politicians also argued that because farm labor is cyclical and seasonal and because its products are subject to the variable temporality of perishability, it would be unduly constrained by time-based wage and maximum-hours regulations.[40] Farmworkers were thus largely excluded from the requirement that piece-rate wages be translated into their hourly equivalent until the 1966 amendments: even after those amendments, farmworkers remain excluded from most maximum-hours rules, and farmworkers on smaller farms are still excluded from minimum-wage laws entirely.[41]

Contrary to the claim that farm work was fundamentally preindustrial or nonindustrial, however, piece-rate wages were common in agriculture precisely *because* the sector was in the process of becoming industrialized. As a result of technological and scientific innovations, agricultural labor had been deskilled and rationalized enough that effort was increasingly more important than experience or skill. Yet the sector was still very labor intensive, and significant parts of the labor process (picking delicate fruit, for instance) were difficult or even impossible to mechanize. Agricultural workers were also too spatially dispersed to be constantly and directly supervised. As rural sociologist Ronald Mize notes, piece-rate wages were thus an effective form of direct domination in semi-industrialized agriculture. "Force and intimidation," Mize argues, are used to "increas[e] the duration and intensity of work while decreasing wages to the lowest feasible rate."[42]

Mid-century agricultural labor thus blended industrial-type mechanization, deskilling, and rationalization with "preindustrial" intensification, sweating, and piece-rate wages. This brutal mix of technology and technique combined with legal informalization and racial exclusion under the Mexican Farm Labor Agreement, later called the

Migrant Labor Agreement, but widely known as the Bracero Program.[43] From 1942 to 1964, the Bracero Program allowed Mexican migrant hand laborers to work seasonally in the United States, mostly in agriculture. The braceros were supposedly guaranteed wages equivalent to those paid to American workers in similar jobs. However because agricultural work was excluded from minimum-wage laws—and because piece-rate compensation was used alongside unregulated working hours—"the few workers who could earn what was guaranteed to them did so only by working extremely long hours," Mize suggests.[44] Braceros were prohibited from working with machines or even driving tractors (the term *bracero*, Spanish for "a person who works with his arms," was intended to emphasize this requirement). In fact, however, mechanization and even automation were crucial to the program. Growers depended on technology to discipline the large, decentralized workforce made available by the Bracero Program, a history vividly described by Curtis Marez in *Farm Worker Futurism*.[45] Moreover, it was only because mechanization had *already* deskilled certain tasks that formerly skilled farmwork jobs could be legally reclassified as unskilled "bracero" fieldwork. Technological innovation and the use of superexploited migrant piece-rate labor thus went hand in hand. The partial automation of lettuce harvesting in the 1950s, for instance, *raised* demand for piece-rate migrant labor: the machines that now packed the lettuce in the field replaced the unionized, citizen laborers who had formerly packed it in sheds and warehouses, but they also required more deskilled hands to work in the fields.[46] Precisely by raising the supply of cheap labor, Marez explains, the Bracero scheme "made the development and deployment of agricultural technology possible and productive."[47]

During the same decades when the Bracero Program was deploying piece rates as a form of racialized superexploitation, piece-rate wages were also serving as a useful managerial affordance for low-waged clerical work, which was similarly becoming more and more mechanized. Throughout the early twentieth century, clerical work maintained at least some of its once-privileged "craft" status.[48] But as factories and commercial enterprises alike came to require ever-greater numbers of clerical workers, office managers began to realize that they, too, needed to "systematize and control" their labor process.[49] Taylorists William Leffingwell and Lee Galloway published fat tomes on the importance of scientific management in the office. Even as they insisted on the easy applicability of factory-type efficiency to offices, however, the Taylorists also worried that it would be hard to subject mental labor to the kinds of rationalization already common in manufacturing. As Galloway observes, "it was impossible to determine whether or not the [clerical] employees were living up to the standard of a fair day's work."[50] If office work was going to become more mechanized, it would be necessary to track and incentivize workers' productivity even in a labor process notoriously resistant to quantitative measures of output.

Office managers and experts solved this problem the same way agribusiness did, that is, by implementing task-rate wages. Leffingwell's chapter titled "The Compensation of Office Employees" opens with an epigraph from his colleague Henry Gantt: "There are only two methods of paying for work—one is for the time the man spends on the work, and the other is for the amount of work he does."[51] It should come as no surprise that the Taylorists favored the latter, and office managers began to use the same sorts of sweating practices that had once shaped textile work, forcing workers to strain for ever-greater levels of efficiency, only so that managers could then increase the standard and lower the rate.

Task-rate payment in clerical work was also tied to the sector's feminization. Female machine operators who processed time cards and did typing or punch carding, Sharon Strom explains, were now the brain of the entire corporate structure, and their "unmechanized hand operations" could easily be "counted and subjected to speed-up and piece rate," such that deskilled and highly rationalized women's work could be used to "break the hold of the male craft workers."[52] Piece-rates were also perceived as a way to inculcate new female workers into habits of productive efficiency. Leffingwell, for instance, narrates the story of one "Miss Slowly," the "girl who had the lowest [efficiency] record in the office" and whose manager, after discovering that she "hadn't much interest in the work," coached her into the highest productivity in the office by "pointing out the possible rewards." Soon, he reports, she was three times faster than before, and all the other girls were soon forced to keep up with the new standard she had established.[53] "Scientific" piece-rate systems also helped office managers develop new technologies that would monitor workers' speed and output even *without* the direct supervision of human managers. Leffingwell, for instance, describes typewriters fitted with "a mechanical contrivance which automatically counts the strokes made on the typewriter and records them on a dial."[54] Mid-twentieth-century office work thus came to look increasingly like nineteenth-century manufacturing insofar as it relied on the pairing of labor-saving technologies with labor-sweating techniques: the typewriter meter was the equivalent of manufacturing devices such as the mechanized peach pitter, which allowed canneries employing immigrant women to monitor each worker's piece rate while also speeding up the labor process itself.[55]

New innovations in data processing and computing eventually allowed a version of what Braverman calls "machine-pacing" even in office work, and by the 1950s, most clerical employees were subject to the same kinds of federal wages-and-hours regulation that protected manufacturing workers.[56] As a result, employers had to find other opportunities to reduce labor costs while increasing productivity, and they did so not by redefining "commerce," as they had in the in-person-service sector, but instead by redefining "employee." By mid-century, more and more US corporations were relying on flexible, temporary, subcontracted clerical workers hired via "temp" agencies such as Manpower. In the 1970s, firms began shifting clerical workers out of agency-based temp work and into even more informal subcontracting arrangements. Under the "homework" model of subcontracting, for instance, large numbers of mostly female workers performed deskilled service work such as envelope stuffing or typing in their homes and were paid task-rate wages in the tradition of the sweated seamstresses of the nineteenth century.[57]

Employers insisted that these clerical "homeworkers" were independent contractors, not employees covered by wage-and-hour protections. To legitimate this informalization, firms yet again emphasized the nonstandard temporality, task-oriented process, and autonomy of clerical homework. Using arguments that recall the debates about domestic labor described in Chapter 1, as well as the discussions of farmwork recounted above, they insisted that clerical homework is fundamentally different from manufacturing labor: it is small-scale, unalienated, make-work performed by women who (as one lawyer argued) "cannot accept definite working hours" and prefer to "work solely at their own convenience free from direction."[58] By the mid-1980s, more and more companies were relying on these contingent "independent contractors," who provided their own computers, worked at home, and were almost entirely unprotected by federal labor standards or regulation. As labor historian Eileen Boris explains, the productivity pressures of a piece-rate payment system required these women to "sweat themselves" just like the nineteenth-century outworkers. As one typist put it, "If you don't type, you are just not paid for it. There is absolutely no pay for the time you have to collate, stable, count, put together your work."[59]

By the late 1990s, the deskilling, tempification, and subcontracting of clerical service work was complete, and the only remaining cost-saving innovation would be to do with clerical work what had already been done in manufacturing: outsource it. Companies such as Xerox and AmEx began to set up offshore business process outsourcing (BPO) operations, what Sarah Roberts describes as "large-scale operations centers with technological infrastructure... to provide numerous services, often on a 24/7 business cycle."[60] Located in underdeveloped regions of India, Singapore, and the Philippines, BPOs allowed companies to hire deskilled clerical service workers for less than they had been paying their US temps and homeworkers.[61]

Improvements in telecom bandwidth, satellite services, and high-speed internet led to even greater use of BPOs in the first decade of the twenty-first century, but today, the fastest-growing sector of outsourced digital labor—generating roughly $25 billion globally—is not in traditional BPOs (which require a centralized location outfitted with computers and other infrastructure), but instead what is often called "platform labor" or "online outsourcing."[62] Platform labor is typically task based or project based, and the work is done in workers' own homes (or in libraries, internet cafés, shopping centers, and other public spaces). Much as temp firms such as Manpower helped companies take advantage of unused office space by hiring temps to work at night, platform labor leverages the flexibility of a newly global digital workforce and allows temps to work from home while also requiring them to provide their own computer, their own internet connection, and their own workspace. Some online outsourcing involves skilled labor in jobs such as IT, finance, or sales: Upwork—the largest online outsourcing platform focusing on skilled subcontracting work—transacts over a billion dollars of this kind of "knowledge work" annually. The kind of online-outsourced work typically referred to as "microwork" or "crowdsourcing," however, is much more deskilled. In microwork, Roberts explains, "tasks are broken into their smallest component parts," and "compensation is often on the order of pennies per task completed."[63]

Although microwork is not always outsourced, it is intimately connected to the kinds of core-periphery inequalities that have been produced by outsourcing, inequalities that eventually rebound to workers in the core, as well.[64] The very term "microwork" comes not from Jeff Bezos, but from a nonprofit development foundation called SamaSource, whose founder, Leila Janah, sought to do to BPO what Mohammed Yunus had done with "microfinancing" a few decades earlier. Based in San Francisco, SamaSource provides "impact sourcing": their platform, SamaHub, subcontracts digital services for large US and European companies (eBay, Getty Images, Walmart, and others) to microwork centers in underdeveloped countries with high rates of poverty such as Pakistan, Uganda, and Haiti.[65] As if to rebut the charge that they were actually *contributing* to global inequality, however, in 2016, SamaSource announced a new project. Noting that "parts of the US resemble subsistence-farming African villages," they explained that they were starting a pilot project in Dumas, Arkansas, whose economic base had been steadily and devastatingly eroded by the mechanization of cotton farming.[66] Three years later, the project was quietly ended with virtually no successes to report. It failed, of course, because of the outsourcing competition that SamaSource itself had already enabled. As people around the world began to bid for tasks, the average wage rates plummeted even further, making it impossible for untrained US microworkers to compete.[67]

Today, at least 20 million people across the globe perform some form of digital microwork, and most of them do it on AMT. Increasingly, AMT workers are being hired to perform work that was previously centralized in BPO centers, especially "content moderation" services. One survey of Turkers described tasks including "'sexual image analysis'; 'moderate photos from adult dating sites'...'watch pornographic movies up to 30 minutes long'...'categorize images from pornographic site'...'describe images of dead people, full of blood.'"[68] (Unlike BPO workers, Turkers typically know nothing about who is hiring them or about the larger project to which their individual "human intelligence task," their HIT, is contributing.) As for Amazon itself, it profits from the service by charging requesters a fee: until 2016, Amazon charged 20 percent of whatever the requester was paying in wages; in 2016, it doubled its base rate, which workers say caused their wages to decrease by an equivalent amount.[69] Most HITs are outsourced by corporations, but not all: according to a Pew Research Study from 2015, the largest group of requesters on AMT that year (36 percent) was neither large corporations nor tech companies, but "academic groups, professors, or graduate students."[70] Every year since 2008, many thousands of academic studies relying on AMT labor are published with little oversight over the wages or working conditions of Turkers, despite the use of public or nonprofit grant funding to pay them.[71] Medical and social scientists use AMT workers as survey participants, while scholars in fields such as natural language processing, computational linguistics, library sciences, music theory, and anthropology hire Turkers to perform tedious work such as semantic tagging or word searching, as well as more sophisticated work such as transcription and translation.[72] Multiple digital humanities initiatives, publications, and organizations have done projects using AMT labor.[73] AMT labor is, as one group of scholars puts it, "extremely inexpensive relative to nearly every alternative other than uncompensated students," allowing academic researchers to outsource not only deskilled data entry, but also traditionally higher-waged work such as transcription and translation to informalized microworkers all over the globe. [74]

As its use by academics suggests, platform microwork both depends on and produces an increasingly global division of knowledge work. For the first few years of AMT's existence, only workers with US bank accounts could be paid in currency; workers outside the United States were paid in Amazon credit. Beginning in 2009, however, Amazon started allowing workers in India to be paid in rupees; in the years since, they have steadily added more currencies to the list.[75] There are significant wage gaps between the Global North and Global South: one study calculates that US Turkers earn on average $3.01/hour, whereas Indian workers earn less than $1.50/hour.[76] In this way, contemporary microwork suggests the enduring effects of the racialization of piece-rate wages, a racialization now applied not to immigrant workers, but instead to the victims of global labor outsourcing. It also recalls the association of piece-rate payment with productivist ableism: a majority of workers on AMT report having at least one disability.[77]

Microworkers are not subject to the rigid time discipline of industrial management (an aspect of the work often ideologically reframed as "flexibility" or entrepreneurial autonomy). But like tipwork and gigwork, microwork's task-rate structure ensures that much of Turkers' work time—from searching for tasks to revising work—is "unac-

Figure 2.1. A list of HITs on AMT.

counted for and unremunerated," as Veena Dubal puts it.[78] Figure 2.1 is an example of the screen a Turker might see as they search the site looking for "good" HITs.

The task times range from one to two seconds to multiple hours, while the pay per task runs as low as one to two cents. Considering the time it takes to find the task, click on it, and request payment, a worker doing only these kinds of tasks would earn less than fifty cents an hour. Indeed, knowing which tasks to accept and which to reject is necessary to surviving on AMT.[79] In a study of AMT "expert" workers, for instance, one described why they rejected a given HIT this way:

> You have to open a link, find 2 pieces of information, copy and paste on another page, plus you have to copy and paste at least one, maybe 2 urls. I highly doubt all of this can be done in 30 seconds or less. If you can do it all in 1 minute, that's .05 a minute which is 3.00 an hour and to make that you have to work really fast, like a machine and do many of them. If you

> can't find the info or the link doesn't work, you have wasted time and have to return the hit to insure you don't get a rejection. It's a waste of time to even look at this hit and an insult because of the low pay.[80]

On the other side of the labor relation, AMT allows "requesters" to reject a Turker's work if it is not performed according to certain specifications. Requesters can claim "poor quality" after receiving the product of hours of a Turker's work, or they can require Turkers to perform unpaid "screening" work before accepting or rejecting them for a job. The structure of task-rate payment on AMT creates information and power asymmetries that are entirely to the advantage of the employers: Turkers describe things like an "'8 minute survey' took around twenty" or "4 days, still waiting for my dime."[81]

AMT also depends on what is often called "decomposition" or "unbundling," or the ability to break up a process into algorithmically managed sequences of tasks. (I will return to these terms when considering university labor in the Coda.) Like the Taylorists before them, designers of decomposed work flows have discovered all kinds of efficiency gains through rationalization. One study describes the computational infrastructure of the platform as a Taylorist's utopia: "the dream to measure every motion at every point throughout the workday and beyond is not only doable, but trivial... modern crowd work [measures] every click, scroll, and keyboard event."[82]

Microwork platforms such as AMT thus bring together the outsourcing affordances of BPO; the labor-cost savings that come from rationalization, deskilling, and mechanization; and the nontemporal forms of work discipline innovated by temp and homeworking arrangements in the clerical service sector. Platform technology speeds up not just the labor process but also the process of getting the workers in the first place. In figure 2.1, for instance, we see references to "qualifications" or "quals." Some of these quals are preset by the requester (for instance, a survey might exclusively want Turkers located in India), but most can be earned by completing tests for which the Turker is not paid. These tests check for everything from the worker's accuracy at performing deskilled click labor to numerical literacy. Most often, quals are used to make workers outside the United States demonstrate their English-language abilities. AMT workers in non-Anglophone countries must have considerably more language proficiency than many "professional" workers in the United States possess, which is a good reminder that when we say "deskilled," we are referring to a process of rationalization and efficiency, and not to a fundamental quality of the work or the worker. Moreover, by making quals the responsibility of the worker—and by ensuring, via the use of task rates, that the employer doesn't have to pay for training—the managerial tasks of hiring, training, and sorting are turned over to the algorithm.[83]

Twenty-first-century microwork is thus shaped by complex and overdetermined connections between productivity, technology, and wages. Microwork draws on task rates as an unregulated, informalized method of wage payment in which the productivity risk is borne almost entirely by the worker.[84] Multiple empirical studies have suggested that task-rate pay is associated with "increased accident and injury risk as well as poor health outcomes," including depression, elevated heart rate, back problems, and repetitive stress injury. In the developing world, task-rate workers "report worse physical and emotional health than workers paid by the hour" due to everything from increased wage uncertainty to higher rates of worker abuse and sexual harassment.[85] Put simply, task-rate workers aren't subject to the time discipline of hourly wages, but can be forced to work both harder *and* longer. Yet although task-rate wages often resemble preindustrial forms of labor subordination based on direct domination, they also allow coercion to be accomplished indirectly through the impersonality of the method of wage payment, which becomes its own form of scientific management.

As I have suggested, piece-rate and task-rate wages are most likely to be used for work that is not fully mechanized, but is industrially organized; that is indirectly managed, but still subject to intense productivity pressures; that has variable output, but is nonetheless highly rationalized.[86] Task-rate wages serve as an alternative to centralized production and direct supervision, but *also* work in concert with modern scientific management.[87] From the bracero workers laboring alongside the machines that would soon replace them to the homeworkers whose labor would soon be outsourced via the technology of the platform, superexploitative piece-rate and task-rate wages are not an *alternative* to technological innovation, but instead the method of wage payment best suited to a labor process in the midst of rapid technological change.

PIECE-RATE POETICS

On AMT, task-rate wages combine superexploiting technique and rationalizing technology. Perhaps more surprisingly, we find that same combination in what is arguably the best-known AMT artwork, Fred Benenson's *Emoji Dick*. As the title suggests, Benenson's project is a rewriting of Herman Melville's *Moby-Dick*, whose titular whale has often been interpreted as an allegory for the "fearful mechanical power" of an emergent industrial capitalism.[88] *Emoji Dick* is similarly interested in platform outsourcing as an innovative labor technology, but it lacks the fierce political critique of its namesake. To create *Emoji Dick*, Benenson divided Melville's novel into its constituent ten thousand sentences. He paid three different Turkers to "translate" each sentence into emojis. The three translations of each sentence were then read by three additional Turkers, who voted on which version should be used for the book. Most of the "translations" were brief—three or four emojis—whereas others, like figure 2.2, were longer.

To fund the project, Benenson raised $3600 through Kickstarter, of which he was a cofounder—like Koblin, Benenson is not just an artist, but also someone professionally embedded in the tech industry. Whereas other AMT artists foreground the low wages paid on the platform in order to critique them, Benenson seems to use AMT's piece-rate wage form to *obscure* how little he paid his "collaborators."

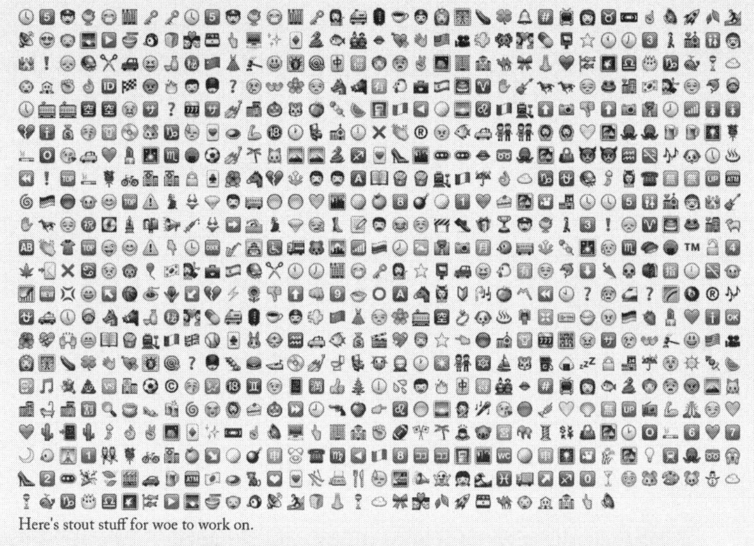

Figure 2.2. "Here's stout stuff for woe to work on," from Fred Benenson's *Emoji Dick*.

In describing the project, he says that he paid "five cents per translation and two cents per vote" and that it took "approximately 3,795,980 seconds working to create this book." The reader who has not worked on AMT herself will probably have no idea whether a rate of five cents per task would ultimately add up to a living wage, any more than she is likely to know that 3,795,980 seconds is 1,110 hours. One would thus have to perform multiple calculations to realize that this book, which sold for $40 in paperback and $200 in hardcover, was produced by piece-rate workers earning an average of $3.24 an hour.[89] In any case, Benenson's interest is in emojis, not wages, and he has described *Emoji Dick* as a basically unreadable "conceptual piece," instead of a crowdsourced translation. Readable or not, the work has garnered attention from digital humanities, book history, communications, and media studies scholars, including a long essay by literary critic Lisa Gitelman, who describes *Emoji Dick* as a "pleasurable, perverse object" that "offers a ludic contact zone between human intelligence and algorithmic processing."[90]

As Beneson's description of *Emoji Dick* suggests, conceptual art has long been interested in the problem of labor. Helen Molesworth's *Work Ethic* argues that postwar conceptual artists "came to see themselves... as workers in a capitalist America."[91] Julia Bryan-Wilson's *Art Workers: Radical Practice in the Vietnam Era* describes 1960s- and 1970s-era conceptual art as a critique of "the large-scale workplace and economic transitions that inaugurated postindustrialism."[92] Benjamin Buchloh argues that conceptual art replaced pop art's "aesthetic of industrial production and consumption with an aesthetic of administrative and legal organization" and connects conceptual artists' interest in routinized procedures to the increased rationalization of professional labor.[93] Dave Beech suggests that conceptual artists were particularly interested in using "mechanical or automatic processes" because they feared that machines were "breaking down the old order of the author, the artist, the genius" and replacing human creative labor with technology.[94] Jasper Bernes, in turn, takes up the relationship between conceptual art and the deskilling of knowledge work: the substitution of the "craft-based elements of making" with "an administrative... manipulation of automated process." Bernes argues that the conceptual artists of the 1960s and 1970s used typewriters, tape recorders, fax machines, and photocopiers to explore the deskilling of "knowledge work." More contemporary conceptual poets, he writes, use the affordances of the internet to "expos[e] the deep 'unfun' of the workplace, its reality as routinized, mechanical information management."[95]

Since the 1960s, then, conceptual art and poetry have been broadly interested in how mental and "creative" service labor has, like industrial work, become subject both to intensified technological mediation and to intensifying techniques of command. Yet a more recent body of "neoconceptual" poetry has departed from the conceptual tradition of critique to explore the aesthetic *opportunities* afforded by new information and communications technology. Sometimes, this is merely "labor-saving" technology. Describing his own poetics of appropriation, for instance, Kenneth Goldsmith argues that the boring "manual labor" once required to "retype an entire book" can now be performed using word processors and the internet, what Craig Dworkin calls "slacker cut-and-paste tools."[96] Other poets in this neoconceptual tradition are interested in automating the act of writing itself, producing what poet Christian Bök terms "robopoetics." Bök uses RACTER, an early AI writing program created in 1984, to produce poems that "confound the metaphysics of authorship" by demonstrating that "the involvement of an author in the production of literature has henceforth become discretionary." "Why hire a poet to write a poem," Bök wonders, "when the poem can write itself?"[97] Joshua Clover thus reads neoconceptualism's fetish for "machinic virtuosity" as a techno-utopian fantasy of full automation.[98]

In its aesthetic form as well as its historical context, neoconceptual poetry evokes the aesthetic category Sianne Ngai calls the "gimmick." Works such as Goldsmith's *Printing Out the Internet* clearly suggest the formal ambivalence Ngai associates with the gimmick: it is at once a clever joke and an intentionally cheap trick, an "occasion for comedy and a catalyst for debate."[99] The gimmick is also, she notes, a name for a technological device, as likewise suggested by neoconceptual art's interest in algorithms and automatic processes. But Ngai's account of the gimmick also suggests a third dimension of neoconceptual work captured neither by Goldsmith's idea that "copy-paste" produces works without work nor by Bök's idea of the poem that "write[s] itself." The gimmick, she writes, "saves us labor," but also "does *not* save labor." Indeed, it often "intensifies" labor—it is "a device that strikes us as working too little" (slackers) but also a "device that strikes us as working too hard" (Turkers).[100] *Emoji Dick*, similarly, is explicitly about the work Benenson does *not* perform, but it is implicitly about the work that AMT pieceworkers *do* perform. In this sense, *Emoji Dick*, like the other AMT artworks I consider below, reflects a final turn in conceptual practice, one away from the idea that poets are no longer necessary since machines can do the same thing and toward an interest in using machines to outsource cheap labor to write the poem for you.[101]

From Oulipo's procedural poetics, to Bök's liberating algorithms, to Goldsmith's computerized copy-paste, and finally to Benenson's piece-rate outsourcing, conceptual poets often insist that the point is not to produce an expressive, authentic, creative artwork, but instead to perform an empty, contentless set of procedures or concepts. As the titles of Goldsmith's volumes—*Against Expression* and *Uncreative Writing*—suggest, conceptual poetry resists the Romantic individualism associated with the lyric poem and "creative" writing. The creators and theorists of conceptual poetry often cite Sol LeWitt's remark that "what the work of art looks like isn't too important" because "the idea or concept is the most important aspect of the work."[102] As such, conceptual poetry is a "labor-saving" genre in yet another way: it doesn't require the reader's effort, either. "The best thing about conceptual poetry," Goldsmith notes in an interview, "is that you don't have to read it."[103]

But what if we *did* read these works? *Emoji Dick* might seem to be a limit case for this procedure, but let's return to the very long emoji sentence quoted above. The AMT translator turned an eight-word sentence into an almost eight-hundred-emoji sequence. We might, of course, read this sequence as an overly diligent attempt to produce a correct translation. Alternatively, we might read it as an example of what new media scholars call a "glitch aesthetic," a failure or accident that unsettles the smooth functionality of digital life. But in light of the previous section's account of task-rate wages and the deskilling or informalization of digital clerical work, we might also read it as an example of what labor organizers call "work-to-rule."[104] Work-to-rule is a kind of labor refusal typically undertaken by workers who have neither formal representation nor labor organization and can protest their working conditions only by intentionally following rules so precisely that they disrupt the product or process. This suggests a different approach to the idea of "rule-based" procedural aesthetics in conceptual art and poetry. By producing "sentences" that can barely be accommodated by the constraints of the concept itself, the long-winded emoji translator flips the script on the aesthetic practice Claire Bishop terms "delegated performance"—where the artist hires a nonprofessional to perform some sort of task—by producing something that cannily violates the spirit, but never quite the letter, of the informal labor contract.[105] Digital studies scholar Zach Whalen has also noted that a single nine-character "sentence" appears more than four hundred times in *Emoji Dick*. Observing that the sequence has no discernible meaning, Whalen describes the work of this anonymous Turker as a form of "scamming."[106] Yet I think we can better understand the four-hundred-times-repeated sentence not as a scam, but as part of the piece-rate-beating practices long employed in secret by deskilled workers. Like the early twentieth-century stenographers who used the space bar, instead of the tabulator key to increase the count on their piecework, the "scamming" Turker takes advantage of the fact that no one is reading the conceptual art they are producing to reuse the same "sentence" over and over.[107]

We can find even more explicit resistance to AMT (and even to the artists who use it) by reading for the voices of workers in Nick Thurston's well-reviewed 2013 conceptual poetry project *Of the Subcontract*.[108] *Of the Subcontract* comprises 100 poems written by anonymous AMT poets, ordered numerically from 1 to 100. These numbers correspond to how many cents each worker was paid for their poem.[109] Instead of treating *Of the Subcontract* as a single conceptual work by Thurston, I want to read it as an anthology of superexploited microworker poetics. My way of reading these poems draws on Maria Damon's idea of "micropoetics." The resonance between "microwork" and "micropoetics" is of course suggestive, but Damon has something broader in mind: both a type of writing and a way of reading. "Micropoetics" for Damon refers both to "all manner of unprofessional, half-formed, emergent, even unintentional, 'failed' or debased poetries" and to "the investigation of poetry as lived cultural experience." The poems in *Of the Subcontract* are somewhat different from the poems Damon describes because they are not straightforwardly outside "poetry's legitimating institutions and mechanisms." Rather, these poems exist *inside* some of the most high-art aesthetic objects imaginable, in conceptual artworks whose own "legitimacy" depends on the professional contexts and institutional processes that lend them significance as art. Yet I want to argue that the poems in *Of the Subcontract* draw on what Damon describes as micropoetry's interest in the "*encounter*"—a moment "in which a trace of the poetic is intuited in an unlikely, out-of-the-way setting"—but render it a scene of class contradiction.[110]

Sometimes, as I will suggest below, these poems reject the ideal of aesthetic autonomy entirely by pointing out how the production of conceptual poetry depends on the superexploitation of labor. Elsewhere, they evoke the ideal of autonomy precisely in order to reveal how poetry's "legitimating institutions" have proven as useless as the "legitimating institutions" of state-based labor regulation when it comes to redressing the superexploitation of microworkers. In this sense, the poems inside *Of the Subcontract* depart from conceptual poetry and instead recall what poet and critic Sean Bonney describes as a "militant poetics," which seeks to capture otherwise "impenetrable" forces, namely, "the invisible lives of migrant workers...and the invisible workings of capital itself, only partially expressed in the lives of the rich." Militant poetics, Bonney contends, attempts to force into view the "destructive unity" of these two apparent mysteries. Unpacking the militant work of *Of the Subcontract*'s micropoetics—understanding how these poems formalize the "destructive unity" between art and exploitation—requires adducing a genealogy for these poems that begins not in the procedural or automatic or delegated aesthetics of conceptual art, but rather in the traditions of proletarian verse and poems about work.[111]

A number of the poems in *Of the Subcontract* grapple with what Margaret Ronda identifies as the linked problems of representation and "disposability": what it means to subsist on the margins without inhabiting a space of pure negation and how to describe the forms of personhood that might emerge from that kind of "wageless life."[112]

These poems take up that problem in a scene of writing and address that is also—even, is *primarily*—a scene of labor. A poem called "Where Do I Start?" offers a compelling example of the kind of vulnerable personhood that emerges as multiple discourses of work—and multiple and uneven laboring conditions—combine in ways that also shape the scene of writing itself.[113]

> Where Do I start? (66 cents)
>
> How should I begin.
> I guess I will just write
> until the very end.
> I could start with my name
> and where I am from.
> Yes, I will start with that
> and then more will come.
> My name is PRIYA
> and I was born in INDIA.
> I am nineteen years old
> but I feel even older.
> . . . .
> I can't think of anything else to say.
> My life in 300 words;
> it is sort of sad in a way.
> My life in one paragraph
> yet I have nothing left to say.
> Well it seems I have begun to rant.
> I hope now you may know me,
> there is not much to see.
> For this is all there is to me.
> In essence of time
> let's bring this to a close.
> And if you are lost, this was my prose
> assignment for my class where we were asked to introduce ourselves.

The poem so closely recalls Langston Hughes's famous and oft-taught "Theme for English B" that the "prose assignment" mentioned in the final line may well have been based on Hughes's poem, which also opens with the idea of the assignment:

> The instructor said,
> *Go home and write*
> *a page tonight.*
> *And let that page come out of you—*
> *Then, it will be true.*

Hughes, addressing the compositional fantasy that "truth" will "come out" immediately on the page, goes on to ask, "I wonder if it's that simple?" The speaker is "the only colored student in my class" and reminds the addressed instructor that "It's not easy to know what is true for you or me."

"Where Do I Start?" similarly draws attention to the occasion of its writing, and similarly reminds us that identity, legibility, and literacy are nonuniversal categories. Like most of the work performed on AMT, *Of the Subcontract* depends on the hegemony of English as the language of the global information economy; although it's likely that many of the poets who contributed to the project lived outside the Anglosphere, all the poems are written in English, presumably because Thurston set English-language competency as a prerequisite for accepting his HIT. As in Hughes's poem, the speaker in "Where Do I Start?" is compelled to speak for or of themselves in someone else's language or style.[114] It also recalls the coerced scenes of English literary instruction—as well as the fetishistic attachment to "self-representation"—that Gauri Viswanathan notes were crucial to the colonial hegemony of the British in nineteenth-century India.[115] But whereas the scene of reading in "English B" is pedagogical, "Where Do I Start?" is occasioned by a labor relation: the work of producing a poem for an unknown reader across the world, a piece-rate assignment whose final product is the "300 words" the poem both recounts and counts. Thus, whereas "Theme for English B" begins with a prompt but ends with a poem, "Where Do I Start?" anxiously deconstructs its own premise and never reassembles it, moving instead toward a pathos of anticlimax; a "life in one paragraph" is inadequate, and the speaker's personhood is diminished when reduced to words. ("I have nothing left to say," "there is not much to see," "this is all there is to me.") Resigned but dutifully efficient, the poem concludes in a manner one might describe as intentionally "workmanlike."

Other poems in *Of the Subcontract* recall literary critic Florence Boos's description of working-class poetry's "transparent appeals for empathy and solidarity," which "give concrete expression to universal human desires for a modest measure of dignity and worth."[116] For instance, a poem titled "But Alas I Am Alone and Poor," for which the writer was paid ten cents, combines the realism of testimonial poetics with the affective language of sentimental verse, yoking social critique to immediate witness.[117] It opens:

> Unlike others, I have many unaccomplished dreams,
> Not 2 be a king or a supreme,
> But 2 be in the world of joy and happiness,
> Understand the essence of life and delightfulness,
> 2 play with the children of my age,
> 2 feel like a bird when freed from a cage

The middle section of the poem goes on to imagine what the speaker would do with money if they had it:

> Spread education, build houses if I have money
> Help in exploring the lost smiles in destitute children,
> Remove their difficulties, problems and pain,
> Raise my voice against the injustice done 2 the people.

The individualizing language of "Unlike others, I" in the first lines gives way immediately to a more utopian imaginary of mutual aid, recalling the tendency Boos discerns in nineteenth-century working-class verse, which "sought solace in solidarity with other [workers] who have struggled, perhaps in vain, to envision a kind of ethical and aesthetic kingdom of ends."[118] A collective working-class life where one might access basic needs such as education and housing without money appears as a lost social world that could be restored only with *infinite* money. The poem never imagines this abundance as the result of waged work, however. In almost all the poems in *Of the Subcontract*, labor is nonredemptive and wholly negative and it appears not just as necessity, but also as inadequacy, something that never guarantees even the minimal predicates of survival. Thus, the poem yields, in the final lines, to a powerfully straightforward articulation of beleaguered constraint via slant rhyme: "This could have been possible if I had money, I'm sure, / But alas I'm isolated, alone and poor."

In "Where Do I Start?" and "But Alas I Am Alone and Poor," poetry becomes a way to articulate what poet Mark Nowak describes the "first-person plural": in these poems, the speaker feels like a *we*, instead of an *I*. In other poems in the volume, however, we find more explicit critiques of AMT poetry *as* poetry. Turkers are far less likely to be hired to write a poem than to be hired to count the number of comments on a webpage, but these poets use the seeming atypicality of their task to insist that the difference is actually negligible. Writing a poem under AMT's conditions, they remind us, is no less a form of deskilled, superexploited labor than the work of counting or clicking or doing CAPTCHAs. The following, for instance, is titled simply "Turk," and it earned the author twenty-nine cents:

> She watches the streams run
> She watches the tide turn.
> Lost again, as if for the first time:
> Picture perfect.
> The last place you look will be the first place I'll go,
> She says,
> The last thing you need will be . . .

She doesn't finish.
She knows you're not listening,
She knows:
River of humanity, concrete jungle, the old metaphors.[119]

Reading between the title, which frames the poem as a meditation on its own production, and the final line, we find both *ars poetica* and postindustrial work poem. The first seven lines hover in banal abstraction. Like the eighteenth-century working-class poets who often satirized high-literary convention, the poem at first defers to familiar pastoral cliché. Yet it then cuts off in a sudden ellipsis: punctuation as labor refusal. The "she" shifts from the subject of the poem to the poet herself who also "doesn't finish." The "you" is now no longer an internal addressee, but an external one: the reader, who in this case is also the employer, is also "not listening." The poet strategically deploys their own alienation, betting that "not finishing" will go undetected because their work is already too deskilled to function as legible content (much like the Turker who submitted the same emoji sequence four hundred times for *Emoji Dick*). For the nonreading "consumer" of conceptual poetry, the tossed-off "old metaphors" are good enough. That includes the poem's own opening metaphor of streams and tides, which the poet depastoralizes (streams become "river of humanity," tides become "concrete") and refuses to revivify aesthetically. Cliché becomes a form of work-to-rule as the poem insistently deconstructs its own status *as* poetry.

A similar resistance from inside the form of the poem appears in different poem also titled "Turk":

Here I sit, and I work,
Being a nasty little Turk,
I hardly get paid and the hours suck,
So give me a fucking buck.[120]

The punchy internal rhyme comes at the cost of mimetic accuracy:

this poem didn't actually earn its author a "fucking buck," but merely twenty-seven cents. But the misprision also registers the experience of piecework, wherein merely sitting in place and working (as the poet does in the first line) does not actually guarantee *any* specific wage. The poem both uses and reorients the practices of syllabic verse and metrical rhythm, materializing traditional modes of poetic "counting" to register the quantification central to piece-rate methods of wage payment. The fantasy of entrepreneurial hustle becomes "I hardly get paid," while the poet satirically describes themselves as a "nasty little Turk." The profanity and the dogged doggerel reject idealisms concerning poetry's autonomy while also providing a "close-enough" approximation to poetry to ensure the author is paid for it. Whereas neo-conceptualism rejects the idea of an autonomous aesthetic realm—of poetry separated from capitalist commodification—these poems evoke poetry's noninstrumentality as an ideal precisely to reveal its relationship to exploitation in the context of AMT.[121]

Attending explicitly to the class contradiction embedded in its own occasion, "Turk" also participates, albeit in a somewhat self-deconstructing manner, in the long tradition of working-class protest poetry. As Boos explains, for instance, the working-class nineteenth-century poet Janet Hamilton exposed the plight of piece-rate tambour-embroidery needlewomen in "A Lay of the Tambour Frame" by addressing the poem to "Selfish, unfeeling men!" who work with "High pay, short hours" while

> She who tambours—tambours
> For fifteen hours a day—
> Would have shoes on her feet, and dress for church
> Had she a third of your pay.[122]

Piece-rate needlewomen such as Hamilton certainly had more opportunities for organizing and a stronger experience of collective working-class life than do contemporary microworkers, who are isolated, dispersed, and informalized. Yet like the microworker poems in *Of the Subcontract*, the poems written by piece-rate seamstresses were addressed not to other workers, but rather to the consumers of the goods they produced. These poems were meant to draw attention to the inequity between those who make goods and those who consume them. Hamilton's "Lay" is addressed to an imagined consumer of both poetry *and* goods, while "Turk" fiercely apostrophizes a reader who is also the consumer of Turkers' labor.[123] Like the gigworkers' inquiries of the next chapter, these poems are a form of testimony, but one in which the relationship between labor and its representation is complexly mediated by the device of AMT itself. On the one hand, the testimony *is* the labor product; on the other hand, the vivid fury of these poems can slip through the "black boxes" of AMT's anonymizing algorithm and of the neoconceptual artwork itself precisely because the labor has been so thoroughly deskilled.

Given the connection between piece-rate wages and semi-industrialized agricultural work developed in the previous section, we might also read some of the poems in *Of the Subcontract* in the tradition of the georgic. In its earliest and most traditional form, critic Tim Burke notes, the georgic celebrated "the human capacity for manipulating natural resources" and thus mirrored the ideology of an emergent capitalist mode of production wherein waged workers were pressed into "ever increased productivity."[124] Traditional georgics also imagined a circular relationship between writing and work. Kevis Goodman has suggestively described the Virgilian *versus* as a reference to the coils and turns of both the poetic line and the agricultural furrow. In the traditional georgic, then, the skilled and unalienated work of writing is both a celebration of and the counterpoint to difficult manual labor. The georgic, Goodman writes, "is about the tending of words," which "requir[e] labor and care"; in it, she suggests, art and work are made complimentary.[125] In her compelling exploration of the early modern georgic, Katie Kadue discerns a similar complementarity, but one that centers on dissatisfaction, instead of care and skill: a "poetics of household activity" that yokes the menial, repetitive labor of housewifery to the "transcendent, high-value" labor of writing.[126]

In the early georgics that Goodman and Kadue describe, however, the connection between the labor of farmwork or housewifery and the labor of writing is largely analogic. The poems in *Of the Subcontract*, by contrast, are about the impossibility of separating microwork poetics from microwork itself. Poetry is here not an alternative to labor, but rather a sign of labor's alienation. In this regard, these poems may have more in common with georgics from a fully capitalist era, as in the late-nineteenth and early twentieth-century agricultural georgic. Writers such as Paul Laurence Dunbar, Ronda argues, came to register a more "disenchanted" understanding of labor—as "difficult, necessary, and often without reward"—by attending to the unevenness of modernization, an unevenness that, as we have seen, bore down particularly on Black and migrant agricultural workers explicitly excluded from "modernizing" reforms such as the FLSA.[127] In these "disenchanted georgics," Ronda argues, the fantasy of virtuous progress embedded in the traditional georgic is replaced by a vividly critical recounting of the tendential immiseration of waged and wageless alike.

The piece-rate poems in *Of the Subcontract* blend the proletarian ferocity of Boos's archive with the "disenchanted georgic" mode of Ronda's account. As Ronda suggests, the late georgic "contemplate[s] poetry's capacity to offset labor's social debasement." These poems take up that same problem while clarifying that the contradictory "possibilities and limitations of poetic redress" dramatized by the work poem are complicated by the fact that in microwork poems, the verse itself is the product of an exploitative labor relation.[128] Another example helps us see these complexities more clearly.

A Poem You Did Not Write (17 cents)

To write a poem for you
That would surely not do
For you to take it and make it your own.

I'd spend all my time
For just a little more than a dime
Giving you line after line of my rhymes.
Rhymes are not free
But they come easy to me
As I believe that by now I have shown.
These rhymes are for you
Do whatever you do
And fake it to make it your own.[129]

The traditional georgic presents the act of writing as a salve for the difficulty of manual labor even as it also celebrates that labor. Written in an age prior to the imposition of capitalist time discipline, the georgic's temporality is the time of history, and the burden of labor lies precisely in its long temporal horizons: its cyclicality, seasonality, and endless, entropic repetition. In piece-rate digital microwork, by contrast, time is enforced by self-management, the compulsion to understand time as potential productivity and thus to work exhaustively.[130] Time in microwork, and in microwork poetics, is measured not by the seasons or by the clock, but rather by the quantifiable number of words or lines produced. The piece-rate georgic "A Poem You Did Not Write" at once plays on and exemplifies these conditions, and the poet must give up "line after line" because their verses become countable insofar as they are purchased with below-survival wages. The rhyme between "time" and "dime" suggests the connection between temporality and wages while also clarifying that the wages do not properly compensate the time or effort spent in work.

Goldsmith describes conceptual writing as "concerned with the choice of what you're presenting," rather "than the thing that you're presenting."[131] But if we reject the conceptual frame entirely and attend to what is actually going on in AMT poems such as "A Poem You Did Not Write," we find a far more canny insistence on the concept's own nonneutrality: to "take it" becomes "to fake it"; to hire is to "rob."

In this way, "A Poem You Did Not Write" gives the conceptual artist's critique of "romantic authorship" a darker cast.

Piece-rate poets also reject the fantasy of visibility encoded in the idea of conceptual art as political critique grounded in "the choice of what you're presenting" instead of in the poem itself. Take, for instance, "Am I Blind or Maybe Dumb," for which the author was paid four cents:

> Am I blind, or maybe dumb?
> To see TWO cents has made me numb.
> Would you do work for this measly amount?
> Would you take it seriously, would it even count.
> This is insulting in so many ways.[132]

In this poem, the reality of working conditions within AMT refuses to be subordinated to the clever conceptual ruse of Thurston's formal conceit. The language of blindness and silence dispenses briskly with the fantasy that these poems illuminate or express superexploitation, while the gesture of sympathy implied by the conceptual project's framing is turned back on itself: "Would *you* do work for this measly amount?" Again, poetry is presented neither as an alternative to deskilled work—an autonomous space of meaning or self-expression—nor as a way to invest deskilled work with dignity, virtue, or purpose. Rather, the poem refuses to separate itself from the exploitative conditions of its production. The work of producing something that looks enough like poetry for it to "count" serves the purposes of the task-rate contract, a job the poem performs diligently, even as it also insists that texts produced under these conditions cannot be "take[n] seriously" *as* poetry. Like the working class, the microwork poem succeeds to the extent that it abolishes itself.

"SO-SO AUTOMATION" AND SABOTAGE

On the title page of Thurston's *Of the Subcontract*, there is a drawing of an eighteenth-century machine, Johann Wolfgang von Kempelen's

Mechanical Turk, whose name Bezos adopted for Amazon's service. Kempelen's Mechanical Turk was a puppet (dressed in a "Turkish" costume) that Kempelen claimed could beat a human player at chess. Although nominally part of what historian Minsoo Kang terms the "automaton craze" of the eighteenth century, Kempelen's device was not *actually* an automaton. Rather, the cabinet on which the puppet sat was designed to look smaller than it actually was, so that a human chess player could crouch inside and control the puppet's movements.[133] Although Kempelen's puppet was a ruse the other technological spectacles of the "automaton craze" not only presaged, but indeed enabled the real technological innovations that would rationalize, deskill, and eventually replace massive numbers of skilled workers and pave the way for the Industrial Revolution. Kempelen's contemporary Jacques de Vaucanson, for instance, is best known today as the inventor of automatons such as the Digesting Duck, but on the strength of those spectacles, he was also tasked with bringing French textile manufacturing up to the productivity standards of other quickly industrializing countries. Vaucanson's design for an automated loom would become the model for Jacques Marie Jacquard's power loom, patented in 1804. The Jacquard loom's effect on the French silk industry was enormous. It introduced an industrial division of labor in textile production that destroyed the guild power of the textile workers and made it possible for machines to displace a mass of skilled artisans with a far smaller number of deskilled workers.

Despite this history, however, most critical accounts of AMT, whether in scholarship or in conceptual art, see Bezos's reference to the original Mechanical Turk as proof that both devices are merely clever diversions and as evidence of the *limits* of mechanization and automation. Edward Jones-Imhotep describes the original Turk as an "illusion," while David Golumbia calls it a "parlor trick." Both suggest that like eighteenth-century audiences duped by the puppet and its cabinet, observers of AMT tend to mistake old-fashioned exploitation for high-tech innovation. Astra Taylor terms Kempelen's and Bezos's devices "fauxtomation" and sees them as proof that "there are still plenty of things egregiously underpaid people do better than robots."[134]

Of course Kempelen's Turk *was* a trick, even though the automaton craze more broadly was vital to the creation of real automation. Likewise, one can certainly understand why these critics want to emphasize the human labor that powers "automated" computational technology. From AI to social media, much digital infrastructure is designed to obscure what Mary Gray and Siddharth Suri evocatively describe as the "ghost work" performed out of view.[135] But I want to suggest that this claim misses something important about the discourse about AMT, and indeed about the platform, namely that *Bezos himself* draws our attention to the human while downplaying the significance of the device. By emphasizing the supposed superiority of human intelligence and commending the "wisdom of crowds," by celebrating projects such as Koblin's *Sheep Market* that realize "the humanity of the creative process," and simply by calling the service an example of "*artificial* artificial intelligence," Bezos focuses on human labor while actively occulting how AMT's technology deskills, outsources, and superexploits that human workforce.[136]

In this final section, then, I want to suggest that descriptions of AMT's technology as a trick or a ruse—as "fauxtomation"—miss the intimate connections between techniques of labor exploitation and technologies of mechanization. Such accounts often treat the superexploitation of microworkers as evidence that there are intractable technological limits to automating clerical work. But in microwork (as in farm work, to return to the comparison of the previous section), superexploitation is not an *alternative to* mechanization. Rather, the use of task-rate wages is itself the sign of an ongoing epochal transformation in clerical service work as well as in professionalized "knowledge work"—a shift from labor-intensive work to a labor process far more vulnerable to automation. Understanding the relationship between historic techniques of intensification and new technologies of automation in microwork, I will suggest, can help us understand technological innovation in service work more broadly.

In making this argument, I am in direct dialogue with two recent influential Marxist accounts of technological stagnation in the service sector, namely, Aaron Benanav's *Automation and the Future of Work* and Jason Smith's *Smart Machines and Service Work: Automation in the Age of Stagnation*. Both books note that we, like the observers of the original Mechanical Turk, are in the midst of a "craze." As Benanav observes, the last decade has seen a familiar cycle of "automation hype," running the gamut from libertarian to liberal to leftist.[137] Smith, for his part, describes contemporary automation talk as a "breathless" rhetoric replete with both "awe and anxiety."[138] Like the critics of "fauxtomation" quoted above, both Benanav and Smith are committed to popping this discursive bubble. Both rightly note that the contemporary global economy shows far more signs of technological and economic stagnation than of technological and economic dynamism.[139] Smith ascribes contemporary economic stagnation to deindustrialization, while Benanav sees it as a consequence of global overcapacity and intensified competition, but both argue that stagnation explains why the economy now relies on the service sector for economic growth and labor demand. Both also draw on economist William Baumol's mid-century account of the inherent "technological stagnation" of service work to explain why the service sector *cannot* adequately power the global economy on its own. In immensely influential 1965 and 1967 essays, Baumol describes manufacturing as "technologically progressive." In manufacturing, he says, technological innovations and economies of scale can increase efficiency and productivity quickly and significantly. The service sector, by contrast, "permit[s] only sporadic increases in productivity." To use Baumol's examples, scientific managers can't direct an orchestra to play faster, and no technology will allow one teacher to teach thousands of students at a time.[140] (I will return to that second example in the Coda.) Smith and Benanav both use Baumol to note that the particular activities performed by contemporary service workers mostly cannot be rationalized, centralized, or deskilled in the manner of industrial manufacturing. Service work's activities "def[y] attempts by business owners to fully subsume these labor processes in a manner resembling the rationalization of manufacturing," Smith notes, and Benanav similarly describes service work as "resistant to industrialization" because it is not "goods-embodied."[141]

Both these accounts of automation debunking are urgent and compelling. Yet Benanav and Smith also tend to depend on somewhat rigid dichotomies: fully automated machines *or* human labor, technological disruption *or* technological limit, outsourcing *or* robots, innovation *or* stagnation. As a way of unpacking some of those oppositions, we might begin with the one that's basic and definitional, namely, Benanav's distinction between "labor-augmenting" mechanization, on the one hand, and "labor-substituting" automation on the other: "Automation may be distinguished from other forms of labor-saving technical innovation in that automation technologies fully substitute for human labor instead of merely augmenting human productive capacities. With labor-augmenting technologies, a given job category will continue to exist, but each worker in that category will be more productive."[142]

If a task can be fully "automated," Benanav argues, the humans who once performed it will be out of work. But if a task is merely "augmented," the firm will still need just as many workers as it did before so long as demand for the now cheaper product increases at an equivalent rate. Yet as Benanav himself concedes, technology that "augments" labor productivity typically causes a sector to need fewer human workers in the long term, not least because demand cannot go up forever. In this sense, the distinction between automation and augmentation seems not just "difficult," as Benanav acknowledges, but potentially counterproductive, especially since the compulsion toward increased productivity (whether labor augmenting or labor replacing) is the defining characteristic of the capitalist mode of production. Even in sectors or jobs where automation is either technically difficult (the job can't be done entirely by machines) or economically unfeasible (the machine would be too expensive relative to the productivity gain it enables), technology can nonetheless be used to "reduce labor time to a minimum," as Marx puts it.[143]

As I have suggested throughout this book, service labor has indeed historically resisted "dynamic efficiency gains." Yet technologies of mechanization such as AMT are clearly deploying new forms of standardization, task decomposition, and intensification to "augment" human productivity in deskilled clerical microwork. The improvements are small, to be sure, yet even in Marx's account, the reduction of labor time enabled by mechanization often occurs via what are, at least initially, small "augmentations" of human productivity: the capitalist's awareness that "moments are the elements of profit" is an imperative fulfilled by a wide range of changes in the labor process, from deskilling to time discipline.[144] And indeed, Amazon as a whole has fiercely pursued precisely these kinds of labor-saving augmentations: in digital platforms such as AMT, in their massive warehouses, in their informalized direct delivery services. "Amazon is continuously trying to increase the delivery speed of its products," Moritz Altenried writes, and knows "precisely how much even small efficiency gains in their labor processes will benefit them." Those benefits, we should note, appear not only in the form of more orders, more customers, and more market share, but also come from reducing labor costs by requiring fewer workers to do the same amount of labor.[145]

But are such small achievements in labor saving really based in technological innovation, or do they simply reveal the *difficulty* of truly industrializing the service sector? Smith suggests the latter, describing efforts to increase productivity in the "technologically stagnant" service sector like this:

> If productivity gains have been won [in the contemporary service economy], it has not been through a revolution in the design of work flows, the replacement of humans by machines, or advances in automation. The true "advances," such as they are, have been in the domination of the

> labor process by employers: their ability to coerce more labor out of a given hour by means of refinements in supervision, oversight, and workplace discipline.[146]

Smith's argument here is important. Like the aforementioned scholars writing about "ghost work," he reveals the truth of postindustrial "immaterial labor," reminding us that many of the technologies designed to increase productivity in the service sector—from the AMT platform to the algorithms and apps I describe in the next chapter—do so not via digital sorcery, but simply by forcing workers to work harder and longer. Yet like Benanav, Smith may overstate the clarity with which we can distinguish between technologies of "discipline" or enforced effort, on the one hand, and truly "revolutionary" productivity enhancements on the other. In fact, such distinctions can even be confounded in the case of prototypically "industrial" technologies such as the assembly line. Consider, for instance, the way a 1921 observer quoted by Braverman described the assembly line at a meatpacking plant: "It would be difficult to find another industry where division of labor has been so ingeniously and microscopically worked out. The animal has been surveyed and laid off like a map; and the men have been classified in over thirty specialties and twenty rates of pay, from 16 cents to 50 cents an hour." This kind of assembly line, Braverman says, gave management "control... over the pace of assembly, so that it could now double and triple the rate at which operations had to be performed and thus subject its workers to an extraordinary intensity of labor," as well as to "more strenuous supervision." [147] This account suggests that even in industrial labor, the distinction between "revolution[s] in the design of work flows" and "refinements... in workplace discipline" is far blurrier than Smith allows.[148] From the "microscopic" decomposition of tasks to the highly detailed division of labor and from the targeted differences in pay rates to the coercive force of speedup and the ever-present watchman, this all sounds remarkably like a description of microwork on AMT.

I am not suggesting, to be clear, that microwork platforms and algorithmic supervision constitute a technological innovation in productivity equivalent to the assembly line. Certainly, they are unlikely to increase the productivity of human labor a hundredfold or more, as Fordist technology did. Yet because both Smith and Benanav insist on firm distinctions between technological innovation (actually automating) and human intensification (merely augmenting), neither acknowledges the extent to which platform technologies have transformed the service sector's labor process both technically and socially.

Moreover, the history of piece rates in partially mechanized sectors demonstrates how "old" techniques of intensification and "new" technologies of mechanization and automation coexist, combine, and shape one another. This was even true in early industrial production: as Marx makes clear, centralized, machine-driven production did not immediately replace superexploited, "sweated" outwork in the textile industry. Nor was the development of mass-scale mechanized production simply uneven, with two coexisting levels of economic development, as is sometimes implied by accounts of the service sector's relative technological backwardness. Outworking did allow employers to hire women, children, and others among the growing surplus of unskilled urban workers, which kept labor costs artificially low.[149] But those low costs and greater flexibility also allowed firms to invest in technology in the parts of the productive process where centralized, mechanized production *would* be profitable.[150] As Linebaugh suggests, piece-rate wages in this period ensured a "fractionation of labor" that facilitated—indeed, compelled—mechanization.[151] As a result, the "uneven" persistence of piece-rate outworking (getting more work for less money) both enabled and eventually had to cede to modern mechanization (getting more output by using machines) as a result of capitalism's fundamentally combined character.

We find a strikingly similar story in the case of the migrant piece-rate laborers hired under the Bracero Program. Time-and-motion studies designed to rationalize the work of braceros were later used to automate it. Research on "single-pass" harvesting conducted during the Bracero Program, for instance, was initially intended to reduce the need for skilled labor, but it also allowed growers to eliminate certain tasks entirely and ultimately led to the development fully automated harvesting machines.[152] Decades of labor cost saving during the program enabled agribusinesses to invest in new technology that significantly increased the sector's productivity and transformed the industry as a whole. As output grew, agricultural employers wanted a small number of trained, skilled workers who could operate machines, instead of a large group of deskilled, low-waged workers prohibited from doing so.[153] By the time the Bracero Program was officially closed in 1964, the change was met with little resistance from growers, since they had effectively achieved the rationalization and "fractionation" of the labor process and were ready to mechanize and automate it more fully.[154]

In short, the history of piece-rate wages suggests a complementary instead of contradictory relationship between superexploitation and automation. We find a similar set of entanglements in the case of AMT. To understand them, we must first understand that AMT is *not* actually an example of things that "people can do better than robots," as Astra Taylor suggests. Many of the tasks performed on AMT are tasks AI *can* do, just not very well. In deciding whether to use AMT or its automated equivalent for a given task, employers use what economists term a "speed-cost-quality" assessment.[155] Human workers clearly lose the "speed" competition, since computers are exponentially faster. For most AMT tasks, humans win when it comes to "quality." But it's the middle term, "cost," that matters most. Since the work done on platforms such as AMT has already been deskilled, explains one study, "the quality of the worker's performance does not yield additional utility to the requester once above a certain quality threshold."[156] Put in simpler terms, although the accuracy or quality of microwork matters, there is a limit to *how much* it matters. For microwork to work, the humans must be better at the "intelligence task" than the machine is, but they don't have to be much better: most employers will be willing to put up with some errors if they can save an equivalent amount of money by allowing AI to perform the task instead. Contra both Bezos *and* the critics of "fauxtomation," in other words, barriers to the automation of many microwork tasks are not primarily technological, but economic. If the wages being paid were even a little bit higher, employing humans would often no longer be worth the small increase in quality and the large decrease in speed compared with having AI do the same thing.

This does not mean, however, that the availability of outsourced microworkers has made technological development less likely, no more than the availability of piece-rate outworkers made textile automation less inevitable. Rather, AMT's access to massive amounts of very cheap labor is *improving* the quality of automated systems. Machine learning—the process whereby AI systems "learn" tasks inductively by being shown millions and millions of examples—relies heavily on microwork. Microworkers identify images of trees and pedestrians to train driverless cars or tag content with "tone" markers so that AI can "learn" what joy or despair sound like.[157] As a result of that work, many tasks where the "speed-cost-quality" formula once favored smarter, slower human labor over AI are now entirely automatable with no meaningful loss in quality.[158] The crowdsourcing platform CrowdFlower, for instance, launched a machine-learning platform to automate certain tasks so that human microworkers could "focus on the harder cases and help the [machine learning] models learn."[159] ImageNet, one of the earliest categorized-image databases, was compiled by tens of thousands of workers contracted via AMT; as a result of this work, tasks such as human image recognition once performed by microworkers can now be performed by AI. In other words, when Turkers perform work such as transcription or semantic tagging, they are not only doing the work for a fraction of what it would have cost only five years ago, they are also helping to train the machine-learning component of these companies' services by providing new examples of how to solve problems.[160]

But does all this mean that AI can achieve the kinds of real productivity gains that have been in short supply during the last five decades of "long downturn"? Or, are we still trapped by what Robert Solow famously describes as a "computer paradox," in which "you can see the computer age everywhere but in the productivity statistics"?[161] In trying to answer those questions, a number of mainstream economists have recently broken with macroeconomic orthodoxy. For more than a hundred years, economists assumed that the loss of some jobs to automation (the displacement effect) would inevitably catalyze a wave of productivity growth that would create an equal or greater number of new jobs (the reinstatement effect). But Daron Acemoglu and Pascual Restrepo, among others, note that something different seems to be happening with the contemporary automation of deskilled clerical and service work. Like Benanav and Smith, Acemoglu and Restrepo acknowledge that most new AI technology provides only "modest productivity gains." Yet whereas Benanav and Smith see that as a hard limit to labor-replacing automation, Acemoglu and Restrepo argue that despite generating only small productivity improvements, these "so-so technologies" nonetheless continue to "threaten employment and wages." Technology such as automated grocery store checkout, for instance, increases productivity only modestly, is "only marginally better" (or, in some cases, worse) in quality, and replaces jobs that were already low waged. As a result, these "innovations" can replace human workers without jump-starting the kinds of productivity effects that have historically driven economic growth in periods of automation.[162]

Put most simply, then, contemporary AI technology amounts to a merely "so-so" innovation in a recalcitrantly stagnant economy—neither technological miracle nor a herald of significant GDP or productivity growth.[163] Increasing productivity only marginally if at all, so-so technology is less a *solution* to technological and economic stagnation than a *symptom* of it, as firms slosh surplus capital into what Acemegolu and Restrepo describe as "excessive automation" in response to global competition for ever-smaller margins of profit.[164] In the meantime, labor-saving intensification and labor-replacing automation are no longer opposites, but twinned compulsions. Older techniques of sweating and informalization combine with the newer affordances of digital service labor through technology that first reduces the quality of human labor and then replaces it. In these ways, so-so automation sets in sluggish motion the process Marx, in his own account of deindustrialization, names "immiseration"—work gets qualitatively worse, and there is also quantitatively less of it.

Historically, this kind of immiseration has led not just to superfluity, but also to struggle, and specifically to sabotage. The "automaton craze" of the late eighteenth century that produced Vaucanson's automated loom and Kempelen's Mechanical Turk also birthed mechanization's most notorious antagonists. The Luddites of early-nineteenth-century northern England struck back against "all Machinery hurtful to Commonality," and specifically automation in the textile industry, by engaging in "collective bargaining by riot," as Linebaugh describes it.[165] Yet the word "sabotage" has a far less theatrical origin: the French *saboteurs* didn't actually throw their wooden shoes (*sabots*) into the machines, as myth would have it, but were metonymically named via the cheap, makeshift shoes they wore for the intentionally shoddy work they performed in protest against deskilling and low wages. A vital genealogy of sabotage thus derives, historian Rebecca Lossin explains, not just from the spectacular "machine breaking" of skilled artisans, but also from sly efforts to gum up the line or reduce productivity in low-waged work. "Going ca'canny"—a tactic of working slowly also known as "Bad Wages, Bad Labor"—was taken up in the twentieth century by organizations such as the Industrial Workers of the World (IWW) precisely because it was available to deskilled and informalized workers. By throwing "a little sand or emery in the gear of those machines which like fabulous monsters mark the exploitation of the workers," one IWW pamphlet observes, workers might render them "palsied and useless." Machines and tools—and, indeed, the entire detailed division of labor—could also be made less efficient by techniques such as the slowdown strategy "work-to-rule" described in in the previous section. Sabotage, Lossin notes, was also sometimes simply a "secret, symbolic, and even whimsical" language of cross-worker solidarity, and she gives the example of a farmer discovering that striking workers had planted "1000 young trees…upside down, their roots waving to the breeze."[166]

Sabotage also has a history in low-waged, deskilled service work, particularly among workers ignored by established craft and industrial unions. For example, IWW-led sabotage tactics were of great importance to the 1912–1913 general strike of hotel workers whose demands included the replacing of insecure and unguaranteed tip wages with an hourly minimum wage. Female hotel workers such as chambermaids and charwomen had been marginalized in prior unionization campaigns, James Woodall explains, not least because they were perceived to be "more 'feminine' and 'servile'" than the "coal miners, factory workers, and longshoremen" seen as the proper vanguard of Progressive-Era working-class struggle.[167] Yet it quickly became apparent to bosses as well as to workers that "in no other industry can sabotage be so successfully employed as in that of preparing and serving food," as one IWW organizer put it. Elizabeth Gurley Flynn's immensely important 1916 book *Sabotage* describes IWW hotel workers realizing they could "get at the boss via the public stomach." "If any of you have ever got soup that was not fit to eat, that was too salty or peppery," Flynn notes, "maybe there were some boys in the kitchen that wanted shorter hours." For those workers, "what they had not been able to win through the strike they were able to win by striking at the taste of the public."[168]

We have probably not yet seen equivalent collective resistance to so-so automation, though it is worth noting that the technologists and bosses and management researchers are somewhat nervous that we might. The "automated" grocery store checkout machine mentioned above, for instance, has increased rates of shoplifting so much that many stores have had to consider whether the loss outweighs the savings; management theorists note that "service sabotage" on the part of workers has risen significantly in service workplaces that have deployed concierge robots or other "contactless" services.[169] To give a recent example of technology sabotage as the "mute evidence of solidarity," striking grad students at the University of California intentionally detoured campus food-delivery "robots" (remotely controlled by off-site human operators, many in the underdeveloped world) and drew them into the picket line. Delayed from their appointed rounds, the robots were covered in prounion fliers, an act that connected the concerns of graduate students about the deskilling of teaching labor to the replacing of on-campus student food-service workers with so-so technology and superexploited taskwork.

Although both covert and overt sabotage are everywhere on AMT, there are as yet few groups capable of *organizing* that sabotage in the way the IWW once did. The Tech Workers Coalition, a radical rank-and-file group of tech workers from salaried professional workers to independent contractors, is mobilizing globally dispersed microworkers into worker coalitions; groups such as the Data Labelers Association have organized and advocated for the rights of workers worldwide contributing to AI; and platforms such as Turkopticon organize mutual aid and resources for piece-rate task workers and provide a community space where microworkers can share information about wage theft and account suspensions. Yet organizing and mobilizing dispersed and deskilled microworkers continues to pose significant challenges. As Phil Jones puts it, "defined by superfluity, exclusion, and informality rather than a wage, microworkers pose a particular challenge to... typical institutions of organized labor."[170]

But microworkers *are* committing one type of sabotage in large numbers: they are having AI do their tasks for them. Describing this practice with the wonderful phrase "Artificial Artificial Artificial Intelligence," one group of researchers recently estimated that since the public launch of ChatGPT, between a third and a half of all summary tasks assigned over AMT were actually performed by AI as microworkers essentially automate their own work while still collecting wages.[171]

We might see this form of sabotage in the long-standing tradition of workers exploiting task-based methods of wage payment by juicing the count. Scientific piece-rate wages were explicitly intended as a solution to the problem of "going ca'canny," or what Taylorism calls "soldiering"—"the common tendency to take it easy." But piece-rate wages also, Taylor admits, raise the incentives for "*systematic* soldiering," a more deliberate attempt to keep the boss "ignorant of how fast work can be done" and thus intentionally to manipulate piece-rate counting systems.[172] As recounted above, female typists paid by the word learned to use the space bar instead of the tabulator key, to increase their word count. Turkers, for their part, use similar tactics, as evidenced not only in *Emoji Dick*'s nonsensically long work-to-rule "sentences," but also, to give another example, in conceptual poet Vladimir Zykov's "I Was Told to Write 50 Words" in which one response to a one-penny HIT asking for a fifty-word poem is just the words "one" to "nineteen" ("one," "two," etc.) followed by the words of the prompt itself ("write" "fifty" "words" "in" "English" etc.). Here, as in the microwork poems described above, we find microworkers responding to the radical deskilling of their labor by knowingly exploiting a system in which the cost-speed-quality formula has determined that quality matters least.[173]

If the only consequence of this small act of sabotage was that "output" decreased a little in quality while workers reappropriated a tiny fraction of an already substandard wage, it wouldn't be very meaningful. However, it turns out that when more and more microworkers are feeding AI-produced data and language back into systems designed to produce data and language to train AI, the results may be quite close to good old-fashioned "machine breaking."[174] An explosive 2024 article published in *Nature* argued that when large language models are "trained" on AI-generated material, instead of human-generated text, it sets in motion a degenerative process called "model collapse": "a cascading effect, in which individual inaccuracies combine to cause the overall error to grow." The researchers give an example of this cascading or degenerating collapse by feeding a prompt about premodern church architecture into a sequence of LLMs, each built entirely from the "inorganic" AI-output of the previous model. The first few outputs sound reasonably close to a Wikipedia entry, making reference to St. John's Cathedral and Pope Innocent. But by the ninth generation, the answer looks more like an unreadable conceptual poem than like actual information: "architecture. In addition to being home to some of the world's largest populations of black @-@ tailed jackrabbits, white @-@ tailed jackrabbits, blue @-@ tailed jackrabbits, red @-@ tailed jackrabbits, yellow @-."[175] By refusing to submit real human inputs to AMT and instead using AI to do the work for them, the machine-breaking Turkers are thus contributing to processes that threaten to destroy AI's language models from the inside.

AMT clearly offers a paradigm for the future of highly rationalized clerical service work, a future in which former "knowledge work" has been fully subsumed into capitalist labor processes and in which small labor-saving productivity gains are achieved via new technologies of intensification, rationalization, and automation. Yet while these changes are transforming the labor process of deskilled clerical service work, the generative-AI axiom "garbage in, garbage out" also suggests the persistently "so-so" qualities of the technology, its output, and its productivity gains. So-so automation will not resolve the looming crisis in capitalism caused by stagnant growth and stagnant technological innovation. That is particularly true when this technology attempts—as capitalist mechanization always has—to destroy the very social life, social worlds, social language, and social labor on which it also depends.

In memory of Joshua Clover

CHAPTER THREE

Control and the Culture of Circulation Gigwork

Be your own boss. This is the by now familiar way transportation network companies such as Uber and Lyft represent gigwork as liberated, autonomous, and independent. The gigworker imagined in the advertisements pictured in figures 3.1 and 3.2 is a self-directed entrepreneur. Unlike other workers, trapped in inflexible nine-to-five jobs under the watchful eyes of bosses, the gigworker is uniquely free—on the move and on their own time. But we find an equally familiar representation of gigwork in figure 3.3, a photograph of the July 2020 "Strike for Black Lives," which protested both police violence and the superexploitation of "essential" gigworkers. Here, gigwork is neither free nor entrepreneurial, but instead a form of modern-day "slave labor." Likewise, figure 3.4—an image of a protest organized by Los Deliveristas Unidos (LDU), which represents tens of thousands of mostly Mexican and Guatemalan immigrant delivery workers in New York City—reframes "entrepreneurial" independence as economic precarity ("Las propinas no son salarios," "Tips are not wages"). Gigwork's "flexibility," in turn, appears as the existential risk of doing one of the city's deadliest jobs.[1]

How can gigworkers be both liberated and enslaved, both dominated and unmanaged, both independent hustlers and vulnerable victims?[2] It is tempting, of course, to say that the claim of freedom in the first two images is pure mystification: the discourse of gigworkers as free to "be their own boss," we might argue, is an ideological fiction concealing realities exposed, in turn, by the protestors. That

Figure 3.1. Gigwork freedom as self-management.

Figure 3.2. Gigwork freedom as temporal flexibility.

Figure 3.3. Gigwork as "modern-day slavery."

Figure 3.4. Gigwork as racialized domination.

explanation is largely true, but it does not answer the question of *why* contemporary gigworkers have become such a powerful and overdetermined symbol for both freedom and control not only in advertisements for gigwork apps, but also in culture, in political discourse, and often in gigworkers' own self-representations.[3]

To understand the longer history of that contradiction, the first part of this chapter suggests, we need to understand how the workers I describe as "circulation gigworkers" (those who transport packages, groceries, dinner, and human beings themselves) came to be classified as "independent contractors" in the first place. Since the late nineteenth century, the statutory definition of "employee" has relied on a legal concept known as the "control test." Grounded in ideas about work, supervision, and domination first articulated in the preindustrial era, the control test holds that for a worker to be considered an *employee*, their labor must be directly and completely controlled by their employer. Workers who maintain control over the "manner and means" of their own labor, by contrast, are *independent contractors*. Mobile, isolated, and in constant movement away from any such centralized supervision, circulation workers, from early-twentieth-century newspaper boys to today's platform gigworkers, have typically been classified as independent contractors and thus excluded from regulations around minimum wages, hours, overtime, and workplace safety. Yet although this classification implies that informalized circulation workers are indeed more "free" than centrally managed and legally formalized employees, transportation and delivery companies have also been able to use technology, instead of human managers, to exert nearly total control over independent contractors' movement, time, and wages. Many of the technologies used to control contemporary circulation gigworkers are new, but surveillance and monitoring technology has been used to manage decentralized circulation and transportation workers for over a century, from fare boxes in railway cars to electronic logging devices in long-haul trucks.

In the complex relationship between labor regulation and labor technology, then, we can begin to see why today's circulation gigworkers seem both free and controlled, both independent and subordinated. Yet to understand fully how debates over regulation and management have shaped contemporary circulation gigwork, we have to look not just at the *management* of circulation gigwork, but also at its *meaning*. In the second part of this chapter, I argue that contemporary circulation gigworkers are uniquely available to fantasies and anxieties about freedom and control in part because of the spatial dimension of their labor, which seems to suggest both circulation and circumscription, both movement and stasis, both constant change and circuitous routine.[4] Alone in their vehicles, yet with their every movement monitored and logged, on the road, yet told where to go and how to get there, contemporary circulation gigworkers have come to represent both the freedom to "be your own boss" and the coercive control of "modern-day slavery."

These same paradoxes show up recent gigwork fiction by Raven Leilani, Priya Guns, and Peter Mendelsund. These novels explore the freedom or unfreedom of gigwork via a vocabulary of motion, speed, and spatial circulation. They take seriously the desire for autonomy, freedom, and independence promised (if often cynically) by circulation gigwork even as they also vividly describe the superexploitation, precarity, and brutal time discipline that define the labor process of informalized gigwork. Yet these novels do not suggest that the solution to informalization is to replace gigwork with formal waged labor. Instead, they link formal "employee" status to the power of managers, bosses, and even the police state to supervise, surveil, and command. By illuminating how control over gigworkers is outsourced to the customer herself (when she rates her driver or tips the person who delivers her food) gigwork fiction offers an expanded vocabulary for thinking about both freedom and obligation via a moral economy of solidarity specific to reproductive labor.

In the final section of this chapter, I pursue the connections between solidarity, circulation, and reproductive labor further by exploring "workers' inquiries" written by circulation gigworkers. This genre, through which workers themselves write about their own working conditions, has traditionally been associated with manufacturing labor but has taken on new meaning and new urgency for contemporary gigworkers. Like the novels described in the previous section, contemporary gigworkers' inquiries keep open the utopian possibilities represented by circulation gigwork's fleeting freedoms even as they also show how control over time and space is a technique of subordination and superexploitation. Developing new versions of the workers' inquiry focused not just on production, but also on reproduction, and not just on wages, but also on subsistence, contemporary service-worker organizing suggests the forms of solidarity and indeed militancy that have replaced the productivist demand for "fair wages."

CONTROL, SURVEILLANCE, AND THE INDEPENDENCE OF CIRCULATION WORK

What are we talking about when we talk about gigwork? The word "gig" in its contemporary usage originates from the argot of jazz musicians, who would describe a one-night booking as a "gig." Linguist Geoff Nunberg suggests that the first use of the term to describe *any* short-term job might be from novelist Jack Kerouac, who writes about putting on his "gig clothes" for a temporary job for the Southern Pacific Railroad, a workplace at which "new engines keep rushing up from the roundhouse, & everywhere in the gray air tremendous excitements of movement of rolling stocks."[5] As Kerouac's breathless style and emphasis on motion suggests, the use of "gig" to describe a temporary job evokes not only the musician's short-term "engagement," but also an earlier meaning of "gig": a small, nimble one-horse carriage, a usage itself related to still-earlier words such as "whirligig" (as well as to *gigolo* and *gigolette,* the feminine and masculine terms for dancing partners hired for a single evening). Sometime in the late 1990s, the immensely influential classified website Craigslist changed the term it used for temporary employment from "1099 freelance" to "gig jobs";

the term "gig economy," from which we derive our current sense of gigwork, originates from 2009, with the founding of Uber. Nunberg selected "gig" as his "word of the year" in 2016, which should not be surprising: most of the new jobs created in the decade after the financial crisis of 2007 were "alternative employment," aka gigwork.

The euphemism "alternative employment" notwithstanding, most US-based gigworkers are not actually "employees" at all, but rather "independent contractors," which is essentially the legal and policy term for "gigwork." The simplest way to define "independent contractor" is probably by negation: independent contractors are not covered by federal unemployment insurance, Social Security, and Medicare provisions; are not covered by the federally mandated wages-and-hours protections of the Fair Labor Standards Act (FLSA); are not covered by state-level regulations about unemployment or workers' compensation; are not protected against employment discrimination under Title VII of the Civil Rights Act, the Age Discrimination in Employment Act (ADEA), or the Americans with Disabilities Act (ADA); are not guaranteed collective bargaining rights under the National Labor Relations Act (NLRA); are not guaranteed leave under the Family and Medical Leave Act; and do not have their retirement and benefits protected by the Employee Retirement and Income Security Act (ERISA). In this section, I detail the history of how "independent contractors" came to be excluded from labor law and regulation. I describe how the control test that distinguished controlled employees from other, more ostensibly "independent" workers was interpreted in a series of important post–New Deal court cases specifically concerned with the status of circulation workers, from the 1944 *Hearst* decision about newspaper delivery boys to important Uber/Lyft cases in 2015. Circulation work, I suggest, uniquely occasioned legal precedent concerning what kinds of work could and should be protected by labor law and regulation. Circulation work was also, I go on to note, the site for technological innovations in surveillance and automated management, and the very mobility that ostensibly made circulation workers legally "independent" was thus effectively managed and mitigated via technology.

As I have suggested, "independent contractors" are defined as those workers who are *not* employees, which means we understand the former only by beginning with the later. Paradoxically, given the exclusion of domestic servants from most modern labor regulation, the legal definition of "employee" derives from the eighteenth-century Master-Servant Acts. Among the earliest efforts to regulate the rights and obligations of workers and those who hired them, the Master-Servant Acts established the terms by which, in William Blackstone's phrasing, "the servant shall serve and the master maintain him."[6] The Master-Servant Acts laid out the various rights and obligations attached to the "the contract of hiring, and purchased by wages": the master's right to "correct" his servant, including with physical force; the servant's obligation to be loyal, an obligation whose breach could be punished by imprisonment; and the master's responsibility for the servant's subsistence and safety, as well as his legal liability for the servant's actions.[7]

Between the mid-eighteenth and the mid-nineteenth century, the Master-Servant Acts were applied to a wide range of employment contexts. As the rules governing domestic servants were expanded to other forms of work, the Master-Servant Acts provided a model of economic subordination and what historian Marc Steinberg calls a "ready form of direct coercion" for a protoindustrial economy newly reliant on wage labor.[8] Eighteenth-century and nineteenth-century employment law translated the "open-ended duty of obedience" permitted under Master-Servant law into the employer's right to control all aspects of the employee's labor process.[9] As historians Simon Deakin and Frank Wilkinson note, these new laws thus allowed employers "to impose a more rigorous system of work discipline" not *just* on servants, but also on manufacturing and agricultural workers.[10] Harsh penal codes that punished even small infractions were increasingly applied to waged artisans and craftspeople who had once had significant autonomy over their labor and working conditions. By the late nineteenth century, employers had expanded and normalized their right to control employees precisely by using master-servant relations as a model.[11]

At the same time, however, the relationship between workers and employers was also swiftly evolving.[12] The rise of centralized industrial manufacturing changed the nature of workplace supervision and authority. The master imagined in common law—the household authority whose position in the hierarchy was singular, natural, and absolute—was being replaced by hired managers who were merely contingent and temporary representatives of the employing firm.[13] Meanwhile, new labor reforms stipulating the rights, obligations, and liabilities of both workers and bosses required clearer statutory distinctions. What distinguished a worker with one permanent employer from an independent artisan or tradesman who might be hired serially (or even simultaneously) by multiple firms to perform a specific service? Whose wages, safety, and laboring conditions had to be protected and guaranteed by the state, and who should be held more personally responsible for the success or failure of their own enterprises?[14]

To answer those questions, the courts invented what came to be known as the "control test." Established in British law in the early nineteenth century, the control test was adopted by the US Supreme Court in 1889. In *Singer v. Rahn*, a case concerning a carter paid on commission to sell sewing machines door to door using a horse and cart provided by the Singer Company, the Supreme Court ruled that "the relation of master and servant exists whenever the employer retains the right to direct the manner in which the business shall be done, as well as the result to be accomplished, or, in other words, not only what shall be done, but how it shall be done."[15] The language is still that of master and servant, but this test was intended to distinguish "employees" (here, "servants") from "independent contractors." Employees, the courts held, sell their labor power and are protected by legal regulations. Independent contractors, by contrast, sell a service or the product of their work and are largely *not* protected by federal regulations.

The control test expanded the idea of a household master who personally oversaw the labor of his employees: endowed with the "*right* to direct" the labor process, a modern industrial employer might accomplish that direction indirectly, via the mediation of a hired manager or even through technology. (An assembly line, for instance, can control "the manner in which [work] shall be done" even without human oversight.) But the control test also made clear that *some* wage workers could determine for themselves "how" to perform their own labor, especially when the nature, location, or duration of their work made direct supervision impractical or impossible.[16] Some of these "independent" workers were skilled artisans or professionals who could command high prices for their specialized services and thus ostensibly didn't require regulatory protection. Yet under the terms of the control test, even low-wage workers could be excluded from wages-and-hours laws if their work was not directly supervised and controlled. The piece-rate "sweated" workers described in Chapter 2, for instance, were "free" to work whatever hours they wanted to because they labored in their own homes or in small sweatshops, instead of under the supervision of the manufacturer, who simply purchased their output from a subcontractor.[17] In this way, as Linder explains, the control test both adopted and adapted common law, becoming "an appropriate standard for core capital-labor relations in which the employer dominates the employee sociotechnologically within the process of production."[18]

There was a relatively straightforward fit between this new "sociotechnological" version of the control test and the centralized, rationalized, scientifically managed industrial work of the early twentieth century.[19] Yet over the next few decades, new social legislation such as the NLRA and the FLSA made the distinction between "employee" and "independent contractor" far more meaningful because only the former would receive protection and benefits under new employment laws and regulations. As employee status was codified in regulations, its definition came under intense scrutiny that the regulations themselves often did not resolve. Many New Deal reforms neither embraced nor rejected the control-test definition of "employee," instead providing only their own confoundingly tautological definitions: the FLSA, for instance, defines "employee" simply as "anyone employed by an employer." That lack of definition was particularly problematic when it came to manufacturing workers who were intimately involved in the production process, but whose "manner and means" of work were not directly overseen by managers, as in the case of "inside contractors" hired to perform transportation services such as delivery or carting. Soon after the passage of the FLSA, then, the Supreme Court was called upon to clarify the status of the control test in defining employee classification.[20]

The most significant case of this period was the 1944 *NLRB v. Hearst Publications*, which concerned the employment status of paper-delivering "newsboys."[21] The Hearst company claimed the newsboys were independent contractors, not employees, and thus ineligible for unionization. In a description that we might just as easily see used by a company such as Uber today, *Hearst* argued that the newsboy was "free to sell his newspapers in the ways, methods and manner that he may see fit." The court ultimately disagreed and ruled that the newsboys were employees.[22] Although the decentralized labor process of newspaper delivery meant the newsboys were not directly managed, the court agreed with the lower court ruling that Hearst Publications nonetheless "exercise[d] control and direction over the manner and means in which the newsboys perform their selling activities."[23] Three years later, the 1947 *United States v. Silk* case, which concerned the employee status of piece-rate workers for a company that unloaded coal from railroad cars, likewise expanded the definition of "employee" to include another group of mobile delivery workers. The court determined that the coal unloaders were indeed employees, and not independent contractors, because the company "exercised all necessary supervision over [the workers'] tasks."[24]

In passing the antilabor Taft-Hartley Act in 1947, however, the first post–New Deal Republican Congress called for a return to the "ancient common-law definition" of control derived from master-servant law, rejecting the minimal expansions of the control test in *Hearst* and *Silk*.[25] Under Taft-Hartley, a worker was an employee only if their employer provided instructions over precisely how work was to be done *and* the work was done within the employer's direct view.[26] Taft-Hartley thus significantly reduced the number of workers covered under federal employment regulations. These limits would be challenged in the 1950s and 1960s as the courts tried yet again to liberate modern regulatory norms from the old common-law control test. Nonetheless, the idea that managerial control defines the employee-employer relation was so enduring and persistent that in 1989, it would become the basis for yet another crucial decision in *Nationwide Insurance Co. v. Darden*. In *Darden*, the court once more called for a return to the common-law interpretation of control as a situation wherein "the employer plans out tasks, gives orders, and monitors performance."[27] The ruling emphasized the presence or absence of managerial control as the most important factor defining employment status and continues to be applied to cases dealing with the classification of gigworkers today.[28]

As this history suggests, the control test has been conceptually and legally "sticky": whether directly or indirectly, it continues to define much worker classification in the United States.[29] One of the many long-term consequences of this stickiness is the persistent declassification—and thus informalization or regulatory exclusion—of in-person service work. The fact that service workers have been excluded from classification as employees is of course a rich historical irony: as we have seen, the control test was itself derived from the Master-Servant Acts, and throughout the early twentieth century, the words "servant" and "employee" were almost entirely synonymous in US labor law.[30] Yet as the control test was repurposed for an industrial economy, it was often used to exclude in-person service workers from employee status and protections for reasons very similar to those discussed in Chapter 1's account of time discipline, management, and wages in service work.[31] By the time the expansion of the FLSA was being debated in the 1970s, legislators could argue that domestic workers were *not* employees because they were instead "'servants' in the old sense," as Senator Jacob Javits put it.[32] Today, many domestic workers are still considered independent contractors under the NLRA, the Civil Rights Act, the ADEA, ERISA, and workers' compensation. A definition of "employment" that originated in Master-Servant Act common law thus was repurposed to deny employee status to those whose work *most* resembled the preindustrial conditions of domestic servants.

Even more than in-person service, however, it was circulation work (the labor of moving goods or people) that particularly shaped—and vexed—legal debates over the use and interpretation of the control test. In Britain, many of the early nineteenth-century cases enshrining the control test concerned someone hired to make a delivery: a cattle drover, a "master carter" at a warehouse, and two cases involving horse-drawn carriages.[33] In the United States, as we have seen, the control test was first used to define "employee" in the 1889 *Singer* case, about traveling salesmen. By the mid-twentieth century, transportation and delivery work likewise featured prominently in US legal cases involving the definition of "employee." I have already described the significance of the *Hearst* decision, about newspaper delivery, and *Silk*, which concerned truck unloaders and was adjudicated alongside *Harrison v. Greyvan*, a case about truck drivers.[34] As these cases suggest, circulation workers—drivers, deliverers, cabbies, and others—posed a problem for a control-test definition of "employee." Throughout the twentieth century and into the twenty-first, the NLRB thus frequently attempted to replace the control test with frameworks that would allow circulation workers to be classified as employees. Because the control test was by then fully embedded in labor law and regulation, however, these efforts were often overruled. In cases such as the 1978 *Local 777 v. NLRB*, involving taxi drivers; *CC Eastern, Inc. v. NLRB*, a 1995 case involving delivery drivers; and *FedEx Home Delivery v. NLRB* in 2009, the NLRB extended employee protections to drivers, only to be later overturned on the grounds that the drivers were not subject to direct managerial control.[35] The final ruling in *Local 777*, for instance, asserted that the employer's "right to control the *physical* movements of the employee" was "the most important element to be considered" in determining employee status, effectively making it impossible ever to treat taxi drivers as employees.[36] *FedEx Home Delivery*, likewise, was overturned because the appeals court determined that the company did not control drivers' "hours of work, whether or when [they] take breaks, what routes they follow, or other details of performance" and did not "subject [them] to reprimands or other discipline."[37]

The judges in these cases often acknowledged that there was a profound mismatch between a twenty-first-century labor market and what one called a "twentieth-century" control test (though as we have seen the control test is actually far older than that).[38] But because they reflected shifting and often inconsistent interpretations and standards, these cases did not clarify what a world without the control test would look like.[39] That problem became even more complicated with the rise of platform labor and the gig economy. The first attempts to adjudicate the status of Uber/Lyft drivers legally (the 2015 US District Court cases *Cotter v. Lyft* and *O'Connor v. Uber*) produced only confusion: some aspects of the drivers' labor process seemed to indicate they were clearly employees, yet their "minimal contact with... management"[40] suggested they should be independent contractors. In another case involving delivery workers, the landmark *Dynamex Operations West, Inc. v. Superior Court* case of 2018, the California Supreme Court sought a solution to the broader problem of classification by replacing the control test with what came to be called the "ABC Test." The ABC test included freedom from control as one criterion for independent contractor status, but added two additional criteria that must also be met for a worker to be classified as independent: their work must be outside the scope of the hiring entity's usual business, and workers must be "engaged in an independently established trade."[41]

Following *Dynamex*, in 2019 the ABC test was written into California law in Assembly Bill 5 (AB5). However, AB5 was successfully challenged in 2020 via Proposition 22, a ballot initiative funded by the rideshare companies. Prop. 22 provided a specific carve-out for platform workers and argued that drivers are independent contractors because the companies do not "unilaterally prescribe" working hours, do not require drivers to pick up certain rides, and do not prevent them from using other apps or doing other nondriving jobs.[42] Using the old common-law control test as its legal and political basis, Prop. 22 thus ensured that gigworkers would remain classified as independent contractors and be denied even the minimal protections of employee status.

As we saw in the advertisements at the beginning of this chapter, gigwork companies claim to provide workers with two kinds of "flexibility": the ability to "be your own boss," free from managerial oversight, and the ability to decide your own schedule and working hours. Behind these fantasies, of course, are the realities of intensified surveillance, deskilling, sweating, and a model of temporal subordination that requires gigworkers to be constantly available, even during time they are not being paid. Those forms of control are possible because despite the California Supreme Court's insistence that gigworkers have "minimal contact with management," in reality, an "algorithmic boss" exerts intense control over circulation gigwork.[43] In the rest of this section, I want to think about how indirect, technologically mediated forms of control shape contemporary circulation work. These technologies, I suggest, have enabled both the informalization of gigwork and its superexploitation via atemporal time discipline and nonhourly wages.

From punch clocks to heat-sensing cameras, there is a long history of monitoring and controlling workers with technology. This chapter cannot detail this history in full, but it's worth noting the particularly strong link between the history of technological control or surveillance and the management of workers who transport goods and people. How to control the movements of the workers who move things has long been a central question in scientific management, which is fundamentally concerned with the "flow" of the overall productive process, not just *over time*, but also *in space*. In Frederick Taylor's classic *Scientific Management*, the first example given is not a worker on the factory floor, but a worker traveling to work: "The writer has timed a naturally energetic workman who, while going and coming from work, would walk at a speed of three to four miles per hour," but "on arriving at his work he would immediately slow down to a speed of about one mile an hour."[44] Historian Dana Orenstein likewise quotes a 1915 Ford Motor Company report noting that the main efficiency problem in automobile manufacturing was "transportation within the factory walls."[45] However whereas the worker traveling to a factory or moving things across a factory posed a difficult but resolvable challenge to scientific management, the worker who moved things outside a factory was a more intractable problem. The very thing that made circulation workers easy to informalize legally—their decentralized "independence"—made them hard to supervise or manage. Circulation workers are typically isolated in the box of their carriage, the cabin of their train, the cab of their truck, or the driver's seat of their car. Prior to the invention of GPS and in-vehicle monitoring, these workers typically had control over their routes and over the order and operation of their tasks. In constant movement away from any centralized hub of management, they could not be subjected to the kinds of direct monitoring and deskilling that had been used to control and increase the efficiency of both manufacturing and retail workers.

Labor historian Jennifer Luff thus argues that modern technological workplace control originated not in the factory, but on trains. The isolation of passenger-train conductors made supervision difficult, so the railroad company subcontracted undercover "spotters" known as Pinkertons (after Allen Pinkerton, the contractor who hired them) to function as "remote managers." When the public, as well as the courts, began to express sympathy for the conductors and hatred of the Pinkertons, the companies turned instead to a "technological fix": devices such as the fare box and the "bell punch," which sounded each time a ticket was punched and which outsourced management to the customer because it made a noise when correctly used by the conductor.[46] Like the peach pitter and typewriter return key discussed in Chapter 2, these technologies were designed to track and control workers' output, but they were also used to automate the labor process: the fare box, for instance, allowed companies to reduce the total number of human conductors required on trains.

The managerial and legal fix of technology was also crucial to employers' capacity to exert control over long-distance truckers. Long-haul trucking promised not just better pay and better working conditions, but also the autonomy of life on the open road. Like contemporary circulation gigwork, trucking was perceived as a profession where one could do the job without being constantly watched and bossed around.[47] The reality, of course, was rather different. As Karen Levy points out in her study of surveillance technology and trucking, truckers are typically paid by the mile and thus "are economically incentivized to drive for as long as possible." As a result, drivers often attempt to evade overtime regulations designed to ensure road safety. Instead of restructuring the method of wage payment to deincentivize this risky behavior, however, the industry instead became an early adopter of technological monitoring and surveillance, collecting "fine-grained data about truckers' behaviors, bodies, braking patterns, even brainwaves."[48] This surveillance also became a technique for deskilling, since it often goes hand in hand with the replacement of "road knowledge" by prescribed routes. When used in concert with pay-per-mile compensation, surveillance allowed companies to increase drivers' productivity while keeping their wages as low as possible.[49]

In the case of circulation gigwork, similarly, technology has been used to preserve the fiction of gigworkers' independence while simultaneously ensuring ever-greater levels of technological subordination. Surveillance technology allows circulation gigworkers' every move to be tracked, while detailed information about those movements is collected and analyzed in real time. "Driving style" algorithms, for instance, are used by most rideshare companies to monitor speed, braking, and acceleration.[50] Delivery drivers for large delivery companies such as FedEx and AmazonFlex work in vans stuffed with hundreds of sensors. These telematic devices monitor their every move, collecting data not just on speed and acceleration, but also the number and length of toilet breaks, how fast they open the door, how many times they have to back the vehicle up or make a left turn. AmazonFlex uses an app that not only manages the labor process, but also evaluates workers' performance, including customer satisfaction metrics.[51] Gigwork companies use GPS to enable an "algorithmic panopticon," where digital maps monitoring drivers' location are an "indirect," but omniscient way to track and control them in real time.[52] Because these transportation and delivery companies exert control over the "manner and means" of labor through technology, instead of through human managers, however, the companies can still claim that these workers are not directly managed "employees," but independent contractors.

Technology is used not only to surveil and control gigwork, but also to rationalize it. UPS workers receive driving directives from ORION (On-Road Integrated Optimization and Navigation), an algorithm developed by UPS to optimize the length and speed of delivery routes.[53] FedEx drivers undergo an intensively Taylorized training, Moritz Altenried explains, "learn[ing] a huge number of protocols relating to how to save time, such as how to start the truck with one hand while buckling with the other."[54] Gigwork algorithms are used to set baseline delivery times, which are then steadily decreased so that workers are forced to keep up (a practice Taylor himself warned could have negative long-term effects if paired with piece-rate incentive systems). Instantaneous data also allows consumers and customers themselves to participate in supervision. Like the bell punch used on early twentieth-century trains, tracking technology gives customers a sense of control and forces employees to conform to the rhythms of consumer demand.[55] A journalistic exposé of food delivery workers in China published by *Renwu* notes that in 2016, the maximum time allowed for a three-kilometer delivery was one hour, but by 2018, it had been reduced to thirty-eight minutes. As in factory work, this speedup is enabled not just by machine pacing, but also by deskilling the whole labor process. As the *Renwu* inquiry notes, platform algorithms seek to "replace the human brain to the greatest extent possible."[56]

Put simply, the technologies used in contemporary circulation gigwork enable an extreme form of intensification, forcing workers to work harder, faster, and longer for lower wages.[57] As in industrial mechanization, the rationalization and subordination of circulation gigwork combines technological innovation with labor intensification. Indeed, algorithms enable forms of time discipline in circulation work similar to Marx's distinction between the "porous" working day, in which output sometimes slows or ceases, and the "dense" working day, in which technology is used to ensure that production never stops; a process Marx describes (quoting the factory inspectors) as a "'petty pilfering of minutes'" guided by the capitalist's understanding that "'moments are the elements of profit.'"[58]

Yet management by algorithm in the circulation sector also draws on forms of discipline and subordination specific to service work. As we have seen in previous chapters, E. P. Thompson's account of industrial work discipline does not adequately describe this form of subordination: industrial labor relies on "straightforward time measurement[s]," presumes "a distinction between [the] employer's time and [the worker's] 'own' time," and is highly "synchronized" and regular.[59] The time control over deskilled circulation gigwork, by contrast, deploys management by algorithm as well as the method of wage payment to control work time with a great degree of specificity, using nonstandardized or "flexible" forms of discipline and measurement to ensure that gigworkers are not paid for all the time they spend working. Circulation gigworkers are typically paid a mix of task-rate wages and tips: the company guarantees a "per delivery" or "per ride" rate that is then supplemented with customer tips. The calculation of "base rates" changes according to miles traveled, traffic, or fluctuations in supply and demand, and these calculations are rarely transparent to gigworkers. As mentioned in Chapter 1, for instance, gigwork companies often apply tips toward the payment of base rates or otherwise steal wages and time from gigworkers. Circulation gigwork thus repurposes the master's total and perpetual authority over the servant's time and labor. Yet whereas the eighteenth-century master was responsible to feed, house, and clothe his servant—"when there is work to be done as when there is not," in Blackstone's words—contemporary circulation gigwork platforms force workers to wait, unpaid, for work.[60] Waiting, scholars of gigwork have argued, is fundamental to the everyday rhythms of delivery work and "central to the economic logic of platform-mediated gig work more generally." As a result, gigwork "can require dizzying speeds... but it can also mean many minutes, hours, and days of simply waiting."[61]

Labor law scholars Guylaine Vallée and Dalia Gesualdi-Fecteau describe this form of postindustrial time discipline as an "obligation to be available."[62] The regulatory and managerial framework for the obligation to be available (without being paid) can be traced in part to care work and other forms of in-person service. In Chapter 1, for instance, I described the legal debate about tips versus time-based wages in which legislators and industry lobbyists claimed it is unfair to pay restaurant employees for time spent waiting for customers to finish their meal or on other "unproductive" tasks, such as folding napkins.[63] But circulation gigwork's time-control techniques were most explicitly innovated in the management of long-haul trucking, a subsector in which workers are traditionally paid by miles traveled, instead of by time. An exemption for rural truckers in the Motor Carrier Act of 1935 shielded trucking firms from federal regulation and unionization, and as a result, truckers were (and still are) explicitly excluded from the FLSA's wages and overtime protections.[64] Truck drivers thus perform a range of tasks for which they are not paid, including waiting at customs, being stuck in traffic, and vehicle maintenance. They often spend days or weeks on the road while not being paid for time spent sleeping, eating, or taking mandated rest breaks.[65] Over the last decade, a massive increase in the online purchasing of consumer goods has meant that truckers have to spend more and more time waiting at ports, borders, and other kinds of checkpoints. Truckers in the United States lose over a billion dollars in wages every year for time spent waiting.[66]

We find a strikingly similar legal-managerial strategy in circulation gigwork. Prop. 22, we recall, was a California ballot initiative funded by the rideshare companies in response to the *Dynamex* decision. The language of Prop. 22 notes that the app companies do not "unliterally prescribe specific dates, times of day, or a minimum number of hours" during which the worker must work. But Prop. 22's disavowal of managerial control over the driver's working time is paired with a definition of "engaged time" that determines gigworkers' wages. Uber and Lyft claimed that Prop. 22 would ensure drivers were paid more than California minimum wage for "engaged time" and would provide health-care subsidies for drivers who averaged at least twenty-five "engaged" hours per week. But "engaged time" is defined in Prop. 22 as "the period of time ... from when an app-based driver accepts a rideshare request ... to when the app-based driver completes that rideshare request." Roughly half of rideshare drivers' working time is *not* "engaged," by this definition.[67] Thus while the companies use "engaged time" to claim that drivers earn an average wage of $20.00 to 30.00 an hour, most gigworkers earn less than $15.00 an hour, and many earn even less than the federal minimum wage of $7.25 an hour.[68] Dubal describes this algorithmically individualized payment structure as a "new racial wage code" when she links Prop. 22's highly specific carve-out for transportation and delivery workers—who are overwhelmingly Black and Brown—to the FLSA's exclusion of Black and Brown domestic and agricultural workers.[69] Migrant and undocumented workers are especially targeted by gigwork's promise of quick income and exploited by its nonhourly wage structures. Already informalized via their citizenship status, these workers are often conscripted into becoming fungible day laborers for the apps.[70]

All of this helps us understand the truths behind the Uber and Lyft advertisements with which I began. Using the logic of the control test, the gigwork companies can indeed claim that gigworkers are able to "be their own boss" while also subjecting them to surveillance, deskilling, and uncertain wages. As the protestors demonstrated, there is a deep connection between circulation gigwork and the legacy of tips and piece rates as "subminimum" wages associated with the racial logics of chattel slavery and migrant exploitation. Across a juridico-political archive of legal cases, state regulations, and management practices, circulation work has been the site of both legal innovations in the informalization of work and technological innovations in the control of workers. As a result, circulation workers themselves appear at once free and coerced, autonomous and governed, hustling entrepreneurs and vulnerable victims. In this way, they also figure a broader ambivalence about service work in general and indeed about waged work as such. The collective desires encoded in images of circulation workers' freedom, independence, and mobility are thus not reducible to merely a demand for more state regulation, for legal formalization, or for the kinds of direct oversight that still ground protected "employee" status under the law. To understand these contradictions, the next section will turn to a literary archive wherein fictions of spatial freedom offer a more complex vocabulary for understanding both freedom and control in circulation gigwork.

FICTIONS OF CIRCULATION

Circulation gigworkers exercise a strong hold on contemporary culture, scholarship, and politics. The work these workers perform sometimes seems invisible—in part because the companies disavow their own managerial control by not providing uniforms or company vehicles—yet because they traverse urban and suburban space constantly, circulation gigworkers themselves are highly visible. Circulation gigworkers are often represented as figures of pathos ("modern-day slaves"), but most of us—including many people who are also circulation gigworkers themselves—at least occasionally rely on the labor of drivers or delivery workers to deliver our packages or our dinner, to pick us up at the airport, or do our grocery shopping. As in the images this chapter began with, the circulation gigworker tends to be represented either as a free, hustling entrepreneur or as a superexploited servant or slave. Caught between the critique of informalization and the critique of waged work, the circulation gigworker is both a vulnerable figure in need of formal regulatory protection and a reminder that formalization has historically been associated with more intensive and direct control by both management and the state.[71]

Recalling the origins of the term "gigwork" described above—its relationship to the spinning whirligig, the speeding gig carriage, and the "tremendous excitements of movement" described by Kerouac—it is little wonder that the contradictions embedded in and embodied by circulation gigwork have specifically coalesced around the cultural form of the road narrative. To understand both how ideals and anxieties around gigwork are mediated by the image of the open road, we must first contend with how gigwork firms themselves have instrumentalized fantasies of freedom and independence using images of spatial mobility. We might begin in no better place than a series of short films funded by Uber and directed by Spike Lee.

Titled *Da Republic of Brooklyn*, the series comprises five films, each one approximately ten minutes long and featuring the story of an individual Uber driver. Although described as "documentaries," these short films are essentially aestheticized propaganda for Uber. Released in July 2018, the films clearly reflect the company's position in the wake of the April 2018 *Dynamex* ruling, which had reclassified gigworkers as employees. The same month *Da Republic of Brooklyn* was released, Uber joined forces with Lyft, Instacart, DoorDash, and TaskRabbit in lobbying California legislators to blunt the impact of *Dynamex*. In August 2018, the companies partnered with the California Chamber of Commerce's (CCC) I'm Independent coalition, which sponsored lobbying initiatives such as a rally at which, in the words of the CCC, "speakers told moving stories about why they choose to be independent contractors and how that choice benefits them and their families."[72]

This description could just as easily be attached to *Da Republic*, whose "moving stories" of gigworkers aestheticize the fantasy of entrepreneurial independence through the visual language of movement and the road. "Good things happen when people can move, whether across town or towards their dreams," Uber's marketing language for the film avers. In Lee's film, the fantasy of spatial freedom as economic freedom finds an overlapping metaphor in the image of the road: one driver is said to be "discovering a new-found independence while traveling on a journey toward an even bolder future"; another "uses art as a vehicle" to capture the "continuous motion" of Brooklyn; while a third is said to be characterized by a "movement that can only be described as relentless." Lee's emphasis on the diversity of the drivers' experiences—their status as citizens of the heterogeneous "Republic of Brooklyn"—is likewise recuperated for a fantasy of migrant "upward mobility." Most importantly, Lee's film reflects the company's legal claim about the informality of drivers' employment. The language of Prop. 22 emphasizes drivers' right to "maintain flexibility to decide when, where, and how they work." In Lee's "documentary," in turn, the drivers repeat Uber's own claim that it exerts no managerial oversight, that its technology is fully in the driver's control, that drivers themselves prefer scheduling freedom to guaranteed wages. Driver Domingo Nolasco favorably compares his work for Uber with his previous job working for a car service, where he had to "get messages from dispatch"; with Uber, by contrast, he has the option "to work as much as I want." Another subject describes Uber as "the opportunity to be free, literally.... It doesn't feel like a grind, it feels like I'm having a long, adventurous day.... Uber is such a flexible open schedule. No interference, I don't have to say 'Hey bossman, I got this thing, can I go?' It's very free in that sense."

Lee's film is clearly compromised, an example of the worst kind of collusion between a celebrity "content creator" and a corporation. But it also registers a set of contradictions common across both cultural and political representations of gigwork, particularly a profound ambivalence about the desirability of formal employment. One version of this ambivalence, of course, is the kind sometimes described as "neoliberal": opposition to regulation on the grounds that formalizing gigworkers' labor will curtail individual entrepreneurial opportunity. (As Chapter 1 suggested, this is not in fact a "new" belief: the ideal of independent proprietorship has long been central to the American national imaginary, and popular beliefs that labor regulation would simply enshrine the permanent dependency of "wage slavery" date to at least the mid-nineteenth century.) Like trucking companies before them, circulation gigwork platforms have conscripted gigworkers into the companies' fight against regulatory reform. But when the drivers in Lee's film positively compare gigwork to other jobs, they also articulate a different kind of critique: a resistance to the embodied control exerted by bosses everywhere. Obviously, the gigwork companies' insistence that drivers are free from managerial control is purely strategic. It's also not true, given that surveillance and other tech does the work of human managers. Yet by evoking the "bossman" of formalized labor, the drivers in Lee's films force us to acknowledge that most workers do indeed *want* control over the "manner and means"—the time and the space, the processes and the products—of their own labor. They also remind us that the control tests used to determine modern employee status were rooted in the coercive management and "total subordination" of master-servant relations.

To explore how these competing critiques and divergent desires show up in texts more explicitly critical of gigwork, I turn to three recent novels about gigwork that are likewise deeply curious about the paradoxes of freedom and coercion represented by contemporary circulation gigwork. I begin with Raven Leilani's 2020 novel *Luster*. Winner of the 2020 Kirkus Prize for Fiction as well as the National Book Critics Circle award and The Center for Fiction First Novel Prize, *Luster* is a bildungsroman about Edie, a twentysomething Black woman who begins a relationship with an older white man in an "open marriage" and ends up moving temporarily into his house, where she becomes an object of fixation for his wife and a friend to his adopted daughter, Akila, who is also Black. As the novel opens, Edie is a painter with massive student debt. When she loses her job at a publishing company (where she experiences both sexual harassment and racial aggressions), she is forced to work as a platform-based delivery rider to make her rent. As Leilani puts it in an interview, money—even more than sex—is at the heart of the novel because she "need[s] to know how [her] characters eat and pay rent." Unlike other novels, in which money can remain unmentioned precisely because the characters "have enough of it where it is a given and so almost an invisible entity," *Luster* explicitly reflects Leilani's own experience being Black, broke, and working as a courier for Postmates. The novel's "frantic energy," Leilani says, reflects her own economic anxiety: "I was writing feeling like: Please God, let this work, let this book help me be able to go to the dentist."[73]

To hear what precarity sounds like in the novel, here is a representative passage describing Edie's work as a courier:

> Most of the time, I stay in Brooklyn. I get the first orders of no-pulp orange juice and champagne out of the way. Make pit stops for vanilla Juul pods, small orders of LaCroix and Pampers. I make my home base Holy Cross Cemetery so I can hydrate in relative peace, and also because it's smack-dab in the middle of Flatbush, the orders come in on all sides. . . . Everyone is excited to see me, and I am sort of excited to see them, the habitual Bensonhurst McFlurries, the Gen X brownstoners who, for some reason, use the app to order pizza . . . the West Indian pockets of Eastern Parkway and their cash-only ackee and coco bread, beaucoup tips on the days I wear the company hat and beat the average time, though occasionally I take the bridge over and field requests by Canal, where I try to protect orders of squid from all that direct sun.[74]

What Leilani describes as the novel's "frantic energy" appears here in both form and content. The breathless parataxis—its random juxtapositionality sharpened by both the specificity and the variety of the items she delivers—mirrors Edie's movement across Brooklyn. Leilani's use of catalogue and her attention to the "excite[ment]" of life in a diverse, dynamic city recalls what Kaitlyn Greenidge describes as the "privileged anonymity" of the *flaneur*, who celebrates both free movement and urban everyday life.[75] In *Luster*, transportation is also translation, and Leilani remixes and celebrates a heteroglot popular vernacular: note the linguistic playfulness and sonorous rhythms of a phrase such as "cash-only ackee and coco bread, beaucoup tips on the day I wear the company hat."

Moreover, Edie's protagonicity depends on her centrality to a narrative of commercial circulation. Her euphoric catalogues of small human details position her as a privileged observer of urban life whose interactions with others are, like service work itself, at once intimate and anonymous: "Five bundles of kale for a customer in an eighth-floor walkup in Flatiron. A vial of rosewater for a customer in Greenwich Village.... Band-Aids and cigarillos for a customer who runs out of the Strand with a stiletto clutched in each hand.... Three black wigs made of virgin Malaysian hair for a half-human, half-turquoise customer on Bowery."[76] The opening of the door that makes private lives momentarily visible further expands the worlds Edie moves through as witness, while the use of listing and parataxis registers the harried seriality of these encounters as she observes the diverse peoples of the city by bringing them the equally diverse commodities they want.[77] *Luster*'s narrative voice thus not only recounts but also is made possible by Edie's work as a courier—by the freedom of her movement, by her spatial autonomy, by her ability to listen in on the rhythms and speech of the city as she moves through it. Edie is both in motion and a still point around which the city's "breakneck, multilingual carousel" turns as she waits for another order and observes details of the world around her: "The neighborhood is fragrant and alien, all the hamlets in Maplewood bracketed in soft, emerald grass. Every half mile, there seems to be a golf course, with some improbable fauna, cranes and hares, circling little white carts along the fairways."[78] Here, the shift from movement to stillness foregrounds Edie's role as an observer. Elsewhere, the transition into motion, registered by Leilani's propulsive syntax, formalizes the kind of "dashing" or "relay" running the apps are named after, as the traversing of space becomes subject to the dictates of the app: "despite the businessmen marching into my path and the physical assault of glass and steel and scary wooden trains in Upper East Side toy stores, I don't feel like I'm moving even while I'm on my feet, up and down and in and out... as the orders come one, two, six."[79] Here we see what gigworker scholars describe as the "fragmented rush" of gigwork's time discipline.[80] Yet Leilani associates the speed of gigwork not just with exhaustion and overwork, but also with a kind of propulsive momentum that affords freedom, adventure, and indeed narrative itself.

But what does it mean that *Luster*'s representation of circulation gigwork echoes many of the terms of Lee's pro-Uber documentary (freedom, autonomy, flexibility, variety, community) even as it also registers the ways and means by which gigwork is superexploited and harried to the point of exhaustion? *Luster,* I am suggesting, both registers and reframes a contradictory set of cultural meanings around circulation gigwork, identifying it as the site of both anxieties *and* fantasies about freedom and control and confronting complex questions about the limits of formalization. If it does not cynically valorize the gigworker's "independence," as Lee/Uber do, neither does it entirely disavow the desire for independence and autonomy.

Nor, importantly, does it suggest that Edie's formally waged, semiprofessionalized office work was less exploited, less racialized and feminized, or less precarious than her gigwork. Edie's courier work *does* liberate her from the office, where she is subject to racism and sexual harassment and where she feels pinned under the "blue computer light," working at a desk positioned "so the manager can see [her] face" and able to survive only by disassociating: "if a person comes to rote work with the expectation that she will be demeaned, she can bypass the pitfalls of hope and redirect all that energy into being a merciless drone."[81] Acknowledging the oppressive, "merciless" tedium of this labor—especially being subject to the surveilling eyes of management as a Black woman—the novel refuses to idealize a regulatory fix that would make gigwork like other kinds of work and instead reminds us of the subjugation associated with managerial control.[82] Leilani thus radicalizes a familiar critique of "rote work" and managerial repression by yoking the manager's structural domination to histories of racialized and gendered violence.

Luster associates labor-process control not just with the oppressive oversight of bosses, but also with the police. These same connections were made, of course, by the "Strike for Black Lives" with which this chapter began. Domination and exploitation in the service sector, protestors suggested, was in fact a necessary part of anti-Black police violence and anti-immigrant state violence, and vice versa. *Luster* likewise builds toward a culminating scene of racist police violence, first foreshadowing this sequence in the half dozen or so casual asides wherein Edie remarks on the presence or threat of police and describes herself as "too much fuck the police" for office work.[83] In the final pages of the novel, Edie and Akila, the adopted teenage daughter of Edie's lover and his wife, are stopped by the cops. Edie, who notes that she been taught and trained in the techniques of dealing with the cops as a Black woman, makes an effort to "appear casual," but she simultaneously realizes that Akila—who is Black, but who has been raised in a white family—"doesn't know the words" to the "script" of this encounter. "There's a part of me that sees her ease, her self-possession, and is frustrated for what she hasn't been told," Edie notes. The scene proceeds in a set of remarkable sentences:

> I know that the moment between when a black boy is upright and capable of speech and when he is prostrate in his own blood is almost imperceptible, due in great part to the tacit conversation that is happening beyond him, that has happened before him, and that resists his effort to enter

> it before it concludes. I know that the event horizon is swift because of the gulf between the greeting and the pavement, but in real time, as they press Akila to the ground, every second is long. . . . Akila, surprised and clumsy and afraid, [is] so conspicuously a child that I run over without thinking and try to get them off, the whites of her eyes bright in the porch light before an officer lifts me into his arms and presses me down into the grass and says *Stop resisting*, which my ears receive as Greek but also as déjà vu, because not even in what is feasibly my last moment can I be free from the internet and the digital hall of mirrors in which orders are issued unironically to dying women and men. For a moment, I only hear geese, and somewhere, an ice cream truck.[84]

Here we find not just the images and themes, but indeed the very rhythms of the earlier passages about gigwork reframed and repurposed to describe the experience of anti-Black state violence. The slowing of time that turns Edie from a participant in the scene into merely its witness is punctuated by the intensified temporality of terror and panic registered by the long sentence that makes up most of the second part of what I've quoted. Shuddering across the language of movement and freedom, the arrest (in both senses of the word) leaves Edie and Akila immobile, "prostrate," "press[ed] to the ground," "press[ed] to the grass" as Edie remarks on the horrifying irony embedded in the police encounter: being "order[ed]" not to fight for one's very life.[85]

In this passage, control is a form of violence that appears not only in labor management but also in the form of the police, the law, and the state. By evoking these multiple forms of control, Leilani shows how state control over nonwhite (and noncitizen) subjects is tied to the particular managerial forms common in circulation gigwork, which may depend legally and materially on the spatial "independence" of workers, but which has also innovated its own forms of disciplinary control. In an age of decentralized circulation work, Joshua Clover argues, the police are often the most visible—and the most violent—representation of an otherwise abstract and invisible "economy."[86] *Luster* extends this insight by describing how police and state control over gigworkers must itself be flexible and variable. Sometimes the security state and the service sector work together to close off or differentiate space. (Despite being a novel of free *flanerie*, *Luster* is equally vivid when describing the phenomenological experience of moving through racially segregated space.) At other times, however, the state and the service sector collaborate to open urban space up to investment, so that circulation gigwork itself can become part of the infrastructure of a city. *Luster* thus suggests that the violence and precarity of circulation gigwork cannot be resolved simply by classifying gigworkers as "employees" under the control test or by expanding forms of state regulation whose legitimacy is based on the state's police power. In this way, the novel both reframes and sharpens the desires for freedom and autonomy (and the critique of control across domains) figured by circulation gigwork.[87] Recalling Chapter 1's account of the picaresque as the genre associated with informal/wageless employment, we might read *Luster* as an effort to acknowledge both sides of a contradiction Sal Nicolazzo identifies in their marvelous account of picaresque parataxis not as "a form of mobile, capacious, and flexible vagrant subjectivity," but rather as a violently capricious mode of legal power. Similarly, *Luster* suggests that these two forms of flexibility are inevitably coconstituting, both the dream and the nightmare of informalized, mobile labor. In this way, the novel imagines a way to move beyond the binaries with which this chapter began, in which the promise of freedom from control could appear only as the ideology of gigwork ("Be your own boss"), while the critique of gigwork as racialized exploitation ("modern-day slavery") could be registered only as a demand for greater regulatory and managerial control.[88]

Gigwork's relationship to both state and managerial control takes on a more explicitly "outlaw" cast in Priya Guns's *Your Driver Is Waiting*. Named a "most anticipated book of the year" by at least a dozen outlets—including *Vogue*, *Esquire*, and *Rolling Stone*—Guns's debut novel was described by the publisher as a "gender-flipped reboot of the iconic 1970s film *Taxi Driver*." Opening with the memorable line "If you're going to be a driver, you'd better hide at least one weapon in your car," *Your Driver Is Waiting* remediates *Taxi Driver*'s Travis Bickle as a queer South Asian woman named Damani who drives for a gig-work company called RideShare.[89] The reference is pointed. In *Taxi Driver*, the desire for freedom and the fear of constriction intersect on the roadways of intraurban travel. "Travis, a feverish combination of cowboy, terrorist, soldier, and street warrior, is the common man traveling through a world of filth and injustice," Jefferson Cowie notes in his study of 1970s-era working-class culture.[90] A similar mood haunts the laconic toughness of *Your Driver Is Waiting*: "There is something about driving at night, stone cold sober while all the world relaxes, that makes me horny. I want it all. The lights, the fear, the surging electricity. The moon watches while the city fills with madness. I am always safest in my car before a passenger climbs in. After that, I welcome madness in, and it pays me to stay."[91] Recalling *Taxi Driver*'s fantasy of vigilante justice, the novel's narrative climax occurs when Damani drives her car into a police station during a protest because she is chasing her ex-girlfriend, a white "ally" who has betrayed Damani and her friends by telling the cops about their "terrorist" plans for a protest:

> Jolene ran like a fucking horse. . . . I was glad I could keep up with her, driving parallel. I lowered the window some more and could hear demonstrators from a few blocks away crescendo even louder. . . . She ran faster. She ran on the road, unafraid of vehicles, unafraid to die. She cut off another car, and I saw my opportunity. I hit the gas to follow her. . . . The police station was ahead . . . she ran faster and faster and I had no choice but to show her that she wasn't shit compared to my B16A engine. I drove forward, switched gears and pressed on the gas. I saw how my revolutions per minute pushed to the right. She looked at me from behind her shoulder. I pressed even harder on the gas and closed my eyes.[92]

Here, Guns reappropriates themes common to 1970s-era representations of working-class masculinity under threat: a desire for vigilante justice, a legitimating pride in her skills and a moral identification with the tools of her trade, and an outlaw attitude resistant to the rules of both bosses and the state. As Cowie argues, *Taxi Driver* emphasized the "exaggerated pathologies of violent, angry white men" to "explain the 'blue collar blues'" consequent on the end of the postwar economic boom and the collapse of the manufacturing sector. Films such as *Taxi Driver* represented the desire for (white, male) working-class autonomy promised by jobs such as trucking and taxi driving, even as they also registered the hopelessness of "a dying era" in which "the promise of modernity itself [was] slipping out of reach."[93] Guns deploys those tropes while revising our sense of the "typical" figure of contemporary work and exploitation: the white working-class Vietnam vet wracked by antisocial rage and political despair becomes a queer, migrant woman whose own rage and despair register the political and economic contradictions of her own moment with equivalent—and similarly ambivalent—force. Guns's novel thus does not reject, but instead reframes and radicalizes gigworkers' desires for autonomy, mobility, adventure, and freedom from supervision.

Make no mistake, however: *Your Driver Is Waiting*'s politics are not the revanchist white male resentment of *Taxi Driver*. It is not by accident that Damani drives right into a police station in the middle of a riot protesting the superexploitation of gigworkers, migrant deportation, racialized police violence, and gentrification. As Clover influentially argues, riots are themselves "struggle[s] to control space and passage through it" and thus are the *volte face* of logistics and circulation. Whereas the strike and industrial production are fundamentally temporal, the riot and circulation work are spatial and thus particularly available to the spatial genre of the circulation narrative.[94] No surprise, then, that *Your Driver Is Waiting* turns to riots. When the video of her destruction of the police station goes viral, Damani becomes known as "The Taxi Driver": the rioters "use the car as a barrier . . . set it on fire and barbeque the insides," galvanizing a series of uprisings led by "everyone in transport and gigworkers from all over."[95] These protests, notably, are *not* about formalization: as Damani's gigworker comrade Shereef puts it, "we don't just want fair wages.... They'll put us on contracts with a low hourly rate and still make money off us.... Plus who says a driver doesn't have the ability to manage themselves?"[96] Here, the novel invokes the political demands of gigworkers themselves, which do not turn on the desire for contracts and managers and legal recognition, but rather emphasize the desire for autonomy, independence, and a wage adequate to their subsistence. Turning the tool of her labor, her car, into a way to push back against state and bosses alike, Damani evokes the tradition of "machine breaking" and sabotage common in periods of class decomposition, even as she also weaponizes and repurposes her pride in her skills as a driver.[97]

Both *Luster* and *Your Driver Is Waiting* thus identify the police and the state as agents of spatial discipline over circulation gigworkers—indeed, as substitutes for the kind of direct managerial control formerly legitimated by labor regulation. By associating control not just with the boss and the corporation, but also with the cop and the state, they give us a more radical and more totalizing register through which to interpret gigwork's fantasy of freedom. But they also remind us that another figure exerts a more direct and indeed intimate control over circulation gigworkers: the customer. The opening sentence of Guns's novel quoted above, about the need to have a hidden weapon, immediately frames the passenger as constant potential threat, "Especially," she goes on, "if you're a driver that looks like me. Not because I'm dashing or handsome, but because I am a woman, of course."[98] The customers described in the novel are mostly characterized only by their rating and how much they tip or how they behave: for instance "Derek (3.4 stars)"; "Rob (4.4 stars) who did a line of coke off his left sleeve"; and "Steven (3.6 stars)" who gets in the car with his friend, "Leather Jacket," and attempts to assault Damani sexually.[99] As the novel proceeds, riders often don't have names, but only numbers: "There were passengers 4 and 5, and 6 and 7, and by then three of them had tipped me more than $2. Passenger number 7 (4.9 stars) said what many say: that drivers have insight like no one else in the country. His ride was only $7.30, zero in tips."[100] In *Luster*, Edie's encounters with those to whom she delivered are often vividly replete with the diversity of both human and commodity detail (the brownstoners and West Indians, the McFlurries and ackee), but in *Your Driver Is Waiting*, customers are reduced to their numerical rating: they are only either threat or tip. In this way, Guns reminds us that gigwork outsources control not only to algorithms and surveillance technology, but also to customers, an intimate (if depersonalized) relation that embeds both economic and bodily risk.

But what are we to make of Guns's reference to a customer who goes on and on about gigworkers' "insight," but doesn't tip, or of her description of passengers who talk "about how I was exploited, my RideShare was the devil of all companies, but they had to use my services *just this one time*," or of the moment when Damani gets a bunch of requests for rides from people coming home . . . from a protest against gigwork?[101] In these passages, Guns forces us to consider the complex relations of complicity that attend the "outsourcing" of managerial domination to customers, including to customers who may *also* be gigworkers or service workers. To explore how this complexity might show up at the level of narrative form, let's turn to Peter Mendelsund's *The Delivery*.

Mendelsund's 2021 novel is mostly told from the perspective of an unnamed "delivery boy" working for an urban delivery company. As its use of an unnamed protagonist suggests, *The Delivery* is minimalist and experimental—much more of a philosophical novel than *Luster* or *Your Driver Is Waiting* and less likely to reference a Scorsese film than to borrow from Ludwig Wittgenstein's *Philosophical Investigations*. (Wittgenstein is frequently quoted in the novel, and his work is referenced, for instance, in Mendelsund's use of character names such as "N," the secret beloved of the "delivery boy.")[102] Yet it shares other features, both thematic and formal, with Leilani's and Guns's novels. The relationship between the spatial mobility of gigwork and its temporal discipline is formalized via Mendelsund's use of white space and minigraphs separated by lines, as here:

Little-to-no-traffic. Few customers.

———

(Slow time.)

———

The rain let up.[103]

Later, the delivery boy realizes "He was ahead. / 1. Ahead in terms of money. 2. Ahead in terms of time": although "the dispatch girls clocked distance-and-time per delivery," he is ahead of schedule and so can spend a few minutes at a museum. But when a customer delays him, "the seconds and the minutes tick by, each one counting against the supply the delivery boy had in trust."[104] Mendelsund's attention to time as something measured, controlled, stored, hoarded, and lost—a relationship to time the book's minimalist, dilatory style also formalizes—figures circulation gigwork as both highly variable or episodic *and* intensely routinized; sometimes rushed to the point of exhaustion, at other times a drag through the dead space of waiting for work. Elsewhere, the frantic, self-harried motion imposed on circulation gigworkers reappears via a fragmented parataxis (as in *Luster*) that registers the world the delivery boy passes as he pedals through the city, not so much a part of the circulation of commodities as a witness to it: "People streaming in and out of oversized chrome doors, thumping music leaking out with the air conditioning. Cars double-parked (always a hazard for delivery boys) and generally lawless sidewalks. People bustling, arguing, sulking. A child wailing."[105] Like *Your Driver Is Waiting, The Delivery* describes customers simply via the quantification of ratings and tips, instead of as round characters: the first chapter of the book, for instance, is simply "Delivery 1: **." Later, we find "Fourth customer: *"; "(The sixth customer had smiled also, in the manner of the lad earlier, and had tipped him generously)"; and "Customer nine: decent tip, no comments. **** / Comments, if they were good, were the best for a delivery boy's average and his prospects. The Supervisor took you into the office with the barred door if he became aware of negative comments."[106] Like Guns, Mendelsund reduces customers to numbers and stars to convey the simultaneously intimate and impersonal quality of these encounters, while the reference to the "comments" as a substitute for "the Supervisor's" gaze clarifies the power relation.

But the most interesting—and vexing—aspect of Mendelsund's novel is its metafictionality. At several moments in the text, an authorial voice intrudes on the intimacy of the close third-person narration, as here:

> (It certainly did not occur to the delivery boy that much of this jewelry was paste.... Even at my age, now, I can't tell real from fake. I don't know why we should expect the delivery boy to have been able to make such difficult assessments. Anyway, some of the jewelry was valuable, certainly, but it was practically impossible to tell which pieces, among so much imitation. So.)[107]

These authorial interruptions increase in frequency as the text progresses until, in the final fifty pages or so, they become something else, in passages such as like this one:

> The delivery boy peered into the darkening orchard,
> and saw
> (A picnic.)
> (No.)
> (Sorry.)
> (That doesn't go here.)
> (But still.)
> (It was the fall, and I was with my parents. Beer foam on my mother's upper lip... She wiped it away, cross, then amused....)[108]

Here, the intruding narrator isn't just the author, commenting metafictionally on his own writing process, but a new character who narrates the parenthetical aside beginning "It was the fall..." and extending into a full parenthetical paragraph wherein the narrator remembers a picnic with his parents. Later, a relatively long twelve-page chapter narrates this character's own traumatic migration, an experience that he says connects him to the delivery boy because they both speak "an amputee language—a language in which whole tenses had been lopped off."[109]

While the book was well reviewed in general, many reviews saw this metafictional device as a flaw. A *New York Times* review, for instance, describes the novel as "often exquisite," however, the review goes on to note, "Unfortunately, the novel picks up an annoying passenger: the narrator, who goes from unobtrusive chronicler to unruly guest."[110] Other reviewers concurred. *Complete review* describes the first-person narrator's "parenthetical asides of commentary but also personal disclosure" as "a curious shadowy presence."[111] Elliot Frank, writing for the *Chicago Review of Books*, opens by noting Mendelsund's interest in puppet shows and uses this analogy to describe how the narrator starts out "silently pulling the strings of the narrative," but eventually becomes "so participatory as to interrupt the delivery boy's quest with his own parenthetical story."[112]

A "shadowy presence," a semivisible "puppeteer," an "annoying passenger"—who *is* this additional narrator and what is he doing in the novel? As a reader, I share these reviewers' sense that the metafictional device disrupts *The Delivery*'s formal coherence. But what if this intruding narrator isn't a formal flaw, but instead a way to register both the author's and readers' shared status as "annoying passengers"? After all, nearly half of all US adults have been driven somewhere by a rideshare worker, while more than 70 percent have received a delivery from a grocery or food delivery app. Most of us, in other words, participate in the "servant economy" as masters. In this context, we should understand Mendelsund's intruding narrator as the formal correlative of our collective complicity in circulation gigwork—a way of registering in the novel's narrative structure the problem of being at once critical of and complicit in the exploitation of circulation gigworkers.

The experience of discomfiting complicity in the exploitation of others is not new to circulation gigwork, of course. Bruce Robbins, among others, has described what it feels like to realize "that one is the beneficiary of an unimaginably vast and complex social whole" in which we depend on the exploited labor of workers at great distance from us.[113] Robbins emphasizes the sublime scale of global production, whose vastness makes us feel both cognitively overwhelmed and politically powerless. Yet circulation gigwork provokes a somewhat different kind of discomfort. The complicity we experience when we put on the shirt with the "Made in Thailand" label (to use Robbins's example) is different from the feeling of stepping into a rideshare driver's car or receiving hand to hand the groceries or the dinner they are delivering to us. The idea of being a distant "beneficiary" does not adequately describe this experience because we are directly and immediately implicated in the exploitation of the circulation gigworker. As I have suggested, both the legal framework and the labor model of circulation gigwork shift managerial control over workers to cameras and sensors and GPS systems and algorithms, but they also conscript the customer herself into this role. Whether she likes it or not, the customer is the gigworker's manager, boss, and "puppeteer": commanding their labor, rating their performance, and paying most of their wage via tips.

The feeling of discomfort that results from this kind of complicity, *The Delivery Boy* suggests, is not the overwhelming experience of vastness and distance, but rather the discomforting awareness of intimacy and proximity. The intruding narrator feels a deep kinship with the delivery boy, but he also knows that he controls both the delivery boy's movements and his story. In the first half of the novel, the narrator highlights his own privilege relative to the delivery boy, acknowledging that his education, language skills, and cultural capital make them fundamentally different. Yet by the end of the novel, as in the passage above about "amputee language," the narrator tends to disavow those distinctions and instead to draw analogies between their shared experiences as migrants. Mendelsund thus seems anxious to reframe the intimate control involved in circulation gigwork by imagining it as an opportunity for connection.

I don't mean this as a critique of Mendelsund's novel or of the more general effort by nongigworkers or ex-gigworkers to write about gigwork (including me), or even of the millions of people who occasionally employ circulation gigworkers (including me). Nor do I interpret the scene in *Your Driver Is Waiting* when Damani observes that the anti-gigwork protestors themselves use RideShare as a "gotcha" moment. Instead, I would argue that both novels are reckoning with the contradictory nature of complicity in the context of circulation gigwork. As Anastasia Eccles notes in a beautiful essay about complicity as a political feeling, complicity is often understood as an effort to "shed or disavow" our fundamental "condition of being-together." Anxiety about complicity as an intolerable degree of connection or mutuality is thus related both to the liberal-individualist ideal of "independence" enshrined in labor law and to the ideology of entrepreneurial self-reliance that occults real precarity and domination in circulation gigwork.[114] But what if, Eccles wonders, we imagined complicity not as a way to ensure our own "distance or independence," but rather as a sign of our abiding condition of "unfulfilled involvement and obligation"? Complicity in this sense, she suggests, would make totality perceptible by offering "a view of a world not from above or outside, but from within."[115]

This view from within is the understanding of complicity we find in Leilani, Guns, and Mendelsund's novels. Given an economy in which 80 percent of all waged workers labor in the service sector, they suggest, complicity is neither a moral failure nor an embarrassing dependency, but rather evidence of our collective interdependence. As Clover notes, "consumer and worker are not two opposed, much less successive, classes," but rather "two momentary roles within the collective activity required to reproduce a single class: the emergent modern proletariat, who must make their way within the wage-commodity nexus."[116] What appears as complicity might thus actually be solidarity, a solidarity that is even more urgent when most of us are both beneficiaries *and* providers of the labor of social provisioning—when the bicycle deliverer tips the barista or the nurse gets home from work by calling a car that might in turn be driven by a teacher working her second shift. Instead of the omniscient view from above of Robbins's "sweatshop sublime"—or the "cognitive maps" that, for Fredric Jameson, attempt to represent otherwise "abstract conceptions of the geographic totality"[117]—these novels instead explore the political as well as narrative possibilities of immediacy and intimacy: the temporary, but vital, forms of obligation created when class is formed not at the point of production, but at the site of consumption. In this way they recall E. P. Thompson's idea of a moral economy, that is, the "popular consensus" as to "social norms and obligations" that reflects a "definite, and passionately held, notion of the common weal." For Thompson, such popular resentment could also become radical when the sense of reciprocity necessary for truly collective action emerges and a mass or mob of people recognizes "an outrage to [shared] moral assumptions." In these struggles, workers are bound together not by some common identity or even position within capital accumulation, but instead by their shared dispossession. The tactics of such struggle thus address not the workplace, but the marketplace: the places where workers eat and drink, the way they get to work or get their groceries—the places, that is, of circulation gigwork.[118]

GIGWORKER INQUIRIES AND THE POLITICS OF POSTPRODUCTIVITY LABOR

I have suggested that contemporary fiction about circulation gigwork explores the tension between freedom and control through narratives of spatial movement. This archive reimagines the everyday intimacy of circulation gigwork as the basis for a radical politics centered on reproduction and relation, instead of production and regulation. But novels aren't the only places where we find the language of movement and the problem of reproduction being applied to the conditions of circulation gigwork. We also find it in recent "workers inquiries" written by circulation gigworkers themselves.

The term "workers' inquiry" refers to the production of knowledge about work, class, and exploitation by workers themselves. Some workers' inquiries are inquiries "from above": in his "Working Day" chapter, for instance, Marx uses a range of sources, including direct accounts of workers, to peer into the "hidden abode of production." More commonly, however, workers' inquiries come "from below": they are written by workers themselves, often as part of a collaborative or collective process. Contemporary gigworker inquiries, I will contend, use the genre to articulate both the individual experience of contemporary circulation gigwork *and* its relation to larger totalities and longer histories. Like the novels described in the previous section, contemporary gigworker inquiries keep open the utopian possibilities represented by circulation gigwork's fleeting freedoms while also demonstrating that control over time and space functions a key technique of subordination and superexploitation. They also, I will suggest, begin to theorize the forms of solidarity and militancy that might emerge from the contemporary service sector, especially in an age wherein a productivist demand for "fair wages" has proven inadequate.

Before I turn to contemporary gigworkers' inquiries, it's worth understanding the history of the workers' inquiry more broadly, and especially how it has changed to reflect transformations in the mode of production as well as in class composition. The term originates with Marx, who used it to describe a questionnaire he wrote in 1880 for *La Revue socialiste* in hopes of generating a detailed statistical record of the situation of the working class in France.[119] Marx's "workers' inquiry" didn't get enough responses from the French workers to be practically useful, however, and the project of the workers' inquiry languished until the 1940s, when it was rediscovered and reinvented by the breakaway post-Trotskyist group the Johnson-Forest Tendency (JFT).[120] Named for founders C. L. R James, who wrote under the pseudonym

J.R. Johnson, and Raya Dunayevskaya, who wrote under the name Freddie Forest, the JFT was responsible for two crucial contributions to the genre: *The American Worker*, published in 1947 and cowritten by autoworker Phil Singer and philosopher Grace Lee Boggs, and *The American Revolution: Pages from a Negro Workers Notebook*, published in 1963 and written by autoworker and theorist James Boggs. Whereas Marx's inquiry had involved an empirical survey to be given to workers, the JFT's inquiries were more worker directed and more narrative: as Asad Haider and Salar Mohandesi suggest, the JFT's inquiries "allowed workers to raise their own unique voice, express themselves in their own language."[121] In the early 1950s, the French radical collective Socialisme ou Barbarie translated some of the JFT's inquiries into French, and later in the decade, a group of Italian radicals describing themselves as "workerist" (*operaisti*) translated the JFT texts into Italian and used them as a models for their own inquiries. In this way, the JFT would establish the enduring features of the genre: most twentieth-century and twenty-first-century workers' inquiries involve a detailed description of a particular labor process written by a worker (sometimes in collaboration with a "theorist"). While most inquiries focus on an individual worker's subjective experience of their labor, they also attempt to generalize across other workers' experiences in the same job or sector.

Between the 1960s and the twenty-first century, the project of the workers' inquiry was once again forgotten.[122] Yet in the aftermath of the 2008 financial crisis and with the rise of gigwork and logistics labor, interest in the workers' inquiry as an empirical, theoretical, and organizing genre surged once again. Multiple scholar-organizers have used workers' inquiries to produce thick descriptions of contemporary work, for instance, Jamie Woodcock's 2016 *Working the Phones*, about call center work, and Kruskaya Hidalgo Cordero's 2022 *Domestic Code in the Flesh*, about migrant domestic and care workers. Marcelo Hoffman's 2019 *Militant Acts* offered the first book-length scholarly history of the genre.[123] *Viewpoint Magazine*, *ephemera*, and *Notes From Below* have published issues devoted to collections of contemporary workers' inquiries, and the 2020 edited collections *Workers Inquiry and Global Class Struggle* and *Struggle in a Pandemic* compiled a range of inquiries, including some from outside the United States and Europe.[124] Workers' inquiries are also being used by service workers in a range of organizing contexts. Labor groups such as Amazonians United are currently using workers' inquiries for power mapping.[125] Other collectives are drawing on the affordances of creative genres.[126] Workers participating in the Workers Writers School, for example, have produced inquiries using poetic forms such as haiku, as in the collection *Coronavirus Haikus*.[127] The Workers Speculative Society (WSS) project has turned to nonrealist narrative modes for its inquiries, guiding rank-and-file Amazon workers to use sci-fi plots to think about the "special insights and intuitions of how to resist and rebel" that might be "encoded in their very bodies" and to imagine narratively "The World After Amazon."[128]

Whereas the workers' inquiry was once intimately linked to industrial labor, contemporary workers' inquiries are primarily focused on service work: the examples above feature jobs such as domestic work, warehouse work, microwork, freelance journalism, adjunct teaching, bartending, hospitality work, call-center work, taxi driving, and delivery.[129] Drawing on the importance of informalized service work to the project of the contemporary workers' inquiry and vice versa, I focus specifically on inquiries written by circulation gigworkers: the bike courier inquiries "Notes from the Road" and "Cycling in the City"; "Far from Seamless," about working for Deliveroo; and *Class Power on Zero Hours*, about grocery delivery.

Like fictional representations of gigwork, gigworker inquiries often play with the association between circulation work and narratives of mobility. Alex Marshall's inquiry "Notes from the Road," for instance, opens by evoking both the spatial imagery of the road narrative and the temporal horizons of endless work: "Eight years on the road. Eight winters endured. One Beast from the East. One record breaking hottest day. And this year: one global pandemic. Throw in the various crashes, bicycle mechanical failures, I am still a courier."[130] The road narrative's emphasis on change and event confronts the exhaustion of labor that can only be "endured," like a winter. Likewise, the immediacy of testimonial address is pressured by the alienating force of the labor process: though Marshall's inquiry is written in the first person, it lacks a syntactic subject until the very end of the sixth sentence, where the "I" is finally attached to the occupation and to the temporality of weathering hard work ("I am *still* a courier").

"Notes from the Road" focuses on how workers endure the unpredictable hazards involved in road work. By contrast, "Far from Seamless" (a workers' inquiry cowritten by a Deliveroo bike deliverer under the pseudonym Facility Waters and scholar/labor organizer Jamie Woodcock) emphasizes the difficulty of enduring the routine of delivery work. Like Leilani's novelistic account of circulation gigwork, routinization in this text appears not only in the experience of grinding repetition, but also in the ultimately circular movement of the delivery worker, who continuously cycles back and forth across the same terrain:

> [I] see where I actually need to go, and it is straight uphill. Six minutes later I get to the customer's address, walk up their steps, and wait at the door. I give them their food and swipe through to see the next address: straight over the hill, down to a gated apartment building in Dulwich, and hand over the food to the next customer 5 minutes after the last.... [Then] the app tells me to make my way back to the zone center and wait to repeat the process.... It is easy to memorize your route, and drift off into a daydream, only awaken as you get to the house though sometimes after the door has shut and the customer has taken their food, and often hours will pass and the daydream will go outside of the cognitive threshold of the repetitive, rhythmic movements towards the next point in a journey without any coherent direction other than its next point.[131]

The numbingly syncopated parataxis ("I see"/"I go"/"I get"/"I wait"/ "I give"/"I swipe"/"I hand"/"I go") registers the intense Taylorization of circulation gigwork. The impersonal but absolute subordination of algorithmic management, in turn, appears as a kind of corporate personhood: "Deliveroo knows exactly when and where I am at all times.... This means that when discipline is applied... it is operating along vectors of authority." Even though Deliveroo is personified here, however, the company's ability to discipline the gigworker is described in the passive voice ("discipline is applied"), as if registering at the level of syntax the company's claim that it does not control its workers.

Whereas "Far from Seamless" represents movement in circulation gigwork as nothing more than routinized, circular repetition, *Class Power on Zero Hours* acknowledges both the thrill and the danger of delivery driving.[132] Consider a passage that could easily come from *Your Driver Is Waiting:*

> Driving is a strange form of mental and physical exhaustion.... You manoeuvre a four-ton heavy metal bullet at life-threatening speed through tight spaces, surrounded by, but insulated from, other drivers of bullets [as well as] flesh-and-bone pedestrians.... You feel like crying or killing.... The combination of having loads of (horse) power, but being static in traffic jams causes frustration. Then the clock's ticking in the background, you're running late for the next delivery.... But then let's be honest, driving can be the most wicked thing ever. On a good day, bass booming, freedom breezes through the window, you glide along and watch the scenery.... I laugh about my street-sweeping ex-workmates as I roll past them and make them eat dust. You feel young and you get paid for it....
>
> But then it fucks you up. Toxic masculinity and toxic air ain't a good combination.[133]

The passage vividly describes the intensity of time discipline in a job where you aren't compensated for time spent waiting, but it also acknowledges the freedom of delivery work, the excitement of fast movement through space. The contrast between "(horse) power" and "being static" recapitulates the themes of freedom and control discussed above, as does the turn on the metaphor of "toxicity," here both the lived condition of road labor and the affective state required of those forced to drive all day. Indeed, the inquiry's language play reminds us that the term "metaphor" comes from Greek word *metapherein*, meaning to carry or transport, as *Zero Hours* evokes what Harris Feinsod terms "the mobility of vehicular language."[134]

As befits the genre of the workers' inquiry, *Zero Hours* also does not distinguish between the experience of work and the experience of *writing* about work: writing here is not abstract contemplation, but rather something embodied, social, and immediate. Working as a delivery driver, *Zero Hours* notes, means "You sometimes have breathing space, you can call friends, you can read and write (for example this sentence here)."[135] Because the inquiry itself was written while working, *Zero Hours* is at once *about* labor and a product *of* it. Circulation gigwork doesn't just give workers the time and opportunity to write; it also provides a unique vantage point for narrative. As in the circulation gigwork novel, in the gigworkers' inquiry, delivery workers have access to an imaginative vision inaccessible to other people. "If you think Tracey Emin's bed is art," *Zero Hours* notes, being a delivery driver allows "a permanent exhibition trip into people's private sphere." The inquiry goes on to describe customer interactions in language that recalls the passages from Leilani's *Luster* evoking the poetics of commerce:

> There was the guy on the White City estate who loaded the 99 iceberg salads and dozens of courgettes straight into his market van.... There is an old man in an estate in Acton who only orders vodka and soup, the flat is filled knee-deep with rubbish, much of it Tesco receipts.... The old man in nappies sits in front of a fan, you have to put the chilled and frozen in the fridge for him.... The Black Island Studios in Acton, they order the cheapest no name products to fill a supermarket scene, the carpenters are still working on it. A Hasidic teenage girl in Golders Green with too much lipstick practices flirting, using an American accent. Kids come running excitedly: "The Tesco-Man, the Tesco-Man!!!"[136]

The reference to conceptual artist Tracey Emin, known for her projects of self-exposure, emphasizes the peek into private space that has long been central to the imaginary of in-person service work. Yet the passage also expands its view outward, into what Marx called the "noisy sphere of circulation," as the delivery driver is afforded a privileged view of the idioms and object worlds that constitute a diverse and teeming social life.

Although the travel narrative's association with mobility and independence appears across these gigworkers' inquiries, the inquiries also insist that gigwork is "free" only by comparison to even worse jobs. Marshall's inquiry, for instance, describes the pleasure of knowing "there are not many rules you have to abide by," yet these seem quite modest forms of freedom: the freedom to find new places to eat lunch or new places to hide out from bad weather. As in Leilani's novel, the pleasure of independence appears exclusively in contrast to office work, where offices are "the epitome of rules and regulations," while couriers can "skip in and out of places where people are . . . bound to desks."[137] In Alice Barker's "Cycling in the City," the "freedom" of circulation gigwork is likewise evident only in contrast to the constraints of in-person service: "it wasn't just another minimum wage bar job" where "you're micromanaged by senior staff," she writes.[138] Many gigworker inquiries similarly evoke a kind of trade-off logic in describing circulation gigwork—less mental alienation, but also less safety; more flexibility, but also more precarity—in a way that refuses to privilege formalized labor. "Far from Seamless," for instance, notes that in gigwork, there is an "illusion of freedom" that comes from the absence of managerial surveillance and "the supervisory gaze" and asserts that "being able to legitimately refuse work is a cause worth fighting for." As in Leilani's and Guns's novels, the critique of circulation gigwork here is not reducible to a demand for more formalized, regimented working conditions, but rather articulates a desire for autonomy across classifications.[139]

Circulation gigworkers' inquiries also tend to explicitly evoke the potential revolutionary power of the postindustrial proletariat. "Far from Seamless" and *Zero Hours* both reject the idea that gigwork is "the highest point of alienation" ("Far From Seamless") or that contemporary postindustrial workers are merely "robots, slaves, the destitute and victims" (*Zero Hours*).[140] All these inquiries acknowledge the challenges to cross-sectoral organization, especially the obstacles produced by outsourcing and informalization. Barker, for instance, considers the exploitation of workers in other parts of the gigworker's labor process, such as the outsourced HR workers who have "a script they must stick to."[141] *Zero Hours* likewise notes the difficulty of organizing between "zero hours" point-of-sale deliverers and logistics workers, who are separated not only spatially but also by the processes of informalization and outsourcing.[142] Yet they also emphasize the political opportunity afforded by the connections that circulation gigworkers create with other workers on the supply chain. Thus, "Far from Seamless" suggests that the spatiality of circulation gigwork might also be reframed as a cartography of solidarity, a map of connections between the workers in restaurants and the gigworkers who deliver the food they make, between the informally employed and the unemployed, and even between gigworkers and their customers: "we produce a topographical layer, where we converge intermittently . . . where we can nod or wave as we pass, or chat during waiting periods," producing a "social field" or "a densely acquired network of familiarity." *Zero Hours* likewise imagines the familiarity and solidarity produced by workers whose labor mediates between production and (working-class) consumption: "[W]e met some truck drivers from Punjab through the solidarity network. . . . We helped them and, in return, they supported us in our organising drive. . . . They could talk to workers in Punjabi and increased the level of trust between us and workers there."[143] In this context, then, the genre becomes a way of thinking about solidarity both analytically and strategically. The gigworkers' inquiry reframes circulation gigwork's network of connections—its transversal relations of interdependence and mutual obligation—as the site of potential political intervention.

Read in this way, the gigwork inquiry reveals the relationship between logistics and what Jasper Bernes has influentially termed a “counterlogistics”: “a logistics against logistics, a counterlogistics which employs the conceptual and technical equipment of the industry,” but puts it to revolutionary ends.[144] In Bernes’s account, that “conceptual equipment” requires a view from above quite similar to Robbins’s “sweatshop sublime,” from whose vantage we suddenly can see the scale and horror of a “world economic system of notoriously inconceivable magnitude and interdependence.”[145] As scholars such as Charmaine Chua, Stefan Yong, and Kyle Stine have argued, the spatially expanding and just-in-time economy of supply-chain capitalism indeed produces images of the networked whole as “both a technical and aesthetic effect,” a “logistical sublime” whose “fearsome, monstrous smoothness” captures the “overwhelming scale and multilayered complexity” required to extend the world market by making the passage of goods across it as fast as data itself.[146] Counterlogistics, Bernes notes, seizes on the logistical sublime’s capacity to see the interconnected totality of the capitalist world system “in order to identify and exploit bottlenecks, to give our blockaders a sense of where they stand within the flows of capital.”[147] In mapping the networks of exploitation that both connect and separate bike couriers from outsourced call-center workers and migrant truck drivers, these inquiries produce an omniscient “gigworkers-eye view,” using the conceptual and technical equipment of the industry against itself to imagine opportunities for solidarity and insurrection.

But the alternative forms of connection mapped in these inquiries also suggest a form of tactical, political, and even affective connection that is nearer and more intimate. Such connections don’t just illuminate the discomfort of being a consumer in the same gig economy that exploits you. Nor do they result exclusively from the “inconceivable” and “overwhelming” scale of the supply chain as a whole. Instead, as in the novels described in the previous section, gigworkers’ inquiries focus on the powerful forms of mutuality and solidarity that might be animated precisely because the networks linking the restaurant worker and the delivery driver and the customer are smaller, more intimate, and more various than the "logistical sublime." In a matter-of-fact sociological mood notably different from *The Delivery*'s handwringing about the differences and similarities between exploited gigworkers and those they serve, *Zero Hours* notes, "You see how their diets differ and you notice that some people's kitchens are bigger than other people's whole flat. In some houses you are greeted... by malnourished cats and their run-down owner."[148] Most important, of course, are the cross-network relations between workers, yet here, too, the language is often about intimate connection, instead of a shared attachment to a political identity such as "working class." In his workers inquiry from food delivery app Deliveroo, for instance, Callum Cant describes circulation gigwork's "highly heterogenous workforce" as the site of radical proletarian community not reducible to producerist fantasies of a shared hegemonic "culture": "Deliveroo's workforce was a varied mass of deskilled labour, not a community of subcultural workers with 'courier' identities. Instead, more common points of connection were music and religion."[149]

The gigworker of the gigworkers' inquiry recalls an earlier class of informalized laborers held together by transversal spatial alliance: the "motley crew" of eighteenth-century and nineteenth-century maritime labor. "Without genealogical unity," Peter Linebaugh and Marcus Rediker note, maritime laborers "spoke [their] own speech... slang, cant, jargon, and pidgin." This class "was *planetary*, in its origins, its motions, and its consciousness. It was "*self-active, creative*; it was—and is—alive; it is onamove."[150] For Linebaugh and Rediker, the scale and consciousness of the planetary can coexist with the scale and consciousness of the street and the dock and the ship, with workers living "onamove," as mobile as the commodities they deliver. Likewise, precisely by offering a view from the ground, from the driver's seat, from the person knocking on the door, the gigworkers' inquiry, a genre of both theory and strategy, moves between the workplace struggle for freedom and the marketplace struggle for subsistence. Marx's survey of manufacturing workers sought to reveal the relationship between the factory floor and the tenement, between time spent working and time spent restoring the body to work again, between wages and the cost of food or housing. By contrast, contemporary gigworkers' inquiries describe labor that already bears a direct and intimate relation to the reproduction of everyday life. In this sense, the genre of the workers' inquiry—which illuminates and activates connections between immediate experience and broader social relations—is the formal correlative of a type of labor that likewise blurs distinctions between production and reproduction, worksite and marketplace, connecting labor to reproduction, work to consumption, proletarian driver to proletarian passenger.

Of course there is another difference between the factory labor represented in workers' inquiries from the late nineteenth through the mid-twentieth century and the service work represented in contemporary gigworkers' inquiries: its productivity. As this book has suggested throughout, there are intractable limits to how much service-sector productivity can be improved by technology. Manufacturing technologies from the automated loom to the assembly line quickly increased output thousandsfold. These same technologies made it possible for manufacturing labor to be regulated and paid hourly wages and even allowed some political compromises between capital and labor when it came to sharing the value of those increases in productivity. In the previous chapter, I described how current innovations in generative AI are allowing "so-so automation" in formerly stagnant sectors, particularly semiskilled or fully deskilled work in language, data, and information processing and higher-waged work such as human resources and teaching. Yet because these technologies increase productivity only marginally, they are not capable of driving significant or sustained economic growth of the kind that shaped the industrial period from the 1930s to the 1960s. Instead of leading to greater regulation, these techniques rely on informalization and outsourcing; instead of reinstating new, higher-waged labor elsewhere, they simply displace workers into even lower-waged work; instead of increasing labor's share of output, they enable gains so modest that they are fully absorbed by capital. Whether it is shaped by so-so automation or by technologies of intensification, across service work we thus find declining real wages and stagnant output. Indeed, the growth of deskilled, low-waged personal services as a portion of the occupational field means that today's labor market often resembles what Jason Smith describes as a "servant economy."[151] Or as *Zero Hours* puts it, gigworkers actually "have one of the oldest professions in human class history: being a water carrier (often literally) for the better off."[152]

Put simply, then, the era of rising productivity that produced not only the US industrial boom of the mid-century, but also the forms of labor regulation specific to manufacturing work—from industrial unions to hourly minimum wages—is over. In its wake, the connection between labor output and wages has likewise vanished. The infrastructure of regulated, formalized, collectively bargained hourly wages adequate to rising costs of subsistence depended on the boss's ability not only to quantify and measure workers' output objectively, but also to increase it meaningfully and consistently. So what becomes of that infrastructure in a sector, indeed an age, of low productivity?

One answer to that question can be found in one of the maps described in "Far from Seamless." The inquiry explains that the map, which shows the worker's delivery zone for a day, doesn't account for his commute into the zone territory itself: "like many people in cities, where I can afford to live, is not where I was working." It shows up, too, in the inquiries by care workers collected in *Domestic Code in the Flesh*, which tie the rising cost of living to low wages:

> It is not a fair price, and with inflation, it is getting worse.... Everything is very expensive and the cost of living is absurd. [The wage is] sometimes not even enough to buy the food for the day.... Many of us work with an empty stomach, many do not eat.... Many workers... work with a bag of salt in their wallets so that their blood pressure doesn't drop or because they don't have time to stop.[153]

Here we can begin to understand what declining "real wages"—or even superexploitation wages—mean in practice: workers unable even to ensure their own reproduction by paying for housing, food, child care, elder care, education, and other basic goods. We might borrow the idea of "metabolic rift" from Marxist ecological thought to theorize and politicize the crisis that results from these conditions. For eco-Marxists such as John Bellamy Foster, "metabolic rift" describes "how large-scale industry and large-scale agriculture combined to impoverish the soil and the worker," producing a "rift" in the "social metabolism" whereby the soil was sapped of the minerals and the laborer separated from nature and thus from subsistence.[154] Marx's "Working Day" chapter compares the "limitless draining away of labor-power" and the extension of the working day to the "exhaust[ion] of the soil" that necessitated colonial incursions into Peru and the Caribbean to obtain guano for fertilizer. Service workers today, I would posit, experience a kind of "*reproductive* rift" insofar as they are deprived of the very sustenance and social care they labor to provide for others. In that rift's gaping chasm we find domestic workers who can't afford their own housing; child-care workers who can't pay for child care; delivery gig-workers who can't afford groceries.

What might proletarian organizing might look like in a postproductivity world—a world in which wages can no longer rise alongside output? What would it mean for worker demands to center not on the productivist ideal that workers should receive their "just share" of output, but rather on the shared condition of reproductive rift? To begin to answer that question, I want to conclude by looking briefly to one last set of inquiries. Here I focus not on workers' inquiries, but rather on "tenant inquiries." Addressing the problem not of work itself, but working-class housing, the tenant inquiry, like service-worker organizing itself, is necessarily detached from the productivism of manufacturing labor and its regulation. Yet like the workers' inquiry, tenants' inquiries are committed to limning the intimate relationship between work and survival, between production and reproduction.[155] Tenants' inquiries thus define proletarian life not in terms of exploitation by capital, but as the contingency of reproduction and as separation from the means of subsistence—the poverty and precarity of what Michael Denning terms "wageless life."[156]

Here, I focus on the tenants' inquiry *Cuadra a Cuadra: A Un Mundo Sin Rent / Block By Block: For a World Without Rent*, produced by tenants-led housing justice organization Los Angeles Tenants Union (LATU). LATU explains that their tenants' inquiries "reflect on and analyze our collective experiences to inform . . . strategy and tactics" and to "critically engage and learn from contradictions."[157] LATU began with one-on-one interviews and then moved to a process unique to the community-organizing model of tenant organizing, namely, discussion circles and collective dialogue. As an example, they describe asking the question "What's an example where a landlord was vulnerable that your Local identified and used in a struggle over the last year?" At first, LATU explains, "Many responded that the landlords have no vulnerabilities. Yet as the discussions unfolded, members talked about how our collective tactics, such as protesting at landlords' homes and organizing tenant associations, exploit certain weaknesses of landlords. These discussions reminded us that landlords do have vulnerabilities and that our unity is their weakness."[158] LATU coresearchers then held listening sessions where they played short excerpts from those sessions, naming themes and contradictions. They ultimately accumulated "a small archive of 'sound objects' (clips of one to two minutes in length)" that allowed the process of listening to the inquiries to be as collective as the process of producing them.[159]

Using the genre of the workers' inquiry but repurposing it for renters, LATU both clarifies and politicizes the gap between wages and subsistence costs. Describing LATU's work doing food distribution during the pandemic, for instance, *Cuadra a Cuadra* says, "Tenants would ask what they should do about rent since most people lost their jobs. [Politicians] told people to prioritize paying rent. . . . [W]e told people to prioritize food, not rent. We told them we would stand with them . . . against the landlords."[160] Here, the idea of what a "union" means is both expanded and radicalized, used to articulate communal demands for housing justice and security. Workers' struggles are imagined not just as struggles over the wage, but as defenses of social welfare and as efforts to reorganize or reappropriate the means of social reproduction. Extraeconomic violence and immiseration are shown to function in tandem with economic compulsion. Such struggles can then broaden what "worker" means to include the informally waged, gigworkers and part-timers, people with disabilities, illegalized migrants and criminalized subjects, the unemployed, and unwaged care workers.

This kind of political reframing is happening not only in "tenants unions" such as LATU, but also in more traditional worker unions: from hotel workers with UNITE-HERE to fast-food workers engaged in the "Fight for Fifteen," more and more union campaigns are linking traditional wage demands not to the idea of compensation equivalent to productivity—the productivist demand for the "full fruits of one's labor"—but instead to the need for wages adequate to rising subsistence costs, especially in the context of a national housing bubble and high inflation.[161] Such radical platforms, sometimes not centered on wages at all, are becoming ever more common among the radical rank and file of service-worker unions: demands for access to good housing, child care, and education; for the rights of workers with disabilities or chronic illnesses; for the rights of queer and trans workers to gender-neutral bathrooms or gender-affirming health care; for police abolition or justice for noncitizen workers.[162] Graduate student workers at the University of California and University of Michigan systems, for instance, have fought for compensation to be tied directly to the cost of living, for rent subsidies, to get cops off campus, and for disability access. In 2024, UC grad workers went on strike demanding divestment of the university from genocide in Palestine, the first explicitly "political strike" of a major union in the United States since the Taft-Hartley Act of 1947. Teachers' unions have demanded justice for the families of the students they teach, including sanctuary schools and anticarceral restorative justice. In 2024, the Chicago Teachers Union's bargaining included a demand to end student homelessness by creating ten thousand new affordable housing units prioritizing Chicago public school households.[163] Amazon warehouse workers in Chicago demanded child-care accommodations for Black and Brown single parents forced to work "megacycles" during the pandemic; in California, they called for transport solutions for workers commuting across the border from Tijuana; in Minnesota, they fought for housing for Somali immigrant women workers priced out of superinflated real estate.[164] Amazon warehouse workers and tech workers have come together to call for decarbonization and climate justice.[165] Starbucks workers organized with Workers United have called for solidarity with the victims of genocide and displacement in Palestine, while the International Alliance of App-Based Transportation workers is demanding that transportation employers be carbon neutral.[166] Perhaps most promisingly, SEIU-1199NE—a historically radical health-care workers union representing nurses, home health-care workers, and others—has joined forces with the Connecticut Tenant's Union to create a dual campaign around collectively bargained leases for SEIU members, describing this as a "twenty-first century, integrated movement for working-class rights" that includes "the ability to have shelter fit for human beings to live in."[167]

These examples are both small scale and scarce, of course. Some unions have cynically used these kinds of demands to galvanize the rank and file only to abandon the demand later as "unbargainable," which suggests the extent to which much labor organizing remains bound to the ideologies and economies of a long-gone industrial age. Yet service workers are increasingly forging new imaginaries around the wage and what it does (and doesn't) afford in an era in which wages are more than ever delinked from productivity. Much as gigworkers are taking seriously the desire for independence and autonomy, instead of simply calling for an extension of traditional state regulation and greater levels of managerial control, organizations such as LATU, the rank-and-file militants of traditional unions, and communities of historically marginalized and criminalized service workers such as the Sex Workers Organizing Project and the Haymarket Pole Collective are organizing not by demanding productivist "fair wages" or even reproductivist "living wages," but instead around larger and more revolutionary demands for equality, autonomy, community, and freedom.

It is hard to critique precariously waged and informalized work without seeming to imply that waged, regulated, and formalized work *does* ensure workers' livelihoods and security. It can even be difficult to remember that wage regulations have long failed to protect *most* workers, let alone all of them. This book has tried to describe the history of racialized and gendered exclusion without seeming to imply that the solution is simply to expand existing regulations or to provide hourly wages or employee status to all workers. In that context, it is useful to remember that those policies were designed in and for a period of high-productivity industrial growth, an age that is now over and unlikely to return. A popular consensus among low-waged service workers—a popular consensus that might also show up in popular culture—will thus have to leave dystopian demands for inflexible hours, managed subordination, and "minimum" wages entirely behind. Only in this way can we demand the richer maximums afforded by life not beneath, but rather beyond the wage.

CODA

Ed Tech and the Labor of Teaching

This book has sought to define contemporary service work through its vulnerability to deskilling, intensification, superexploitation, and informalization. This led me to focus on three kinds of work that I have argued are emblematic of current service-labor conditions: in-person tipwork, clerical microwork, and circulation gigwork. Such a focus has of necessity left out many other kinds of low-waged service work that are critically important both to the contemporary economy and to contemporary labor politics. These include fast-food workers and other hourly food-service workers; janitors, cleaners, and maintenance workers; warehouse workers and other formalized logistics workers; and grocery and retail workers. I have not discussed semiprofessionalized service jobs such as nursing and home health-care, jobs that Gabriel Winant has identified as "labor-intensive, low-productivity, low-wage" work typical of the postindustrial service economy.[1] And I have not yet touched on teaching, despite the fact that K-to-12 teaching is no longer a predictably stable, professionalized, middle-class job, but has been, as Eric Blanc notes, "steadily subjected to job intensification and deskilling."[2]

One book cannot possibly address all these forms of work, unfortunately. However because I am a teacher myself, I *can* testify firsthand to the ways that teaching labor has increasingly been opened to deskilling, intensification, superexploitation, and informalization. In the spirit of Chapter 3's interest in the workers' inquiry—a genre of writing and knowledge production through which workers themselves explore their own labor process and working conditions—I want to use this coda to produce a workers' inquiry about my own service work. More specifically, I want to unpack the relationship between teaching and technology in the contemporary university.[3] Historically, teaching has been relatively untouched by labor-saving and labor-replacing technology. Today, however, contemporary higher-ed labor is undergoing a series of changes that strongly bind it to the forms of superexploited service work I have explored in the previous chapters. The aim of this workers' inquiry is not simply to argue that labor-saving technology in higher ed threatens to degrade teachers' labor and students' education. It is also to make the case for a common struggle among tenure-track instructors, informalized and graduate student instructors, undergraduate students, and the communities from which our students come and in which they live.

Teaching has long been considered immune to full automation and even to major improvements in productivity. Jason Smith helpfully describes the problem of tech in teaching:

> Teachers... are no more productive today than they were one hundred years ago, since the labor process they perform resists technological innovation of the sort implemented in, say, an iPhone factory.... Teachers are service providers who operate, by contemporary capitalist standards, with a great deal of autonomy in the workplace. The unity of the labor process in their case remains relatively intact, immune as it is from the highly differentiated detail division of labor characteristic of capital-intensive industries.... The teacher creates a product—instruction—that requires a relatively low and historically stable teacher-to-student ratio.... The actual labor process required in the delivery of education services has changed very little over decades, or even longer, whatever enthusiasm administrators might have for introducing new technologies in the classroom.[4]

As Smith notes, teaching has historically been protected from rationalization, outsourcing, and automation. It cannot be subjected to significant time-saving innovations, cannot be moved overseas or transformed via economies of scale, is relatively autonomous, and continues to require skill and expertise. Although Smith is describing contemporary teaching, he builds on the influential work of mid-century macroeconomist William Baumol. In a canonical essay, "On the Performing Arts: An Anatomy of Their Economic Problems," Baumol and his coauthor, William Bowen, concluded that musicians are paid poverty wages because "the live performing arts" are unable to implement transformative "technological economies."[5] A follow-up essay in 1967 extended this analysis by dividing all economic activities into two types: "technologically progressive activities," where technological innovations and economies of scale allowed "output per man hour" to increase progressively, and "nonprogressive" activities, "which by their very nature, permit only sporadic increases in productivity."[6] In the later essay, Baumol's central example of a "nonprogressive" activity isn't violin playing, but teaching. Teaching is fundamentally resistant to "economies of large-scale operation," he argues, and it is relatively untouched by technology. Besides "closed circuit television and a variety of other innovations," he notes, there is as yet no fully automated "teaching machine."[7]

For more than half a century, Baumol's theory of technological stagnation has been used by orthodox economists and policy experts to explain the rising costs of higher education and health care.[8] Yet using my own experience in the postpandemic university as evidence, I will suggest that the meteoric rise of ed tech in general and online education (OLE) has upended the Baumolian account on which Smith draws. OLE, I argue, is making possible a massive and hyperaccelerated shift in academic labor, belying Baumol's certainty that teaching labor cannot be rationalized, deskilled, or automated. Or, better put, contemporary OLE belies Baumol's optimism that rationalization, deskilling, and automation could not possibly happen in higher ed because no one would accept the inevitable degradation in quality.

Studies of ed tech "innovation" often begin with the massive online open-access course (MOOC). In the early 2010s, university presidents and critical university studies scholars all seemed equally sure that these open-access, asynchronous online courses—courses where students access lectures on their own time—portended the future of higher education, whether for better (per the presidents) or for worse (per the scholars). Of course "remote" or "distance" education wasn't invented with the MOOC. For-profit correspondence schools date to the late nineteenth century and have long been used to take advantage of groups underserved by traditional universities, from working parents to incarcerated students. As David Noble explains in his prescient 2001 book *Digital Diploma Mills*, early-twentieth-century correspondence schools relied on a labor model remarkably like the superexploited piece work performed in sweatshops at the dawn of industrialization: "Many firms preferred 'sub-professional' personnel, particularly untrained older women," he notes. These women "were paid on a piece-work basis per lesson or exam (roughly twenty cents per lesson in the 1920s)," and they had to work long hours at lightning speed to earn even close to a living wage.[9] Throughout the twentieth century, distance-learning programs relied on communications technology, from radios and telephones to TVs and VCRs. In 1989, in-home internet connectivity allowed the for-profit University of Phoenix (UOP) to launch the first online college program. At its peak in 2010, UOP enrolled around half a million students in a single year.[10]

The MOOC drew on this history of correspondence school "disruption." Using the new affordances of online video streaming, as well as the ability to automate aspects of assessment via learning management systems (LMSs), the MOOC allowed a single instructor to teach tens of thousands of students all at once and around the globe, tuition free. Excited by this possibility, the *New York Times* rather peremptorily declared 2012 "The Year of the MOOC." Recalling previous "automation crazes," what Richard Grusin aptly describes as "MOOC mania" showed up in both celebrations and critiques of MOOCs.[11] The MOOC was seen as "'solving' the problems of education through computational automation," as Ian Bogost puts it.[12] Yet although hundreds of universities rushed to produce MOOCs between 2011 and 2014, by 2013, the original MOOC innovator himself, former Stanford University professor-cum-ed-tech-entrepreneur Sebastien Thrun, announced he was "pivoting away" from the MOOC idea, in large part because the promise of "access" had run aground on the reality that only around 5 percent of students were actually completing the courses.[13] It seemed as if Baumol had correctly identified at least one barrier to increased productivity in teaching: there were indeed "fairly firm limits to class size."[14]

Of course, other things were happening in higher ed over those years, too, especially its skyrocketing cost. Between 2005 and 2015, average tuition at private universities increased by more than 40 percent, while in-state tuition at public universities increased more than 80 percent.[15] In other words, universities were realizing the truth of yet another Baumolian axiom, namely, that students and their families will continue to pay for higher education even if the price continues to rise. Consistent growth in the demand for higher ed found its supply via expanded access to student loans enabled by financial deregulation and securitization. As a result, universities had little incentive to offer part of their product for free via MOOCs, particularly given that most had justified their rising prices by building fancy dorms and gyms and computer labs for the in-person campus experience.

Universities were also realizing that it was far cheaper and easier simply to hire cheaper, more causalized adjunct instructors than it was to transform the whole model of higher education. The portion of courses taught by adjuncts and other part-time and contingent instructors skyrocketed during the half decade of MOOC mania, and by 2014, part-time and nontenure-track instructors made up 75 percent of the instructional workforce in degree-granting institutions.[16] Like the deprofessionalized women who worked for the early twentieth-century correspondence schools, adjuncts are typically paid neither by work time nor with a full-time guaranteed salary, but per course: as a 2014 congressional report notes, "contingent faculty usually are paid a piece rate, a fixed amount of compensation for each unit produced, regardless of how much time it takes to produce." The median compensation for an adjunct in 2014 was $22,000—barely above the poverty line for a family of three.[17]

In a nutshell, then, during the very same years a lot of critical university scholars (including me) were spilling a lot of ink about the MOOC as a form of automation, what was *actually* happening was a far less "innovative" but also far more successful process of casualization and intensification.[18] In 2015, Thrun himself announced that having abandoned the MOOC, his ed-tech start-up Udacity now wanted to be "Uber for Education," offering "nanodegrees" that provided education in "small portion sizes, on demand and in a mobile app."[19] As the Uber reference suggests, Thrun's new business model was less like innovative tech development and more like the standard-issue deskilling and informalization increasingly common across app-based labor. In a nanodegree program, students pay a few hundred dollars for a course on coding, programming, or app building, and a global network of piece-rate "code reviewers" grades students' work. The ambitious scale and disruptive promise of "massive" online education was thus reduced to the "small portion sizes" of programs relying on outsourcing and casualization, instead of high-tech innovation.

This isn't to say that ed tech in general wasn't booming during these years. It was, and in a way that would ensure that the farce of the MOOC could become the tragedy of OLE. "Decade of the For-Profit LMS" probably sounds less sexy than "Year of the MOOC," but the former would be a more accurate way to describe the innovations of the 2010s. Revisions to federal education policy allowed public schools to outsource more of their technological services to for-profit companies, and universities began to replace the LMSs, admissions management software, online bulletin boards, and email clients they had previously built in-house with for-profit LMSs and other technology and digital services.[20] The billions of dollars that began to flow into the ed-tech sector increased the privatization of public and nonprofit universities.[21]

OLE was also already on the rise in this period. A 2006 change to the Higher Education Act allowed fully online degree programs to receive federal aid, and by 2012, more than half of students at for-profit institutions were taking all of their classes online.[22] In 2018, the Trump administration's Department of Education loosened requirements on online education still further, and by 2019, OLE had become "the fastest growing segment of postsecondary education."[23] Yet OLE was still largely limited to for-profit institutions and portions of the community college system, and proposals to expand OLE in not-for-profit institutions were typically met with skepticism and pushback. As a result, until 2020, the looming problem of higher ed's technological and economic stagnation was being "solved" not with new kinds of technological automation, but instead with more old-fashioned forms of dispossession, from skyrocketing student debt to labor casualization.

And then came the pandemic. The speed of OLE's growth went from fast to breakneck as hundreds of millions of postsecondary students and teachers suddenly shifted their in-person courses online. In 2021–22, more than 60 percent of college students took at least one online course, while 30 percent of college students took all their classes online, more than doubling prepandemic numbers.[24] Although these changes were initially made out of pure exigency, they would not be temporary. Institutions of higher education quickly realized that online teaching promised cost savings on everything from infrastructure to labor. According to a 2023 report, most "chief online officers" (COOs) at US universities say that their current strategic plans and resource allocations focus on significantly expanding online learning. Almost all community colleges and 63 percent of public four-year institutions currently "widely use" online asynchronous courses for undergraduates.[25] My own institution, UC Irvine, recently announced in its strategic plan that it had a goal of "diversifying pedagogical options" by having at least 25 percent of regular academic-year courses offered in an exclusively online format by 2030.

Fully online degree programs are also on the rise. In 2022–23, primarily online institutions grew their enrollments nearly twice as fast as overall higher-ed enrollment growth. In the past, growth in fully or primarily online degree programs was mostly driven by for-profit institutions and by community colleges; today it's mostly four-year public colleges and universities.[26] In 2024, multiple public institutions announced that they would be converting to totally online, including three branch campuses in the University of Wisconsin system. In early 2024, the University of California Office of the President and the UC Regents overrode a policy set in place by the faculty senate in order to allow fully online undergraduate degree programs in the UC system.[27]

One primary motivation for the shift to online is obvious: tuition revenue. Online classes and programs are a great way for colleges to reach out-of-state and international students. Because asynchronous online courses provide students more scheduling flexibility, expanded online offerings also allow colleges to market themselves to "nontraditional" students. And expanding the potential student body is more important now than ever before as colleges across the country worry about the so-called "demographic cliff." The US birth rate dropped substantially during the financial crisis of 2008–2009 and has failed to recover in the decades since, meaning the potential number of US college attendees is estimated to decline significantly as of the late 2020s. Of course, descriptions of the "demographic cliff" are often overstated or misstated because the problem is not so much an *absolute* drop in the number of eighteen-year-olds, but rather a decline in the number of presumed "college-going" high school graduates. For instance, the decline seems "inevitable" only if one assumes that there are no opportunities for improving the rate of college-going among Latine students. Nonetheless, in many regions and for many institutions, demographic changes have already had a major impact, especially at four-year, nonelite institutions.[28]

Tuition isn't the only financial incentive for OLE, of course. It's also much cheaper to expand the online student population than to grow the on-campus student population. Whereas colleges and universities once justified their high tuition by offering high-end campus facilities such as dorms and gyms and movie theaters, many are now moving away from these kinds of investments, especially in cities where population density and skyrocketing real estate prices have created hard limits to the expansion of physical infrastructure. In 2022, for instance, UC Berkeley was forced to freeze enrollments due to a long-standing legal battle with "Save Berkeley Neighborhoods," a NIMBY group of Berkeley homeowners concerned about how the construction of more student housing would affect their property values. To solve the problem, UC Berkeley invited thousands of admitted first-year students to enroll exclusively in online courses for a year to reduce the pressure on campus housing and infrastructure. With fully online courses, you can achieve economies of scale without even having to build and maintain a huge lecture hall. These economies of scale aren't just at the level of individual classes, but also across a system. For instance, UC Online (as well as similar programs in Wisconsin, Texas, Colorado, and many other public university systems) allows students to take online courses offered by any campus in the system, creating the opportunity for "systemwide efficiencies": why have foreign language departments, or courses in classics, or gender studies faculty on all the campuses, when you can offer them online to students across the state from a single campus?

OLE also comes with its own costs, but those costs have been either obscured or justified in the name of "innovation." By making massive investments in ed tech, university administrators and decision-makers are effectively channeling federal and state funds, as well as student tuition, into the private ed-tech sector—an estimated $20 billion is spent annually on ed tech in higher ed, while tens of billions more are being paid to third-party vendors of enrollment management and online program management (OPM) software.[29] Critical university studies scholars describe these arrangements as a form of "privatization by obfuscation"—a way to conceal the for-profit arrangements behind apps and other pedagogical tech from students and instructors alike.[30] When my research collaborator, Louise McCune, and I looked into ed-tech contracts at UCI in 2022, we found that most of the contracts UCI and the UC system had signed with for-profit apps were approved by a very small number of noninstructional staff with no faculty input and that these agreements were often completed without the requisite step of negotiating a full contract with the vendor, let alone any attempt to protect student and faculty privacy or intellectual property rights. OLE's entire infrastructure is subtended by such agreements between nonprofit institutions of higher education and the third-party, for-profit OPM vendors that run 85 percent of all online programs for public universities.[31] OPMs typically require not just fees, but also revenue-sharing arrangements, meaning that universities are directly funneling tuition dollars into companies backed by venture-capital and private-equity investment, which prioritize enrollment and revenue growth over student outcomes.

The "access" argument is never explicitly framed as a way to increase revenues and privatize services while decreasing labor and infrastructure costs, of course. Instead, it cynically tends to wear the mantle of "equity and inclusion," where campuses such as my own, which have historically made it very difficult for nontraditional or part-time students to enroll and succeed, are now suddenly eager to "serve a broader population" via online offerings. Faculty opposed to OLE are thus often accused of being inadequately concerned with equity and access. In fact, Black and Latine students, Pell Grant recipients, and first-generation college students were already concentrated in online programs even before the pandemic.[32] This process has been described as "predatory inclusion" analogous to credit markets. Much as subprime mortgages and high-interest student loans were disproportionately offered to nonwhite borrowers, OLE targets historically excluded and working-class students and their families, offering them a shittier version of the higher ed they were once shut out of entirely.[33] OLE also disproportionately disadvantages these students, producing lower grades, worse outcomes in future courses, and increased likelihood of dropping out.[34] One study found that Black and Pell-Grant-receiving OLE students are significantly less likely to graduate on time and more likely to be delinquent on their student loans.[35] Another study notes that "the performance decrement of online (versus face-to-face) classes has been significantly larger for students from disadvantaged backgrounds" and that male students, Black students, Hispanic students, and low-performing students suffered the largest performance difference.[36] Education scholars have suggested that online education tends not to resolve, but instead to "exacerbate educational inequities" and that "moving vulnerable students online will widen attainment gaps rather than solving the seemingly intractable problem of unequal educational opportunity."[37] Growth in OLE will likely reentrench existing institutional hierarchies. Large public-serving institutions from community colleges to research universities will eventually offer more online courses than in-person ones, whereas elite private institutions and small liberal arts colleges will market themselves as providing a higher-quality, more personalized, "artisanal" in-person experience.

Differences in outcomes between in-person and online courses are not attributable solely to resource inequalities among students. Across *all* student groups, data suggest that it is simply not possible for online courses (especially asynchronous courses) to substitute for the pedagogical affordances of in-person teaching. Multiple studies confirm that "online learning is often hindered ... by the lack of interpersonal interaction" and that "students in online courses persistently report feelings of disconnectedness, distraction, and lack of personal attention, which have negative effects on course persistence and learning performance."[38] "Nearly all causal studies find negative effects of online course taking on student course performance or, at best, null results," education scholars Di Xu and Ying Xu note, citing the fact that online students face significantly "greater difficulties in enabling effective human interactions."[39]

Most postpandemic research on OLE outcomes emphasizes the difference between fully online courses and "hybrid" courses, which combine online and in-person instruction. Hybrid courses don't entirely mitigate the problems of OLE for vulnerable students, but most studies suggest that partially online courses in which material is taught synchronously and in which students also have consistent in-person interactions with the instructor and with their peers produce significantly better outcomes than fully-online, asynchronous courses. Hybrid courses also allow the kinds of scheduling flexibilities administrators evoke in defending OLE as a student-serving project. Yet hybrid courses don't offer universities the same cost savings and economies of scale that fully online courses do. As a result, fully online asynchronous courses—significantly the worst option pedagogically and in terms of measurable outcomes—are "by far the most common," a 2023 study notes, because "the convenience of fully asynchronous provision still outweighs the pedagogic variety afforded by mixing in synchronous or in-person elements."[40]

Often, faculty are reassured that because we retain intellectual property (IP) over curriculum, our course content can't be used without our permission. A 2011 law review article by Nathaniel Strauss notes "the near-universal assumption... that professors own the works they create."[41] The reality, unfortunately, is more complex. The "work made for hire" doctrine, which the American Association of University Professors (AAUP) describes as the "default starting point for copyright policies within universities," offers few IP or copyright protections for teachers.[42] A "teacher exception" once exempted instructors from work-for-hire rules, but universities' interest in owning patents, technology, and other potential commercial products has led to significant erosion of this exception since it was established in the mid-1970s. Because OLE, Strauss notes, "depends on such materials and attracts both educational non-profit and for-profit entities," the "teacher exception" has by now been thoroughly dismantled.[43] Universities themselves have also begun finding ways to work around faculty IP rights even without the expense of a legal case. On my own campus, for instance, faculty are enticed to create online courses by being offered additional research funds, but to receive those funds, we must preemptively sign over our curricular IP rights. Other institutions have changed their policy on faculty curricular IP by fiat: in 2020, in the middle of the pandemic, Purdue University simply issued a memo claiming the right to all courseware and online material in perpetuity.[44] Campuses can even potentially "capture" recorded instructional content without the instructor's permission by using the affordances of the LMS and in-classroom camera systems.[45]

Despite these fairly clear messages from higher-ed administration across the country, in conversations with my colleagues I have often been met with skepticism when I suggest that we are on the brink of being automated out of work—or, at least, of being subject to drastic transformations in our labor process and likely drastic cuts in the number of us required. My colleagues' objection to this prediction is basically the same as Baumol's. For Baumol, automated "teaching machines" are impossible because "the labor itself is the end product." In the classroom, as at the symphony, we judge the value of the product by how many hours of labor went into making it. Similar problems, Baumol argues, attend economies of scale in education. Because "class size (number of teaching hours per student) is taken as a critical index of quality," no one would accept the "college lecture attended by 2000 underclassmen."[46] My colleagues often say a version of the same thing: that the University of California would lose prestige and standing were it to become a majority online institution, because the caliber of instruction (and hence the university's reputation) would suffer. But the problem with applying Baumol's argument to the contemporary university is that Baumol, like my colleagues, assumes pedagogical "quality" will continue to matter above and beyond the university's other imperatives, namely, to take in more tuition revenue while reducing the cost of instructional labor.

In fact, however, the problem of "quality" allows us to connect a longer history of deskilling and casualization in higher education to more recent efforts to transform teaching labor via technology. The analogy to microwork is again useful here. For jobs such as translation or transcription to be outsourced and turned into microwork, they must first be deskilled and rationalized: a big project must be broken up into a series of very small tasks, each of which requires less training or experience to complete than does the whole. The same is true for teaching, where the rationalization and division of labor is accomplished via what is sometimes called "unbundling." Unbundling separates the elements of teaching into discrete parts—curricular development, content delivery, interaction, grading, student support, and advising—often so that some of these tasks can be performed by less skilled or trained professional staff.[47] As Robert Ovetz notes, unbundling was first theorized in the mid-1970s, when the separation of teaching from research was used to create a new labor hierarchy between casualized "teaching faculty" and tenured "research faculty," but it didn't become central to pedagogical theory until ed-tech technology such as LMSs made it possible to realize this Taylorist vision of teaching as task-work fully.[48] The justification for unbundling often appears in the "pedagogical" language of competencies, outcomes, pathways, standardization, and modularity. Unbundling also allows pedagogy to be outsourced to for-profit entities, and Ovetz gives the example of digital "coursepacks," which promise "Our content, your course," thus disarticulating content knowledge from the labor of teaching. The more that course design is handed over to ed tech or for-profit companies, the more control the university has over it, which in turn leads to more deskilling. But the real aim of unbundling is to increase labor productivity by turning the complex intellectual and emotional labor of teaching into a series of discrete, technologically mediated tasks and to reduce labor costs by shifting as many of these tasks as possible to low-waged adjuncts, graduate students, and even undergraduate tutors and graders. Because proponents of unbundling suggest it is no longer necessary to teach skills which, Ovetz notes, are "notoriously difficult to assess," and instead emphasize "competent completion of tasks, which are immensely easy to observe, record, and measure," unbundling is a form of pedagogical rationalization, allowing teachers' "output" to be quantified and subjected to efficiency pressures.[49]

It is *so* easy to measure task completion in the unbundled course, in fact, that the measurement can often be fully automated. Here, too, quality is often evoked rhetorically, but ignored in practice. Proponents of automated grading often cite its salutary "impartiality," that is, "AI grading systems take away the possibility that human biases will affect the grading process" and ensure that "the review process is neutral and fair," *The Princeton Review* says in a marketing email I received. In reality, of course, this claim is laughable. As many scholars and critics have reminded us, because AI is "trained" via human-made data sets, it is at least as biased as any human assessor—it's just harder to track and mitigate the bias embedded in an ostensibly "objective" technology.[50] As a result, AI simply reflects what Ruha Benjamin describes as the "interlocking forms of domination" shaping the society from which it steals.[51]

Proponents of automated assessment also praise its capacity for "personalized feedback": "the true power of AI grading lies in its ability to provide personalized feedback to individual students," *The Princeton Review* says.[52] Of course, human teachers have been providing "personalized feedback" since the dawn of time, as my own students might write before I give them personalized feedback about how to avoid that kind of cliché. Yet decades of casualization, deskilling, and rationalization have almost certainly had their effect on both the quantity and the quality of instructor "feedback": the nontenure-track instructor teaching hundreds and hundreds of students indeed cannot offer much personalized assessment. A crisis created by labor-cost-saving techniques can then be "solved" by labor-cost-saving technology. Once assignments have already been reduced to tasks that can be assessed by someone teaching hundreds of students at the same time for less than a living wage, those tasks can probably also be assessed by a chatbot or an ed-tech "tool" such as PackBack, a "Digital TA" that uses AI language models to produce "instant, personalized feedback" on student writing, "Khanmigo," an AI-guided chatbot "tutor" developed by Kahn Academy, or LearnLM, Google's new "AI tutor."[53]

In the UC system, I saw the link between the degradation of instructional quality and the push toward automation most clearly after the graduate student worker strike of 2022–2023. Because of the labor militancy of the radical rank and file described briefly at the end of Chapter 3, the strike led to a significant increase in the compensation of graduate student instructors. These increased labor costs were largely not funded by systemwide leadership, however, and were instead passed down to campuses and individual departments. Almost immediately, then, provosts and deans and chairs began trumpeting three seemingly different, but in fact deeply imbricated, solutions for maintaining high-quality teaching without having to pay for it. The first solution was to increase the faculty-to-student ratio (intensification). The second was to increase the use of undergraduate "Learning Assistants" who receive no compensation because they are concurrently enrolled in the class themselves (deskilling). The third was automation. A UC Berkeley chief operating officer, questioned in spring 2023 about how his campus would pay for the increases in graduate student instructor stipends, said that campuses would start "automating grading using machine learning" to save on the labor costs of graduate student instructors.[54]

Unbundling and automated assessment can thus be used both to degrade the quality and to increase the quantity of "output" in teaching far more than Baumol ever imagined. Automated proctoring, automated assessment, and automated course management via LMS tools are enabling labor-saving mechanization even in "traditional" in-person classrooms. But it is again asynchronous OLE that promises to reshape instructional labor most profoundly, leading to outcomes that are in fact quite close to full automation. Once fully developed, after all, an online course can be run without the university having to pay the instructor who developed it. Course curriculum is embedded in the campus-controlled LMS and campus-funded ed-tech apps, and recorded asynchronous lectures can be reused year after year and across different campuses in the same university system. It's not even necessary for the original faculty member to be alive to continue to run an online course. In 2021, a student at Concordia University in Montreal discovered that the professor for the course he was taking online had died two years earlier. The dead faculty member's recorded lectures and curriculum provided the course content, while the grading was done by low-waged graduate student TAs.[55]

In some ways, the story of the TAs running the class of their dead professor from behind the scenes suggests that the real threat to university labor today comes not from new technological innovations, but rather, as in the days of MOOC mania, from more familiar dangers, namely, adjunctification and the exploitation of low-waged graduate students. Such an argument might draw on Mary Gray and Siddharth Suri's idea of "ghost work": the low-waged, precarious, outsourced labor that enables online infrastructure, from the precariously employed "remote proctors" watching students' webcams from call centers in India to the low-waged outsourced laborers in Bogota and Medellín paid two dollars an hour to control remotely the "food delivery robots" that are now omnipresent on US campuses.[56] However, as I have already suggested in my account of the complementary relationship between deskilling/rationalization and automation, such an argument overstates the purely *technological* limits to automating this kind of work. Indeed, OLE is perhaps the best example there is of the "so-so automation" I described in Chapter 2, a technology whose quality is lower than its human equivalent and that generates relatively small increases in productivity, but that nonetheless profoundly threatens both employment and wages.

Baumol believed that it would be impossible to automate or mechanize instructional labor "without a complete revolution in our approach to teaching."[57] I have suggested here that we are currently in the midst of just such a revolution. Teaching is now being rationalized, intensified, and deskilled in ways previously not thought possible.

This process began before the advent of asynchronous online learning as adjunctification and economies of scale laid the groundwork for administrators, faculty, and students to accept the "so-so automation" that is now firmly in place in the education sector, from casualization and increased class sizes to AI tutors and prerecorded lectures.

So what is to be done? A number of modest practical solutions present themselves, including stronger faculty governance, especially over curricular modalities, defenses of instructional intellectual property for all teachers, and contractual protections against the use of tech to deskill or replace faculty labor. None of these solutions seems likely in the absence of strong tenure-track faculty unions ready to work side by side with other unionized instructors, solidarity and organizing that I would hazard are the only things standing between us and our own obsolescence. As in almost all prior waves of rationalization and automation, efforts to degrade teaching labor have come first for the teachers whose marginal institutional status or job insecurity already made them vulnerable. Those forces are now coming for the once more-protected members of the faculty, a fact that ought to make crystal clear the necessity of forging common cause across these ever-blurrier professional distinctions. Such common cause must also extend to our students and to the communities they come from—communities that are themselves made up of many different kinds of service workers.[58] Here, too, the loss of access to a quality education is primed to do the most damage to historically excluded and otherwise vulnerable students. In this way, focusing on the quality of educators' work is not a way of saying our work is special. It is a way of calling our attention to the fact that our work serves many communities both within and beyond the university.

Service work—the work conducted in what Marx calls the "noisy sphere of circulation"—is far more visibly and inextricably embedded in our daily lives than other kinds of labor. We relate to the labor of the manufacturing worker primarily through the products they produce at a great distance from us. Our relationship with service workers, by contrast, is intimate and implicated. Service work's embeddedness in daily life has been exploited by service-sector employers and the intimacy thus often feels (as I suggested in Chapter 3) like complicity. But we might also think of it as the basis for solidarity. Whereas the feeling of complicity mystifies our interconnectedness, the fact of solidarity politicizes it. Tenured faculty have long resisted seeing ourselves as workers. In the context of the present fight, this resistance—still disappointingly common—meets a more specific reluctance to place our working conditions in the context of longer histories of work: the histories, indeed, of capitalism's own "moving contradiction," which always and everywhere seeks to throw human workers out of work. University educators, too, are workers whose labor process is subject to the pressures of superexploitation, deskilling, intensification, and automation. In that sense, solidarity is not optional. For professors are not simply distanced observers or complicit users of service workers. We are ourselves part of the service-working class.

Acknowledgments

The earliest seeds of this book were planted when, while sitting in on a course on welfare economics, I learned how much mainstream microeconomists prefer "performance pay" to guaranteed hourly wages. I was able to take that course—and a bunch of others like it—through the support of a Mellon New Directions Fellowship, and I am deeply grateful for that opportunity. My research was also supported by a University of California Humanities Research Institute residential research fellowship and a University of California Irvine Humanities Center publication grant. Portions of this project originally appeared in *Post45 Journal* and the University of Minnesota Press volume *Insecurity*, edited by Richard Grusin.

I am also grateful for the useful feedback I have gotten when I have presented material from this project at the University of California, Davis, the University of Michigan, Ann Arbor, Yale University, Post45 @ USC, the California Labor Lab, the Duke University Critical Theory Institute, the University of Pittsburgh Humanities Center, the Critical Finance Studies Conference, Goldsmiths University, Queen Mary University, the Finance and Fiction Conference at CalArts, the After Marxism Conference at UC Berkeley, the University of Wisconsin-Madison, the 21st Century Studies Conference at the University of Wisconsin-Milwaukee, and the Penn State American Cultures series.

As I have presented material from this project, I have had many opportunities to talk to graduate students about their working conditions and their labor organizing—the insights I gained from those candid, thoughtful, moving conversations were incredibly important to my thinking. This book also would never have been possible without the theory and praxis of many labor groups in the service sector, especially One Fair Wage, the Restaurant Opportunity Center, Los Deliveristas, Gigworkers Rising, Domestic Workers United, Amazonians United, the Sex Workers Organizing Project, the Haymarket Pole Collective, and the LA Tenants Union. Proceeds from this book will be donated to these groups in gratitude for their work.

I am deeply grateful to everyone at Zone Books, especially Meighan Gale and the astonishingly thorough Bud Bynack. Michel Feher has provided engaged, insightful comments at multiple points along the way and has been an invaluable interlocutor. Wendy Brown has been a generous and kind advocate—I am deeply grateful for her support over many years. Sarah Osment's incisive suggestions were crucial as I was completing the manuscript. An early draft of part of this book was read by two brilliant peer reviewers, Harris Feinsod and Jason Smith, whose interventions made it far better. The cover image, a painting titled *Sans Titre,* is part of an extraordinary series of portraits of gigworkers by the painter Arnaud Adami, who generously allowed me to use his work.

Two amazing graduate-student scholars also shaped this project. Jon-David Settel was my coauthor and coconspirator for an essay on service work and sex work published in *SAQ.* Working together was a bright light in the darkness of lockdown, and I learned a great deal from him about sex work and mutual aid. Louise McCune was my research collaborator in the summer of 2022 as we dug into contracts for ed-tech apps in the UC system. I could not have written the coda to this book without Louise's careful, cogent research—she is a model of what it means to be both intellectually and politically committed to the work of teaching.

At UCI, I have been lucky to be part of a supportive and collegial department. My colleagues Richard Godden, Joe Jeon, Chris Fan, and Michael Szalay provided feedback on much of this material in its earliest drafts. The pandemic-era WAP group was of vital importance at the beginning of this project. I was also fortunate to find a tiny space on the internet for good conversations about Marxism and labor history, especially with Gabe Winant, who I feel like I know even though we've never met offline, and with Jasper Bernes, Nate Holdren, Madeline Lane-McKinley, and Sarah Brouillette, who I have deeply missed seeing in-person over these last few years.

Several institutional collaborations shaped my life during the period in which this book was written. I want to particularly acknowledge the students in the 2021–2023 Black Studies Cohorts and the students and faculty in UCI-LIFTED: all have helped remind me why teaching and community matters. The same goes for the Marxist Institute for Research (MIR). Conversations with students at "Marx camp" have been some of the smartest, most inspiring intellectual discussions I've had in years, and a workshop with the MIR "hub faculty" changed the introduction to this book in meaningful ways. MIR wouldn't be possible without Chris Chen, Rob Nichols, Wendy Matsumura, Yousuf al-Bulushi, and especially Colleen Lye, who is now a dear friend and collaborator, but who I will never stop thinking of as the terrifyingly brilliant badass I met when I entered her grad seminar classroom in fall 2003. Speaking of terrifyingly brilliant badasses, Charmaine Chua is one, too: Charmaine's rigor, political commitment, and trivia skills are inimitable, and I feel lucky to know her.

I am fortunate that my fam has had a bounty of dear friends here in So-Cal who have made life more joyful and more communal. For laughter, sympathy, walks, evening hangouts, and family dinners, I am grateful to Amy and Chris, Chelsea, Joe and Young-min, Kyle and Valentina, Maria and Melanie, Meka and JB, Michael and Andrea, Natalie and Ricky, Richard and Rhiann, Sri, Tamara and Ben, and Tara and Jesse. Tobias Menely is a beloved devil's advocate. Liron Mor,

James Robertson, and Rania Robertson are the absolute best and an absolute necessity—their good hearts, good humor, and good cooking have been vital sustenance in tough times.

Before moving to the final dedications of this book, I want to say that the most important part of the last few years of my life was finding political hope in a hopeless place. The comrades of my heart in IFA and FSJP have taught me the truth of what Kristen Ross calls "communal luxury": "free and equal companions, oblivious to the existence of old boundaries, helping each other in peace from one end of the world to the other." Those who are part of that work and that solidarity are—astonishingly—too numerous to list, but that's OK: you know who you are.

I am enduringly lucky to have three amazing siblings: my beautiful, strong, wise sisters, Cait and Kris, and my radical and brilliant brother Bill. Much love to all y'all. I am also grateful for the loving and welcoming extended Martin clan, especially Fran.

Near the very end of this book's writing, my dear friend Joshua Clover passed away. I miss him beyond words, and he contributed more than anyone to the ideas in this book, much of which he read and responded to with characteristic generosity and rigor. His comradeship and commitment are ideals in the truest sense: impossible to live up to, impossible not to try. Chapter 3, which engages his work most directly, is in his memory.

This book is dedicated to three people. It's dedicated to Margaret Ronda, my travel companion, my conversant during untold hours of phone calls, and my dearest friend. Her sympathy and wisdom have been sustaining graces. It's dedicated to Lulu McClanahan, my extraordinary daughter and the kindest, funniest, most luminous person I know. I want to make the world better for her; she makes the world better simply by being in it. And it's dedicated to my mom, Cia White, who helped me be the person I am simply by modeling the kind of person I wanted to be—and by loving me the whole time.

Finally, and with a strong sense of not having words adequate to the task, I want to thank my beloved partner, Ted Martin. Nothing passes through my mind or heart that I don't want to immediately share with him—his sympathy, wit, brilliance, and patience are boundless and abiding, and I couldn't possibly love him more.

Notes

INTRODUCTION

1. Denning defined being "wageless" as distinct from being "unemployed" and already began to suggest the challenge of distinguishing between "waged" work and work paid a regulated, contracted, hourly wage, defining the "wageless" as "casual labourers and service providers who work for others in the intricate disguises of contracted and piece-rate jobs." Michael Denning, "Wageless Life," *New Left Review* 66 (November–December 2010), p. 93.

2. As Jairus Banaji puts it, "a liberal-individualist notion of wage-labour as essentially free labour, labour based on the 'consent' of the individual worker and the free bargain that embodies that 'consent'... is in sharp contrast to Marx whose references to free labour have a profoundly delegitimating intent." Jairus Banaji, "The Fictions of Free Labor: Contract, Coercion, and So-Called Unfree Labor," *Historical Materialism* 11.3 (2003), pp. 74–75.

3. US Department of Labor Wages and Hours Division, "The Fair Labor Standards Act of 1938, as Amended" (May 2011), https://www.dol.gov/sites/dolgov/files/WHD/legacy/files/FairLaborStandAct.pdf.

4. This idea is particularly important because jobs once protected from those processes are now increasingly vulnerable to them (including formerly professionalized service work such as my own, university teaching). It can also help us better understand what is currently happening in underdeveloped economies because of what development economists call "premature deindustrialization." Countries in the Global South are now running out of opportunities for industrial growth far faster and at far lower income levels than did the

Global North in its own, earlier industrial booms. As a result, many underdeveloped economies are not passing through the expansive industrial phase that (for reasons this book theorizes) produced the regulated, formal, hourly wage as a political norm. Instead, more and more countries are transitioning directly from an agricultural economy to a service (or "tertiary") economy, where wages tend to be lower, more informal, and more precarious.

5. Karl Marx, *Capital, Volume One,* trans. Ben Fowkes (New York: Penguin, 1976), p. 342.

6. For more on the "voice" in this chapter, see Rosalind C. Morris, "Dialect and Dialectic in 'The Working Day' of Marx's *Capital,*" *boundary 2* 43.1 (2016), pp. 219–48.

7. Arlie Hochschild, *The Managed Heart: Commercialization of Human Feeling* (Berkeley: University of California Press, 1983), pp. 3–6, 45–46, 9–10.

8. Cameron Macdonald and Carmen Sirianni, "The Service Society and the Changing Experience of Work," in Cameron Lynne Macdonald and Carmen Sirianni, eds., *Working in the Service Society* (Philadelphia: Temple University Press, 1996), p. 4.

9. Bram Ieven, s.v. "Immaterial Labor," in George Ritzer, ed., *The Wiley-Blackwell Encyclopedia of Sociology* (Hoboken: Wiley-Blackwell, 2012); Robin Leidner, "Emotional Labor in Service Work," *Annals of the American Society for Political and Social Sciences* 561 (January 1999), p. 85.

10. Leidner, "Emotional Labor in Service Work," p. 87.

11. John Van Maanen and Gideon Kunda, "'Real Feelings': Emotional Expression and Organizational Culture," *Research in Organizational Behavior* 11 (1989), p. 92.

12. Amy Wharton, "The Sociology of Emotional Labor," *Annual Review of Sociology* 35 (2009), p. 159.

13. On the difference between alienation and exploitation in Hochschild's work, see Kathi Weeks, "Life Within and Against Work: Affective Labor, Feminist Critique, and Post-Fordist Politics," *ephemera* 7.1 (2007), pp. 233–49.

14. Mark Fisher, "Suffering with a Smile," *Occupied Times* (June 22, 2013), https://theoccupiedtimes.org/?p=11586.

15. Maurizio Lazzarato, "Immaterial Labour," in Michael Hardt and Paulo

Virno, eds., *Radical Thought in Italy: A Potential Politics* (Minneapolis: University of Minnesota Press, 1996), p. 135; Maurizio Lazzarato, *Signs and Machines: Capitalism and the Production of Subjectivity*, trans. Joshua David Jordan (Los Angeles: Semiotext(e), 2014), pp. 120–21.

16. Frédéric Lordon, *Willing Slaves of Capital: Marx and Spinoza on Desire*, trans. Gabriel Ash (London: Verso, 2014), p. 83.

17. Eva Illouz, *Cold Intimacies: The Making of Emotional Capitalism* (Cambridge: Polity, 2007).

18. Michael Hardt, "Affective Labor," *boundary 2* 26.2 (Summer 1999), p. 90.

19. Michael Hardt and Antonio Negri, *Empire* (Cambridge, MA: Harvard University Press, 2002), p. 293. A more recent group of feminist scholars have theorized service work not from the perspective of labor at all, but rather by reference to the exploitation of nature and land: as the "extraction" or "dispossession" of affect. Kalindi Vora uses the term "biocapital" to describe the "labor of producing and transferring human vital energy... through the work of affect," while Shiloh Whitney describes service as "the work of metabolizing waste affects and affective byproducts." Kalindi Vora, "Limits of 'Labor': Accounting for Affect and the Biological in Transnational Surrogacy and Service Work," *South Atlantic Quarterly* 111.4 (Fall 2012), p. 682; Shiloh Whitney, "Byproductive Labor: A Feminist Theory of Affective Labor Beyond the Productive-Reproductive Distinction," *Philosophy and Social Criticism* (2017), p. 2. Alex Pittman offers an excellent summary of the turn to "extractive" metaphors in "The Reserve Army of Affectivity: Unemployed Labor in William Greaves's Psychodramatic Cinéma Vérité," *Camera Obscura* 37.1 (2022), pp. 31–59.

20. Silvia Federici, *Wages Against Housework* (Bristol: Power of Women Collective / Falling Wall Press, 1975).

21. Leopoldina Fortunati, *The Arcane of Reproduction: Housework, Prostitution, Labor and Capital*, trans. Hilary Creek (Brooklyn: Autonomia, 1995), p. 7.

22. Angela Davis makes a similar—though slightly more skeptical—argument in "The Coming Obsolescence of Housework," noting that "If the industrial revolution resulted in the structural separation of the home economy

from the public economy, then housework cannot be defined as an integral component of capitalist production. It is, rather, related to production as a *precondition*." Angela Davis, "The Coming Obsolescence of Housework," in *Women, Race, and Class* (New York: Vintage, 1983), p. 234.

23. I am indebted to Joshua Clover for this image and for many years of conversation on this topic.

24. Nancy Fraser, "Crisis of Care? On the Social-Reproductive Contradictions of Contemporary Capitalism," in Tithi Bhattacharya, ed., *Social Reproduction Theory: Remapping Class, Recentering Oppression* (London: Pluto Press, 2017).

25. Jason Smith, *Smart Machines and Service Work: Automation in an Age of Stagnation* (London: Reaktion Books, 2020), p. 11.

26. Gabriel Winant, *The Next Shift: The Fall of Industry and the Rise of Health Care in Rust Belt America* (Cambridge, MA: Harvard University Press, 2022), p. 2.

27. Endnotes Collective (Maya Gonzalez and Jeanne Neton), "The Logic of Gender: On the Separation of Spheres and the Process of Abjection," *Endnotes* 3 (September 2013), pp. 56–90, https://archive.org/details/Endnotes3/mode/2up. As Kathi Weeks notes, much of the early Marxist-feminist work on social reproduction "came to hinge on the question of whether domestic labor was best conceived as internal or external to capitalist production proper" and thus remained trapped within an "essentially Fordist industrial framework," including the kind of productivist "metaphyiscs of labor" that this book suggests was used to exclude waged service work from regulation." Kathi Weeks, *The Problem with Work: Feminism, Marxism, Antiwork Politics, and Postwork Imaginaries* (Durham: Duke University Press, 2011), pp. 235–36.

28. Gonzalez and Neton also draw a useful conceptual distinction between "directly market mediated" (waged) and "indirectly market mediated" (unwaged) service work, a distinction that also has material consequences for reproductive work's labor process. The unwaged work of the parental caregiver is directly dominated by the male breadwinner as the representative of patriarchy. However, this kind of unwaged labor is unlikely to be rationalized, deskilled, or subject to forced intensification or speedup because it is not the source of

profit. By contrast, the waged day-care employee is controlled by the abstract, impersonal domination of the market itself: she thus must work "at competitive levels in terms of productivity, efficiency and product uniformity" (p. 64). In the end, however, even these impersonal market pressures meet their intractable limits in the service sector. Because service workers cannot produce either *more* or *more quickly*, they are instead vulnerable to persistent downward pressure on wages. That pressure is possible, Gonzalez and Neton argue, because feminized work has already been devalued by being associated with women and with the household. The essay also maps a powerful account of gender, one that has been compellingly elaborated by Amy De'Ath. Noting that service workers are vulnerable to persistent downward pressure on wages, De'Ath contends that low-productivity, low-waged work determines "how gender is lived temporally," as well as by the long-standing devaluing (and naturalization) of feminized work. Amy De'Ath, "Gender and Social Reproduction," in Bev Best, Werner Bonefeld, and Chris O'Kane, eds., *The SAGE Handbook of Frankfurt School Critical Theory* (London: Sage, 2018), p. 1548.

29. In *Smart Machines and Service Work*, Smith describes the contemporary service sector as a "servant economy" dominated by low-waged, labor-intensive, deskilled activities that "rely on putatively innate (and therefore 'gendered') social and interpersonal knowledges and behaviors." This suggestive phrase evokes a much longer history of service work, but since Smith's book is mostly focused on the present (like almost all the scholarship discussed above), he does not pursue those possible historical continuities. Smith, *Smart Machines and Service Work*, p. 14.

30. Evelyn Nakano Glenn, "From Servitude to Service Work: Historical Continuities in the Division of Paid Reproductive Labor," *Signs* 18.1 (Autumn 1992), p. 3.

31. Adam Smith, *An Inquiry into the Nature and Causes of the Wealth of Nations, Book Two*, ed. Edwin Cannan (Chicago: University of Chicago Press, 1977), p. 439.

32. When there *was* a tangible product from the servant's work, it was not seen as a reflection of their own labor or capacities, but rather of the master's,

what Carolyn Steedman and Bruce Robbins describe as the paradigmatic synecdoche applied to servants perceived solely as a kind of prosthetic "extra hand." In John Locke's famous treatise on property, Steedman notes, the master can claim property not only in goods to which he adds his own labor, but also in "the grass my servant has cut." Carolyn Steedman, "Servants and Their Relation to the Unconscious," *Journal of British Studies* 42.3 (July 2003), pp. 232–33; Bruce Robbins, *The Servant's Hand: English Fiction from Below* (Durham: Duke University Press, 1993), pp. 152–53.

33. Carolyn Steedman, *Master and Servant: Love and Labour in the English Industrial Age* (Cambridge: Cambridge University Press, 2007), pp. 42–43.

34. Marx, *Capital, Volume One*, pp. 575 and 1043–45. On Marx's account of servants as precapitalist, see also Marc Steinberg, "Marx, Formal Subsumption, and the Law," *Theory and Society* 39.2 (March 2010), pp. 73–202.

35. E. P. Thompson, "Time, Work-Discipline, and Industrial Capitalism," *Past and Present* 38.1 (December 1967), pp. 56–97.

36. Eric Hobsbawm, "Custom, Wages, and Workload in Nineteenth Century Industry," in Asa Briggs and John Saville, eds., *Essays in Labor History* (New York: St. Martin's Press, 1966), p. 118.

37. Leonard Schwarz, "Custom, Wages, and Workload in England During Industrialization," *Past and Present* 197.1 (November 2007), p. 156. Joel Suarez makes a related argument in his essay "Temporalities of Emancipation," noting that while "historians have produced a rich literature on the nature of time in the history of capitalism," most of those histories are "defined by debates over 'preindustrial' or 'premodern' temporality and the ruptures caused by the emergence of factory work and mechanical clock." For Suarez, the consequence of this tendency is that work on capitalist time "gives short shrift to labor and time in the latter half of the twentieth century," though Shwarz's text adds the nuance that a focus on factory clock -time also misses important characteristics of eighteenth-century and nineteenth-century capitalist labor. Joel Suarez, "Temporalities of Emancipation: Women, Work, and Time in 1970s America," *Critical Historical Studies* 10.2 (Fall 2023), p. 178.

38. See Steedman, *Master and Servant*, pp. 71–76.

39. Thompson, "Time, Work-Discipline, and Industrial Capitalism," p. 56.

40. William Blackstone, *Commentaries on the Laws of England in Four Books* (Philadelphia: J. B. Lippincott, 1893), chapter 14, "Of Master and Servant," p. 270, http://files.libertyfund.org/files/2140/Blackstone_1387-01_EBk_v6.0.pdf.

41. Thompson, "Time, Work-Discipline, and Industrial Capitalism," p. 61.

42. As Steedman puts it, "Servants are the category of worker around which economic and social historians constructed many of their theories . . . and yet the one about which they remain the most embarrassed—embarrassed at the idea of workers who could not easily be lined up with the 'classic' industrial or craft worker of the historical imagination." Steedman, "Servants and their Relationship to the Unconscious," p. 334.

43. See Willibald Steinmetz, "Was There a De-Juridification of Individual Employment Relations in Britain?," in Willibald Steinmetz, ed., *Private Law and Social Inequality in the Industrial Age: Comparing Legal Cultures in Britain, France, Germany, and the United States* (Oxford: Oxford University Press, 2000); Douglas Hay and Paul Craven, introduction to Douglas Hay and Paul Craven, eds., *Masters, Servants, and Magistrates in Britain and the Empire, 1562–1955* (Chapel Hill: University of North Carolina Press, 2004); Gordon Anderson, Douglas Brodie, and Joellen Riley, *The Common Law Employment Relation* (Cheltenham: Edward Elgar, 2017); Simon Deakin and Frank Wilkinson, *Law of the Labour Market: Industrialization, Employment, and Legal Evolution* (Oxford: Oxford University Press, 2005).

44. Peggie R. Smith, "Regulating Paid Household Work: Class, Gender, Race, and Agendas of Reform," *American University Law Review* 48.4 (April 1999), pp. 855 and 858.

45. Quoted in ibid., p. 899.

46. Quoted in ibid., p. 868.

47. Cecilia Rio, "'A Treadmill Life': Class and African-American Women's Paid Domestic Service in the Postbellum South," *Rethinking Marxism* 20.1 (Fall 2008), p. 95.

48. Jacqueline Jones, *Labor of Love, Labor of Sorrow: Black Women, Work, and the Family from Slavery to the Present* (New York: Basic Books, 2009), p. 110.

49. Sarah Haley, "Like I Was a Man: Chain Gangs, Gender, and the Domestic Carceral Sphere in Jim Crow Georgia," *Signs* 39.1 (Autumn 2013), p. 70.

50. Tera W. Hunter, *To 'Joy My Freedom: Southern Black Women's Lives and Labors After the Civil War* (Cambridge: Harvard University Press, 1997), p. 206.

51. Davis, *Women, Race, and Class*, p. 237.

52. See Robert J. Steinfeld, *Invention of Free Labor: The Employment Relation in English and American Law and Culture, 1350–1870* (Chapel Hill: University of North Carolina Press, 1991).

53. Grace Chang, *Disposable Domestics: Immigrant Women Workers in the Global Economy* (Cambridge, MA: South End Press, 2000).

54. Steedman, *Master and Servant*, pp. 19–20.

55. Sarah Maza, *Servants and Masters in 18th-Century France: The Uses of Loyalty* (Princeton: Princeton University Press, 1983), p. 12.

56. Judith Rollins, *Between Women: Domestics and Their Employers* (Philadelphia: Temple University Press, 1987), pp. 207–32.

57. Ashley Farmer, *Remaking Black Power: How Black Women Transformed an Era* (Chapel Hill: University of North Carolina Press, 2017), pp. 20–49.

58. Eileen Boris and Premilla Nadasen, "Domestic Workers Organize!" *WorkingUSA: The Journal of Labor and Society* 11.4 (December 2008), pp. 423.

59. Magally Miranda, "The Power of Trabajadoras and the Subversion of Capital: Notes on a Domestic Workers Inquiry," *Viewpoint* (March 2017), https://viewpointmag.com/2017/03/07/the-power-of-trabajadoras-and-the-subversion-of-capital-notes-on-a-domestic-workers-inquiry.

60. Harry Braverman, *Labor and Monopoly Capitalism: The Degradation of Work in the Twentieth Century* (New York: Monthly Review Press, 1974). The phrase "labor process" comes from Marx's account of the shift from the "formal subsumption" of labor to its "real subsumption" under industrialization. "Formal subsumption," he explains, refers to the moment when capital first internalizes or takes command of labor by imposing the wage as the only means of survival for those "without reserves." "Real subsumption," by contrast, describes a fully capitalist mode of production that "transforms *the nature of the labor process and its actual conditions*," subjecting workers to a more alienated, rationalized, scientifically managed, and ultimately more mechanized production process. Marx, *Capital, Volume One*, pp. 1034–35.

61. In defining "degradation," Braverman notes that "*the labor process has*

become the responsibility of the capitalist," alienating both the product and the process of labor from the worker. Because the division of labor under scientific management separates "hand and brain," he contends, skill and knowledge are taken from workers and become the domain of professional managers; workers thus lose autonomy over their own labor process and can be paid lower wages. At the same time, advances in technology also increase the productivity of labor and intensify the labor process via speedup, routinization, and temporal discipline. Braverman, *Labor and Monopoly Capitalism*, pp. 140–41.

62. Of *Labor and Monopoly Capitalism*'s twenty chapters, only two are about service-sector work: an immensely useful chapter on clerical work in manufacturing, which I draw on in Chapter 2 of this book, and a shorter and less developed chapter titled "Service Occupations and Retail Trade," which briefly describes "the simplification and rationalization of skills" in service work, a process of deskilling and scientific management that Braverman suggests has made retail workers "closer to factory operatives than anyone had ever imagined possible." Braverman's account of how industrial-type discipline and rationalization have been applied to in-person service work is important, and it echoes some of the arguments made in this book. Yet he fails to address the significant *differences* between how wages and management contribute to exploitation and intensification in the context of service work, and he ignores how time discipline and managerial practices are by necessity different in a technologically stagnant sector. Braverman, *Labor and Monopoly Capitalism*, p. 256.

63. Amy Dru Stanley, *From Bondage to Contract: Wage Labor, Marriage, and the Market in the Age of Slave Emancipation* (Cambridge: Cambridge University Press, 1988).

64. See Leonard Schwarz, "Custom, Wages, and Workload in England During Industrialization," *Past and Present* 197.1 (November 2007), pp. 143–75; Peter Scholliers and Leonard Schwarz, "The Wage in Europe Since the Sixteenth Century," in Peter Scholliers and Leonard Schwarz, eds., *Experiencing Wages: Social and Cultural Aspects of Wage Forms in Europe Since 1500* (New York: Berghahn Books, 2003), p. 15.

65. See Maurice Dobb, *Wages* (Cambridge: Cambridge University Press, 1928).

66. It is worth noting the resonances between my account of how this particular type of wage came to appear as a political, conceptual, and historical norm and Cooper's account of wages in *Family Values: Between Neoliberalism and the New Social Conservatism*. For Cooper, the "Fordist family wage . . . stood at the heart of the mid-century organization of labor, race, and class, defining African American men from their exclusion from the male breadwinner wage and African American women by their relegation to agricultural and domestic labor in the service of white households"; it also produced a "sexual division of labor that relegated women to lower-paid, precarious forms of employment." Of particular importance to Cooper is the Fordist family wage's role as an instrument of redistribution, one that—with the decline of Fordism as a mode of accumulation and the rise of a socially conservative form of neoliberal deregulation—has now been largely replaced by private forms of social welfare and redistribution. She also offers an excellent account of the relationship between the destruction of social welfare programs under President Bill Clinton and the rise of often compulsory low-waged service work, especially among Black, Latine, and migrant women: "The imposition of workfare requirements," she writes, "was bound to have a devastating effect not only on the lives of welfare recipients (who must fund their own childcare needs while they work, or more realistically, turn to the unpaid labor of female relatives), but also on service workers in general, since the state-subsidized supply of free or low-cost labor has inevitably worsened conditions for all service workers, especially those at the lower echelons of the labor market. . . . [T]he effect of workfare has been to brutally reinstate the historically racialized obligations of domestic servitude, in a form that responds to the imperatives of the post-Fordist service economy."

Cooper's book shares my interest in the qualitative features of the wage—of its historical specificity, its political meaning, its relationship to questions of race, gender, ability, and other ascriptive logics. Yet because she takes the Fordist wage as a given, in order to tell the story of its collapse, Cooper does not explain the specific relationship of this kind of wage to the Fordist mode of production. Indeed, her account of the Fordist wage focuses largely on its quantity (whether it was enough to support a family) and not its qualities (hourly, regulated, contractually guaranteed). Nonetheless, this book is in many ways a companion to Cooper's work, insofar as she insists on the embedded relationship of the regulatory state with a given mode of accumulation. Moreover, my account of the productivism inherent to the discourse of "fair" wages and central to the exclusion of service work from regulation rhymes with Cooper's critique of ostensibly leftist political discourses that nostalgically imagine the "restoration" of both the Fordist family and the Fordist wage. Melinda Cooper, *Family Values: Between Neoliberalism and the New Social Conservatism* (New York: Zone Books, 2019), pp. 8–10 and 102. Cooper's account of "welfare reform" also compellingly echoes Sarah Haley's immensely important account of the "domestic carceral" under Jim Crow, through which Black women were forced to work as domestic servants for white families, "giving meaning to the concept of the prison of the home." Haley, "Like I Was a Man," p. 54.

67. Histories of the FLSA rarely spend much if any time on the exclusion of service work from regulation, nor are there many accounts of how and why tips were excluded from the FLSA even after the 1966 expansion of the act to cover most service workers. Meantime, a capacious history such as David Roediger and Philip Foner's *Our Own Time: A History of American Labor and the Working Day* (London: Verso, 1989) says essentially not a single word about service work—and barely anything about other nonmanufacturing sectors, including farmwork—or about tips, or about the relationship between manufacturing's *specific* form of time discipline and productivity and the production of both the hourly wage and the forty-hour week as historical and political norms.

68. Theories of superexploitation are typically associated with Marxist development economics, especially the work of Brazilian economist and sociologist Ruy Mauro Marini. In his 1973 *Dialectics of Dependency*, Marini identifies three key mechanisms of superexploitation: "the intensification of work, the extension of the working day, and the expropriation of part of the labor necessary for the worker to replenish his labor power," that is, paying workers less than what they actually need to subsist. Superexploitation, Marini notes, gives rise to a "mode of production based exclusively on the greater exploitation of the worker, and not on the development of his productive capacity," making it more common in underdeveloped national economies such as those in Latin

America, especially in extractive industries and agriculture. In his later work, however, Marini identified superexploitation as something increasingly generalized to the whole system, including advanced economies; more recently, Andy Higginbottom notes, Marini's theory of superexploitation has resurfaced to describe outsourcing and other forms of global labor arbitrage. Ruy Mauro Marini, *Dialectics of Dependency*, eds. Amanda Latimer and Jaime Osorio, trans. Amanda Latimer (New York: Monthly Review Press, 2022), p. 131; Andy Higginbottom, "Structure and Essence in *Capital I:* Extra Surplus-Value and the Stages of Capitalism," *Journal of Australian Political Economy* 70 (2012), pp. 251–70.

69. Marx, *Capital, Volume One*, p. 275.

70. Ibid., p. 534; Marini, *Dialectics of Dependency*, p. 161.

71. See Farmer, *Remaking Black Power*, chapter 2.

72. Claudia Jones, "An End to the Neglect of the Problems of the Negro Woman!," *Political Affairs* 28.6 (June 1949), p. 53, https://www.marxists.org/history/usa/pubs/political-affairs/1949-06v28n6-political-affairs.pdf.

73. See Thompson, "Time, Work-Discipline, and Industrial Capitalism."

74. Braverman, *Labor and Monopoly Capitalism*, p. 60

75. Accounts of postindustrial time discipline such as Jonathan Crary's idea of "24/7 capitalism" likewise attempt to understand how managerial control and domination works in a sector that cannot be fully rationalized or "scientifically" managed. Yet Crary's focus on salaried professional workers who, like Hoschchild's "double pretending" flight attendant, cannot separate their working self from their "real" self, emphasizes captured or commodified subjectivity, instead of the labor process of service work. Jonathan Crary, *24/7: Late Capitalism and the Ends of Sleep* (London: Verso, 2014).

76. Jason E. Smith, "What Do Digital Bosses Do?", *The Brooklyn Rail* (July–August 2022), https://brooklynrail.org/2022/07/field-notes/What-Do-Digital-Bosses-Do.

77. See Kerry Seagrave, *Tipping: An American Social History of Gratuities* (Jefferson: McFarland, 1998); Ofer Azar, "The History of Tipping—from Sixteenth-Century England to United States in 1910," *The Journal of Socio-Economics* 33.6 (2004), pp. 745–64; Jacqueline Ross and John Welsh, "Service Labor, Freedom, and the Technique of Tipping," *Critical Sociology* 49.4–5

(2022), pp. 725–48; Daniel Levinson Wilk, "The Red Cap's Gift: How Tipping Tempers the Rational Power of Money," *Enterprise and Society* 16.1 (March 2015), pp. 5–50.

78. See Guylaine Vallée and Dalia Gesualdi-Fecteau, "Setting the Temporal Boundaries of Work: An Empirical Study of the Nature and Scope of Labour Law Protections," *International Journal of Comparative Labour Law and Industrial Relations* 32.2 (September 2016), pp. 344–78.

79. Suarez, Temporalities of Emancipation," p. 174.

80. Jodi Dean, "Neofeudalism: The End of Capitalism?," *Los Angeles Review of Books* (May 12, 2020), https://lareviewofbooks.org/article/neofeudalism-the-end-of-capitalism.

81. Aaron Benanav, *Automation and the Future of Work* (London: Verso, 2020), p. 57; Astra Taylor, "The Automation Charade," *LOGIC(S)* 5 (August 1, 2018), https://logicmag.io/failure/the-automation-charade.

82. William Baumol, "Macroeconomics of Unbalanced Growth: The Anatomy of Urban Crisis," *American Economic Review* 57.3 (June 1967), pp. 415–16. Baumol first introduced this idea two years earlier, in a 1965 essay about the context of the "starving artist" and the "strained economic circumstances" facing symphonies and other institutions of the performing arts. See William Baumol and W. G. Bowen. "On the Performing Arts: The Anatomy of Their Economic Problems," *American Economic Review* 55.1.2 (March 1965), pp. 495–502. The 1967 essay, by contrast, has a much bigger ambitions: nothing less than diagnosing "growing urban deterioration." Baumol offers a number of explanations familiar to anyone who has studied the "urban crisis" literature of this period: "externalities" such as traffic and pollution, rising crime and other forms of urban "blight," flight to the suburbs and the resulting decline of the tax base, and so on.

83. Baumol, "Macroeconomics of Unbalanced Growth," p. 416.

84. See Karen Levy, *Data Driven: Truckers, Technology, and the New Workplace Surveillance* (Princeton: Princeton University Press, 2022); Steven Vallas and Juliet Schor, "What Do Platforms Do? Understanding the Gig Economy," *Annual Review of Sociology* 46 (July 2020), pp. 273–94; Mareike Möhlmann and Lior Zalmanson, "Hands on the Wheel: Navigating Algorithmic Management

and Uber Drivers' Autonomy," *Proceedings of the Thirty-Eighth International Conference on Information Systems (ICIS 2017), December 10–13, Seoul, South Korea*, https://aisel.aisnet.org/icis2017/DigitalPlatforms/Presentations/3; Emma McDaid, Paul Andon, and Clinton Free, "Algorithmic Management and the Politics of Demand: Control and Resistance at Uber," *Accounting, Organizations and Society* 109 (August 2023), https://www.sciencedirect.com/science/article/pii/S0361368223000363; Heiner Heiland, "Neither Timeless nor Placeless: Control of Food Delivery Gig Work via Place-Based Working Time Regimes," *Human Relations* 75.9 (2022), pp. 1824–48.

85. Benanav, *Automation and the Future of Work*, p. 6.

86. See Juan F. Perea, "The Echoes of Slavery: Recognizing the Racist Origins of the Agricultural and Domestic Worker Exclusion from the National Labor Relations Act," *Ohio State Law Journal* 72.1 (2011), https://lawecommons.luc.edu/cgi/viewcontent.cgi?article=1150&context=facpubs; Phyllis Palmer, "Outside the Law: Agricultural and Domestic Workers Under the Fair Labor Standards Act," *Journal of Policy History* 7.4 (1995), pp. 416–40; Peggie Smith, "Regulating Paid Household Work: Class, Gender, Race, and Agendas of Reform," *American University Law Review* 48.4 (April 1999), pp. 851–923.

87. For the argument about output and wages, see Hobsbawm, "Custom, Wages, and Workload in Nineteenth Century Industry."

88. Marx, *Capital, Volume One*, p. 348.

89. Dorothy Sue Cobble, "Worker Mutualism in an Age of Entrepreneurial Capitalism," *Labour & Industry: A Journal of the Social and Economic Relations of Work* 26.3 (September 2016), pp. 179–89.

90. Connecting these kinds of movements to a general category of "wagelessness," Phil Jones similarly identifies the "organic demands of a growing number unable to secure their basic subsistence: free healthcare, utilities, housing and food and an end to unnecessary, violent institutions. Taken together, they reveal a hidden utopian horizon. Some might call it Universal Basic Services (UBS), the idea that services fundamental to human survival should be free at the point of access, and should be democratically determined and managed." Phil Jones, *Work Without the Worker: Labour in the Age of Platform Capitalism* (London: Verso, 2021), ebook, unpaginated.

91. Nicholas Brown, *Autonomy: The Social Ontology of Art Under Capitalism* (Durham: Duke University Press, 2019).

92. Mark Nowak, *Social Poetics* (Minneapolis: Coffee House Press, 2020), p. 6.

CHAPTER ONE: TIPWORK AND TV

1. National Restaurant Association, "State of the Industry Report" (2025), https://greatmenusstarthere.com/uploads/files/2025-NRA-State-of-the-Restaurant-Industry.pdf; US Bureau of Labor Statistics, "Employment Projections and Occupational Outlook" (September 8, 2022), https://www.bls.gov/news.release/archives/ecopro_09082022.htm; US Bureau of Labor Statistics "Industries at a Glance: Leisure and Hospitality," https://www.bls.gov/iag/tgs/iag70.htm; National Employment Law Project, "Minimum Wage Basics: Overview of the Tipped Minimum Wage" (April 2015), https://www.nelp.org/app/uploads/2015/04/Basics-Tipped-Minimum-Wage.pdf.

2. Pew Research Center, "The State of Gig Work in 2021," December 8, 2021, https://www.pewresearch.org/internet/2021/12/08/the-state-of-gig-work-in-2021; Saru Jayaraman, *One Fair Wage: Ending Subminimum Pay in America* (New York: The New Press, 2021), ebook, unpaginated.

3. See Jayaraman, *One Fair Wage.*

4. One Fair Wage, "Our Work," https://www.onefairwage.org/our-work.

5. According to OFW, tip wages do not even do what wages are supposed to do as a "market mechanism": they do not guarantee that the worker has an adequate subsistence ensuring that she can herself become a consumer and that she can continue to work day after day; they do not ensure that she does not require the aid of the state; and, because they have been the object of a century of concerted industry lobbying, they are not determined by an unimpeded system of supply and demand.

6. The intimacy and reciprocity of tip payment has fascinated and bewildered microeconomists perplexed as to why any rational actor would bother paying a tip when they didn't have to. "From an economics perspective," one illustrative essay admits, "tipping behavior is hard to understand in terms of pure self-interest," while another describes it as a "unique economic

phenomenon" that disrupts "the traditional assumption of a selfish economic agent who doesn't care about social norms and has no feelings," but that might nonetheless be accommodated by the formal models on which those assumptions are based: tipping "suggests that norms and feelings may be the reasons for other economic behaviors as well," the essay muses incredulously, and, "We should then consider incorporating feelings and conformity with social norms in the utility function." Michael Conlin, Michael Lynn, and Ted O'Donoghue, "The Norm of Restaurant Tipping," Cornell Library eCommons, https://ecommons.cornell.edu/server/api/core/bitstreams/d8248514-d64b-4a33-9cb9-cf4248f74504/content, p. 1.

7. In doing so, OFW moves well beyond mass production unionism and toward something like what Dorothy Cobble terms the "occupational unionism" practiced by waitresses and others. Emphasizing "occupational membership rather than worksite affiliation," Cobble suggests, "create[s] bonds between workers that cross the boundaries of individual workplaces." Dorothy Cobble, "Organizing the Postindustrial Work Force: Lessons from the History of Waitress Unionism," *Industrial and Labor Relations Review* 44.3 (April 1991), p. 433.

8. Arlie Hochschild, *The Managed Heart: Commercialization of Human Feeling* (Berkeley: University of California Press, 1983), p. 45.

9. Joel Suarez makes a related point in "Temporalities of Emancipation: Women, Work, and Time in 1970s America," noting that historians of labor, like historians of time and capitalism, have paid inadequate attention "to labor and time in the latter half of the twentieth century, preferring instead earlier histories of industrialization and work rationalization in the nineteenth and early twentieth centuries." Suarez's essay considers the *two* shifts most women were forced to work after deindustrialization caused the end of the "family wage"—a waged and formal job on top of their unwaged domestic work—and uses this to consider women's proletarianization "amid incipient economic stagnation and profound sectoral reconfiguration." Joel Suarez, "Temporalities of Emancipation: Women, Work, and Time in 1970s America," *Critical Historical Studies* 10.2 (Fall 2023), pp. 177–78.

10. E. P. Thompson, "Time, Work-Discipline, and Industrial Capitalism," *Past and Present* 38.1 (December 1967), p. 61.

11. Ibid., p. 56. For an account of the temporal "porosity" involved in the concept of labor time as "availability," see Urwana Coiquaud, "The Obligation to Be Available: The Case of the Trucking Industry," *International Journal of Comparative Labour Law and Industrial Relations* 32.3 (2016), pp. 322–43.

12. Leonard Schwarz, "Custom, Wages, and Workload in England During Industrialization," *Past and Present* 197.1 (November 2007), p. 156. Peter Scholliers and Leonard Schwarz likewise note that under early industrialization, many wages were paid in kind—in food, beer, or lodging. The rise of the factory system and generalized industrialization did indeed standardize the forms wages took between the late nineteenth and early twentieth centuries, but in the agricultural, extractive, and service sectors, it was not uncommon for wages to continue to be paid in "coal, [wood]chips [that is, by-products], subsidized meals." Peter Scholliers and Leonard Schwarz, "The Wage in Europe Since the Sixteenth Century," in Peter Scholliers and Leonard Schwarz, eds. *Experiencing Wages: Social and Cultural Aspects of Wage Forms in Europe Since 1500* (New York: Berghahn Books, 2003), p. 15. Amy Dru Stanley also reminds us that even in the nineteenth century, labor arrangements tended to rely "on contract rules that were written and unwritten, spoken and unspoken, formal and informal." Amy Dru Stanley, *From Bondage to Contract: Wage Labor, Marriage, and the Market in the Age of Slave Emancipation* (Cambridge: Cambridge University Press, 1988), p. 63.

13. See Simon Deakin and Frank Wilkinson, *The Law of the Labour Market: Industrialization, Employment, and Legal Evolution* (Oxford: Oxford University Press, 2005).

14. Jacqueline Jones, *Labor of Love, Labor of Sorrow: Black Women, Work, and the Family from Slavery to the Present* (New York: Basic Books, 2009), pp. 115 and 132.

15. South Carolina Black Code of 1865, Lowcountry Digital History Initiative, https://ldhi.library.cofc.edu/exhibits/show/after_slavery_educator/unit_three_documents/document_eight.

16. Cecilia Rio, "'A Treadmill Life': Class and African-American Women's Paid Domestic Service in the Postbellum South," *Rethinking Marxism* 20.1 (Fall 2008), pp. 95–96.

17. For different versions of this history, most of which agree on the importance of the history of vails and many of which refer directly to the Samuel Johnson anecdote, see Kerry Seagrave, *Tipping: An American Social History of Gratuities* (Jefferson: McFarland, 1998); Ofer Azar, "The History of Tipping—from Sixteenth-Century England to United States in 1910," *Journal of Socio-Economics* 33.6 (2004), pp. 745–64; Jacqueline Ross and John Welsh, "Service Labor, Freedom, and the Technique of Tipping," *Critical Sociology* 49.4–5 (2022), pp. 725–48; Daniel Levinson Wilk, "The Red Cap's Gift: How Tipping Tempers the Rational Power of Money," *Enterprise and Society* 16.1 (March 2015), pp. 5–50.

18. See Wilk, "The Red Cap's Gift," especially pp. 15–17.

19. Quoted in Seagrave, *Tipping*, pp. 78–79.

20. On racialized submission and tipping, see Evelyn Nakano Glenn, "From Servitude to Service Work: Historical Continuities in the Division of Paid Reproductive Labor," *Signs* 18.1 (Autumn 1992), pp. 1–43. For an excellent account of the discourse of tips as bribery, see Andrew P. Haley, *Turning the Tables: Restaurants and the Rise of American Middle Class* (Chapel Hill: University of North Carolina Press, 2011), pp. 175–81. While Haley and Seagrave each offer a vital history of US tipping practices, and while both narrate extended debates that took place between the late nineteenth century and the 1940s over the abolition of tipping, neither discuss the FLSA and the impact of its exclusion of service workers.

21. Alvin Harlow, "Our Daily Bribe: The Degrading Practice of Tipping," *Forum* (April 1939), p. 231.

22. On the preponderance of Black workers in service at the turn of the twentieth century, see Jayaraman, *One Fair Wage*, pp. 16–18.

23. William Scott, *The Itching Palm: A Study of the Habit of Tipping in America* (Philadelphia: Penn, 1916), n.p.

24. Harlow, "Our Daily Bribe," p. 233.

25. Quoted in "Tips Not Born of Pullman System," *San Francisco Chronicle* April 6, 1915, p. 15. Hungerford was queried as to "the social effect of such a wage which compels men but recently removed from bondage to subsist on gratuities from another race." In response, Hungerford insisted that tips didn't

originate with Pullman, but "seem to always have been a general condition." See also Larry Tye, *Rising from the Rails: Pullman Porters and the Making of the Black Middle Class* (New York: Henry Holt, 1994).

26. See "Pullman Wage Inquiry Begun by US Board," *Christian Science Monitor* (April 6, 1915), p. 8. This was a congressional commission whose mission was to study working conditions in the United States between 1913 and 1915 and whose work would ultimately lead to multiple pre-FLSA labor regulations under the National Industrial Recovery Act.

27. See also "Tips vs Wages for Pullman Porters," *Outlook*, May 19, 1915, p. 120; "Will Robert T. Lincoln Be the Second Emancipator," *Chicago Defender* (May 8, 1915), p. 1; "T. R. Lincoln Favors Tips," *Afro-American* (May 8, 1915), p. 1; "Porters Tips Aid Pullman Profit: Robert Lincoln Justifies System," *New York Tribune* (May 5, 1915), p. 14; and "RT Lincoln Would Raise Porter's Pay: Pullman Chief Holds Public to Blame for the Tipping Evil," *Chicago Daily Tribune* (May 5, 1915), p. 1. I suspect the uncertainty and contradictions within those headlines indicate Lincoln's own ambivalence and attempt to maneuver his way around the question rhetorically.

28. Dorothy Cobble, *Dishing It Out: Waitresses and Their Unions in the Twentieth Century* (Champaign: University of Illinois Press, 1992), p. 42. Like the perceived link between tips and slavery, the association of tips with sex work implied here has a long history. Carolyn Steedman notes that in the eighteenth century, the story "of the failed service career as a direct route to street-walking" was "told everywhere, from religious tract to social realist novel." Carolyn Steedman, *Master and Servant: Love and Labour in the English Industrial Age* (Cambridge: Cambridge University Press, 2007), p. 52.

29. Frances Donovan, *The Woman Who Waits* (Boston: Gorham Press, 1920), pp. 211 and 220. Vanessa May's *Unprotected Labor* notes that domestic service was likewise associated with sexual impropriety: "the delinquent behavior that observers of the 'servant problem' were most concerned would infect middle-class homes was what they viewed as domestics' pronounced proclivity for sexual vice." Vanessa May, *Unprotected Workers: Household Workers, Politics, and Middle-Class Reform in New York, 1870–1940* (Chapel Hill: University of North Carolina Press, 2011), p. 30.

30. Franklin Delano Roosevelt, "Message to Congress," *New York Times* (May 24, 1937), p. 19.

31. May also offers a powerful account of the claim that domestic service "was fundamentally different from other, more public, forms of labor," writing that "casting domestic service as an anachronistic form of labor naturalizes its exclusion from labor reform agendas and state and federal labor laws" and "suggests that domestic service was an entirely private matter, unchanged by the "modern" world developing outside the walls of the middle-class and elite home." May, *Unprotected Workers*, p. 14.

32. Guaranteed minimum wages, they argued, would ensure that workers' subsistence needs were met and thus serve the broader social welfare by ensuring the reproduction of a healthy national body politic. In her history of living-wage and minimum-wage laws in France, historian Dana Simmons argues that living-wage debates involved nothing less than the question of what makes life itself, involving the sciences of ergonomics, physiology, scientific management, reproduction, and nutrition. Dana Simmons, *Vital Minimum: Need, Science, and Politics in Modern France* (Chicago: University of Chicago Press, 2015). If a living wage had to provide for human needs *beyond* mere subsistence, the debates over what amount is necessary were even more complex: what would be the appropriate amount to enable a life replete with activity, educational improvement, decency, comfort, and an "American standard of living"? Even before the invention of the Fordist family wage—which Melinda Cooper explains was central to the New Deal—the "male breadwinner norm" (in Wally Seccombe's phrasing) had long shaped the discourse of nineteenth-century industrial labor. Melinda Cooper, *Family Values: Between Neoliberalism and the New Social Conservatism* (New York: Zone Books, 2019); Wally Seccombe, "Patriarchy Stabilized: The Construction of the Male Breadwinner Wage Norm in Nineteenth-Century Britain," *Social History* 11.1 (January 1986), pp. 51–76.

33. These quotes from the Industrial Welfare Commission of 1916 come from Willis Nordlund, *The Quest for a Living Wage: The History of the Federal Minimum Wage Program* (Westport: Greenwood, 1997), p. 15. My account of the history of living-wage arguments, gender, and the FLSA, relies particularly on the following sources: Ellen Mutari, "Brothers and Breadwinners: Legislating

Living Wages in the Fair Labor Standards Act of 1938," *Review of Social Economy* 62.2 (June 2004), pp. 129–48; Marilyn Power, "Parasitic-Industries Analysis and Arguments for a Living Wage for Women in the Early Twentieth Century United States," *Feminist Economics* 5.1 (December 2010), pp. 61–78; Eileen Boris, *Making the Woman Worker: Precarious Labor and the Fight for Global Standards, 1919–2019* (Oxford: Oxford University Press, 2019); Suzanne B. Mettler, "Federalism, Gender, and the Fair Labor Standards Act of 1938," *Polity* 26.4 (Summer 1994), pp. 635–54; and Laurence Glickman, *A Living Wage: American Workers and the Making of Consumer Society* (Ithaca: Cornell University Press, 1997).

34. Reformers and organizers in the skilled industrial trades feared that, as AFL-CIO president Samuel Gompers put it in congressional testimony given in 1914, support for living wages would "result in a long era of industrial slavery." Samuel Gompers, *The American Labor Movement: Its Makeup, Achievements, and Aspirations* (Washington, DC: American Federation of Labor, 2014), p. 14, https://dn790003.ca.archive.org/0/items/americanlabormovoogomp/americanlabormovoogomp.pdf. See also Glickman, *A Living Wage*, especially pp. 40–49, on anxieties about masculinity.

35. As Nordlund explains, the growth industries in this period (chemicals, rubber, automobiles) were less craft oriented and tended to be deskilled, thus raising fears of automation-driven unemployment. The President's Reemployment Agreement (PRA), passed in 1933 as part of the National Recovery Act, called for firms to comply voluntarily with a reduced work week and a minimum recommended wage for white-collar as well as manufacturing workers. Meanwhile, Northern manufacturing interests were concerned that regional wage differentials were giving the South an unfair advantage when it came to cheap labor. When the PRA and NRA were invalidated by the Supreme Court in 1935, labor conditions swiftly deteriorated, making clear the necessity of more enforceable legislation. See Nordlund, *The Quest for a Living Wage*, pp. 1–30.

36. See Sean Farhang and Ira Katznelson, "The Southern Imposition: Congress and Labor in the New Deal and Fair Deal," *Studies in American Political Development* 19.1 (Spring 2005), pp. 1–30.

37. See ibid.; Juan F. Perea, "The Echoes of Slavery: Recognizing the Racist Origins of the Agricultural and Domestic Worker Exclusion from the National Labor Relations Act," *Ohio State Law Journal* 72.1 (2011), https://lawecommons.luc.edu/cgi/viewcontent.cgi?article=1150&context=facpubs; Phyllis Palmer, "Outside the Law: Agricultural and Domestic Workers Under the Fair Labor Standards Act," *Journal of Policy History* 7.4 (1995), pp. 416–40. Most of the scholarship on these compromises focuses on the exclusion of agricultural workers (to which Chapter 3's account of piece-rate work will return), but the exclusion of "domestic" workers is particularly important to the history of how and why service work—especially in its most racialized and feminized forms—would end up falling outside most labor regulations for decades. The exclusion of Black domestic workers also most clearly belies the claim that these carve-outs were necessary to ensure economic stability: whereas agricultural production was indeed crucial to the national economy, domestic service was not.

38. Quoted in Peggie Smith, "Regulating Paid Household Work: Class, Gender, Race, and Agendas of Reform," *American University Law Review* 48.4 (April 1999), p. 888. Cooper's account of this history is also richly compelling and offers a somewhat different angle than my own by attending to the politics of social welfare. That is, while my history here emphasizes the turn away from explicitly "reproductive" and, indeed, social-welfare justifications for state intervention in wages, Cooper persuasively suggests that the New Deal underwrote—indeed, produced—the Fordist family wage precisely because it was "a mechanism for the normalization of gender and sexual relationships" and was core to a gendered, nationalist understanding of American "family values." In this context, she suggests that the exclusion of agricultural and domestic workers in the South was a means to "defin[e] African American men by the exclusion from the male breadwinner wage and African American women by their relegation to agriculture and domestic labor in the service of white households." Cooper, *Family Values*, p. 8.

39. See Helen Knowles, *Making Minimum Wage: Elsie Parrish Versus the West Coast Hotel Company* (Norman: University of Oklahoma Press, 2021).

40. Congressional Record, House, May 23, 1938, p. H7326.

41. See Knowles, *Making Minimum Wage*, pp. 234–35.

42. Responding to the concern of Southern senators worried that the act as written would apply those employed on cotton farms, for instance, the FLSA was amended to specify that it applied only to those "engaged in the *handling*" of agricultural products, not their initial production: if you turned cotton into textiles in a factory, you were covered; if you harvested cotton in the field, you were not. Katznelson and Farhang, "The Southern Imposition," p. 12.

43. See Mettler, "Federalism, Gender, and the Fair Labor Standards Act of 1938."

44. Due to the obsessive focus on intrastate versus interstate circulation, considerably more time seems to have been spent debating the status of newspaper employees than was ever spent discussing the masses of service workers left out of the act's protections. See the Congressional Record for January 3 to June 16, 1938, vol. 83, https://www.govinfo.gov/app/details/GPO-CRECB-1938-pt12-v83.

45. Richard A. Epstein, "The Regulatory Hour: The History, Law and Economics of Minimum Wage and Maximum Hours Legislation," *New York University Journal of Law and Liberty* 12.3 (2019), p. 497.

46. For the argument about output and wages, see Eric Hobsbawm, "Custom, Wages, and Workload in Nineteenth Century Industry," in Asa Briggs and John Saville, eds., *Essays in Labor History* (New York: St. Martin's Press, 1966).

47. Notably, prior to the FLSA, many industries were less time disciplined than Thompson's essay acknowledges, suggesting that the act made temporally specific work discipline possible (because it was legally necessary), instead of the other way around: a 1943 report explains that "thousands of employers in unorganized industries have never kept data" on hours worked, rate of pay, etc., and "many workers in the low wage industries are illiterate, have no clocks or watches of their own, and have only the vaguest idea of time consumed for particular tasks." Irvine Richter, "Four Years of the Fair Labor Standards Act: Some Problems of Enforcement," *Journal of Political Economy* 51.2 (April 1943), pp. 105–106.

48. Service work in the domestic realm also often tends to blur the lines between "market" and "nonmarket" categorization. In this sense, service work

shares some qualities with other kinds of labor excluded from the protection of the FLSA, including the labor of incarcerated workers. Writing on prison labor, Noah Zatz argues that the FLSA relied on firm distinctions between market work (characterized by "'compensation' and 'control,'" as well as "'short-term monetization' and 'time discipline'") and nonmarket labor (intimately "embedded in a highly particularized relationship among a small number of individuals and often characterized by the worker's identification with... those who benefit from her labor"). Zatz identifies prison labor as a category of labor balanced between these categories (because prison labor is seen to have a primarily social or rehabilitative function). Other types of labor perceived to pose similar categorical problems and thus excluded from federal regulation and protection include in-home domestic labor, apprentice or student labor, and the labor of workers in so-called "sheltered workshops" (the industries managed by charitable organizations to employ those classified as disabled). Incarcerated workers are still unprotected by any minimum wage laws or labor regulation; domestic workers who work in private homes are still excluded from the NLRA and were included in the FLSA only in 1974 (though some exclusions persist), and home health-care and other "companionate workers" were excluded until 2013. Noah Zatz, "Prison Labor and the Paradox of Nonmarket Work," in Nina Bandelj, ed., *Economic Sociology of Work* (Leeds: Emerald Group, 2009). See also Katherine E. Leung, "Prison Labor as a Lawful Form of Race Discrimination," *Harvard Civil Rights-Civil Liberties Law Review* 53.2 (Fall 2018), pp. 681–708; Lan Cao, "Made in the USA: Race, Trade, and Prison Labor," *New York University Review of Law & Social Change* 43.1 (2019), pp. 1–58. On the complex relationships between carceral labor and domestic work, see also Sarah Haley's powerful "Like I Was a Man: Chain Gangs, Gender, and the Domestic Carceral Sphere in Jim Crow Georgia," *Signs* 39.1 (Autumn 2013), pp. 53–77.

49. The railroad and shipping companies also tried to force redcaps to sign agreements claiming they were independent contractors, not employees, so that the FLSA would not apply to them. A 1942 article about the history of the redcap debate makes the "fictitiousness" of this arrangement clear and in terms that uncannily anticipate the legal debate about gigworkers eighty years later (to which we will return in Chapter 3): "Like ordinary factory employees,

redcaps were told by their bosses when to work and when not to work, how and where to do their jobs. They were subject to discipline and discharge; had to wear uniforms." Harry Weiss and Philip Arnow, "Recent Transition of Redcaps from Tip to Wage Status," *American Labor Legislation Review* 32.3 (September 1942), pp. 134–35.

50. "Redcaps Tips at Issue," *New York Times*, October 25, 1938, p. 12.

51. For archival research on the redcaps case, see United States Department of Labor, "Labor Laws and their Administration 1941," bulletin no. 721 (Washington, DC: US Government Printing Office, 1943), https://fraser.stlouisfed.org/files/docs/publications/bls/bls_0721_1943.pdf, and Richter, "Four Years of the Fair Labor Standards Act." There were actually two unions for the redcaps: the AFL's Brotherhood of Railway Clerks and the IBR, led by William Saxby Townsend. The Railway Clerks was a "whites only" union. Although the AFL supported Philip Randolph's historically Black Brotherhood of Sleeping Car Porters, they also permitted local "autonomy" and thus did not require the Railway Clerks to accept Black members. Despite an initial showing of racial unity and pleas for a one-union strategy by Black labor leaders as well as groups such as the Urban League, the minority white members ultimately chose the AFL. Thus, although the redcaps were as a group somewhat more diverse than the Pullman porters, the union itself was largely Black, and on the West Coast, Japanese-American. See Patricia Romero, "The Early Organization of Red Caps, 1937–1938," *Negro History Bulletin* 29.5 (February 1966), pp. 101–102 and 114; Barbara M. Posadas, "The Hierarchy of Color and Psychological Adjustment in an Industrial Environment: Filipinos, the Pullman Company, and the Brotherhood of Sleeping Car Porters," *Labor History* 23.3 (1982), pp. 349–73.

52. "Tips in the Supreme Court," *American Labor Legislation Review* 32.2 (June 1941), pp. 55–56.

53. Mary Anderson, "Tips and Legal Minimum Wages," *American Labor Legislation Review* 31.1 (March 1941), p. 12. See also Mary B. Gilson, "Tips and Social Insurance," *American Labor Legislation Review* 31.2 (June 1941), pp. 67–71; Rae L. Needleman, "Tips Again," *American Labor Legislation Review* 31.1 (March 1941), pp. 109–11.

54. Susan Kocin, "Basic Provisions of the 1966 FLSA Amendments," *Monthly Labor Review* 90.3 (March 1967), pp. 1–4.

55. Congressional Record—House, May 25, 1966, p. H11378. See also Congressional Record, Senate, August 26, 1966.

56. Congressional Record, House, May 24, 1966, p. H11299. The inclusion and regulation of farmworkers was also once again hotly debated in the context of these 1966 amendments. And once again, the central issue raised with farmworkers had to do with whether it was possible or desirable to measure these workers' output or productivity by the hour. From 1966 congressional testimony: "A good example [of the difficulty of measuring agricultural labor by the hour] is sheepherding... a sheepherder may work 2 hours a day or 24 hours a day depending upon the needs of his flock. Obviously it would be next to impossible to keep track of a sheepherder's time on an hourly basis." It's interesting that although this is a discussion of agricultural labor, the language is about the nonclock-based temporality of care work. Congressional Record—House, May 25, 1966, p. H11362.

57. Congressional Record, House, May 25, 1966, p. H11364.

58. Ibid.

59. See Benjamin Meyer, "Mrs. Orville Isn't Trying to Steal Tips: An FLSA Story," *University of Chicago Law Review* 84.4 (Fall 2017), https://lawreview.uchicago.edu/print-archive/mrs-orville-isnt-trying-steal-tips-flsa-story; Susan N. Eisenberg and Jennifer T. Williams, "Evolution of Wage Issues in the Restaurant Industry," *ABA Journal of Labor and Employment Law* 30.3 (Spring 2015), pp. 389–408.

60. Ruthie-Marie Beckwith, *Disability Servitude: From Peonage to Poverty* (London: Palgrave Macmillan, 2016), pp. 108–10. In theory, the subminimum wage for workers with disabilities is supposed to be based on "substandard" productivity, however, as Carli Friedman notes, "research has found that companies utilizing these certificates always end up paying below the minimum wage, regardless of their employees' productivity," and an organization such as Goodwill Industries, which has a total revenue of $5.59 billion, "gets donations and government contracts... while still paying people with disabilities subminimum wage." Carli Friedman, "Ableism, Racism, and Subminimum Wage

in the United States," *Disability Studies Quarterly* 39.4 (Fall 2019), https://doi.org/10.18061/dsq.v39i4.6604. As I observed in a note above, the same is true of prison workers: like the labor of "disabled" workers and apprentices/students, prison labor is seen to have a primarily social or rehabilitative function, and not a market function, and thus, incarcerated workers are likewise still unprotected by any minimum wage laws or labor regulation. On productivity, sheltered workshops and the exclusion from regulation, see also Sarah F. Rose, *No Right to Be Idle: The Invention of Disability, 1840s–1930s* (Chapel Hill: University of North Carolina Press, 2017), and Todd Carmody, *Work Requirements: Race, Disability, and the Print Culture of Social Welfare* (Durham: Duke University Press, 2022).

61. Congressional Record, House, May 25, 1966, pp. H11365–66.

62. See the National Restaurant Association statement read by Puciski, Congressional Record, House, May 25, 1966, pp. H11364–65.

63. Congressional Record, Senate, July 8, 1996, p. S7403.

64. Restaurant Opportunities Center United, "The Other NRA: Unmasking the Agenda of the National Restaurant Association," 2014, https://workercenterlibrary.org/wp-content/uploads/2024/07/The-Other-NRA-Unmasking-the-Agenda-of-the-National-Restaurant-Association.pdf.

65. Congressional Record, House, July 9, 1996, pp. H7118–19. See also Mike Elk, "Herman Cain, the NRA, and the Stagnant Subminimum Wage," *In These Times*, September 26, 2011.

66. Sylvia Allegretto and Kai Filion, "Waiting for Change: The $2.13 Federal Subminimum Wage," Briefing Paper 297, Economic Policy Institute, February 23, 2011, p. 4.

67. Nina Mast, "Tipping is a Racist Relic and a Modern Tool of Economic Oppression in the South," Economic Policy Institute (June 2024), https://files.epi.org/uploads/283447.pdf.

68. Food Labor Research Center / International Human Rights Law Clinic at UC Berkeley, "Working Below the Line: How the Subminimum Wage for Tipped Workers Violates International Human Rights Standards" (December 2015), https://food.berkeley.edu/wp-content/uploads/2015/07/WorkingBelowTheLine_F2.pdf.

69. Jasper Bernes, *The Work of Art in the Age of Deindustrialization* (Stanford: Stanford University Press, 2017), p. 35.

70. According to a Federal Reserve study, in the late twenty-teens, about 30 percent of working-age adults had engaged in gigwork; of those, 40 percent had used it to supplement income from another job, and of those, 65 percent said this extra money was very important to their family income. Board of Governors, "Report on the Economic Well-Being of U.S. Households in 2017," Federal Reserve (May 2018), https://www.federalreserve.gov/publications/files/2017-report-economic-well-being-us-households-201805.pdf.

71. Take it from Edward Lazear, founder of the field of personnel economics, the study of labor incentives and compensation, and author of a very influential study of a glass installation firm that shifted from hourly to piece-rate compensation and saw a productivity increase of 44 percent. An incentive payment scheme "motivates those who want to work at high levels of effort as well as those who choose to work at lower levels of effort. A disadvantage is that a pure piece-rate scheme makes the worker bear risk associated with variations in exogenous factors like business conditions." Edward P. Lazear, "Salaries and Piece-Rates," *Journal of Business* 59.3 (July 1986), p. 421.

72. Juliana Feliciano Reyes and Jason Laughlin, "How Incentives in the Gig Economy Put Workers at Risk," *Philadelphia Inquirer*, May 31, 2018, https://www.inquirer.com/philly/news/gig-economy-worker-safety-independent-contractor-caviar-grubhub-handy-care-uber-20180531.html.

73. See Veena Dubal, "On Algorithmic Wage Discrimination," *Columbia Law Review* 123:7 (October 2023), pp. 1929–92.

74. Data and quotation from Suzanne Specker, "Hun, I Want You for Dessert: Why Eliminating the Sub-Minimum Wage for Restaurant Servers Will Empower Women," *University of Pennsylvania Journal of Law and Social Change* 19.4 (2016), p. 344.

75. One Fair Wage, "The Key to Saving the Restaurant Industry Post-Covid 19," https://static1.squarespace.com/static/6374f6bf33b7675afa750d48/t/6478b90b6da8b82fc69bdb75/1685633291680/OFW_FactSheet_USA.pdf.

76. Niels van Doorn and Darsana Vijay, "Gig Work as Migrant Work: The

Platformization of Migration Infrastructure," *Economy and Space* 56.4 (2021), p. 4.

77. The firm itself offered these "essential heroes"—the "most active shoppers" on the app, most of whom had made between one and three thousand deliveries in a single year during the middle of the COVID-19 pandemic—a $200 grocery shopping credit.

78. Housekeepers earn on average less than $25,000 a year, and a significant majority are women of color or recent immigrants. Marriott—which had reported net incomes for the previous year of more than $600 million, up 10 percent from the year before—was, not surprisingly, eager to participate in an effort promising to raise their employee's incomes (and thus potentially improve their retention rates and productivity) without increasing the corporation's labor costs.

79. Hobsbawm, "Custom, Wages, and Workload in Nineteenth Century Industry," p. 113.

80. Ibid., pp. 114 and 118.

81. Palmer, "Outside the Law," p. 417.

82. Matthew Klein, "The Great American Make-Work Programme," *Financial Times*, September 8, 2016, https://www.ft.com/content/ff20019a-3444-30dd-b479-4ef79b9e860e.

83. See Jasper Bernes, "Character, Genre, Labor: The Office Novel After Deindustrialization," *Post45* 1 (January 10, 2019), https://post45.org/2019/01/character-genre-labor-the-office-novel-after-deindustrialization.

84. Madeline Lane-McKinley, *Comedy Against Work: Utopian Longing in Dystopian Times* (New York: Common Notions, 2022), p. 20.

85. Ella Taylor, *Prime-Time Families: Television Culture in Postwar America* (Berkeley: University of California Press, 1989), pp. 112–13.

86. As Michael Szalay notes, even the most well-discussed "working-class" sitcom of this period, *All in the Family*, treated its protagonist's manufacturing job as an "afterthought," and "the series explored his moonlighting as a taxi-driver before it took us to his day job." Michael Szalay, *Second Lives: Black-Market Melodramas and the Reinvention of Television* (Chicago: University of Chicago Press, 2023), p. 20.

87. Taylor, *Prime-Time Families*, p. 111. See also Michael Tueth, *Laughter in the Living Room: Television Comedy and the American Home Audience* (New York: Peter Lang, 2005). On the relationship between workplace TV and women's work, see also Serafina Bathrick, "*The Mary Tyler Moore Show*: Women at Home and at Work," in Joanne Morreale, ed., *Critiquing the Sitcom: A Reader* (Syracuse: Syracuse University Press, 2003); Elana Levine, *Wallowing in Sex: The New Sexual Culture of 1970s American Television* (Durham: Duke University Press, 2007).

88. Lane-McKinley, *Comedy Against Work*, p. 25.

89. Tueth, *Laughter in the Living Room*, p. 121. See also Taylor, *Prime-Time Families*, pp. 112–13.

90. Szalay, *Second Lives*, pp. 8–9.

91. Michael Z. Newman, "From Beats to Arcs: Towards a Poetics of Television Narrative," *Velvet Light Trap* 58.1 (Fall 2006), p. 23.

92. In this sense, they capture aspirational mobility by way of what Lauren Berlant describes as "a fantasy of endless upwardness." Lauren Berlant, *Cruel Optimism* (Durham: Duke University Press, 2011), p. 5.

93. As Tueth observes, Alex Reiger's status as the "central, mimetic character with whom the viewers could identify" seems directly linked to the fact that he's also the only character who views taxi driving as a vocation. Tueth, *Laughter in the Living Room*, p. 124.

94. By allegorizing the reality of *nondomestic* in-person service work as the fantasy of domestic servitude, these shows might even be said to anticipate the discourse around mid-1990s welfare reform, especially the Personal Responsibility and Work Opportunity Act, which Melinda Cooper describes as "brutally reinstat[ing] the historically racialized obligations of domestic servitude, in a form that responds to the imperatives of the post-Fordist service economy," typically by "subjecting them to new forms of unfree domestic labor *outside the home*," that is, in low-waged jobs in child care or fast food. Cooper, *Family Values*, pp. 102–103.

95. L. S. Kim, *Maid for Television: Race, Class, Gender, and a Representational Economy* (New Brunswick: Rutgers University Press, 2023), p. 7.

96. Quoted in Lisa Diaz-Ordaz, "Real Work: Domestic Workers' Exclusion

from the Protections of Labor Laws," *Buffalo Journal of Gender, Law, and Social Policy* 19.1 (2010–2011), p. 107.

97. Provisions to include in-home direct-care workers were not passed until 2015, and babysitters remain among the only low-wage service occupations explicitly excluded from the FLSA's overtime and wage regulations.

98. *Roseanne*'s interest specifically in managerial labor—managerial labor run along domestic lines, as a "family-owned business"—also anticipates the transformation Szalay locates in quality TV in the wake of the 2001 and 2008 financial crises. These "corporate family melodramas" don't represent the workplace as a family, but rather imagine the family itself as a business, as on shows such as *The Sopranos, Big Love, Weeds, Breaking Bad, Halt and Catch Fire, Empire, Ozark,* and *Succession.* Szalay, *Second Lives*, pp. 8–10.

99. Tueth, *Laughter in the Living Room*, p. 134.

100. As Richard Butsch observes, between 1946 and 1990, "of 262 domestic situation comedies, only 11 series featured a blue-collar employee," and "when clerical and service workers are included, 'working class series' are still a very meager 11% of all series; by contrast, 45% represented professional heads of household." Richard Butsch, "Class and Gender in Four Decades of Situation Comedy: Plus ça change . . . ," *Critical Studies in Mass Communication* 9.4 (1992), p. 389. See also Lynne Spangler, "Class on Television: Stuck in *The Middle*," *Journal of Popular Culture* 47.3 (2014), pp. 470–88.

101. While my account here will focus on the form and content of contemporary service-work TV, rather than its production, the historical shift I am describing might easily be mapped onto changes in the labor practices and processes of the film and TV industry itself. John Thompson Caldwell, among others, has noted that labor in the TV/film industry is very differentiated, including workers governed by a residually "Taylorist industrial" work process and with access to the "labor mystique" of craft work, highly professionalized "creative class" workers with professional legitimacy and a great deal of cultural capital, and an "unregulated" sector of noncontracted assistants and clerical workers without access to either stable craft employment or professional security. For this last type of worker, Caldwell notes, there is "little permanence or job security, and . . . none of the regimentation of production proper." As a

result, he argues, the "trade genres" that self-reflexively capture these workers' experience tend to be "stories that affirm constant interpersonal flexibility, quid pro quo networking, and mutual exploitation as vocational skill-set." John Thornton Caldwell, *Production Culture: Industrial Reflexivity and Critical Practice in Film and Television* (Durham: Duke University Press, 2008), pp. 38, 156, 58–59. Lane-McKinley similarly notes a link between the rise of platform TV—which brought with it new cultures of both production and consumption—and the rise of stand-up comedy specials as well as more "traditional comedian-centered sitcoms" (a category that includes a number of the shows listed above, including *Crashing*, *Insecure*, and *Master of None*). Yet while Caldwell suggests that the most exploited workers in the film and TV industry have a largely mystified, "affirmative" relationship to their own labor conditions—recalling Hochschild's comparison of the in-person service worker to the method actor who is "trying to delude herself and create an illusion for the audience, who accept it as a gift"—Lane-McKinley finds a more dialectical mix of the ideological and the utopian in contemporary service-work TV: "The stand-up artist may embody the gigified work ethic of these times, internalizing the conditions of work and transmuting exploitation into artistic aspirations," she contends, "but not without an undercurrent of antiwork questioning and post-work longing." Lane-McKinley, *Comedy Against Work*, pp. 41 and 46–48.

102. Paradoxically, *Succession* thus turns out to be closer than *Downton Abbey* to the nineteenth-century novel: the servant of the Victorian novel, Bruce Robbins notes, was limited mostly to "mute, expository appearances" and was intended simply to "place the [upper-class] protagonist's life in problematic relation to the laboring community." Bruce Robbins, *The Servant's Hand: English Fiction from Below* (New York: Columbia University Press, 1985), p. 123.

103. Alex Woloch, *The One vs. the Many: Minor Characters and the Space of the Protagonist in the Novel* (Princeton: Princeton University Press, 2003), p. 120.

104. Ibid.

105. As Steedman argues in an extraordinary essay on the figure of the servant and theories of the unconscious, servants have long served as just such a screen—or, better put, as a witness. The servant's "observation and recounting"

affirms the master's "dimensions, [their] shape and form as a person." Carolyn Steedman, "Servants and their Relation to the Unconscious," *Journal of British Studies* 42.3 (July 2003), p. 334.

106. For Sianne Ngai and Lauren Berlant, contemporary comedy captures the indistinction between labor and play: affective work, they suggest, "demand[s] play and fun," and comedy has long found humor in the tension between play and the coercive demand. Sianne Ngai and Lauren Berlant, "Comedy Has Issues," *Critical Inquiry* 43.2 (Winter 2017), p. 236.

107. See Szalay, *Second Lives*, especially pp. 12–15.

108. As Ngai and Berlant's account suggests, comedy is uniquely able to set opposites alongside one another, to forge odd couples, to produce contrary emotional responses (anxiety/catharsis, pleasure/discomfort).

109. Steedman, "Servants and their Relation to the Unconscious," p. 338.

110. Woloch, *The One vs. the Many*, p. 120.

111. Lane-McKinley, *Comedy Against Work*, p. 9.

112. The term *picaro*—a figure Anne Cruz defines as "a lowly rogue living by his wits"—first appeared in a literary text in 1599 (Mateo Aleman's *Guzman de Alfarache*). Anne Cruz, *Discourses of Poverty: Social Reform and the Picaresque Novel in Early Modern Spain* (Toronto: University of Toronto Press, 1999), p. 5. Although some critics date the origins of the picaresque genre as far back as the 1499 *La Celestina*, its codification in Spanish literature is typically dated to the mid-sixteenth-century *Lazarillo de Tormes*; later influential examples in English include Daniel Defoe's *Moll Flanders* and *Roxana* and Tobias Smollett's *Roderick Random*. Often a criminal, the picaro is virtually always a "low-class individual who yearns for a higher social status" and "tries his hand at several professions living by his or her wits," J. A. Garrido Ardila observes. J. A. Garrido Ardila, "Origins and Definition of the Picaresque," in J. A. Garrido Ardila, ed., *The Picaresque Novel in Western Literature* (Cambridge: Cambridge University Press, 2015), p. 11. Although its commitment to realistic description make it an important precursor to the realist novel, the picaresque tends not to follow what Northrop Frye identified as the novel's "hence" structure (a causal and orderly organization of events), but rather to deploy the "and-then" narrative of the romance, where events follow on one another paratactically and in a

potentially interchangeable order. Northrop Frye, *Notebooks on Romance* (Toronto: University of Toronto Press, 2005).

113. Matthew Garrett, "Subterranean Gratification: Reading After the Picaro," *Critical Inquiry* 43.1 (Fall 2015), p. 99.

114. Pierre Vilar, "The Age of Don Quixote," *New Left Review* 1.68 (July–August 1971), p. 70.

115. As critic Stephen Miller writes, "there is no part the picaro will not play.... He assumes whatever appearance the world forces on him.... The picaro is every man he has to be, and therefore no man."Quoted in Ulrich Wicks, "The Nature of Picaresque Narrative: A Modal Approach," *PMLA* 89.2 (March 1974), p. 247. See also Garrett, "Subterranean Gratification," p. 100.

116. Peter Linebaugh, *The London Hanged: Crime and Civil Society in the Eighteenth Century* (London: Penguin, 1991), p. 119.

117. On *White Lotus*, as I noted above, the first season's emphasis on the service workers at a resort expands in the second season to include two sex-working service workers, Lucia and Mia, who must find a way to force a client to pay them what he owes. (Interestingly, Lucia and Mia solve this problem by pretending to have a threatening pimp, when in fact they are more like independent contractors.) We find a similar connection between service work and sex work in two 2022 films about service work, Ruben Ostlund's *Triangle of Sadness* and Mark Mylod's *The Menu*. There is far more to say about these films (both darkly comedic farces in the vein of *White Lotus*) than I can accommodate in a single footnote. Here I will note simply that *Triangle of Sadness* plots its own picaresque reversal of fortunes when the most seemingly abjected service worker on the cruising yacht, "toilet manager" Abigail, gains the upper hand over the other survivors of the shipwreck because she is the only one who knows how to fish and she gleefully revels in her newfound power by turning one of the passengers into her own personal sex worker, paying him "in kind" in pretzels and Evian. In *The Menu*, Margot—one of the guests at the restaurant—is saved from being burned alive along with the other guests when Julian realizes she is not the girlfriend of her date, but rather a hired escort. Clarifying that he must distinguish between "us" (the restaurant staff) and "them" (the guests), Julian tells Margot, "You belong here with your own breed....

With the shit shovelers. You thought I couldn't tell? Oh, I know a fellow service industry worker when I see one." In this way, *The Menu* neither abjects sex work nor uses it as a metaphor. Instead, it simply notes that sex workers are a subset of service workers: both, as Julian says, laboring as "a provider of experiences."

118. Quoted in Wicks, "The Nature of Picaresque Narrative," p. 245.

119. Garrett, "Subterranean Gratification," p. 100.

120. Sianne Ngai, *Our Aesthetic Categories: Zany, Cute, Interesting* (Cambridge, MA: Harvard University Press, 2014), pp. 174–224.

121. In film, this affective (as well as economic) "recession" has been associated with "mumblecore," popularized by *Easy* showrunner Joe Swamberg.

122. The show was originally a web series featuring nineteen five-to-twelve-minute episodes, and HBO produced a second and third season of thirty-minute episodes. The shift from web series to HBO-produced series seems to have led to at least one less than salutary revision: while the webisodes make clear that The Guy is service worker who sees those he delivers to as "customers," an early HBO episode has him answer the question "Why don't you have a loyalty program?" by saying, "My business isn't doing well enough to give out free product"—as if he's a self-employed small-business-owner—and referring not to "customers," but rather to "clients." This change can be read as ideological, but it also might reflect the consequences of the partial decriminalization of weed in New York City in 2013, the year after the web series was released. After this legal change, most deliverers were shift workers for larger operations, with their earnings based on commissions and tips, instead of independent operators.

123. I was reminded of the tradition in some restaurants of "family meal," the meal that "back-of-house" workers sometimes prepare for "front-of-house" workers to get them through the long dinner shift, usually a much more casual, homey, and sustaining style of food than the cuisine being served to customers.

124. Wicks, "The Nature of Picaresque Narrative," p. 242.

125. Dynamex Operations West, Inc. v. Superior Court of Los Angeles County, 4 Cal. 5th 903, 416 P.3d 1, 232 Cal.Rptr.3d 1.

126. Vilar, "The Age of Don Quixote," p. 68.

127. Rebecca Wanzo, "Precarious-Girl Comedy: Issa Rae, Lenham Dunham, and the Abjection Aesthetics," *Camera Obscura* 31.2 (2016), pp. 27–59. *Broad City*'s humor also resembles that of prestige comedies such as *Weeds*, which in Szalay's account registers the abjecting qualities of reproductive labor via grotesque images of bodily violation and bodily fluids, from breast milk to shit. Szalay, *Second Lives*, pp. 85–86.

128. Heather Berg, "Working for Love, Loving for Work: Discourses of Labor in Feminist Sex-Work Activism." *Feminist Studies* 40.3 (2014), pp. 694–95. See also Heather Berg, *Porn Work: Sex, Labor, and Late Capitalism* (Chapel Hill: University of North Carolina Press, 2021), especially pp. 165–70.

129. Mark Fisher, "Suffering with a Smile," *Occupied Times* (June 22, 2013), https://theoccupiedtimes.org/?p=11586.

130. Carl Cederström and Peter Fleming, "If Only I Was Fucked and Left Alone," *Strike! Magazine* (2012), pp. 16–17.

131. Frédéric Lordon, *Willing Slaves of Capital: Marx and Spinoza on Desire*, trans. Gabriel Ash (London: Verso, 2014), p. 81.

132. Peter Fleming, *Sugar Daddy Capitalism: The Dark Side of the New Economy* (New York: Polity, 2019), pp. 6 and 15.

133. For a more considered, feminist account of the connection between service work and sex work, see Maya Gonzalez and Cassandra Troyan, "Heart of a Heartless World," *Blindfield: A Journal of Cultural Inquiry*, May 26, 2016, https://blindfieldjournal.com/2016/05/26/3-of-a-heartless-world; Elizabeth Bernstein, "Bounded Authenticity and the Commerce of Sex," in Eileen Boris and Rhacel Salazar Parreñas, eds., *Intimate Labors: Cultures, Technologies, and the Politics of Care* (Stanford: Stanford University Press, 2010).

134. Hochschild, *The Managed Heart*, pp. 8 and 45.

135. Étienne de La Boétie, *The Politics of Obedience: The Discourse of Voluntary Servitude*, trans. Harry Kurz (Auburn: The Von Mises Institute, 2008), pp. 73–74.

136. Lordon, *Willing Slaves of Capital*, pp. 53 and 81. In a powerfully critical review of Lordon, Chris Taylor notes that the translation of the title is both inaccurate and telling: "What the original French title [*Capitalisme, désir et*

servitude] refers to as neoliberal 'servitude' is posed as qualitatively distinct from the forms of work and domination that precede it. And yet the history of slavery that Lordon wants to bracket off as he fixes his attention on our present symptomatically erupts into his text with a surprising regularity," Chris Taylor, "Plantation Neoliberalism," *The New Inquiry* (July 8, 2014), https://thenewinquiry.com/plantation-neoliberalism.

137. See Daniel Rodgers, *The Work Ethic in Industrial America, 1850–1920* (Chicago: University of Chicago Press, 1979).

138. Quoted in Glickman, *A Living Wage*, p. 12.

139. See ibid., chapters 1 and 2.

140. As I suggested above, OFW deploys what Cobble terms "occupational unionism"—a unionism not connected to a specific work site, but one that enables mobility and portability—a "bread and roses unionism" seeking not just contracts and regulations and to redress systems of exploitation, but also to imagine the provision of care and community and to redress systems of domination (sexual harassment, for instance). Dorothy Cobble and Michael Merrill, "The Promise of Service Worker Unionism," in Marek Korczynski and Cameron Lynne Macdonald, eds., *Service Work: Critical Perspectives* (New York: Routledge, 2009), p. 164.

141. See Sheila Blackburn, "Princesses and Sweated Wage-Slaves Go Well Together: Images of British Sweated Workers, 1843–1914," *International Labor and Working-Class History* 61 (Spring 2002), pp. 24–44; Lori Merish, *Archives of Labor: Working-Class Women and Literary Culture in the Antebellum United States* (Durham: Duke University Press, 2017).

142. Miller's image—the one most clearly evoked by OFW—actually didn't become an iconic or representative image until the mid-1980s. Prior to the 1980s, and especially during the period of World War II, Norman Rockwell's *TIME* cover was the exemplary image of Rosie.

143. As a number of historians note, War Manpower Commission campaigns such as "Rosie the Riveter" were ultimately not especially successful, though they did succeed in hastening the decline of domestic service as the primary form of work available to Black women. Rates of domestic service plummeted during the 1940s and didn't rebound after the war, in part due to

the mid-century rise in consumer durables that fed the US economic boom at the peak of industrial profitability. See William Breen, "Women and Work: The Limits of the War Manpower Commission Policy in World War II," *Australasian Journal of American Studies* 20.2 (December 2001), pp. 62–78; Paddy Quick, "Rosie the Riveter: Myths and Realities," *Radical America* 9.4–5 (July–August 1975), pp. 124–30.

144. "By closing off new job opportunities to a worker," a War Manpower Commission report from 1941 notes, "he can be compelled to remain in his present employment." Technical Service Division, United States Employment Service, US Department of Labor, *A Short History of the War Manpower Commission* (June 1948), p. 113, https://babel.hathitrust.org/cgi/pt?id=uiug.30112011683056&seq=5. Thanks to Jordan Pruett for this citation. The category also appears in labor laws regulating the right to strike and as a way to make the state itself the dispute mediator of last resort. As the International Labour Organization notes, those in "essential services" can be prohibited from striking when doing so would pose "a clear and imminent threat to the life, personal safety or health of the whole or part of the population." See ILO, *Freedom of Association: Compilation of Decisions of the Committee on Freedom of Association*, 6th ed. (Geneva: International Labour Office, 2018), paragraph 836, p. 156, https://www.ilo.org/sites/default/files/wcmsp5/groups/public/@ed_norm/@normes/documents/publication/wcms_632659.pdf.

145. Pandemic-era guidance on the definition of "essential worker" defined "essential" even more broadly than had World War II–era policy: in Arizona, it included employees at golf courses; in Florida, it encompassed those employed by World Wrestling Entertainment. As Andrew Lakoff notes, "The policy was not oriented toward traditional public health activities, whether sanitation and hygiene measures or biomedical interventions. It did not involve the production of knowledge about the disease per se.... Rather, the policy focused on the systems underpinning social and economic life. As [California governor Gavin] Newsom's executive order put it, 'The supply chain must continue.'" Lakoff describes "essential work" as "a new form of social classification, one that interacted in complex ways with existing forms of social inequality," but like the policy itself, he accepts a blurred distinction between "socially essential" and

"economically essential." Andrew Lakoff, "The Supply Chain Must Continue: Becoming Essential in the Pandemic Emergency," *Items: Insights from the Social Sciences* (November 5, 2020), https://items.ssrc.org/covid-19-and-the-social-sciences/disaster-studies/the-supply-chain-must-continue-becoming-essential-in-the-pandemic-emergency.

146. Berg, *Porn Work*, p. 23.

147. Juno Mac and Molly Smith, *Revolting Prostitutes: The Fight For Sex Workers' Rights* (London: Verso, 2020), pp. 7 and 135–36.

148. "My tips also vanished into many hands before they reached mine," writes Rachel Rabbit White, "It was mandatory to tip the 'host', the DJ . . . even the bouncers or managers when they 'hooked you up' with customers. Instead of counting on earning a fair wage, every aspect of working for the club felt designed to put me in debt that my labor paid back." Rachel Rabbit White, "Strippers on Strike," *Commune* 5 (Winter 2020), https://communemag.com/strippersonstrike.

149. See the transcript of "Strippers in the U.S. Want Better Work Conditions. Some Are Trying to Unionize," National Public Radio, September 16, 2022, especially the interview with Cat Hollis of the Haymarket Pole Collective, https://www.npr.org/2022/09/14/1122937491/strippers-in-the-u-s-want-better-work-conditions-some-are-trying-to-unionize.

150. Chris Chen, "The Limit Point of Capitalist Equality Notes Toward an Abolitionist Antiracism," *End Notes 3: Gender, Race, Class, and Other Misfortunes* (September 2013), https://endnotes.org.uk/translations/chris-chen-the-limit-point-of-capitalist-equality. Italics in the original.

CHAPTER TWO: MICROWORK AND PIECE-RATE POETRY

1. Aaron Koblin, "The Sheep Market: Two Cents Worth," MA thesis, UCLA, 2006.

2. Jeff Barr, "10,000 Sheep—Collaborative Art Project," *AWS News Blog*, May 10, 2006, https://aws.amazon.com/blogs/aws/10000_sheep_col.

3. Aaron Koblin, "Visualizing Ourselves . . . with Crowd-Sourced Data," TED, March 2011, https://www.ted.com/talks/aaron_koblin_visualizing_ourselves_with_crowd_sourced_data?language=en. This, obviously, is why *Sheep*

Market could become an Amazon-friendly "cool example" of the "wisdom of crowds."

4. As Amazon Web Service's website puts it, through Amazon's Mechanical Turk, "a crowdsourcing marketplace that makes it easier for individuals and businesses to outsource their processes and jobs to a distributed workforce who can perform these tasks virtually," workers can "complete simple tasks that people do better than computers. And, get paid for it. Choose from thousands of tasks, control when you work, and decide how much you earn." Amazon Web Services, "Amazon Mechanical Turk: Access a Global, On-Demand, 24x7 Workforce," https://www.mturk.com. Koblin's emphasis on humanity resonates with the ideological discourse of microwork as entrepreneurial, unalienated, and liberated. Like Amazon, Koblin frames AMT as a way for workers to "express" their skills, creativity, and intelligence, redirecting our attention away from AMT's technology and gesturing instead toward a transhistorical idea of human collective intelligence.

5. Siou Chew Kuek, Cecilia Paradi-Guilford, Toks Fayomi, Saori Imaizumi, Panos Ipeirotis, Patricia Pina, and Manpreet Singh, *The Global Opportunity in Online Outsourcing* (Washington, DC: World Bank, 2015), p. 1, https://openknowledge.worldbank.org/server/api/core/bitstreams/4444b259-4bd5-5b6f-b0e3-b7e1ab92ebde/content.

6. Quoted in Jason Pontin, "Artificial Intelligence, with Help From the Humans," *New York Times*, March 25, 2007, https://www.nytimes.com/2007/03/25/business/yourmoney/25Stream.html.

7. Paul Hitlin, "Research in the Crowdsourcing Age, a Case Study," Pew Research Center (July 2016), https://www.pewresearch.org/internet/2016/07/11/research-in-the-crowdsourcing-age-a-case-study.

8. International Labor Organization, "How to Define a Minimum Wage?," 1.7, "Piece Rate Pay," https://www.ilo.org/resource/17-piece-rate-pay.

9. See Vern Baxter and Susan Mann, "The Survival and Revival of Non-Wage Labor in a Global Economy," *Sociologia Ruralis* 32.2–3 (August 1992), pp. 231–47.

10. In underdeveloped countries that moved directly from agriculture to an informalized service economy and thus skipped generalized

industrialization—the stage in which, for reasons Chapter 1 explained, time-based wage regulations could transform manufacturing labor (and vice versa)—piece-rate wages have simply remained the norm. For data on the prevalence of piece-rates, see Fay Hansen, "Currents in Compensation and Benefits," *COMPFLASH News and Analysis* 42.6 (November 2010), pp. 3–15, https://journals.sagepub.com/doi/10.1177/0886368709355652, and Nicholas Bloom and John Van Reenen, "Human Resource Management and Productivity," National Bureau of Economic Research Working Paper 16019 (May 2010), https://www.nber.org/papers/w16019.

11. Darren Wershler, afterword to Nick Thurston, *Of the Subcontract, or Principles of Poetic Right* (York: Information as Material, 2013), p. 135.

12. Mark McGurl, *Everything and Less: The Novel in the Age of Amazon* (London: Verso, 2021).

13. Aaron Benanav, *Automation and the Future of Work* (London: Verso, 2020); Jason Smith, *Smart Machines and Service Work: Automation in an Age of Stagnation* (London: Reaktion Books, 2020).

14. In E. P. Thompson's account, piece rates occur in manufacturing contexts where there are "irregular work rhythms" and informal "taken work" conducted outside the normativizing lash of the regular work week. Hobsbawm's account of time wages and rationalization is markedly different in this respect. For Hobsbawm, the shift from a diversity of payment methods (including some based on custom and others on productivity) to a singular, time-based wage contributed to the process whereby industrial workers could learn "'the rules of the game'" when it came to setting the price of labor, a "fair day's wage for a fair day's work." That is, while Thompson sees time discipline as an alienating rationalization—and as the *differentia specifica* of the capitalist labor process—Hobsbawm argues that by learning "to regard labor as a commodity" with a potentially standardizable (instead of solely customary) price, workers could demand compensation more equivalent to their contribution. Like Thompson, however, Hobsbawm suggests a straightforward association between time-based wages and the rationalizing force of scientific management and increased mechanization: employers responded to workers' new conceptions of their bargaining power by creating more "efficient ways of utilizing

their workers' labor time" and increasing productivity via the "scientifically calculated and controlled output norm per time unit" made possible by technology. E. P. Thompson, "Time, Work-Discipline, and Industrial Capitalism," *Past and Present* 38.1 (December 1967), pp. 56–97; Eric Hobsbawm, "Custom, Wages, and Workload in Nineteenth Century Industry," in Asa Briggs and John Saville, eds., *Essays in Labor History* (New York: St. Martin's Press, 1966).

15. Karl Marx, *Capital, Volume One*, trans. Ben Fowkes (New York: Penguin, 1976), pp. 692–96. The chapter titled "Piece-Wages" is somewhat contradictory. Marx initially argues that difference between time rates and piece rates is not particularly important relative to the more urgent distinction between the price of labor power and its use value. The opening sentence of the chapter notes that "the piece-wage is nothing but a converted form of the time-wage." But Marx goes on to argue that piece-rate wages are fundamental to the emergence of capital labor discipline and mechanization—moreover, the claim that they are the purest form of capitalist wage also suggests that they might not be an exception or a prehistory, but rather a norm to which capitalism tends.

16. Ibid., p. 695.

17. John Ramsay McCulloch, *A Treatise on the Circumstances Which Determine the Rate of Wages and the Condition of Labouring Classes* (London: G. Routledge, 1854), pp. 70–71.

18. Peter Scholliers and Leonard Schwartz, *Experiencing Wages: Social and Cultural Aspects of Wage Forms in Europe since 1500* (New York: Berghahn Books, 2003), pp. 114–15.

19. James Schmiechen, *Sweated Industries and Sweated Labour: The London Clothing Trades, 1860–1914* (London: Croom Helm, 1984), pp. 8–9.

20. Mechanization in factories forced deskilling and extended the working day for outworkers, too, while low piece-rate wages pushed down wages across the board. In periods of labor unrest (for instance, in the wake of a large 1834 textile strike) many organized day-rate factory workers were replaced by decentralized piece-rate outworkers. Nor was piece-rate sweated labor untouched by the pressures of mechanization. The sewing machine, which could speed up the work of seam sewing by 500 percent, was also small enough that it could be used in homes and small tenement workshops and was often sold on brutal

installment plans that made it available to small-scale producers, thus making the mechanization even of piece-rate outwork possible. See Wally Seccombe, *Weathering the Storm: Working-Class Families from the Industrial Revolution* (London: Verso, 1993), especially chapters 1 and 2.

21. Peter Linebaugh, *The London Hanged: Crime and Civil Society in the Eighteenth Century* (London: Penguin, 1991), pp. 226–27 and 400–401.

22. Linebaugh argues that they thus complete the "despotism of capital" by ensuring that "the 'task' itself comes under the control of capitalist definitions." Ibid., pp. 400–401.

23. Sometimes, of course, fixed and regular wages are better than task-rate wages simply for reasons of rational efficiency and reducing bureaucratic and management costs. Thus, Ronald Coase's immensely influential essay "The Nature of the Firm" defines firms primarily via the difference between an enterprise that hires employees and offers guaranteed compensation (a firm) and one that contracts out to independent contractors (an entrepreneurial project). Ronald Coase, "The Nature of the Firm," *Economica* 4.16 (November 1937), pp. 386–405.

24. Frederick Winslow Taylor, *Scientific Management: Comprising Shop Management, the Principles of Scientific Management, and Testimony Before the Special House Committee* (New York: Harper, 1947), pp. 30–31.

25. Clarence Bertrand Thompson, *Scientific Management: A Collection of the More Significant Articles Describing the Taylor System of Management* (Cambridge, MA: Harvard University Press, 1914), p. 709, emphasis mine.

26. Edward P. Lazear, "Performance Pay and Productivity," *American Economic Review* 90.5 (December 2000), p. 1350. See also Edward P. Lazear, "Salaries and Piece Rates," *Journal of Business* 59.3 (July 1986), pp 405–31.

27. As historians Martin Brown and Peter Philips put it, piece rates were a way to "exploit the tolerance of hand-production technology for a wide range of labor productivity." Martin Brown and Peter Philips, "The Decline of the Piece-Rate System in California Canning: Technological Innovation, Labor Management, and Union Pressure, 1890–1947," *Business History Review* 60.4 (Winter 1986), p. 569.

28. David Montgomery, *Workers Control in America: Studies in the History of*

Work, Technology, and Labor Struggles (Cambridge: Cambridge University Press, 1979), pp. 37–39.

29. Claudia Goldin, for instance, found that in manufacturing work in the late nineteenth century, women were 3.5 times more likely to be paid by the piece compared to men. Claudia Goldin, "Women's Employment and Technological Change: A Historical Perspective," in Heidi Hartmann, ed., *Computer Chips and Paper Clips: Technology and Women's Employment, Volume 2* (Washington, DC: National Research Council, 1987).

30. See Ian Smith and Trevor Boyns, "Scientific Management and the Pursuit of Control in Britain to c. 1960," *Accounting, Business, and Financial History* 15.2 (July 2005), pp. 187–216. Chapter 3 will explore the relationship between management, control, and the method of wage payment in more detail, but it's worth noting that Linebaugh also connects piece rates not only to the "despotism of capital," but to the more direct violence of the police. He describes the River Thames Police—London's first centralized police force and forerunners of the Metropolitan Police formalized in the mid-nineteenth century—as "accepting direct responsibility for the payment of wages" to the informalized day-laborer work crews of the docks, "setting piece-rates," managing the workers, and thus as "directly responsible for the quantitative exploitation of the river working-class." Linebaugh, *The London Hanged*, pp. 433–34.

31. Brown and Philips, "The Decline of the Piece-Rate System in California Canning," p. 580. The shift away from piece rates was technological, but it also had a bearing on managerial technique: "When production becomes highly mechanized . . . the motivational aspects of incentive wages are greatly diminished." Ibid., p. 572. A historical study of Bureau of Labor Statistics data on piece rates notes significant declines in their use in manufacturing beginning in the 1940s: for instance, 60 percent of metalworkers were paid by the piece in 1942, but by 1961, the number had dropped to only 8 percent. See Earl Lewis, "Extent of Incentive Pay in Manufacturing," *Monthly Labor Review* 83.5 (1960), pp. 460–63.

32. Richard A. Epstein, "The Regulatory Hour: The History, Law and Economics of Minimum Wage and Maximum Hours Legislation," *New York University Journal of Law and Liberty* 12.3 (2019), p. 497. Even this solution provoked

debate, of course: the proposal to create a racial differential based on the substandard productivity ascribed to Black workers, for instance, was one effort to reject this kind of averaging or equalizing framework. In Chapter 1, similarly, I quote a senator making the case for excluding domestic work from regulation because the hour worked by the feminized careworker who might sit and "have a Coke with the family" or otherwise "enjoy herself" was fundamentally different from an hour worked by a male worker laboring hard with his body.

33. See United States v. Rosenwasser, 323 U.S. 360 (1945), p. 323.

34. In 1966, the FLSA allowed competitive employers to pay only 50 percent of the minimum wage. The 1986 amendments made it such that subminimum wages paid to workers with disabilities were no longer indexed to the prevailing minimum wage at all. Instead, employers of workers with disabilities were require simply to pay a "commensurate" wage indexed to the employee's "productivity." In the ableist logic that justified this exclusion, we find the same set of anxieties about productive efficiency that had convinced employers that piece-rate wages were a good way to manage immigrant workers and women. As Sarah Rose argues in *No Right to Be Idle: The Invention of Disability*, "mechanization and the drive for efficiency... provided employers with new notions of what made a good worker." Sarah F. Rose, *No Right to Be Idle: The Invention of Disability, 1840s–1930s* (Chapel Hill: University of North Carolina Press, 2017), p. 11. These new ideas about productivity and efficiency were also built into the FLSA, in part because the act's narrowly productivist definition of "industry" and "commerce" meant that only those "engage[d] in... the production of goods" would be covered and in part as a result of the exclusion of "individuals whose earning capacity is impaired by age or physical or mental deficiency." Yoked to the long-standing producerist and ableist ideologies about disabled workers' capacities, these new regulations allowed for even greater wage theft, since piece-rate wages based on measured productivity were, Ruthie-Marie Beckwith explains, "prone to error and/or deliberate manipulation." Ruthie-Marie Beckwith, *Disability Servitude: From Peonage to Poverty* (London: Palgrave Macmillan, 2016), p. 84. See also Carli Friedman, "Ableism, Racism, and Subminimum Wage in the United States," *Disability Studies Quarterly* 39.4 (Fall 2019), https://dsq-sds.org/index.php/dsq/article/view/6604/5465, and

Todd Carmody, *Work Requirements: Race, Disability, and the Print Culture of Social Welfare* (Durham: Duke University Press, 2022).

35. See Lee J. Alston and Robert Higgs, "Contractual Mix in Southern Agriculture Since the Civil War," *Journal of Economic History* 42.2 (June 1982), pp. 327–53.

36. See Sean Farhang and Ira Katznelson, "The Southern Imposition: Congress and Labor in the New Deal and Fair Deal," *Studies in American Political Development* 19.1 (Spring 2005), pp. 1–30; Juan F. Perea, "The Echoes of Slavery: Recognizing the Racist Origins of the Agricultural and Domestic Worker Exclusion from the National Labor Relations Act," *Ohio State Law Journal* 72.1 (2011); Phyllis Palmer, "Outside the Law: Agricultural and Domestic Workers Under the Fair Labor Standards Act," *Journal of Policy History* 7.4 (1995); Veena Dubal, "The New Racial Wage Code," *Harvard Law and Public Policy Review* (September 30, 2021).

37. Quoted in Autumn L. Canny, "Lost in a Loophole: The Fair Labor Standards Act's Exemption of Agricultural Workers from Overtime Compensation Protection," *Drake Journal of Agricultural Law* 2 (Summer 2005), p. 370. The white supremacist claim that plantation-style racialized labor was necessary to Southern agrarian "tradition" was thus strategically reframed as an argument about the importance of keeping labor costs low in a sector whose "traditional" working conditions were fundamentally different from the conditions of Northern industrial manufacturing.

38. "Statement of Ivan McDaniel, Representing the Agricultural Producers' Labor Committee—Resumed," *National Labor Relations Act and Proposed Amendments: Hearings Before the Committee on Labor, US Senate, Seventy-Sixth Congress, First Session*, part 16 (July 11, 12, and 13, 1939), p. 3638. Like domestic-service workers, farmworkers were described as having a uniquely "intimate," personal, and nonconflictual relation to their employers. Thus, the Social Security Board's 1937 report *Social Security in America* claimed that regulations were hard to enforce in the case of both "farm labor and domestic servants in private homes" because of "the close relationship which exists between employer and employee." Quoted in Larry Dewitt, "The Decision to Exclude Agricultural and Domestic Workers from the FLSA," *Social Security Bulletin*

70.4 (2010), p. 57. As Phyllis Palmer explains, agricultural lobbying groups appealed to "the images and ideology associated with the family farm, evoking a familial work relationship based on mutual interests and properly exempt from public scrutiny and interference" and emphasizing the "pre-industrial nature of growing and the paternal relationship" between bosses and employees. Palmer, "Outside the Law," p. 421.

39. Quoted in Canny, "Lost in a Loophole," p. 365.

40. See Harry S. Kantor, "A Minimum Wage for Farm Workers," *Monthly Labor Review* 83.7 (July 1960), pp. 677–85.

41. See Canny, "Lost in a Loophole."

42. Ronald L. Mize, "Mexican Contract Workers and the Capitalist Agricultural Process: The Formative Years, 1942–1964," *Rural Sociology* 71.1 (March 2006), p. 95.

43. For instance, tomato growers in California and in Baja California, on the other side of the border, both employ an almost entirely Mexico-born labor force. But the California growers whose workers are Mexican migrants use piece-rate much more often than operations based in Mexico as a result of assumptions about piece-rate and immigrant labor similar to those that informed early twentieth-century manufacturing. See Carol Zabin, "U.S.-Mexico Economic Integration: Labor Relations and the Organization of Work in California and Baja California Agriculture," *Economic Geography* 73.3 (July 1977), pp. 337–55.

44. Mize, "Mexican Contract Workers and the Capitalist Agricultural Process," p. 103. In her account of piece-rate strawberry workers, Julie Guthman argues that piece rates are a form of both social and technological discipline in agriculture. Much as Marx described sweated tenement workers incentivized "to strain [their] labor-power as intensely as possible," Guthman characterizes piece-rate wages in agricultural labor as "inadequate, unless workers toil very hard" and the equivalent of an hourly wage only "if they work very, very hard." Julie Guthman, "Paradoxes of the Border: Labor Shortages and Farmworker Minor Agency in Reworking California's Strawberry Fields," *Economic Geography* 93.1 (January 2017), p. 39.

45. Curtis Marez, *Farm Worker Futurism: Speculative Technologies of Resistance* (Minneapolis: University of Minnesota Press, 2016).

46. See Don Mitchell, "Taylorism Comes to the Fields: Labor Supply, Labor Process, and the Twilight of Fordism in California Agribusiness," *Economic Geography* 99.4 (March 2023), pp. 341–62. As in nineteenth-century textile manufacturing, piece-rate wages in agriculture were the form that "absolute surplus value extraction" (more work for lower wages) took when subject to the simultaneous pressure of "relative surplus value extraction" (more output via technological innovation).

47. Marez, *Farm Worker Futurism*, p. 21.

48. By the end of the 1940s, one in four working women was a clerical worker. Eileen Boris, *Home to Work: Motherhood and the Politics of Industrial Homework in the United States* (Cambridge: Cambridge University Press, 1994), p. 308. See also Sharon Hartman Strom, "'Light Manufacturing': The Feminization of American Office Work, 1900–1930," *Industrial and Labor Relations Review* 43.1 (October 1989), pp. 53–71.

49. Harry Braverman, *Labor and Monopoly Capitalism: The Degradation of Work in the Twentieth Century* (New York: Monthly Review Press, 1974), p. 210.

50. Lee Galloway, *Office Management: Its Principles and Practices Covering Organization and Operation with Special Consideration of the Employment, Training, and Payment of Office Workers* (New York: Ronald Press, 1919), p. 569.

51. William Leffingwell and Edwin Robinson, *Textbook of Office Management* (New York: McGraw-Hill, 1923), p. 483. I am grateful to Charles Gunn for introducing me to Leffingwell's work.

52. Strom, "'Light Manufacturing,'" p. 60.

53. William Leffingwell, *Scientific Office Management* (New York: A.W. Shaw, 1917), pp. 52–53.

54. Ibid., p. 149.

55. See Brown and Philips, "The Decline of the Piece-Rate System in California Canning,"

56. See Braverman, *Labor and Monopoly Capitalism*, p. 230, and Boris, *Home to Work*.

57. Innovations in data processing as well as the microlevel subdivision of labor enabled by the Taylorization of clerical service work described above made workers themselves seem interchangeable. As in agriculture, moreover,

mechanization and informalization in clerical work were complementary processes: automated offices still needed human attendants, and temps could do that work for significantly lower wages than permanent workers. Plus, they could easily be fired and rehired as needed. See Braverman, *Labor and Monopoly Capitalism*, chapter 15, and Louis Hyman, *Temp: How American Work, American Business, and the American Dream Became Temporary* (New York: Viking, 2018), pp. 125–41.

58. Boris, *Home to Work*, p. 317.

59. Ibid., p. 332. See also Mann and Baxter, eds, *Computer Chips and Paper Clips*.

60. Sarah Roberts, *Behind the Screen: Content Moderation in the Shadows of Social Media* (New Haven: Yale University Press, 2019), p. 42.

61. Many of these centers provide customer service, from direct-call centers to content moderation, and the health-care industry makes up the fastest-growing portion of BPOs. The World Health Organization estimated in 2015 that BPOs would gross around $20 billion in revenue by 2020, and today, almost all US employers—not just multinational corporations, but mid-size companies, as well as public-sector institutions such as universities—outsource at least one business service. See Jamie Peck, *Offshore: Exploring the Worlds of Global Outsourcing* (Oxford: Oxford University Press, 2017), especially chapter 5.

62. On the displacement of BPOs by online outsourcing, see Kuek, et al, *The Global Opportunity of Online Outsourcing*.

63. Roberts, *Behind the Screen*, pp. 42–43.

64. See Nick Bernards, *The Global Governance of Precarity: Primitive Accumulation and the Politics of Irregular Work* (London: Routledge, 2018).

65. For glowing coverage of Samasource, see, for instance, Francesca Gino and Bradley R. Staats, "The Microwork Solution," *Harvard Business Review* (December 2012), https://hbr.org/2012/12/the-microwork-solution, and Kerry Dolan, "Google Gives a Boost to Microwork Nonprofit Samasource," *Forbes* (December 14, 2011), https://www.forbes.com/sites/kerryadolan/2011/12/14/google-gives-a-boost-to-microwork-nonprofit-samasource/. For criticism of SamaUSA, see Sarah Kessler, "The Unequal Geography of the Gig Economy,"

Atlantic, June 15, 2018, https://www.theatlantic.com/business/archive/2018/06/gig-economy-inequality/560942: and Kessler, *Gigged: The End of the Job and the Future of Work* (London: St. Martins Press, 2018). For more on microwork and the global division of labor's integration with the security state, see Miranda Hall, "The Ghost of the Mechanical Turk," *Jacobin* (December 16, 2017), https://jacobin.com/2017/12/middle-east-digital-labor-microwork-gaza-refugees-amazon.

66. Maria Konnikova, "Bringing the Rural Poor into the Digital Economy," *Pacific Standard Magazine*, November 19, 2015, https://psmag.com/education/bringing-the-rural-poor-into-the-digital-economy.

67. Much as microcredit soon became a lucrative business for banks and speculative lenders, Janah's company transitioned in 2019 from a nonprofit to a for-profit company now called simply Sama. In 2022 Sama and Meta (Facebook's parent company) were sued in Kenya for rights, health, and privacy violations surrounding content-moderation labor.

68. Bruno Moreschi, Gabriel Pereira, and Fabio Cozman, "The Brazilian Workers in Amazon Mechanical Turk: Dreams and Realities of Ghost Workers," *Contracampo: Brazilian Journal of Communication* 39.1 (2020), p. 58, https://periodicos.uff.br/contracampo/article/view/38252/pdf.

69. In this way, AMT resembles delivery apps such as Instacart that likewise black-box their wage formulas and then, after ensuring a steady supply of and demand for workers, increase their own share of the total amount spent by customers on labor.

70. Hitlin, "Research in the Crowdsourcing Age, a Case Study," n.p.

71. As policy researcher Vanessa Williamson writes: "In the course of my graduate work at Harvard University, I paid hundreds of Americans living in poverty the equivalent of about $2 an hour. . . . I was not alone, or even unusual, in basing Ivy League research on less-than-Walmart wages; literally thousands of academic research projects pay the same substandard rates." Vanessa Williamson, "Can Crowdsourcing Be Ethical?", *Brookings Institute*, February 8, 2016, https://www.brookings.edu/articles/can-crowdsourcing-be-ethical/. A very few scholars have similarly suggested that AMT poses a serious ethical problem to researchers and have suggested that journal editors should commit

to publishing only articles where the authors pay a living wage, while grants, Institutional Review Board approval, and general disciplinary protocols should require similar transparency and ethics. Many others have pointed out some of the methodological "challenges" of using AMT, especially epistemological or methodological questions of representativeness, quality, accuracy, and anonymity.

72. Researchers concerned about the use of AMT in computational linguistics analyzed the Association of Computational Linguistics Anthology, which hosts papers on the study of computational linguistics and natural-language processing, and turned up eight-six papers using AMT labor in a single year. Karen Fort and Gilles Adda, "Amazon Mechanical Turk: Gold Mine or Coal Mine?," *Computational Linguistics* 37.2 (June 2011), pp. 413–20. A few examples focused especially on the humanities and literature: Phillip Massey, Patrick Xia, and Noah Smith, "Annotating Character Relationships in Literary Texts," Cornell University arXivLabs (2015), https://arxiv.org/pdf/1512.00728; David Plans Casal, "Crowdsourcing the Corpus: Using Collective Intelligence as a Method for Composition," *Leonardo Music Journal* 21 (2011), pp. 25–28; Mike Thelwall, Kevan Buckley, and Georgios Paltoglou, "Sentiment in Twitter Events," *Journal of the American Society for Information Science and Technology* 62.2 (February 2011), pp. 406–18; Smitha Milli and David Bamman, "Beyond Canonical Texts: A Computational Analysis of Fanfiction," in Jian Su, Kevin Duh, and Xavier Carreras, eds., *Proceedings of the 2016 Conference on Empirical Methods in Natural Language Processing* (Austin: Association for Computational Linguistics, 2016); Saif Mohammad and Peter D. Turney, "Emotions Evoked by Common Words and Phrases: Using Mechanical Turk to Create an Emotion Lexicon," in *Proceedings of the Workshop on Computational Approaches to Analysis and Generation of Emotion in Text* (Los Angeles: Association for Computational Linguistics, 2010); Piotr Marecki, "Crowdsourcing and Literature: A Report from the Project 'Wiersze za sto dolarów,'" *World Literature Studies* 3.9 (2017), pp. 79–86; Andrew Land and Joshua Rio-Ross, "Using Amazon Mechanical Turk to Transcribe Historical Handwritten Documents," *Code4lib* 15 (October 31, 2011), https:// journal.code4lib.org/articles/6004. Researchers in political science have written methodological essays about the usefulness of AMT, as have scholars in psychology and statistics. See, for instance. Nicole

Lazar, "The Big Picture: Crowdsourcing Your Way to Big Data," *Chance* 32.2 (2019), pp. 43–46; Adam Berinsky, Kai Quek, and Michael Sances, "Conducting Online Experiments on Mechanical Turk," *Newsletter of the APSA Experimental Section* 3.1 (2012), https://titiunik.github.io/papers/Titiunik2012-Experimental Newsletter.pdf; Michael Buhrmester, Tracy Kwang, and Samuel D. Gosling, "Amazon's Mechanical Turk: A New Source of Inexpensive Yet High-Quality Data?", *Perspectives on Psychological Science* 6.1 (January 2011), pp. 3–5.

73. *Digital Scholarship in the Humanities* has published at least four articles using AMT labor. The Berkeley D-Lab's AMT projects have included The University of California Cliometric History Project and the Online Hate Index Research Project. The Berkeley D-Lab has multiple AMT-sourced projects and offers consulting services geared toward helping scholars use it. Stanford's Center for Spatial and Textual Analysis (CESTA) has a whole partnership, funded by the Mellon Foundation, to explore crowdsourcing in the humanities and has partnered with the Stanford Literary Lab on AMT-exploiting projects such as RyanHeuser, Franco Moretti, and Erik Steiner, *The Emotions of London*, Literary Lab Pamphlet 13 (October 2016). Columbia University English Professor Nick Dames used AMT workers for "Extracting Social Networks from Literary Fiction," produced with David K. Elson and Kathleen McKeown and published in Jan Hajič, Sandra Carberry, Stephen Clark, and Joakim Nivre, eds., *Proceedings of the 48th Meeting of the Association for Computational Linguistics* (Uppsala: Association for Computational Linguistics, 2010). Influential media theory scholar Lev Manovich's Cultural Analytics institute uses AMT labor for projects such as selfiecity, "Interactive web app for exploring a dataset of 3200 Instagram selfie photos." Other digital humanities labs have produced tools allowing other scholars to use AMT more easily, such as the Berkeley D-Lab's TextThresher and various emotion lexicons. One widely reported study used low-waged AMT labor to map the relation between the "literary misery index" in twentieth-century Anglophone novels and the "economic misery index" of the location where they were set: one component of "economic misery" was (you guessed it!) low wages. Alexander Bentley, Alberto Acerbi, Paul Ormerod, and Vasileios Lampos, "Books Average Previous Decade of Economic Misery," *PLOS One* 9.1 (January 8, 2014), https://journals.plos.org

/plosone/article?id=10.1371/journal.pone.0083147. Another study used AMT for pedagogical purposes: students were assigned to "inherit the uncomfortable position of capitalist management" by hiring AMT workers to create a digital art piece exploring the immiserating conditions of industrial labor described in Rebecca Harding Davis's 1861 novel *Life in the Iron Mills*: xtine burrough and Sabrina Starnaman, "A Digital Korl Woman: Students and Workers Recover the Spirit of *Life in the Iron Mills* from the Digital Factory to the Classroom," *Transformations: The Journal of Inclusive Scholarship and Pedagogy* 27.2 (2017), pp. 121–41. As these examples suggest, humanities researchers may feel a bit queasy about using AMT, but they continue not only to do so, but also to defend it. Suzanne Keen, writing on digital humanities methods for *Narrative*, describes AMT as contributing to diversity because it allows researchers "to reach a large and diverse pool of paid research subjects" (although they virtually all require proof of English competency before they'll pay a Turker for HITs). Suzanne Keen, "Pivoting Towards Empiricism: A Response to Fletcher and Monterosso," *Narrative* 24.1 (January 2016), p. 109.

74. Adam Berinsky, Gregory Huber, and Gabriel Lenz, "Evaluating Online Labor Markets for Experimental Research: Amazon.com's Mechanical Turk," *Political Analysis* 20.3 (January 4, 2017), p. 354.

75. In other countries—most notably, Brazil, where high unemployment has produced a large supply of microworkers—AMT workers are still paid in US dollars, which adds yet another form of risk to their wage structure: currency fluctuation. See Moreschi, Pereira, and Cozman, "The Brazilian Workers in Amazon Mechanical Turk," p. 52, and Kuek et al., *The Global Opportunity in Online Outsourcing*, pp. 56–57.

76. See Joel Ross, Lilly Irani, Six Silberman, Andrew Zaldivar, and Bill Tomlinson, "Who are the Crowdworkers? Shifting Demographics in Amazon Mechanical Turk," *Proceedings of the 28th International Conference on Human Factors in Computing Systems, CHI 2010, Extended Abstracts* (New York: Association for Computing Machinery, 2010), pp. 2863–872. If an Indian AMT worker worked full time and earned that amount consistently—which for reasons I lay out below would actually require significantly more than forty hours a week on the platform—their monthly take-home pay would be roughly equivalent to the

minimum wage for semiskilled workers there, although the majority of global microworkers have at least some college education and, as I note below, multi-language competency.

77. Stephen Uzor, Jason T. Jacques, John J, Dudley, and Per Ola Kristensson, "Investigation the Accessibility of Crowdwork Tasks on Mechanical Turk," *Proceedings of the 2021 CHI Conference on Human Factors in Computing Systems* (New York: Association for Computing Machinery, 2021), pp. 1–14.

78. Dubal, "The New Racial Wage Code," p. 5. See also Vili Lehdonvirta, "Flexibility in the Gig Economy: Managing Time on Three Online Piecework Platforms," *New Technology, Work and Employment* 33.1 (March 2018), pp. 13–29.

79. Most Turkers understand that the platform "works" by stealing workers' time unless they are very careful about which tasks they take on and can perform those they select at incredible speed. As one study of worker knowledge noted, a HIT that a novice worker rated as "fair" was quickly rejected by a more experienced worker: "This could take a maximum of 30 minutes and 55 questions for 8 cents, that comes out to $0.16 an hour, no way I would touch it." This canniness on the part of microworkers belies the fiction that they actively enjoy the freedom and flexibility of the platform. For instance, one academic paper defending researchers' use of AMT claimed that "most participants do not find MTurk stressful" and that "MTurk offers flexibility and benefits that most people value above other options for work." Benjamin V. Hanrahan, Anita Chen, JiaHua Ma, Ning F. Ma, Anna Squicciarini, and Saiph Savage, "The Expertise Involved in Deciding which HITs Are Worth Doing on Amazon Mechanical Turk," *Proceedings of the ACM on Human-Computer Interaction* 5.128 (April 2021), p. 14. Aaron J. Moss, Cheskie Rosenzweig, Jonathan Robinson, Shalom N. Jaffe, and Leib Litman, "Is It Ethical to Use Mechanical Turk for Behavioral Research?," *Behavior Research Methods* 55.2 (May 2023), https://osf.io/preprints/psyarxiv/jbc9d_v1. (Of this study of the "ethics" of using AMT, it's worth noting that the "Conflicts of Interest" stated on the PsyArXiv website where this article appears states that "The authors of this manuscript have the following potential competing interests: all authors are employed at CloudResearch (formerly TurkPrime). CloudResearch provides online research

tools and services, including tools that allow researchers to run studies on Mechanical Turk.")

80. Hanrahan et al., "The Expertise Involved in Deciding which HITs Are Worth Doing on Amazon Mechanical Turk," p. 19.

81. Ibid., p. 9.

82. Ali Alkhatib, Michael S. Bernstein, and Margaret Levi, "Examining Crowd Work and Gig Work Through the Historical Lens of Piecework," *Proceedings of the 2017 CHI Conference on Human Factors in Computing Systems* (New York: Association for Computing Machinery, 2017), p. 4605.

83. The crowdsourcing platform MobileWorks even automates the selection of HITs themselves: whereas AMT allows workers to select from a menu of HITs, MobileWorks claims to make microwork less frustrating by assigning tasks algorithmically, rather than requiring workers to choose. See Lehdonvirta, "Flexibility in the Gig Economy."

84. Economist Joseph Stiglitz, for instance, argues that by paying hourly wages, the firm "reduc[es] the risk faced by the worker" while "increas[ing] the risk to the firm." For Stiglitz, the risk shift is salutary, but it's clearly far less of a positive for workers themselves. Joseph Stiglitz, "Incentives, Risk, and Information," *Bell Journal of Economics* 6.2 (Autumn 1975), p. 558. Dubal describes piece-rates as an "unpredictable and inconsistent wage calculation system" that sometimes means workers labor for no wages at all. Dubal, "The New Racial Wage Code," p. 6. Political economist Paul William Matthews dubs piece rates "tyrannical" because of the power inequalities between workers and employers: workers are given quotas, and if they cannot meet them for any reason—including "absence, sickness, injury, lack of ability, broken machinery, or lack of raw materials"—they "may have to borrow from [their] boss against future labor." Paul William Mathews, "Piece Rates as Inherently Exploitative: Adult/Asian Cam Models as Illustrative," *New Proposals: Journal of Marxism and Interdisciplinary Inquiry* 7.2 (March 2015), pp. 67–69.

85. See Daniel C. Ganster, Christa E. Kiersch, Rachel E. Marsh, and Angela Bowen, "Performance-Based Rewards and Work Stress," *Journal of Organizational Behavior Management* 31.4 (Fall 2011), pp. 221–35; M. E. Davis and E. Hoyt, "A Longitudinal Study of Piece Rate and Health: Evidence and

Implications for Workers in the US Gig Economy," *Public Health* 180.2 (October 2020), pp. 1–9; Mary Davis, "Pay Matters: The Piece Rate and Health in the Developing World," *Analysis of Global Health* 82.5 (September 2016), pp. 858–65.

86. As its critics suggest, because piece-rate wages seem to coordinate the interests of bosses and workers neutrally and impersonally, they are a powerful tool of managed subordination. Ironically, however, because piece-rate workers *seem* to be autonomous and self-managed, they are sometimes described as having more control over their own working conditions than hourly workers. (We will return to this problem of control in Chapter 3.) In this context, Marx describes liberal social reformer John Watts's argument that piece workers resemble independent artisans because they "are their own masters." Conflating freedom with the compulsion to "chose" to work ever-longer days, the discourse of piece-rate workers' autonomy anticipates the contemporary representation of gigworkers as independent, entrepreneurial self-starters.

87. For Marx, piece rates produce a competition among workers that prevents collective organization; for Michael Burawoy, they "manufacture consent" by eliciting the kinds of social and individual pleasures to be had in "the play of the game"; for Harry Braverman, likewise, they are an attempt to "enlist the worker as a willing accomplice in his own exploitation." Michael Burawoy, *Manufacturing Consent: Changes in the Labor Process Under Monopoly Capitalism* (Chicago: University of Chicago Press, 1982), especially chapter 5; Braverman, *Labor and Monopoly Capitalism*, p. 43. See also Michael Burawoy and Janos Lukacs, *The Radiant Past: Ideology and Reality in Hungary's Road to Capitalism* (Chicago: University of Chicago Press, 1992), especially chapter 2.

88. C. L. R. James, *Mariners, Renegades, and Castaways: The Story of Herman Melville and the World We Live In* (London: Allison and Busby, 1985), p. 17. See also Cesare Casarino, *Modernity at Sea: Melville, Marx, Conrad in Crisis* (Minneapolis: University of Minnesota Press, 2002).

89. Promotional material for *Emoji Dick*, https://www.emojidick.com.

90. Lisa Gitelman, "*Emoji Dick* and the Eponymous Whale, An Essay in Four Parts," *Post45*, July 7, 2018, https://post45.org/2018/07/emoji-dick-and-the-eponymous-whale-an-essay-in-four-parts.

91. Helen Molesworth, *Work Ethic* (State College: Penn State University Press, 2003), p. 27.

92. Julia Bryan Wilson, *Art Workers: Radical Practice in the Vietnam War Era* (Berkeley: University of California Press, 2009), pp. 4–5.

93. Benjamin Buchloh, "Conceptual Art 1962–1969: From the Aesthetic of Administration to the Critique of Institutions," *October* 55 (Winter 1990), p. 107.

94. Dave Beech, *Art and Postcapitalism: Aesthetic Labour, Automation, and Value Production* (London: Pluto Press, 2019), pp. 68–70.

95. Jasper Bernes, *The Work of Art in the Age of Deindustrialization* (Stanford: Stanford University Press, 2017), pp. 4–5 and 141–49.

96. Craig Dworkin, "Poetry in the Age of Consumer-Generated Content," *Critical Inquiry* 44 (Summer 2018), p. 674. Kenneth Goldsmith and Craig Dworkin, eds., *Against Expression: An Anthology of Conceptual Writing* (Evanston: Northwestern University Press, 2011), p. xix. Goldsmith also celebrates "the new environment of textual abundance" in which it's not necessary to write new poems, because there are so many texts out there already. "We aren't hammering on typewriters," Goldsmith writes. Here, he seems to acknowledge the transformed—which is to say fully industrialized—experience of deskilled clerical work that Bernes describes, but then he pivots to a techno-utopian description of contemporary networked labor: we are "focused all day on powerful machines with infinite possibilities, connected to networks with a number of equally infinite possibilities." Kenneth Goldsmith, *Uncreative Writing: Managing Language in the Digital Age* (New York: Columbia University Press, 2011), p. 24.

97. Christian Bök, "The Piecemeal Bard Is Deconstructed: Notes Toward a Potential Robopoetics," *Object 10: Cyberpoetics* (2002), p. 10.

98. Joshua Clover, "The Technical Composition of Conceptualism," *Mute*, April 2, 2014, https://www.metamute.org/editorial/articles/technical-composition-conceptualism.

99. Sianne Ngai, *Theory of the Gimmick: Aesthetic Judgement and Capitalist Form* (Cambridge, MA: Harvard University Press, 2020), p. 4

100. Ibid., p. 72.

101. In this sense—and drawing on Bernes's account of neoconceptual poetry as the aesthetic correlative of internet trolling—we might see these works as an elaborate "troll" of the art practices that Leigh Claire La Berge describes in her illuminating book *Wages Against Artwork*. In La Berge's account, contemporary social-practice art draws on feminist theory and aesthetics to resist the commodification of labor and the wage and to expose the material relations between precarious art workers and other equally precarious postindustrial wage laborers. La Berge locates deindustrialization and financialization—and the fact that "we will work more and more for less and less, and in some cases even for nothing"—as the context for an aesthetic "grounded in labor's decommodification." I do not disagree with this as a broad description of much contemporary art, but the pieces and microtraditions I discuss here are clearly taking a different approach to the same set of historical conditions. Leigh Claire La Berge, *Wages Against Artwork: Decommodified Labor and the Claims of Socially Engaged Art* (Durham: Duke University Press, 2019), p. 16.

102. The quote appears in Dworkin's introductory essay for *Against Expression*, in Goldsmith's *Uncreative Writing*, and in Marjorie Perloff's "Conceptual Poetry and the Question of Emotion," https://www.humanities.uci.edu/sites/default/files/document/ConceptualPoetryforIrvineseminar.pdf, among other places.

103. Poets.org, "Against Expression: Kenneth Goldsmith in Conversation," June 17, 2011, https://poets.org/text/against-expression-kenneth-goldsmith-conversation.

104. For this reading of "glitch," see Hugh Manon and Daniel Temkin, "Notes on Glitch," *world picture* 6 (2011), http://worldpicturejournal.com/article/notes-on-glitch.

105. Claire Bishop, *Artificial Hells: Participatory Art and the Politics of Spectatorship* (London: Verso, 2012), pp. 219–39.

106. The description is certainly suggestive, After all, the massive increase in globally connected phone-scamming operations over the last five years is a result of the concomitant rise in BPOs (the largest US investigation of Indian scam-call centers was called "Operation Outsource," and even the scam syndicates themselves employ subcontractors). Zach Whalen, "Some Notes

on Analyzing the Content of *Emoji Dick*," June 26, 2022, https://www.zachwhalen.net/notes/note-1656258366.

107. On piece rates and stenographers, see Braverman, *Labor and Monopoly Capitalism*, p. 213.

108. Nick Thurston, *Of the Subcontract, or Principles of Poetic Right* (York: Information as Material, 2013).

109. John Guillory's *Cultural Capital* famously highlights the pathos of an unread canon of working-class writing by describing it as like undiscovered gems that "do not circulate but nevertheless have value, a kind of *unvalued* value." These poems circulate under the name not of aesthetic or commodity value, but rather under the sign of the *wage*. John Guillory, *Cultural Capital: The Problem of Literary Canon Formation* (Chicago: University of Chicago Press, 1993), p. 86.

110. Maria Damon, "Micropoetries," *Oxford Research Encyclopedia of Literature* (May 24, 2017), https://oxfordre.com/literature/view/10.1093/acrefore/9780190201098.001.0001/acrefore-9780190201098-e-63.

111. Sean Bonney, "Notes on Militant Poetics," *Journal of British and Irish Innovative Poetry* 14.1 (2022), https://poetry.openlibhums.org/article/id/9255.

112. Margaret Ronda, "'Not Much Left': Wageless Life in Millennial Poetry," *Post45: Contemporaries* (October 9, 2011), https://post45.org/2011/10/not-much-left-wageless-life-in-millenial-poetry.

113. Thurston, *Of the Subcontract*, pp. 102–104.

114. Much as Hughes's poem contests the universality of the lyric "I," the anonymous poet who wrote "Where Do I Start" begins with the speaker's proper name and location; much as "English B" distances the twenty-two-year-old speaker from the "older" instructor, "Where Do I Start" implies that even that quantitative details such as age might be experienced quite differently across sites and subjects because the speaker is nineteen, but "feel[s] even older."

115. Gauri Viswanathan, "The Beginnings of English Literary Study in British India," *Oxford Literary Review* 9.1–2 (1987), p. 20. I am grateful to Harris Feinsod for pointing this out.

116. Florence Boos, s.v. "Poetry, Working-Class," in Dino Felluga, Linda K. Hughes, and Pamela Gilbert, eds., *The Encyclopedia of Victorian Literature*

(Chichester: Wiley Blackwell, 2015). They recall, too, Mark Nowak's account of "social poetics," in which context "poems written by migrant workers whose primary occupations are neither poetry nor academia might be bolder, more imaginatively militant" than the canon. Mark Nowak, *Social Poetics* (Minneapolis: Coffeehouse Press, 2020), p. 142.

117. Thurston, *Of the Subcontract*, p. 33.

118. Boos, "Poetry, Working-Class"; Nowak, *Social Poetics*, pp. 177–200.

119. Thurston, *Of the Subcontract*, p. 59.

120. Ibid., p. 56.

121. In this sense, neoconceptual works such as Thurston's resemble what Joanna Drucker terms "complicit formalism," which involves a "knowing compromise" that "counters the basis on which autonomy could be assumed." In evoking or even defending the special status of art against this compromise, the Turkers who contributed to Thurston's project expose the bad faith behind this gesture. This also puts them in an interesting relation to Leigh Claire La Berge's fascinating account of how artistic critiques of autonomy—whether in art or theory—are *always* in a complex relation (what she terms "oppositional independence") to the very ideals they resist. For La Berge, social-practice art dialectically appeals to the special status of the art object to illuminate the conditions of work that "cannot be sold." "Turk," likewise, demands that the reader attend to the brutal inadequacy of the price of commodified labor on AMT. Like the institution of the art school (paid for by student debt) that La Berge describes, AMT here becomes a kind of medium of its own through which claims to autonomy must by processed and in which they are entangled. I return to questions of complicity in Chapter 3. See Johanna Drucker, *Sweet Dreams: Contemporary Art and Complicity* (Chicago: University of Chicago Press, 2005); La Berge, *Wages Against Artwork*, especially chapters 1 and 2.

122. Boos, "Poetry, Working-Class."

123. Unlike Hamilton, the author of "Turk" knowingly writes for an audience of one or even none; hence, I think, the affective mix of rage and resignation we find in this and the other AMT poems. Nonetheless, to respond to this poem *as if* one has been addressed is to begin to understand the complex relations of both complicity and (potential) solidarity produced by global microwork.

124. Tim Burke, "The Romantic Georgic and the Work of Writing," in Charles Mahoney, ed., *A Companion to Romantic Poetry* (London: Wiley Blackwell, 2011), pp. 142–43.

125. Kevis Goodman, *Georgic Modernity and British Romanticism: Poetry and the Mediation of History* (Cambridge: Cambridge University Press, 2005), p. 11.

126. Katie Kadue, *Domestic Georgic: Labors of Preservation from Rabelais to Milton* (Chicago: University of Chicago Press, 2021), pp. 11–16.

127. Margaret Ronda, "'Work and Wait Unwearying': Dunbar's Georgics," *PMLA* 127.4 (October 2012), pp. 863–78.

128. Margaret Ronda, "Georgic Disenchantment in American Poetry," *Genre* 46.1 (Spring 2013), p. 61.

129. Ibid., p. 41.

130. See Dubal, "The New Racial Wage Code," p. 12.

131. Poets.org, "Against Expression: Kenneth Goldsmith in Conversation," Academy of American Poets, June 17, 2011, https://poets.org/text/against-expression-kenneth-goldsmith-conversation.

132. Thurston, *Of the Subcontract*, p. 26.

133. See Minsoo Kang, *Sublime Dreams of Living Machines: The Automaton in the European Imagination* (Cambridge, MA: Harvard University Press, 2011).

134. Edward Jones-Imhotep, "The Ghost Factories: Histories of Automata and Artificial Life," *History and Technology* 36.1 (2020), pp. 3–29; David Golumbia, "The Amazonization of Everything," *Jacobin* (August 5, 2015), https://jacobin.com/2015/08/amazon-google-facebook-privacy-bezos/; Astra Taylor, "The Automation Charade," *Logic(s)*, no. 5, August 1, 2018, https://logicmag.io/failure/the-automation-charade. For other examples, see also Kris Paulsen, "Shitty Automation: Art, Artificial Intelligence, and Humans in the Loop," *Media-N: Journal of the New Media Caucus* 16.1 (March 2020), https://iopn.library.illinois.edu/journals/median/article/view/227; Shawn Wen, "The Ladies Vanish," *New Inquiry*, November 11, 2014, https://thenewinquiry.com/the-ladies-vanish. An exception to this tendency to misdescribe microwork's reliance on tech is Phil Jones' excellent book *Work Without the Worker: Labour in the Age of Platform Capitalism* (London: Verso, 2021), ebook, unpaginated,

which situates AMT in a long history of technological rationalization and which describes microwork as "informalized... badly paid, erratic piecework" sundered from the "regulatory frameworks that legislate pay and rights." Jones also contrasts the decentralization of microwork with the urban centralization of platform gigworkers described in the next chapter: microworkers, he writes, are "tucked away in bedrooms and internet cafes" and "remain invisible to one another and to the institutions that might otherwise organise them. Workers are geographically dispersed, rarely if ever brought together in physical space"; the organization of circulation gigworkers, by contrast, has required "meeting in town and city centres [as] a central tenet of organisation."

135. Mary Gray and Siddarth Suri, *Ghost Work: How to Stop Silicon Valley from Building a New Global Underclass* (New York: Harper Collins, 2019).

136. Interestingly, this may mirror Kempelen's own intentions. As Kang explains, Kempelen did not in fact intend to deceive audiences into thinking his device was real. Rather, Kang argues, by staging a device doing things most audiences believed "a clock-work machine could not possibly do," Kempelen intended to demonstrate "the *impossibility* of man as machine" and to celebrate the distinct capabilities of "human guidance and reason." Kang, *Sublime Dreams of Living Machines*, p. 182.

137. Benanav, *Automation and the Future of Work*, pp. 1–2.

138. Smith, *Smart Machines and Service Work*, p. 15.

139. Benanav, *Automation and the Future of Work*, p. 29.

140. See William Baumol and W. G. Bowen. "On the Performing Arts: The Anatomy of their Economic Problems," *American Economic Review* 55.1.2 (March 1965), pp. 495–502; William Baumol, "Macroeconomics of Unbalanced Growth: The Anatomy of Urban Crisis," *American Economic Review* 57.3 (June 1967), pp. 415–26.

141. Smith, *Smart Machines and Service Work*, p. 81; Benanav, *Automation and the Future of Work*, pp. 59–60.

142. Benanav, *Automation and the Future of Work*, p. 5.

143. Karl Marx, *Grundrisse*, trans. Martin Nicolaus (New York: Penguin Books), p. 706.

144. Marx, *Capital, Volume One*, p. 352.

145. Moris Altenried, *The Digital Factory: The Human Labor of Automation* (Chicago: University of Chicago Press, 2022), pp. 52–53.

146. Smith, *Smart Machines and Service Work*, pp. 111–12.

147. Braverman, *Labor and Monopoly Capitalism*, pp. 81 and 148.

148. Indeed, the assembly line as a technology has often blurred the distinction between technological "revolution" and old-fashioned "domination." Take, for instance, the opening image of Elizabeth Esch's *The Color Line and the Assembly Line*, a description of Ford production manager Charles Sorensen in 1932 as painted by Diego Rivera: "Sorensen—popularly known among workers as the 'slave-driver'—[is] pressing workers through fear and the threat of force to work faster on the assembly line." He is "clutching the clipboard that—like the stopwatch—signified Ford's constant surveillance of workers' movements," and his "fierce and hovering presence is a potent representation of how power was wielded and production was achieved on Ford's assembly lines." Elizabeth Esch, *The Color Line and the Assembly Line: Managing Race in the Fordist Empire* (Berkeley: University of California Press, 2018), p. xi. As Smith says, even the assembly line—the technology most associated with the "replacement of humans by machines"—was *also* a way to "coerc[e] more [human] labor out of a given hour."

149. Gareth Stedman Jones argues that outwork allowed for a great deal of flexibility: it "removed all necessity to iron out irregularity of production" and thus "accentuated the advantages of small-scale production." Gareth Stedman Jones, *Outcast London: A Study in the Relationship Between Classes in Victorian Society* (London: Verso, 2014), pp. 38–42.

150. Thus, Marx writes, "the scattered handicrafts and domestic industries" were "a broad foundation" of mass-scale industrial production: outworking and more centralized, formalized, and mechanized labor not only combined, but also exerted wage and productivity pressures on one another until finally, "the basis of the old method, sheer brutality in the exploitation of the workers," proved inadequate, and "the hour struck for the introduction of machinery." Marx, *Capital, Volume One*, pp. 601 and 599.

151. Linebaugh, *The London Hanged*, pp. 226–27 and 400–401.

152. Michell, "Taylorism Comes to the Fields," p. 352.

153. This is often explained as the shift from a price-competition model (which tends to be friendly to piece-rate wages, as producers seek to maximize quantity by hiring a lot of workers and paying them as little as possible) to a quality-competition paradigm (which incentivizes greater fixed capital investment, as producers seek to maximize quality by hiring fewer skilled workers to operate machines).

154. See Margaret FitzSimmons, "The New Industrial Agriculture: The Regional Integration of Specialty Crop Production," *Economic Geography* 62.4 (1986), pp. 334–53. Similarly, legislators and lobbyists insisted that excluding Black agricultural workers from minimum-wage laws would *prevent* those workers from losing their jobs to machines. But in fact, the mechanized cotton picker fully automated most of the hand labor in cotton harvesting a decade *before* agricultural workers were included under federal minimum wage laws, and not primarily for reasons of labor shortage or increased costs. Instead, as in textiles, farmers were able to innovate new technology—often simply for reasons of "prestige" or "personal convenience"—in part because they had saved money by paying below-subsistence wages to human workers. See Gilbert Fite, "Recent Progress in the Mechanization of Cotton Production in the United States," *Agricultural History* 24.1 (January 1950), pp. 19–28; James Street, "The 'Labor Vacuum' and Cotton Mechanization," *Journal of Farm Economics* 35.3 (August 1953), pp. 381–97.

155. Alexander J. Quinn, Benjamin B. Bederson, Tom Yeh, and Jimmy Lin, "CrowdFlow: Integrating Machine Learning with Mechanical Turk for Speed-Cost-Quality Flexibility," Human-Computer Interaction Lab 27th Annual Symposium, 2010, https://www.cs.umd.edu/hcil/about/events/symposium2010/Abstracts%20for%20Website/32_alex.pdf.

156. Yaron Singer and Manas Mittal, "Pricing Tasks in Online Labor Markets," in Association for the Advancement of Artificial Intelligence Workshop, *Human Computation: Papers from the 2011 AAAI Workshop (WS-11-11)*, https://citeseerx.ist.psu.edu/document?repid=rep1&type=pdf&doi=f075c8604ef175aaa422514b1390c81635030f89.

157. Louis Hyman, "Digital Migrants, Virtual Reality, and Machine Learning," *Medium*, April 3, 2018, https://medium.com/whats-at-stake-in-a-fourth

-industrial-revolution/digital-migrants-virtual-reality-and-machine-learning-d5a61346d5c9.

158. An increasing number of AMT applications are about what researchers describe as a "symbiotic relationship between humans and computers": tools such as CrowdFlower, a programming library, helps employers chose, on a task-by-task basis, between AMT workers and a fully automated system, often on the basis of the "speed-cost-quality" formula described above. Quinn et. al., "CrowdFlow," n.p.

159. Hope Reese and Nick Heath, "Inside Amazon's Clickworker Platform: How Half a Million People Are Being Paid Pennies to Train AI," *TechRepublic*, December 16, 2016, https://www.techrepublic.com/article/inside-amazons-clickworker-platform-how-half-a-million-people-are-training-ai-for-pennies-per-task.

160. The other relevant form of automation involved in AMT is the automation of management. Here, too, it's worth considering the relationship between piece rates and the labor cost of scientific management itself. Theories of scientific management are replete with anxieties about the "monitoring costs" involved in paying managers to surveil the labor process and keep track of output and productivity. "Is not the expense burden of maintaining the planning department equal to all the savings it can make?" early twentieth-century scientific management gurus Frank and Lillian Gilbreth ask rhetorically. Frank Gilbreth, *Primer of Scientific Management* (New York: D. Van Nostrand, 1912), p. 41. (Todd Carmody's work on the Gilbreths' use of film and photography implies that visual motion studies were themselves a labor-saving device not primarily for factory or office workers, but for scientific managers: "Before specializing in filmic analysis," he writes, "the Gilbreths' approach was a pen and paper affair . . . grounded in painstaking observation and description. . . . It was only when the Gilbreths turned to Marey's light bulb method that industrial motion study would begin to . . . distinguish between efficient and inefficient at a glance." Carmody, *Work Requirements*, pp. 138–41). Lazear goes further, acknowledging that the cost savings that come with piece-rate wages disappear "as the cost of the more precise monitoring rises"; that is, as the work of managers become more and more "scientific" and professionalized,

managers might become so expensive that they cost more money than they save. AMT resolves these problems easily by using platform algorithms in place of an HR department and AI surveillance in place of human managers. Edward P. Lazear, "Salaries and Piece Rates," *Journal of Business* 59.3 (1986), pp. 405–31. As Lilly Irani writes, "For AMT to be scalable, the effort that goes into using AMT—setting up tasks, choosing workers, communicating with workers, and deciding who gets paid and who doesn't—must be manageable for someone who might commission 10,000 workers in the span of a few hours": AMT users are thus "constantly refining techniques to automate the management of this workforce." Lilly Irani, "Microworking the Crowd," *Limn* 2 (2012), https://limn.press/article/microworking-the-crowd. Amazon itself has been secretly developing a means to automate its own HR services, a plan that was first exposed when it turned out that because the AI had been created with data from the tech industry's human hiring practices over the previous ten years, the model had trained itself to reject applications from women. Jeffrey Dastin, "Amazon Scraps Secret AI Recruiting Tool That Showed Bias against Women," *Reuters Business News*, October 9, 2018, https://www.reuters.com/article/world/insight-amazon-scraps-secret-ai-recruiting-tool-that-showed-bias-against-women-idUSKCN1MK0AG.

161. Robert Solow, "We'd Better Watch Out," *New York Times*, July 12, 1987, p. 36.

162. Daron Acemoglu and Pascual Restrepo, "Automation and New Tasks: How Technology Displaces and Reinstates Labor," *Journal of Economic Perspectives* 33.2 (Spring 2019), pp. 5, 10–11, 27.

163. Acemoglu predicts only "modest gains" in both GDP and "total factor productivity" over ten years. See Daron Acemoglu, "The Simple Macroeconomics of AI," *Economic Policy* 41.131 (January 2025), pp. 13–58.

164. Daron Acemoglu and Pascual Restrepo, "Artificial Intelligence, Automation, and Work," National Bureau Of Economic Research, NBER Paper 24196 (January 2018), p. 2.

165. Peter Linebaugh, *Ned Ludd and Queen Mab: Machine Breaking, Romanticism, and the Several Commons of 1811–12* (Oakland: PM Press, 2012), p. 8.

166. Rebecca Lossin, "The Point of Destruction: Sabotage, Speech, and

Progressive-Era Politics," PhD diss., Columbia Journalism School, Columbia University, 2020, pp. 23–30.

167. James Wyatt Woodall, "New York's Taste of Sabotage: Waiters, Wobblies, the 'Peculiar Industry,' and the 1912–13 New York City Hotel Workers' Strike," *Historia Nova: The Duke Historical Review* 1.1 (Fall 2018), pp. 28–47.

168. Elizabeth Gurley Flynn, *Sabotage: The Conscious Withdrawal of the Workers' Industrial Efficiency* (Chicago: IWW Publishing Bureau, 1917), https://www.marxists.org/subject/women/authors/flynn/1917/sabotage.htm.

169. Management theorists Lloyd Harris and Emmanuel Ogbonna note the very high prevalence of what they describe as "intentional, deviant, antiservice behaviors" in contemporary service workplaces, while management scholars Chunhao Ma and Jian Ye note that the introduction of AI and automation only increases the likelihood of service worker sabotage. Lloyd Harris and Emmanuel Ogbonna, "Exploring Service Sabotage: The Antecedents, Types and Consequences of Frontline, Deviant, Antiservice Behaviors," *Journal of Service Research* 4.3 (February 2002), p. 165; Chunhao Ma and Jian Ye, "Linking Artificial Intelligence to Service Sabotage," *Service Industries Journal* 42.13–14 (2022), pp. 1054–74.

170. Jones, *Work Without the Worker,* n.p.

171. Veniamin Veselovsky, Manoel Horta Ribeiro, and Robert West, "Artificial Artificial Artificial Intelligence: Crowd Workers Widely Use Large Language Models for Text Production Tasks," arXiv, June 13, 2023, https://arxiv.org/pdf/2306.07899.

172. Taylor, *Scientific Management,* p. 30.

173. Collected in Goldsmith and Dworkin, *Against Expression,* p. 585.

174. We find a witty representation of this tactic in a surprising place: a TV advertisement for Cadbury chocolate produced and circulated in India. Titled "Make A.I. Mediocre Again," the campaign opens with an office worker receiving a call from his boss, who asks when the project will be done. When the worker responds "Two days?" the boss rejoins, "Use some AI and finish it fast. Send it to me in 10 minutes." "Is AI really helping us work less," a voiceover asks, "or is it making us work even faster?" As if in visual response, a room full of workers stare numbly at their computer screens, responding to requests

from an AI system giving them deadlines in five-second intervals. "If we're forced to keep pace with superefficient AI," the ad inquires, "Will we ever get to sit back and just do nothing?" "Make A.I. Mediocre Again," the ad proclaims alongside a pixelated and intentionally glitchy image of raised fists. "We've built the world's first server farm dedicated to filling the internet with thousands of confusing websites.... And since all AIs train from the internet, the more nonsense the AIs pick up, the more mistakes they start making.... And the more time we'll get to eat [candy bars] and do nothing."

175. Ilia Shumailov, Zakhar Shumaylov, Yiren Zhao, Nicolas Papernot, Ross Anderson, and Yarin Gal, "AI Models Collapse When Trained on Recursively Generated Data," *Nature* 631 (July 24, 2024), p. 758.

CHAPTER THREE: CONTROL AND THE CULTURE OF CIRCULATION GIGWORK

1. On the risks of bike delivery work during the pandemic, see Maria Figueroa, Ligia Guallpa, Andrew Wolf, Glendy Tsitouras, and Hildalyn Colón Hernández, "Essential but Unprotected: App-Based Food Workers in New York City," Cornell University School of Industrial and Labor Relations (ILR) Workers Institute (2023), https://hdl.handle.net/1813/113534.

2. These contradictions recall debates (elaborated in Chapter 1) about the supposedly unalienated quality of in-person service work: domestic work, for instance, was often described as unalienated and unrationalized, healthy and natural, self-managed and self-paced, and thus not in need of regulations designed for industrial work. Yet for reasons I suggest here, the particular tension between freedom or autonomy, on the one hand, and control or subordination, on the other, is specific to the discourse (and the legal status) of gigwork, and especially circulation gigwork. On the contradictions between different conceptions of freedom at work in gig economy discourse, see Deepa Das Acevedo, "Unbundling Freedom in the Sharing Economy," *Southern California Law Review* 91 (2017), pp. 793–838.

3. It is worth briefly articulating both the overlaps and the differences between my argument here and recent essays on "radical flexibility" by Michelle Chihara and Heather Berg. I differ from them by putting

contemporary gigwork in historical context, specifically, the long legal history of direct and indirect control as problems of regulation and management that bear, too, on the legal status of service work in general. At the same time, I admire both essays for their commitment to understanding what Chihara terms a "willful reappropriation" of flexibility and what Berg describes as "the politics of refusal." In this light, Berg contends, "the refrain—'gig work is not, actually, a space of freedom'—does less to shed new light on current conditions than it does to obscure workers' creative maneuverings within them." Berg's essay reframes the critique of gigwork as a critique of work as such, reminding us not to fall into a kind of "exceptionalism" whereby gigwork is a uniquely degrading or otherwise anomalous type of work. Chihara's focus on "flexibility" (for example, her description of workers as "loyal" to "flexible work") is also useful for thinking about the desire for a life not subject to time discipline. Yet it tends to obscure the fact that the vast majority of workers require flexibility not because they "prefer" flexibility in the abstract (as implied by her framing of "radical flexibility" as a utopian demand), but simply because their material circumstances require it. She also does not explore the relationship between temporal flexibility and the self-harrying and overwork that become visible when one considers the larger regulatory/material context of postindustrial service work, especially around issues of informalization. Here, examination of the exploitation of migrant and particularly migrants without work permits seems of vital importance. So, too, is this chapter's concluding focus on the politics of reproduction in a postproductivity era. Michelle Chihara, "Radical Flexibility: Driving for Lyft and the Future of Work in the Platform Economy," *Distinktion: Journal of Social Theory* 23.1 (November 2021), pp. 3, 8, 10. Heather Berg, "Reading Gigs Dialectically," *Critical Historical Studies* 9.1. (Spring 2022), pp. 39–40.

4. My use of "circulation" to describe the work of truckers, "last-mile" delivery workers, and app-based service workers for platforms such as Uber and Doordash is both broader and narrower than some uses of the term. It is narrower in the sense that I focus only on the circulation of finished consumer goods to "end consumers," and not on the supply chains that provide raw materials or that enable production and assembly to be distributed globally. It

is also narrower than Joshua Clover's immensely influential account of circulation as the site of both accumulation and struggle. For Clover, following Giovanni Arrighi's famous account, "circulation" names an epoch wherein capital accumulation depends on mercantile or finance capital. It is broader in the sense that I include not only casualized delivery workers for companies such as FedEx and Amazon, but also workers for app-based services such as DoorDash and Instacart, as well as Uber and Lyft, that deliver humans themselves. These jobs, I suggest, combine features of industrial-type logistics labor with aspects of in-person service work. On the one hand, circulation gigwork's use of technology and its intensely rationalized labor process resemble the industrial-type labor discipline and mechanization common in logistics more than they recall the labor process of domestic servitude. On the other hand, circulation gigwork is clearly part of what Jason Smith terms the contemporary "servant economy" through which consumers across classes can access the private drivers and personal shoppers once available only to the rich. See Deborah Cowen, *The Deadly Life of Logistics: Mapping Violence in Global Trade* (Minneapolis: University of Minnesota Press, 2014), especially chapter 3, "Labor of Logistics"; Joshua Clover, *Riot Strike Riot: The New Era of Uprisings* (London: Verso Books, 2016); Jason Smith, *Smart Machines and Service Work: Automation in an Age of Stagnation* (London: Reaktion Books, 2020), p. 14.

5. Geoff Nunberg, "Goodbye Jobs, Hello Gigs," NPR, January 11, 2016, https://www.npr.org/2016/01/11/460698077/goodbye-jobs-hello-gigs-nunbergs-word-of-the-year-sums-up-a-new-economic-reality; Jack Kerouac, *Lonesome Traveler* (San Francisco: Grove Press, 1960), p. 68.

6. William Blackstone, *Commentaries on the Laws of England in Four Books* (Philadelphia: J. B. Lippincott, 1893), chapter 14: "Of Master and Servant," vol. 1, p. 270, http://files.libertyfund.org/files/2140/Blackstone_1387-01_EBk_v6.0.pdf. See Marc Linder, *The Employment Relation in Anglo-American Law: A Historical Perspective* (New York: Greenwood Press, 1989). Writing on an earlier period, Urvashi Chakravarty also finds a connection between common-law regulation of service and the development of slavery, contending that "in early modern England, freedom and servitude, far from being opposites, are mutually enabling concepts. Further, although service and slavery are located

not on a spectrum of labor but rather as mutually distinct categories, they are also repeatedly coarticulated. This twinned appearance of service and slavery compels us to revise, definitively, not only where we look for the archives of histories of slavery but also how we understand the insistent conjunction of service and slavery." Urvashi Chakravarty, *Fictions of Consent: Slavery, Servitude, and Free Service in Early Modern England* (Philadelphia: University of Pennsylvania Press, 2022), p. 8. As I implied in Chapter 1's account of the racialization of service as distinctly abject, "servile," and unfree, we might see the "coarticulation" of service and slavery in the early modern period as the origin for the later association between service and slavery and their use in constructing (via opposition) the "fictions of consent" embedded in industrialized wage dependency.

7. Blackstone, *Commentaries on the Laws of England in Four Books*, vol. 1, pp. 272 and 271.

8. Marc Steinberg, "Marx, Formal Subsumption and the Law," *Theory and Society* 39.2 (March 2010), p. 182.

9. Gordon Anderson, Douglas Brodie, and Joellen Riley, *The Common Law Employment Relation* (Cheltenham: Edward Elgar, 2017), p. 16. See also Carolyn Steedman, *Master and Servant: Love and Labour in the English Industrial Age* (Cambridge: Cambridge University Press, 2007), pp. 17–18; Simon Deakin and Frank Wilkinson, *Law of the Labour Market: Industrialization, Employment, and Legal Evolution* (Oxford: Oxford University Press, 2005), pp. 43–61. Deakin and Wilkinson argue that contract thus did not replace "status," but rather extended and reinforced the kinds of domination previously forged in precapitalist common law and practice. In this way, they differ from previous histories—by thinkers from Max Weber to Karl Polanyi to E. P. Thompson—in which a precapitalist "household" model of direct domination (limited only by the "moral economy" of practice, tradition, and customary rights) was entirely supplanted by industrial capitalism's particular combination of mechanization, scientific management, and formal contract.

10. Deakin and Wikinson, *Law of the Labour Market*, pp. 65 and 71. See also Steinberg, "Marx, Formal Subsumption and the Law."

11. See Linder, *The Employment Relation in Anglo-American Law*, pp. 53–78.

12. In part, this was because the existence of slavery made it necessary to draw clearer ideological distinctions between the (unfree) chattel slave and the (free) waged worker, a distinction threatened by the persistence of laws that allowed employers to subject waged workers to things such as corporal punishment. As Chakravarty argues, in the early modern period, "fictions of consent underpinned a range of practices which conscripted their participants into forms of [labor] insistently framed as free," ultimately racializing the distinction between "free" labor and the unfreedom of slavery. The same thing was true centuries later, too, of course: being perceived as a "free laborer" would, for instance, be chief among what W. E. B. Du Bois describes as the "public and psychological wages" of whiteness itself. Chakravarty, *Fictions of Consent*, p. 6; W. E. B. Du Bois, *Black Reconstruction: An Essay Toward a History of the Part Which Black Folk Played in the Attempt to Reconstruct Democracy in America, 1860–1880* (New York: Harcourt Brace, 1935), p. 700.

13. See Linder, *The Employment Relation in Anglo-American Law*, pp. 60–65.

14. See Guy Davidov, Mark Freedland, and Nicola Kountouris, "The Subjects of Labor Law: 'Employees' and Other Workers," in Matthew Finkin and Guy Mundlak, eds., *Comparative Labor Law* (Cheltenham: Edward Elgar, 2015); Linder, *The Employment Relation in Anglo-American Law*, pp. 19–20.

15. Singer Manufacturing Co. v. Rahn, 143 U.S. 518 (1889), p. 523.

16. See Oscar Kahn-Freund, "Servants and Independent Contractors," *Modern Law Review* 14.4 (October 1951): pp. 505–506.

17. Deakin and Wilkinson, *Law of the Labour Market*, pp. 89–91. This test also borrowed from Blackstone's distinction between the servant, who was paid by the year (and/or mostly in kind) and whose work time was unlimited because they were bound to be available "when there is work to be done as well [as] when there is not," and the "laborer," paid by the day or week and more able to control their own work process and work time.

18. Linder, *The Employment Relation in Anglo-American Law*, p. 15. See also Davidov, Freedland, and Kountouris, "The Subjects of Labor Law"; Simon Deakin, "Decoding Employment Status," *King's Law Journal* 31.2 (July 2020), pp. 180–93.

19. This chapter focuses almost exclusively on US labor law and regulation. For a good account of the relationship between British common law

(specifically the Master-Servant Act codes) and employee classification in the UK, see Barry Collins, "Defining the Employee in the Gig Economy: Untangling the Web of Contract," in Rebecca Page-Tickell and Elaine Yerby, eds., *Conflict and Shifting Boundaries in the Gig Economy: An Interdisciplinary Analysis* (Leeds: Emerald Publishing Limited, 2020).

20. See Gerald Stevens, "The Test of the Employment Relation," *Michigan Law Review* 38.2 (December 1939), pp. 188–204; Karen R. Harned, Georgine M. Kryda, and Elizabeth A. Milito, "Creating a Workable Legal Standard for Defining an Independent Contractor," *Journal of Business, Entrepreneurship & the Law* 4.1 (2010), pp. 93–117.

21. Richard Carlson offers an excellent summary of the history of employment classification and its common-law origins, with particular attention to *Hearst*. Richard R. Carlson, "Why the Law Still Can't Tell an Employee," *Berkeley Journal of Employment and Labor Law* 22.2 (2001), pp. 295–368.

22. See also Linder, *The Employment Relation in Anglo-American Law*, pp. 187–208. The court's intention in this case was to update the definition of protected "employees" to include all workers who were *economically* dependent on their employer. This purposive reading of the NLRA sought to go beyond the common-law tradition of the control test by offering a political framework attuned to the *intention* of labor regulation rather than merely a technical interpretation of statutes. Yet despite the call for a more expansive definition based on economic dependency, rather than merely managerial oversight, the case still hinged on the question of whether the Hearst Company determined not just "what" the newsboys did, but also "how." As a result, Linder argues, the court "failed to distinguish rigorously between personal dependence, in the sense of the control test, and economic dependence." Ibid., p. 195.

23. NLRB v. Hearst Publications 322 U.S. 111 (1944); Hearst Publications v. National L. Relations Board, 136 F.2d 608 (9th Cir. 1943), p. 611

24. United States v. Silk, 331 U.S. 704 (1947). In both *Hearst* and *Silk*, the court was ostensibly affirming a more capacious, even definition of "employee" beyond the control test by defining it as anyone "dependent upon the business to which they render service," as the court put it in reaffirming the *Silk* decision. However, in both cases a substantial portion of the reasoning suggests

the court did not *replace* control as the primary criterion for employment but instead *revised* it. See Linder, *The Employment Relation in Anglo-American Law,* pp. 193.

25. Linder, *The Employment Relation in Anglo-American Law,* p. 206.

26. See Micah Prieb Stoltzfus Jost, "Independent Contractors, Employees, and Entrepreneaurialism under the National Labor Relations Act: A Worker-by-Worker Approach," *Washington and Lee Law Review* 68.1 (Winter 2011), pp. 311–52.

27. For an account of how *Darden* affects contemporary Uber classification, see Paul M. Secunda, "Uber Retirement," *University of Chicago Legal Forum* (2017), https://legal-forum.uchicago.edu/print-archive/uber-retirement.

28. See Susan Provenzano, "Worker Classification Conundrums in the Gig Economy," *Pacific Law Review* 54.1 (2023), pp. 67–80.

29. For more on the "stickiness" of the control test, see Acevedo, "Unbundling Freedom in the Sharing Economy."

30. See Carlson, "Why the Law Still Can't Tell an Employee," p. 309.

31. See Linder, *The Employment Relation in Anglo-American Law,* p. 13

32. Quoted in Molly Biklen, "Healthcare in the Home: Reexamining the Companionship Services Exemption to the Fair Labor Standards Act," *Columbia Human Rights Law Review* 35.1 (Fall 2003), p. 124.

33. See Stevens, "The Test of the Employment Relation."

34. Taxi companies were among the first businesses nationwide to use the common-law control test to insist that their employees were independent contractors. See Biju Mathew, *Taxi: Cabs and Capitalism in New York* (Ithaca: ILR Press, 2008); Veena Dubal, "An Uber Ambivalence: Employee Status, Worker Perspectives, and Regulation in the Gig Economy," in Deepa Das Acevedo, ed., *Beyond the Algorithm: Qualitative Insights for Gig Work Regulation* (Cambridge: Cambridge University Press, 2021)

35. For accounts of the problems of classification after the control test focusing specifically on the "entrepreneurship" test in *FedEx* and other recent cases, see Griffin Pivateau, "Rethinking the Worker Classification Test: Employees, Entrepreneurship, and Empowerment," *Northern Illinois University Law Review* 34.1 (2013), pp. 67–108; John A. Pearce II and Jonathan P. Silva, "The Future of

Independent Contractors and Their Status as Non-Employees: Moving on from a Common Law Standard," *Hastings Business Law Journal* 14.1 (2018), pp. 1–36.

36. Local 777, Democratic Union Organizing Committee v. NLRB, 99 L.R.R.M. 2903,603 F.2d 862,195 U.S.App.D.C. 280, para. 25 my emphasis.

37. FedEx Home Delivery v. NLRB, 563 F.3d 492 (D.C. Cir. 2009), p. 498. Many of these decisions also hinged on whether compensation was paid by the hour (in which case the worker was indeed a subordinated "employee" selling their labor time) or by the task (in which case the worker was an autonomous "independent contractor" selling a service). As the Judge in *FedEx* put it, if workers had the opportunity to take the "economic risk . . . to profit from working smarter, not just harder," then they were independent contractors, not employees. Ibid., p. 503. It is worth noting here how the ruling hinges on the apparent problem of distinguishing between entrepreneurial effort (profits from "working smarter") and pay by output (profits from "working harder"). This apparent link between piece-rate sweating and entrepreneurial hustle goes all the way back to Marx's nineteenth century, as Marx quotes political economist John Watts: "The system of piece-work illustrates an epoch in the history of the working-man; it is halfway between the position of the mere day-labourer depending upon the will of the capitalist and the co-operative artisan, who in the not distant future promises to combine the artisan and the capitalist in his own person. Piece-workers are in fact their own masters, even whilst working upon the capital of the employer." Karl Marx, *Capital, Volume One*, trans. Ben Fowkes (New York: Penguin, 1992), p. 692 n. 1.

38. Acevedo, "Unbundling Freedom in the Sharing Economy," p. 795.

39. For an account of the problem of the control test in crowd work and the on-demand economy—relevant to questions of the classification of microworkers, for instance—see Adrian Todoli-Signes, "The End of the Subordinate Worker? The On-Demand Economy, the Gig Economy, and the Need for Protection of Crowdworkers," *International Journal of Comparative Labor Law and Industrial Relations* 33.2 (January 21, 2017), pp. 241–68. See also Veena Dubal, "Winning the Battle, Losing the War? Assessing the Impact of Misclassification Litigation on Workers in the Gig Economy," *Wisconsin Law Review* 4 (2017), pp. 739–802.

40. Cotter v. Lyft, Inc. 60 F.Supp.3d 1067 (N.D.Cal. 2015), p. 1081.

41. Dynamex Operations West, Inc. v. Superior Court of Los Angeles County, 4 Cal. 5th 903, 416 P.3d 1, 232 Cal.Rptr.3d 1, p. 57.

42. See "Text of Proposed Laws; Proposition 22," https://www.lalawlibrary.org/pdfs/PROP_1102_22.pdf. Although riders' groups challenged the constitutionality of the proposition and won in the lower courts, a 2023 appeals court ruled on behalf of the rideshare companies and kept Prop 22 largely intact.

43. Algorithmic control isn't just a technical and legal fix; it also "depriv[es] workers of the relational spaces that have traditionally made it possible... to challenge managerial authority." Because many circulation workers interact neither with management nor with coworkers, they are led to "feel that they are working for an abstract 'system,'" instead of an organization. There are no opportunities for workers to negotiate working conditions: "companies are rarely motivated to disclose the underpinning criteria of their algorithms and are sometimes unable to fully explain the results themselves." Steven Vallas and Juliet Schor, "What Do Platforms Do? Understanding the Gig Economy," *Annual Review of Sociology* 46 (July 2020), p. 278; Mareike Möhlmann and Lior Zalmanson, "Hands on the Wheel: Navigating Algorithmic Management and Uber Drivers' Autonomy," *Proceedings of the International Conference on Information Systems (ICIS 2017), December 10–13, Seoul, South Korea*, p. 5, https://www.researchgate.net/publication/319965259_Hands_on_the_wheel_Navigating_algorithmic_management_and_Uber_drivers'_autonomy.

44. Frederick Winslow Taylor, *Scientific Management: Comprising Shop Management, the Principles of Scientific Management, and Testimony Before the Special House Committee* (New York: Harper, 1947), pp. 31–32.

45. Dana Orenstein, *Out of Stock: The Warehouse in the History of Capitalism* (Chicago: University of Chicago Press, 2019), p. 49.

46. Jennifer Luff, "Surrogate Supervisors: Railway Spotters and the Origins of Workplace Surveillance," *Labor: Studies of Working-Class History* 5.1 (February 2008), pp. 47–74.

47. See Jason Smith, "What Do (Digital) Bosses Do?," *Brooklyn Rail*, July–August 2022, https://brooklynrail.org/2022/07/field-notes/What-Do-Digital-Bosses-Do.

48. Karen Levy, *Data Driven: Truckers, Technology, and the New Workplace Surveillance* (Princeton: Princeton University Press, 2022,) pp. 3–9.

49. Ibid., p. 58.

50. Because this device makes drivers feel constantly surveilled, they also come to fear that other forms of surveillance might also come with the app, including access to the mic and camera on their cellphone. See Emma McDaid, Paul Andon, and Clinton Free, "Algorithmic Management and the Politics of Demand: Control and Resistance at Uber," *Accounting, Organizations and Society* 109 (August 2023), pp. 8, 11, 12.

51. Moritz Altenried, *The Digital Factory: The Human Labor of Automation* (Chicago: University of Chicago Press, 2022), p. 57.

52. See Heiner Heiland, "Neither Timeless nor Placeless: Control of Food Delivery Gig Work via Place-Based Working Time Regimes," *Human Relations* 75.9 (2022), pp. 1824–48; Aaron Shapiro, "Between Autonomy and Control: Strategies of Arbitrage in the 'On-Demand' Economy," *New Media & Society* 20.8 (2018), pp. 2954–71.

53. Alexandra Mateescu and Aiha Nguyen, "Algorithmic Management in the Workplace," *Data & Society* (February 2019), p. 7. These algorithms solve what information scientists aptly name the "Traveling Salesman Problem" (TSP). First pondered by mathematicians in the late eighteenth century, the TSP presents the complexity of finding the shortest route between multiple stops. It was taken up by marginalist economist Karl Menger in the early twentieth century; in the 1950s, RAND Corporation mathematicians used computers to offer faster and more efficient solutions. Mathematicians and theorists of "network flow" have treated the TSP mostly as a paradigmatic "hard problem" for understanding combinatorial optimization, but the name comes from an 1882 German manual for traveling salesmen that posed a version of the problem as it faced real salesmen and their employers. Like carters and taxi drivers, traveling salesmen have also long posed a problem for employment classification. A 1953 legal theory essay detailing the history of inconsistent and contradictory rulings on the employment status of traveling salesmen concludes with a powerful argument against the control test, an argument that could be quite easily applied to today's deregulated gigworkers. Noting that there is no true

"independence" when the worker is subordinated to the imperative to earn a living, the author observes that a better control test would acknowledge the "indirect but effective control which the economic whip of discharge furnishes an employer." Robert Schmid, "Traveling Salesman—Employee or Independent Contractor," *Utah Law Review* 4 (Fall 1953), p. 489; Nigel Cummings, "A Brief History of the Traveling Salesman Problem," The Operational Research Society, is no longer available online.

54. Altenried, *The Digital Factory*, pp. 120–25.

55. Shenglan Li and Lihuan Jiang, "New Forms of Labor Time Control and Imaginary Freedom: A Study of the Labor Process of Food Delivery Workers," *Journal of Chinese Sociology* 9.8 (2022), p. 10. See also Vallas and Schor, "What Do Platforms Do?," p. 275. Because customers might decide to choose a different app if the estimated delivery time listed is too long, network apps sometimes intentionally give customers an inaccurate estimated time of arrival—if the driver cannot keep up, they will receive negative reviews or not get tipped, but the company still gets to pocket the delivery fee. Some apps also allow other drivers to "grab" an order, if the original driver is unlikely to make it on time, creating what Li and Jiang term a "competition over time" between workers as they scramble for marginally better wages by pushing themselves to work faster than their peers. Li and Jiang, "New Forms of Labor Time Control and Imaginary Freedom," p. 11.

56. Chuang, "Delivery Workers, Trapped in the System," *Renwu*, November 12, 2020, https://chuangcn.org/2020/11/delivery-renwu-translation. On food delivery apps such as Caviar, likewise, "tasks are broken down into their component parts, and couriers enter information at each step (order payment, acceptance, location of pick-up, location of delivery." Shapiro, "Between Autonomy and Control," p. 2959.

57. This is Jason Smith's argument in "What Do (Digital) Bosses Do?"

58. Marx, *Capital, Volume One*, p. 352.

59. E. P. Thompson, "Time, Work-Discipline, and Industrial Capitalism," *Past and Present* 38.1 (December 1967), pp. 61 and 80.

60. Blackstone, *Commentaries on the Laws of England in Four Books*, p. 270.

61. See Kafui Attoh, Katie J. Wells, and Declan Cullen, "The Work of

Waiting: Migrant Labour in the Fulfillment City," *Journal of Ethnic and Migration Studies* 50.15 (July 2024), p. 2.

62. Guylaine Vallée and Dalia Gesualdi-Fecteau, "Setting the Temporal Boundaries of Work: An Empirical Study of the Nature and Scope of Labour Law Protections," *International Journal of Comparative Labour Law and Industrial Relations* 32.2 (September 2016), p. 346.

63. Scholar Louise Boivin describes how the "obligation to be available" works in in-home care work: "The first manifestation [of this obligation] pertain[s] to time . . . considered to be 'free' time but during which these workers were unable to engage in any pre-planned personal activities on account of their variable and unpredictable working hours. . . . The second manifestation pertain[s] to time . . . spent carrying out work-related tasks, including travelling for work, while nevertheless being excluded from these workers' paid work time through a densification of work." For Boivin, "just-in-time" models of labor organization in the care-work sector combine subcontracting and other forms of legal informalization with the intensification of work time itself. She describes intensification as a form of temporal "densification" and gives as an example the exclusion from compensated work time of tasks such as "break times, time spent putting on one's uniform, and time spent opening and closing the cash register." Louise Boivin, "'Just in Time' Labour: The Case of Networks Providing Home Support Services in Quebec," *The Journal of Comparative Labour Law and Industrial Relations* 32.3 (2016), p. 307. See also Kyle Bigley, "Between Public and Private: Care Workers, Fissuring, and Labor Law," *Yale Law Journal* 132.1 (October 2022), pp. 250–325, for an excellent overview of the problem of classification with respect to care workers.

64. Shane Hamilton, *Trucking Country: The Road to America's Wal-Mart Economy* (Princeton: Princeton University Press, 2008), pp. 13–42.

65. See Urwana Coiquad, "The Obligation to Be Available: The Case of the Trucking Industry," *International Journal of Comparative Labour Law and Industrial Relations* 32.3 (September 2016), pp. 322–43.

66. See Levy, *Data Driven*, pp. 48–49.

67. The delivery and rideshare companies themselves acknowledge that 33 percent of drivers' working time does not count as "engaged time," while

drivers suggest that it's around 50 percent. See Veena Dubal, "The New Racial Wage Code," *Harvard Law and Policy Review* 15 (May 27, 2021), p. 533, https://journals.law.harvard.edu/lpr/wp-content/uploads/sites/89/2022/05/3-Dubal.pdf.

68. See Ben Zipperer, Celine McNicholas, Margaret Poydock, Daniel Schneider, and Kristen Harknett, "National Survey of Gig Workers Paints a Picture of Poor Working Conditions, Low Pay," Economic Policy Institute, June 1, 2022, https://www.epi.org/publication/gig-worker-survey/. Prop. 22 also clarifies that gigwork companies are not "required to provide a particular amount of compensation . . . for any given rideshare or delivery request": instead, the "guaranteed wages" mentioned in the legislation refers to net earnings averaged over an earnings period. This has allowed companies such as Instacart, DoorDash, and AmazonFlex to count tips toward guaranteed wages or (as we saw in Chapter 1) toward per-ride base pay. Drivers call this "shaving." Some drivers have even reported tip and surge shaving happening via *negative* base rates. For discussions of it among drivers advocates and YouTubers, see The Rideshare Guy's "Uber Upfront SHAVING Is Raging with Tips Now?," https://www.youtube.com/watch?v=1kmCd3Xwr5A, and "Uber NEGATIVE Base Fare Now in Deliveries?!," https://www.youtube.com/watch?v=RkVgueZYCOg.

69. Dubal, "The New Racial Wage Code." See also Zephyr Teachout, "Algorithmic Personalized Wages," *Politics & Society* 51.3 (2023), pp. 436–58.

70. As Niels Van Doorn and Darsana Vijay argue, even migrants who have language or documentation barriers find gig platforms to be relatively "accessible components of [their] arrival infrastructure." Investigating the food delivery platform Relay, they note that migrants become "prey" for the app, which, they write, takes advantage of "the potential labor supply embodied in the city's large population of undocumented migrants" by using social networks to recruit Mexican and Central American couriers. Relay uses New York's subminimum tip-credit wage system, paying an hourly wage of $12.50 (less than the state minimum wage of $15) plus tips, but subjects the scheduling of workers to algorithmic control, ensuring that only workers who are always available, never turn down a delivery, and never take more than fifteen minutes per delivery get the work. Niels van Doorn and Darsana Vijay, "Gig Work as Migrant

Work: The Platformization of Migration Infrastructure," *Environment and Planning A: Economy and Space* 56.4 (2021), pp. 11346 and 1139.

71. Attoh, Wells, and Cullen describe this paradox clearly: "a narrow focus on employment relations [that is, reclassification of gigworkers] is destined to fall short. Not only do such efforts ignore all the ways in which the 'legal status of employment is by no means a safe haven from precarity' but they ignore the deep ambivalence that many migrants express toward the prospects of more formal employment. The reasons behind that ambivalence may be obvious. Beyond the fact that formal employment 'has frequently failed to secure the livelihoods and dignity of low wage workers,' the benefits of gig work in terms of flexibility and autonomy remain real. A focus on reclassification may benefit some migrant workers but may push others into even more precarious or degrading work as they seek more hours, greater flexibility, or an escape from the rules around language acquisition that may come with more formal status. Thus, any attempt to address the precarity of migrant workers in the platform-based gig economy will require addressing the state's role in producing the conditions that make migrants exploitable and that push them toward precarious work in the first place." Attoh, Wells, and Cullen, "The Work of Waiting," p. 4. Altenried, *The Digital Factory*, p. 12; Niels van Doorn, Fabian Ferrari, and Mark Graham, "Migration and Migrant Labour in the Gig Economy: An Intervention," *Work, Employment and Society* 37.4 (2023), p. 1104.

72. CalChamber, "I'm Independent Coalition Rally Urges Legislators to Protect Independent Contractors," *Advocacy*, August 16, 2018, https://advocacy.calchamber.com/2018/08/16/im-independent-coalition-rally-urges-legislators-to-protect-independent-contractors.

73. Raven Leilani, interview with Jennifer Wilson, "Raven Leilani Needs to Know How Her Characters Pay Rent," *Lux Magazine* 2, August 2021, https://lux-magazine.com/article/raven-leilani-needs-to-know-how-her-characters-pay-rent

74. Raven Leilani, *Luster: A Novel* (New York: Farrar, Straus and Giroux, 2020), pp. 86–87.

75. Kaitliyn Greenidge reads *Luster* as "a novel about what it means to be a black female flaneur," beautifully detailing how Leilani uses the flaneur's anonymity not only to describe the city she moves through, but also to explore

the racial logics of seeing and being seen. However, Greenidge does not attend to the connection between Edie's status as an "incessant traveler, watching the worlds she passes through" and her struggle for economic survival as a circulation gigworker. Kaitlyn Greenidge, "Sex in the City: The Black Female Flaneur in Raven Leilani's *Luster*," *Virginia Quarterly Review* 96.2 (Summer 2020), pp. 210–11.

76. Leilani, *Luster*, p. 90.

77. Edie thus records not just physical space, but also what literary critic Kirsten Ortega describes, in an essay on the literary representation of the "black *flaneuse*" as "paths through... labyrinths of social interaction and consumer transaction." Kirsten Ortega, "The Black Flaneuse: Gwendolyn Brooks's 'In the Mecca'" *Journal of Modern Literature* 30.4 (Summer 2007), p. 141.

78. Leilani, *Luster*, pp. 108–109.

79. Leilani, *Luster*, pp. 90–91.

80. See Attoh, Wells, and Cullen, "The Work of Waiting."

81. Leilani, *Luster*, p. 70.

82. Drawing on the association of sailors with slavery in the nineteenth century, Leon Fink makes a similar argument: that "the racial connections to maritime employment and regulation" were more complex than simple homologies might suggest, not least because "despite certain parallels in the mistreatment of slaves and sailors... the sea often represented a realm of relative freedom for African Americans." Leon Fink, *Sweatshops at Sea: Merchant Seamen in the World's First Globalized Industry, from 1812 to the Present* (Chapel Hill: University of North Carolina Press, 2011), p. 50.

83. Leilani, *Luster*, p. 22. Greenidge explains that in this way, *Luster* evokes not only the "anonymity" associated with the white, male *flaneur*, but also the specific experience of traveling while Black: "The flaneur, the white-male version at least, is not self-aware enough to realize that in his observations of the city, he may also be being observed back," she writes, "But Edie is hyper-aware, at all times, of the impression she is making or that she believes she is making around her." Greenidge, "Sex in the City," p. 214.

84. Leilani, *Luster*, pp. 214–15.

85. Moreover, much as both entrepreneurial "independence" *and* formal-

ized wage labor can seemingly be defined only in contrast to "wage slavery," the racially differentiated right to "self-possession" here becomes visible only in its violation, as Akila is introduced to the pedagogy of police violence.

86. Clover, *Riot Strike Riot*, pp. 125–26.

87. Sal Nicolazzo, *Vagrant Figures: Law, Literature, and the Origins of the Police* (New Haven: Yale University Press, 2020), pp. 67–69.

88. There is an intimate historical connection between the state's police power and its regulatory power that complicates the idea that the regulatory state has purely benevolent motives. In Chapter 1, I mentioned that the early defenses of labor regulation depended on the constitutional authority of the police power, and the ability of the state to regulate private interests, including labor contracts, on behalf of the public safety, morals, order, and welfare had its roots in the expansion of the police power nationally. In his early twentieth-century treatises *The Police Power* and *Legislative Regulation*, Ernst Freund —architect of the transformation of the police power into modern legislative regulatory authority—argues that "the growing power, scope, and complexity" of the industrial economy necessitated state action in the public interest, making it necessary to expand the police power as the basis for the state's authority to "promot[e] the public welfare by restraining and regulating the use of liberty and property." The connection to industrialization and the regulation of industrial labor is particularly important to this story, Mariana Valverde notes, since "the police power flourished because . . . the differentiation of time increased in importance as regulatory strategies, beginning with maximum hours" laws. Freund, *The Police Power: Public Policy and Constitutional Rights* (Chicago: Callahgan, 1904), quoted in William Novak, "Police Power and the Hidden Transformation of the American State," in Markus D. Dubber and Mariana Valverde, eds., *Police and the Liberal State* (Stanford: Stanford Law Books, 2008), p. 63; Mariana Valverde, "Police, Sovereignty, and the Law," in ibid., p. 25.

89. Priya Guns, *Your Driver Is Waiting: A Novel* (New York: Doubleday, 2023), p. 1.

90. Jefferson Cowie, *Stayin' Alive: The 1970s and the Last Days of the Working Class* (New York: New Press, 2010), p. 331.

91. Guns, *Your Driver Is Waiting*, p. 47.

92. Ibid., pp. 280–81.

93. Cowie, *Stayin' Alive*, pp. 10–12.

94. Clover, *Riot Strike Riot*, p. 30.

95. Guns, *Your Driver Is Waiting*, pp. 295–96.

96. Ibid., pp. 118 and 199.

97. See Eric Hobsbawm's famous description of a period of transition in the eighteenth century when "the class is a mob not an army" and recurred to "Luddism and sabotage." Eric Hobsbawm, "The Machine Breakers," *Past & Present* 1.1 (February 1952)," p. 61.

98. Guns, *Your Driver Is Waiting*, p. 1.

99. Ibid., pp. 22 and 81–82.

100. Ibid., p. 157.

101. Ibid., p. 21.

102. For Wittgenstein, "every proposition is the result of successive applications of one logical operation—the so-called 'N-operator'—to a base of elementary propositions." Ian Proops, "Wittgenstein's Logical Atomism," n. 2, in Edward N. Zalta and Uri Nodelman, eds., *The Stanford Encyclopedia of Philosophy* (Fall 2022 edition), https://plato.stanford.edu/entries/wittgenstein-atomism/notes.html.

103. Peter Mendelsund, *The Delivery: A Novel* (New York: Farrar, Straus and Giroux, 2021), p. 5.

104. Ibid., pp. 48–54.

105. Ibid., p. 179.

106. Ibid., pp. 3, 14, 18–19.

107. Ibid., p. 153.

108. Ibid., pp. 252–53.

109. Ibid., p. 252.

110. Andy Newman, "Numbers, Speed, Mystery: The World of the Delivery Worker," *New York Times*, February 9, 2021, https://www.nytimes.com/2021/02/09/books/review/peter-mendelsund-delivery.html.

111. M. A. Orthofer, "Peter Mendelsund's *The Delivery*," *the complete review* (February 3, 2021), https://www.complete-review.com/reviews/usx/mendelsund p2.htm.

112. Elliot Frank, "'The Delivery' is a Meta-Fictional Puppet Show with Little to Say," *Chicago Review of Books*, February 15, 2021, https://chireview ofbooks.com/2021/02/15/the-delivery-is-a-meta-fictional-puppet-show-with -little-to-say.

113. Bruce Robbins, "The Sweatshop Sublime," *PMLA* 117.1 (January 2002), p. 84.

114. The same thing is true of attempts to regulate the "independent" status of gigworkers by making them more like other waged workers. As legal scholar Deepa Acevedo notes, many contemporary debates about independent contractor status offer only a "classically liberal understanding of freedom as non-interference." Framed by the logic of the control test, this definition of individual freedom forecloses a thicker and more radical ideal of freedom as nondomination—an ideal that could be applied to all waged work. Acevedo, "Unbundling Freedom in the Sharing Economy," p. 796.

115. Anastasia Eccles, "Feeling Complicit in William Godwin's *Caleb Williams*," *Romantic Circles*, December 2021, https://romantic-circles.org /praxis/publicfeeling/praxis.2021.publicfeeling.eccles.html.

116. Clover, *Riot Strike Riot*, p. 15.

117. Fredric Jameson, *Postmodernism, or, The Cultural Logic of Late Capitalism* (Durham: Duke University Press, 1991), p. 52.

118. E. P. Thompson, "The Moral Economy of the English Crowd in the Eighteenth Century," *Past &* Present 50 (February 1971), pp. 79 and 120.

119. Karl Marx, "A Workers' Inquiry" (1880), Marxists.org, https://www. marxists.org/archive/marx/works/1880/04/20.htm. Asad Haider and Salar Mohandesi describe Marx's survey as purely objective and mechanical, that is, as a means to produce a strictly "scientific knowledge" that would also be so particular to an individual trade or subset of the working class (or even to an individual worker) that it could not possibly be generalized. But this does not feel entirely accurate to me. For one thing, any actual scientist would reject out of hand a survey with leading questions such as "don't your employers or their clerks resort to trickery, in order to swindle you out of part of your wages?" or "If you are paid piece rate, isn't the quality of the goods used as a pretext for wrongful deductions form your wages?" or "Do you know of cases when the

government made unfair use of the armed forces, to place them at the disposal of the employers against their wage workers?" More important, the survey is not at all simply about quantifiable data, asking about the particular work in which the worker is engaged, for instance, Marx asks for a description "not just of the technical side but also the muscular and nervous strain required"; he asks what is taught in the schools for workers' children (if they exist); whether the worker must "depriv[e] [them]self of things [they] need"; and what are the "general physical, intellectual and moral conditions of life of the working men and women employed in your trade." See Asad Haider and Salar Mohandesi's "Workers' Inquiry: A Genealogy," *Viewpoint Magazine* 3 (September 27, 2013), https://viewpointmag.com/2013/09/27/workers-inquiry-a-genealogy.

120. See Marcelo Hoffman, *Militant Acts: The Role of Investigations in Radical Political Struggles* (Albany: State University of New York Press, 2019), pp. 9–19. As Hoffman notes, Lenin did use a questionnaire to interview workers in the late nineteenth century, and Mao performed inquirylike investigations into the peasant movement and rural life in the late 1920s and early 1930s.

121. Haider and Mohandesi argue that the JFT's turn toward more "narrative" modes of expression meant that "measured generalization" became "untenable overgeneralization" because the JFT's inquiries presumed the experiences of *one* worker could stand in for the experiences of *all* workers, thus undermining the "scientific" imperative of the genre.

122. Robert Ovetz, introduction to Robert Ovetz, ed., *Workers Inquiry and Global Class Struggle* (London: Pluto Press, 2021), p. 3.

123. Jamie Woodcock, *Working the Phones: Control and Resistance in Call Centres* (London: Pluto Press, 2017); Kruskaya Hidalgo Cordero, *Domestic Code in the Flesh: Stories of Workers in Cleaning Services Apps*, trans. Renata Laureano (2022), https://www.codigodomestico.com/en/pdf/domestic_code_in_the_flesh.pdf; Hoffman, *Militant Acts.*

124. *Viewpoint Magazine* 3, "Workers' Inquiry: A Genealogy," September 30, 2013, https://viewpointmag.com/2013/09/30/issue-3-workers-inquiry; *ephemera: theory & politics in organization* 14.3, "The Politics of Workers' Inquiry" (August 2014), https://www.ephemerajournal.org/sites/default/files

/pdfs/issue/14-3ephemera-aug14.pdf; *Notes from Below* 1, "No Politics Without Inquiry," (January 2018), https://notesfrombelow.org/issue/no-politics-without-inquiry; The Editorial Collective of Notes from Below, *From the Workplace: A Collection of Worker Writing* (Notes from Below Publishing, 2020); Robert Ovetz, ed., *Workers Inquiry and Global Class Struggle* (London: Pluto Press, 2021); Workers Inquiry Network, *Struggle in a Pandemic: A Collection of Contributions on the COVID-19 Crisis* (London: Workers Inquiry Network, 2020).

125. On Amazonians United, see Spencer Cox, "Neoliberalism's Last Days: Amazon and the Rise of America's New Working Classes," PhD diss., Department of Geography, Environment, and Society, University of Minnesota, 2022.

126. This interest in the literary qualities of the workers' inquiry has led literary critics to write about the genre: in a lovely essay on the JFT's inquiries as literature, Daniel Hartley suggests that they contributed to a "subterranean current of proletarian *literary* internationalism," and we find a similar interest in using "literary" modes to register the "political unconscious of the workplace" in contemporary workers' inquiries. As a result, many of the above-named texts also complicate and confound some of the distinctions Haider and Mohandesi set out in their account, blurring the line between organically worker-produced inquiries and those cowritten with theorists, between empirical surveys and qualitative narratives, and between descriptive and prescriptive language. Daniel Hartley, "Militant Structures of Feeling: Raymond Williams, Claude Lefort, and Workers' Inquiry," in Benjamin Kohlmann and Ivana Perica, eds., *The Political Uses of Literature: Global Perspectives and Theoretical Approaches, 1920–2020* (London: Bloomsbury, 2024), pp. 121 and 131.

127. Workers Writers School founder Mark Nowak describes this work as a response to the JFT's call for "more working-class chroniclers": what he terms "social poetics" engages "working people themselves in a new conjunction of aesthetic practice and political action." Mark Nowak, *Social Poetics* (Minneapolis: Coffee House Press, 2020), pp. 6–7; Worker Writers School, *Coronavirus Haikus*, ed. Mark Nowak (Kenning Editions, 2021).

128. Reimagining Value Action Lab, *The World After Amazon: Speculative Stories from Amazon Workers*, p. 15.

129. In this sense, these texts are part of an imaginary of labor that, I have

suggested throughout this book, decades of labor history, labor organizing, and especially, labor regulation unreflexively treated as a historical norm, to the exclusion of service work and other nonindustrially organized forms of labor. The Phil Singer / Grace Lee Boggs and James Boggs inquiries were both written in the boom years of US and industrial growth, the period in which that imaginary would become fully reified. However, we can also read these texts in light of the history of service work, resituating the labor processes of *non*industrial work as our conceptual frame and using the insights that result to understand industrial work, too, in new ways. These mid-century workers' inquiries and the politics of the militant theoretical movements with which they were associated then lead to a new and expanded set of political, conceptual, and historical insights. We then can also expand our archive of mid-century workers' inquiries to include writing about and/or by Black working-class women, for instance, literary writers such as Alice Childress, author of the 1956 novel *Like One of the Family: Conversations from a Domestic's Life*, and Beulah Richardson, actor, CPUSA activist, and author of the galvanizing 1951 poem "A Black Woman Speaks." Both Childress and Richardson were inspired in their writing by the work of contemporary Black Marxist-feminist organizers such as Claudia Jones, whose account of superexploitation deeply informs this book, and both their texts, while not strictly speaking workers' inquiries, draw on the genre's testimonial form and its mix of first-person particularity and typifying generalization.

130. Alex Marshall, "Notes from the Road," in *From the Workplace*, p. 32.

131. Facility Waters and Jamie Woodcock, "Far from Seamless: A Worker's Inquiry at Deliveroo," *Viewpoint Magazine*, September 20, 2017, https://viewpointmag.com/2017/09/20/far-seamless-workers-inquiry-deliveroo.

132. "Zero hours" is the term used in the UK to describe independent contractors: because it refers to the lack of guaranteed paid hours, it recalls the argument made throughout this book about the atemporal time discipline of service work.

133. AngryWorkers, *Class Power on Zero Hours* (2020), "Driving," in chapter 10, "Working and Organising at a Tesco Customer Fulfilment Centre," https://

files.libcom.org/files/2023-03/Class_Power_on_Zero_Hours.pdf. (This ebook is unpaginated, so I cite the chapter and the section within that chapter in which the quoted language appears.)

134. Harris Feinsod, "Vehicular Networks and the Modernist Seaways," *American Literary History* 27.4 (Winter 2015), p. 686.

135. AngryWorkers, *Class Power on Zero Hours*, "Customers," in chapter 10.

136. Ibid.

137. Marshall, "Notes from the Road," p. 33.

138. Alice Barker, "Cycling in the City," in *From the Workplace*, p. 49.

139. They also show how exploitation in the circulation sector depends on a mismatch between time (as excruciatingly extended shifts) and wages ("irregular and unpredictable" because it is typically paid by the job): piece rates, Marshall reminds us, are a way of forcing workers to "work long hours and full weeks," while Barker notes that "waiting times"—which are often unpredictable and outside the worker's control—"are not paid." Marshall, "Notes from the Road," pp. 34, 41, 54; Barker, "Cycling in the City," p. 52.

140. "Far from Seamless," AngryWorkers, *Class Power on Zero Hours*, "Introduction."

141. Barker, "Cycling in the City," p. 53.

142. AngryWorkers, *Class Power on Zero Hours*, "Struggles in Distribution Centers," in chapter 9, "Food Distribution in Capitalism."

143. "Far from Seamless," AngryWorkers, *Class Power on Zero Hours*, "Introduction."

144. Jasper Bernes, "Logistics, Counterlogistics and the Communist Prospect," *Endnotes* 3 *Gender, Race, Class, and Other Misfortunes* (September 2013), https://endnotes.org.uk/articles/logistics-counterlogistics-and-the-communist-prospect, n.p.

145. Robbins, "The Sweatshop Sublime, p. 85.

146. Stefan Yong, "The Sublime and the Logistical: Containment Strategies in the Aesthetics of Circulation," in Mathies Denecke, Holger Kuhn, and Milan Sturmer, eds., *Liquidity, Flows, Circulation: The Cultural Logic of Environmentalization* (Zurich: Diaphenes Press, 2022), p. 28; Charmaine Chua, "The Chinese Logistical Sublime and Its Wasted Remains," *The Disorder*

of Things (February 7, 2015), https://thedisorderofthings.com/2015/02/07/the-chinese-logistical-sublime-and-its-wasted-remains.

147. Bernes, "Logistics, Counterlogistics, and the Communist Prospect," n.p.

148. AngryWorkers, *Class Power on Zero Hours*, "Customers," in chapter 10.

149. Callum Cant, "The Warehouse Without Walls: A Workers' Inquiry at Deliveroo," *ephemera: theory & politics in organization* 20.4 (November 2020), https://ephemerajournal.org/contribution/warehouse-without-walls-workers%25E2%2580%2599-inquiry-deliveroo.

150. Peter Linebaugh and Marcus Redikker, *The Many-Headed Hydra: Sailors, Slaves, Commoners, and the Hidden History of the Revolutionary Atlantic* (Boston: Beacon Press, 2000), p. 333.

151. Smith defines the "servant economy" as "smaller, spatially dispersed workplaces, where they carry out labor-intensive production processes that, because they rely on putatively innate (and therefore 'gendered') social and interpersonal knowledges and behaviors, are deemed low-skill occupations and are therefore poorly paid." Smith, *Smart Machines and Service Work*, p. 14.

152. AngryWorkers, *Class Power on Zero Hours*, "Training," in chapter 10.

153. Cordero, *Domestic Code in the Flesh*, p. 30.

154. John Bellamy Foster, "Marx's Theory of Metabolic Rift: Classical Foundations for Environmental Sociology," *American Journal of Sociology* 105.2 (September 1999), p. 379.

155. As Alisa Del Re writes in an essay on the workers' inquiry and reproductive labor, the inquiry allows us to consider "the characteristics of life and the historical memory of women"—and others for whom racialization, feminization, or marginalization has made them vulnerable to superexploitation—"producing an idea of society as a whole, starting from their strategic position and from the totality of their lives." Alisa Del Re, "Workers' Inquiry and Reproductive Labor," *Viewpoint Magazine* 3, September 23, 2013, https://viewpointmag.com/2013/09/25/workers-inquiry-and-reproductive-labor.

156. Michael Denning, "Wageless Life," *New Left Review* 66 (November–December 2010), pp. 79–97.

157. Los Angeles Tenants Union, *Cuadra a Cuadra / Block by Block: To a World Without Rent* (2022), pp. 26–27.

158. Ibid., p. 28.

159. Ibid., p. 29.

160. Ibid., p. 64.

161. As Magally Miranda notes in a powerful essay about domestic workers, "The super-exploitation of... feminized immigrant care workers in particular points toward elements of a radical political platform [as well as] towards new ways of building power in opposition to neoliberal and nativist hegemony." Magally Miranda, "The Power of Trabajadoras and the Subversion of Capital: Notes on a Domestic Workers Inquiry," *Viewpoint Magazine* (March 2017), https://viewpointmag.com/2017/03/07/the-power-of-trabajadoras-and-the-subversion-of-capital-notes-on-a-domestic-workers-inquiry.

162. Connecting these kinds of movements to a general category of "wagelessness," Phil Jones similarly identifies the "organic demands of a growing number unable to secure their basic subsistence: free healthcare, utilities, housing and food and an end to unnecessary, violent institutions. Taken together, they reveal a hidden utopian horizon. Some might call it Universal Basic Services (UBS), the idea that services fundamental to human survival should be free at the point of access and should be democratically determined and managed." Phil Jones, *Work Without the Worker: Labour in the Age of Platform Capitalism* (London: Verso, 2021), ebook, unpaginated.

163. Sarah Lazare, "The Chicago Teachers Union Wants to End Student Homelessness at the Bargaining Table," *Nation*, March 25, 2024, https://www.thenation.com/article/activism/chicago-teachers-union-homelessness; International Alliance of Transportation Workers, "Who We Are," https://www.iaatw.org.

164. I'm grateful to Charmaine Chua for helping me find these examples of Amazon organizing. See Joe DeManuelle-Hall, "Dispersed but Undaunted, Chicago Amazon Workers Win Megacycle Pay Nationwide," *Labor Notes*, June 15, 2021, https://labornotes.org/2021/06/dispersed-undaunted-chicago-amazon-workers-help-win-megacycle-pay-nationwide; Lauren Kaori Gurley, "Amazon Workers Who Commute Across the Border Are Organizing for Better Working Conditions," *Vice*, July 8, 2022, https://www.vice.com/en/article/amazon-workers-who-commute-across-the-us-mexico-border-every-day-are

-organizing-for-better-working-conditions; Maximillian Alvarez, "How Immigrant Workers Took on Amazon and Won," *Real News Network*, August 9, 2023, https://therealnews.com/how-immigrant-warehouse-workers-in-minnesota-took-on-amazon-and-won.

165. See Amazon Employees for Climate Justice, https://www.amazonclimatejustice.org/.

166. See Jonathan Rosenblum, "How the Palestinian Justice Movement Helped Starbucks Workers United," *Nation*, March 11, 2024, https://www.thenation.com/article/activism/starbucks-gaza-israel-union-organizing.

167. Quoted in Fran Quigley, "It's Not Charity: Labor Unions and Tenants Unions Join Forces," Housing Is a Human Right substack, June 4, 2024, https://housingisahumanright.substack.com/p/its-not-charitylabor-unions-and-tenants.

CODA: ED TECH AND THE LABOR OF TEACHING

1. Gabriel Winant, *The Next Shift: The Fall of Industry and the Rise of Health Care in Rust Belt America* (Cambridge, MA: Harvard University Press, 2022), p. 2.

2. Eric Blanc, *Red State Revolt: The Teachers' Strike Wave and Working-Class Politics* (London: Verso, 2019), and Jennifer Berkshire, "Naught for Teacher," *The Baffler* 73 (April 2024), https://thebaffler.com/outbursts/naught-for-teacher-berkshire. While this coda will focus on higher ed teaching, instead of primary and secondary, Berkshire notes that one of the hottest trends in public education today is "microschools," in which small clusters of students are taught online by "minimum-wage 'guides' who are able to pass a background check," a description that echoes this Coda's account of online education in higher ed.

3. The most developed version of the argument appears in William Baumol, "Macroeconomics of Unbalanced Growth: The Anatomy of Urban Crisis," *American Economic Review* 57.3 (June 1967), pp. 415–26. See also William Baumol and W. G. Bowen. "On the Performing Arts: The Anatomy of Their Economic Problems," *American Economic Review* 55.1–2 (March 1965), pp. 495–502.

4. Jason Smith, *Smart Machines and Service Work: Automation in an Age of Stagnation* (London: Reaktion Books, 2020), pp. 73–74. While I focus here mostly on higher-ed teaching, Smith's account is focused somewhat more on K-to-12

instruction. I strongly suspect those who work in that field would contest many aspects of this description, especially about questions of autonomy and deskilling.

5. Baumol and Bowen, "On the Performing Arts," p. 495.

6. Baumol, "Macroeconomics of Unbalanced Growth," pp. 415–16.

7. Ibid.

8. See William Baumol et. al, *Cost Disease: Why Computers Get Cheaper and Health Care Doesn't* (New Haven: Yale University Press, 2012).

9. David Noble, *Digital Diploma Mills: The Automation of Higher Education* (New York: Monthly Review Press, 2001), pp. 8–9. Because correspondence school teaching was thus deprofessionalized, it was considered significantly lower quality than in-person instruction. Distance learning wasn't just a product of for-profit institutions: some of the first correspondence programs, Noble notes, were offered by Columbia, the University of Chicago, and the University of California, which required that their correspondence programs be separate from the "traditional" university because faculty and administrators alike recognized them as the low-quality cash grabs they were.

10. See data compiled in Phil Hill, "University of Phoenix Enrollments Over Time," *On EdTech Newsletter*, April 26, 2023, https://onedtech.philhillaa.com/p/university-of-phoenix-enrollments-over-time.

11. Richard Grusin, "The Dark Side of the Digital Humanities—Part 2," Center for 21st Century Studies, *Thinking C21*, January 9, 2013, https://www.c21uwm.com/2013/01/09/dark-side-of-the-digital-humanities-part-2.

12. Ian Bogost, contribution to "MOOCs and the Future of the Humanities: A Roundtable (Part 1)," *LA Review of Books*, June 14, 2013, https://lareviewofbooks.org/article/moocs-and-the-future-of-the-humanities-a-roundtable-part-1.

13. Tressie McMillan Cotton, "The Audacity: Thrun Learns a Lesson and Students Pay," *Some of Us Are Brave: The Archive*, November 19, 2013, https://tressiemc.com/uncategorized/the-audacity-thrun-learns-a-lesson-and-students-pay.

14. Baumol, "Macroeconomics of Unbalanced Growth," p. 416.

15. Sarah Wood, "A Look at 20 Years of Tuition Costs at National Universities," *US News and World Report*, September 23, 2023, https://www.usnews

.com/education/best-colleges/paying-for-college/articles/see-20-years-of-tuition-growth-at-national-universities.

16. See Glenn Colby, "Data Snapshot: Tenure and Contingency in U.S. Higher Ed," *Academe Magazine*, Spring 2023, https://www.aaup.org/academe/issues/spring-2023/data-snapshot-tenure-and-contingency-us-higher-education; House Committee on Education and the Workforce Democratic Staff, "The Just-in-Time Professor: A Staff Report Summarizing eForum Responses on the Working Conditions of Contingent Faculty in Higher Education," January 2014, https://democrats-edworkforce.house.gov/imo/media/doc/1.24.14-AdjunctEforumReport.pdf.

17. House Committee on Education and the Workforce Democratic Staff, "The Just-in-Time Professor," pp. 5–6.

18. The increased exploitation of low-waged, part-time instructors (including graduate students) does suggest Baumol was wrong to assume that the wages of college instructors would remain high despite the sector's stagnant productivity.

19. Nanette Byrnes, "Uber for Education," *MIT Technology Review*, July 27, 2015, https://www.technologyreview.com/2015/07/27/167002/uber-for-education.

20. Patricia Burch, *Hidden Markets: Public Policy and the Push to Privatize Education*, 2nd ed. (London: Routledge, 2021); Audrey Watters, *The Monsters of Educational Technology 4* (2017), https://monsters4.hackeducation.com. See also Daniel Greene, *The Promise of Access: Technology, Inequality, and the Political Economy of Hope* (Cambridge, MA: MIT Press, 2021).

21. Jon Marcus, "More Colleges and Universities Outsource Services to For-Profit Companies," *The Hechinger Report*, January 8, 2021, https://hechingerreport.org/more-colleges-and-universities-outsource-services-to-for-profit-companies; Christian Michael Smith, Amber D. Villalobos, Laura T. Hamilton, and Charlie Eaton, "Promising or Predatory? Online Education in Non-Profit and For-Profit Universities," *Social Forces* 102.3 (March 2023), pp. 952–77; Laura Hamilton, Heather Daniels, Christian Michael Smith, and Charlie Eaton, "The Private Side of Public Universities: Third-Party Providers and Platform Capitalism," Berkeley Center for Studies in Higher Education

Research and & Occasional Paper Series, 2022, https://herelab.org/images/qt7p0114s8_nosplash_1847d6a649017454cecf88b9e9e9961e-4.pdf.

22. Stephanie Riegg Cellini, "For-Profit Colleges in the United States: Insights from Two Decades of Research," in Brian McCall, ed., *The Routledge Handbook of the Economics of Education* (London: Routledge, 2021).

23. See Smith et. al., "Promising or Predatory?"; Charlie Eaton, Sabrina T. Howell, and Constantine Yannelis, "When Investor Incentives and Consumer Interests Diverge: Private Equity in Higher Education," *Review of Financial Studies* 33.9 (September 2020), pp. 4024–60.

24. National Center for Education Statistics, "Undergraduate Enrollment," *The Condition of Education* (2023), https://nces.ed.gov/programs/coe/pdf/2023/cha_508.pdf; Mellissa A. Venable, *Online Education Trends Report*, 2021, https://www.bestcolleges.com/wp-content/uploads/2021/07/2021-Online-Trends-in-Education-Report-BestColleges.pdf.

25. Richard Garrett, Bethany Simunich, Ron Legon, and Eric Fredericksen, *CHLOE 7: Tracking Online Learning from Mainstream Acceptance to Universal Adoption. The Changing Landscape of Online Education*, Quality Matters and Encoura Eduventures Research (2022), https://www.qualitymatters.org/sites/default/files/research-docs-pdfs/QM-Eduventures-CHLOE-7-Report-2022.pdf.

26. Marcus, "More Colleges and Universities Outsource Services to For-Profit Companies."

27. See Derek Newton, "UC Office of the President: UC Regents May Revoke Faculty Senate's Authority Over Online Degree Program Policy," *Forbes*, December 14, 2023, https://www.forbes.com/sites/dereknewton/2023/12/14/university-of-california-president-regents-may-revoke-faculty-senates-authority-over-online-degree-policy.

28. Jill Barshay, "College Students Predicted to Fall by More Than 15% after the year 2025," *Hechinger Report*, September 10, 2018, https://hechingerreport.org/college-students-predicted-to-fall-by-more-than-15-after-the-year-2025. On the "demographic cliff" debate, see Chris Newfield, "When Are Access and Inclusion Also Racist?", *Remaking II: Long Revolution*, June 28, 2020, https://utotherescue.blogspot.com/2020/06/when-are-access-and-inclusion-also.html; Dan Nemser and Brian Whitener, "Demographic Realism and the Crisis of

Higher Education," *Los Angeles Review of Books*, May 11, 2021, https://lareviewofbooks.org/article/demographic-realism-and-the-crisis-of-higher-education; Matt Seybold, "Putting the 'If' in Demographic Cliff," American Vandal substack, March 4, 2024, https://theamericanvandal.substack.com/p/putting-the-if-in-enrollment-cliff. Many thanks to Matt Seybold for these sources and for discussing the topic with me via email.

29. See Spiros Protopsaltis, and Sandy Baum, "Does Online Education Live Up to Its Promise? A Look At the Evidence and Implications for Federal Policy," *Center for Educational Policy Evaluation*, 2019; Marcus "More Colleges and Universities Outsource Services to For-Profit Companies"; Smith et. al., "Promising or Predatory?"; Hamilton et al., "The Private Side of Public Universities."

30. Hamilton et al., "The Private Side of Public Universities," p. 4.

31. Ibid.

32. Amber Villalobos, "Online College Programs Increasingly Put Black and Hispanic Students at Risk," The Century Foundation, November 17, 2023, https://tcf.org/content/commentary/online-college-programs-increasingly-put-black-and-hispanic-students-at-ris.

33. Smith et. al, Promising or Predatory?"

34. Sandy Baum and Michael McPherson, "The Human Factor: The Promise and Limits of Online Education," *Daedalus* (Fall 2019), p. 148.

35. Smith et al., "Promising or Predatory?"

36. Tamara Tate and Mark Warschauer, "Equity in Online Learning," *Educational Psychologist* 57.3 (June 2022), pp. 192–206.

37. Di Xu and Ying Xu, "The Ambivalence About Distance Learning in Higher Education," in Laura Perna, ed. *Higher Education: Handbook of Theory and Research* 35 (Cham: Springer International, 2020), p. 352; Protopsaltis and Baum, "Does Online Education Live Up to Its Promise?," p. 30.

38. Tate and Warschauer, "Equity in Online Learning," p. 198.

39. Di Xu and Ying Xu, "The Promises and Limits of Online Higher Education: Understanding How Distance Education Affects Access, Cost, and Quality," American Enterprise Institute, March 4, 2019, p. 26, https://www.aei.org/research-products/report/the-promises-and-limits-of-online-higher-education.

40. Richard Garrett, Bethany Simunich, Ron Legon, and Eric Fredericksen,

CHLOE 8: Student Demand Moves Higher Ed Toward a Multi-Modal Future. The Changing Landscape of Online Education, 2023, Quality Matters and Encoura Eduventures Research (2024), p. 6, https://qualitymatters.org/sites/default/files/research-docs-pdfs/QM-Eduventures-CHLOE-8-Report-2023.pdf.

41. Nathaniel S. Strauss, "Anything but Academic: How Copyright's Work-for-Hire Doctrine Affects Professors, Graduate Students, and K-12 Teachers in the Information Age," *Richmond Journal of Law and Technology* 18.1 (2011), p. 7.

42. American Association of University Professionals (AAUP), "Intellectual Property Issues for Faculty and Faculty Unions," April 15, 2020, https://www.aaup.org/sites/default/files/intellectual_property_issues_faculty.pdf.

43. Strauss, "Anything but Academic," p. 8.

44. Elizabeth Townsend, "Legal and Policy Responses to the Disappearing 'Teacher Exception,' or Copyright Ownership in the 21st Century University," *Minnesota Intellectual Property Review* 4.2 (2003), pp. 209–83; Jed Scully, "Virtual Professorship: Intellectual Property: Ownership of Academic Work in a Digital Era," *McGeorge Law Review* 35.2 (2004), pp. 227–76; Colleen Flaherty, "IP Problems," *Inside Higher Ed*, May 18, 2020, https://www.insidehighered.com/news/2020/05/19/who-owns-all-course-content-youre-putting-online.

45. A nontenure-track professor at the University of North Carolina discovered in spring 2024 that his lectures had been recorded by the university without his knowledge or consent after students complained he was sharing his "political beliefs" about diversity and equity. UNC had recorded him by using Panopto, an aptly named camera system they had previously put in classrooms to enable remote instruction. By setting a precedent for recording lectures without knowledge or consent in order to monitor political speech, universities can now also record lectures to make them available for future asynchronous instruction. As in Chapter 2's example of the typewriter return key and Chapter 3's example of the fare box, the technologies of surveillance and discipline go hand in hand with the technologies of automation. Liam Knox, "UNC Fires Professor They Secretly Recorded," *Inside Higher Ed*, June 17, 2024, https://www.insidehighered.com/news/faculty-issues/academic-freedom/2024/06/17/unc-dismisses-professor-after-secretly-recording.

46. Baumol, "Macroeconomics of Unbalanced Growth," p. 416.

47. Sean Gehrke and Adrianna Kezar, "Unbundling the Faculty Role in Higher Education: Utilizing Historical, Theoretical, and Empirical Frameworks to Inform Future Research," in Michael B. Paulsen, ed., *Higher Education: Handbook of Theory and Research* 30 (Cham: Springer International, 2015).

48. Robert Ovetz, "The Algorithmic University: On-Line Education, Learning Management Systems, and the Struggle Over Academic Labor," *Critical Sociology* 47.7–8 (2021), pp. 1066–67.

49. Ibid., p. 1076.

50. Consider, for example, automated exam proctoring. The rise of OLE in the 2010s increased demand for remote exam proctoring, which was typically done via the equivalent of a Zoom call: before beginning the online test, the student would turn on their laptop camera, scan the camera over their workspace, and then would leave the camera on while taking the test. On the other end of the call, a call-center worker (most of them working in business process outsourcing centers in the Global South) would monitor multiple test takers at once, checking each camera to make sure the students' eyes were on their screen and that they weren't using books, calculators, or other prohibited tools. However, when the pandemic caused demand for proctoring to soar even as BPOs were shuttered by national lockdowns, many institutions pivoted to *automated* proctoring services. Automated test proctoring, as one company describes it, uses "advanced AI software" to "detect abnormal student behavior that may signal academic dishonesty." Because they rely on facial recognition software, motion detection, and biometric data calibrated for white skin, these automated proctoring services often cannot "recognize" nonwhite students. Students wearing headscarves, students whose gender expression does not "match" their state-issued ID, and neurodivergent are also often flagged as cheating. When students' complaints over these experiences became the subject of public outcry, a number of US senators threatened an investigation of automated proctoring services, and many campuses immediately discontinued their use. In most cases, however, campuses that cancelled the service were still on the hook to pay for it because they had signed contracts without doing any "ethical tech" research into the product. On my own campus, for instance, we received an email encouraging us to consider "alternative assessment

techniques" instead of automated proctoring, but we were never told that automated proctoring might be discriminatory, nor were the apps removed from the campus learning management system (LMS). Indeed, although faculty have been told that all ed-tech tools integrated into the campus's LMS have been vetted for privacy, with careful contracts outlining the cost and the use of data, my investigations with my research collaborator, Louise McCune, suggest that these reviews, as well as the contracts themselves, were either incomplete and slapdash or essentially nonexistent. Although the UC system as a whole would presumably have a great deal of leverage to request additional measures with respect to privacy and the use of data, we saw absolutely no effort on the part of UC campuses to use that leverage. Virtually all of the contracts we reviewed took the company's own language about their privacy/data/discrimination protections at face value; some didn't even include this language and simply stated that the prevailing policies of the company itself as stated online would apply to the contract. See Jason Kelley, "A Long Overdue Reckoning for Online Proctoring May Finally Be Here," Electronic Frontier Foundation, June 22, 2021, https://www.eff.org/deeplinks/2021/06/long-overdue-reckoning-online-proctoring-companies-may-finally-be-here; Shea Swauger, "Our Bodies Encoded: Algorithmic Test Proctoring in Higher Education," in Jesse Stommel, Chris Friend, and Sean Michael Morris, eds., *Critical Digital Pedagogy: A Collection* (Denver: Hybrid Pedagogy, 2021).

51. Ruha Benjamin, *Race After Technology: Abolitionist Tools for the New Jim Code* (Princeton: Princeton University Press, 2019), p. 46.

52. "The Evolution of Education: How AI is Reshaping Grading," *Princeton Review*, https://www.princetonreview.com/ai-education/how-ai-is-reshaping-grading.

53. Moreover, we should all be highly skeptical of the quality of this "personalized" assessment. As one study puts it, "while some aspects of the judgements that go into evaluating a piece of written work might be readily automated, the breadth of human judgements and expertise that lie behind the act of grading a written assignment [are] irreducible to even to the most contextually rich, complex statistical model"; in particular, they argue, such "tools" are not "sensitive to the social context of the process or practice

being automated." Neil Selwyn, Thomas Hillman, Annika Bergviken-Rensfeldt and Carlo Perrotta, "Making Sense of the Digital Automation of Education," *Postdigital Science and Education* 5 (2023), pp. 1–14, https://link.springer.com/article/10.1007/s42438-022-00362-9.

54. Ally Markovich, "Raises Won During Strike Have $38M Price Tag. How Will UC Berkeley Pay?", *Berkeleyside*, March 14, 2023, https://www.berkeleyside.org/2023/03/14/uc-berkeley-cost-of-strike.

55. Tamara Kneese, "How a Dead Professor Is Teaching a University Art History Class," *Slate*, January 27, 2021, https://slate.com/technology/2021/01/dead-professor-teaching-online-class.html.

56. Mary Gray and Siddharth Suri, *Ghost Work: How to Stop Silicon Valley from Building a New Global Underclass* (New York: Harper Collins, 2019); Emma Rooholfada, "Kiwi Hires Colombian Students to Supervise Kiwibots," *Daily Californian*, October 15, 2019, https://www.dailycal.org/archives/kiwi-hires-colombian-students-to-supervise-kiwibots/article_6065ef5a-0c8f-53d4-8d36-832066668fd72.html.

57. Baumol, "Macroeconomics of Unbalanced Growth," p. 416.

58. Noting that K–12 teachers have been among the most militant sectors of the unionized labor force in the last decade, Jason Smith similarly describes the labor actions of teachers' unions as a "spirited defense of the public sector as a cost necessary for the reproduction of society." Smith, *Smart Machines and Service Work*, p. 141.

Index

Near Futures series design by Julie Fry
Typesetting by Meighan Gale
Image placement and production by Julie Fry
Printed and bound by Maple Press